QuickBooks® Fundamentals 2014

For QuickBooks Pro, Premier and Accountant Version 2014

Copyright © 2014

Product Name	QuickBooks Fundamentals - Version 2014
	978-1-932487-76-3
Trademarks	Intuit, the Intuit logo, QuickBooks, QuickBooks Pro, QuickBase, Quicken, TurboTax, ProSeries, Lacerte, EasyStep, and QuickZoom, among others, are registered trademarks and/or registered service marks of Intuit Inc. in the United States and other countries. QuickBooks ProAdvisor is a trademark and/or service mark of Intuit Inc. in the United States and other countries. Other parties' trademarks or service marks are the property of their respective owners and should be treated as such.
	Terms, conditions, features, service offerings, prices, and hours referenced in this document are subject to change without notice. We at Intuit are committed to bringing you great online services through QuickBooks. Occasionally, we may decide to update our selection and change our service offerings, so please check www.quickbooks.com for the latest information, including pricing and availability, on our products and services.
Copyright	© 2014 The Sleeter Group, Inc.
	All rights reserved
Disclaimer	This material is intended as a learning aid for QuickBooks software users. Under no circumstances shall the author or publisher be liable for any damages, including any lost profits, lost data or other indirect damages arising out of anything written in this document or expressed directly or indirectly by the author or publisher.
Developed and Written By	Douglas Sleeter
Contributing Authors, Testers, and Reviewers	Deborah Pembrook
	David Brewster
	Pat Carson
	Esther Friedberg Karp
	Tricia Lippincott
	Ellen Orr

Table of Contents

Preface vii
   Using This Book vii
   Integrating QuickBooks with other products vii
   Using QuickBooks Student Trial viii
   About the exercise files viii
      Installing the exercise files viii
   Certification ix
   Acknowledgements ix
   Chapter 1   Introducing QuickBooks 1
   Topics 1
   The QuickBooks Product Line 1
      QuickBooks Editions 1
      QuickBooks Releases 2
   Accounting 101 2
      Accounting's Focus 2
      Accounts, Accounts, Everywhere Accounts 2
      Account Types and Financial Reports 3
      Double-Entry Accounting 3
      Accounting Behind the Scenes 4
      Accounting for the Future: Cash or Accrual? 4
      Academy Photography 5
   QuickBooks Files 5
      Creating a New File 6
      Opening a QuickBooks Sample File 6
      Opening Other QuickBooks Data Files 7
      Closing QuickBooks Files 9
      Opening Multiple Files 9
      Closing the QuickBooks Program 9
   Opening Portable Company Files 9
      Creating Portable Company Files 11
   Restoring Backup Files 13
      Backing up Your Data File 13
      Restoring a Backup File 16
   QuickBooks User Interface Features 17
      Home Page 18
      Centers 18
      Snapshots 19
      Icon Bar 19
      Calendar 20
      QuickBooks Mobile 20
   Entering Transactions in QuickBooks 20
      Forms 21
      Lists 22
      Accounts 22
      Registers 23
      Items 24
   QuickBooks Help 25
      Support Resources 25
      QuickBooks Learning Center 25
      Certified QuickBooks ProAdvisors 26
   Review Questions 26
      Comprehension Questions 26
      Multiple Choice 27
      Completion Statements 27
   Introduction Problem 1 28
   Introduction Problem 2 (Advanced) 28
   "From Click to Cart: A Holiday Survival Guide for Small Business Retailers" 30

	New Terminology	30
	Putting New Knowledge to Use	30
Chapter 2	**The Sales Process**	**31**
	Topics	31
	Tracking Company Sales	31
	Setting Up Customers	35
	Job Costing	40
	Recording Sales	41
	Entering Sales Receipts	41
	Undeposited Funds	45
	Creating Invoices	48
	Open Invoices Report	52
	Receiving Payments from Customers	53
	Receiving Payments by Check	53
	Handling Partial Payments	55
	Receiving Payments by Credit Card	55
	Where Do the Payments Go?	56
	Preferences for Applying Payments	57
	Recording Customer Discounts	58
	Making Bank Deposits	61
	Depositing Checks and Cash	61
	Holding Cash Back from Deposits	63
	Printing Deposit Slips	64
	Depositing Credit Card Payments	66
	Income Tracker	68
	Review Questions	70
	Comprehension Questions	70
	Multiple Choice	70
	Completion Statements	72
	Sales Problem 1	73
	Sales Problem 2 (Advanced)	74
	"How to Integrate PayPal into QuickBooks"	76
	New Terminology	76
	Putting New Knowledge to Use	76
Chapter 3	**Additional Customer Transactions**	**77**
	Topics	77
	Recording Customer Returns and Credits	77
	Refunding Customers	78
	Writing Off a Bad Debt	84
	Applying the Bad Debt Credit Memo to an Open Invoice	86
	Create Batch Invoices	87
	Creating Customer Statements	89
	Collecting Sales Tax	91
	Setting up Sales Tax	91
	Sales Tax Codes	94
	Calculating Sales Tax on Sales Forms	97
	Creating Sales Reports	97
	Customer Open Balance Report	97
	Sales by Customer Summary Report	98
	Sales by Item Report	99
	Review Questions	100
	Comprehension Questions	100
	Multiple Choice	100
	Completion Statements	102
	Customers Problem 1	102
	Customers Problem 2 (Advanced)	103
	"Comparing QuickBooks Desktop with QuickBooks Online"	104
	New Terminology	104
	Putting New Knowledge to Use	104

Chapter 4 Managing Expenses ... 105
Topics ... 105
Entering Expenses in QuickBooks ... 105
    The Process of Entering Expenses in QuickBooks ... 105
Setting Up Vendors ... 108
Activating Class Tracking ... 112
Tracking Job Costs ... 114
Paying Vendors ... 115
    Using Registers ... 115
    Using Write Checks Without Using Accounts Payable ... 119
    Managing Accounts Payable ... 120
Printing Checks ... 128
Voiding Checks ... 131
Applying Vendor Credits ... 133
Handling Deposits and Refunds from Vendors ... 136
    Vendor Deposits — When You Use Accounts Payable ... 137
    Vendor Refunds — When You Use Accounts Payable ... 137
    Vendor Refunds — When You Directly Expensed Payment ... 142
Tracking Petty Cash ... 142
Tracking Company Credit Cards ... 143
    Entering Credit Card Charges ... 143
    Paying the Credit Card Bill ... 144
Paying Sales Tax ... 146
    Paying Sales Tax ... 146
Accounts Payable Reports ... 147
    Vendor Balance Detail ... 147
    Transaction List by Vendor ... 148
    Sales Tax Liability ... 148
Tracking Loans using the Loan Manager ... 149
    Setting up a Loan in the Loan Manager ... 149
    Making Loan Payments using the Loan Manager ... 152
Review Questions ... 154
    Comprehension Questions ... 154
    Multiple Choice ... 154
    Completion Statements ... 156
Expenses Problem 1 ... 157
Expenses Problem 2 (Advanced) ... 158
"Hail the Vendor Neutral, Frictionless, Zero Data Entry World!" ... 159
    New Terminology ... 159
    Putting New Knowledge to Use ... 159

Chapter 5 Bank Reconciliation and Bank Transactions ... 161
Topics ... 161
Reconciling Bank Accounts ... 161
Bank Reconciliation Reports ... 167
Finding Errors During Bank Reconciliation ... 168
    Step 1: Review the Beginning Balance Field ... 168
    Step 2: Locate and Edit Incorrectly Recorded Transactions ... 170
    When QuickBooks Automatically Adjusts your Balance ... 173
Handling Bounced Checks ... 173
    When Your Customer's Check Bounces ... 173
    Receiving and Depositing the Replacement Check ... 175
    When Your Check Bounces ... 176
Reconciling Credit Card Accounts and Paying the Bill ... 176
Bank Feeds ... 179
    Bank Feed Setup ... 180
    Processing Online Transactions ... 180
    Opening the Sample File ... 181
    Downloaded Transactions ... 181
Review Questions ... 183

Comprehension Questions 183
Multiple Choice 184
Completion Statements 185
Bank Reconciliation Problem 1 186
Bank Reconciliation Problem 2 (Advanced) 186
"Cloud Accounting Comparison – Introduction" 187
New Terminology 188
Putting New Knowledge to Use 188

Chapter 6 Reports 189

Topics 189
Types of Reports 189
Cash Versus Accrual Reports 190
Accounting Reports 192
Profit & Loss 192
Profit & Loss by Class Report 195
Profit & Loss by Job Report 197
Balance Sheet 198
Statement of Cash Flows 199
General Ledger 200
Trial Balance 201
Voided/Deleted Transactions Summary Reports 201
Business Management Reports 202
Customer Phone List 202
Vendor Contact List 203
Item Price List 203
Check Detail Report 204
Accounts Receivable and Accounts Payable Reports 205
QuickBooks Graphs 207
Building Custom Reports 209
Memorizing Reports 215
Viewing Memorized Reports 216
Contributed Reports 216
Processing Multiple Reports 217
Printing Reports 218
Finding Transactions 220
Using the Find Button 220
Using the Search Command 220
QuickReports 221
Using QuickZoom 224
Exporting Reports to Spreadsheets 225
Exporting a Report to Microsoft Excel 225
Review Questions 227
Comprehension Questions 227
Multiple Choice 227
Completion Statements 229
Reports Problem 1 229
Reports Problem 2 (Advanced) 229
How to Record Sales on Consignment in QuickBooks " 230
New Terminology 231
Putting New Knowledge to Use 231

Chapter 7 Company File Setup 233

Topics 233
Choosing a Start Date – Step 1 233
Creating the Company File – Step 2 234
Express Start 234
Detailed Start 236
Setting Up the Chart of Accounts and Other Lists – Step 3 243
Setting Up the Chart of Accounts 243
Setting Up Other Lists 252

            Add/Edit Multiple List Entries 252
        Setting Up Opening Balances – Step 4 254
            Gathering Your Information 254
            Opening Balances for Accounts 257
            Understanding Opening Bal Equity 260
        Entering Open Items – Step 5 260
            Entering Outstanding Checks and Deposits 260
            Entering Open Bills (Accounts Payable) 261
            Entering Open Invoices (Accounts Receivable) 262
            Entering Open Purchase Orders 264
            Entering Open Estimates and Sales Orders 264
        Entering Year-to-Date Income and Expenses – Step 6 264
        Adjusting Opening Balance for Sales Tax Payable – Step 7 265
        Adjusting Inventory and Setting up Fixed Assets – Step 8 266
            Adjusting Inventory for Actual Counts 266
            Setting up Fixed Assets 267
            Setting up Loans 267
        Setup Payroll and YTD Payroll Information – Step 9 267
        Verifying your Trial Balance – Step 10 267
        Closing Opening Bal Equity – Step 11 268
        Setting the Closing Date - Backing up the File – Step 12 270
            Setting the Closing Date to Protect your Setup Balances 270
        Users and Passwords 270
            Setting Up Users in the Company File 270
            Multi-User and Single-User Modes 274
        Review Questions 275
            Comprehension Questions 275
            Multiple Choice 275
            Completion Statements 277
        Setup Problem 1 278
        Setup Problem 2 (Advanced) 278
        "QuickBooks for Law Firms: Setup" 283
            New Terminology 284
            Putting New Knowledge to Use 284

Chapter 8   Customizing QuickBooks 285
    Topics 285
    QuickBooks Preferences 285
        Setting User Preferences 286
    Customizing QuickBooks Menus and Windows 288
        Favorites Menu 288
        QuickBooks Icon Bar 289
        Customizing the Icon Bar 290
        Open Window List 293
    QuickBooks Items and Other Lists 294
        QuickBooks Items 294
        Printing the Item List 299
        The Terms List 300
        Price Levels 302
    Custom Fields 304
        Adding Custom Field Data to Customer Records 304
    Modifying Sales Form Templates 305
    Review Questions 310
        Comprehension Questions 310
        Multiple Choice 310
        Completion Statements 312
    Customizing Problem 1 312
    Customizing Problem 2 (Advanced) 313
    "Custom Fields in QuickBooks" 314
        New Terminology 315

Putting New Knowledge to Use	315
Chapter 9 Walker Graphic Design Business Scenario	**317**
Description of Company	317
Goals	317
Company Set Up	317
Instructions	318
Business Transactions	318
May 2018	318
Analysis Questions	324
Appendix	**325**
Keyboard Shortcuts	325
Answer Key for End of Chapter Questions	326
Introducing QuickBooks	326
The Sales Process	327
Additional Customer Transactions	328
Managing Expenses	329
Bank Reconciliation	331
Reports and Graphs	332
Company File Setup and Maintenance	333
Customizing QuickBooks	334
Walker Business Scenarios	336
Index	**337**

Preface

This guide introduces you to QuickBooks—Intuit's easy-to-use, powerful accounting system for small businesses. The guide contains 14 chapters including a final business scenario.

This guide is designed to teach you how to use many of the features available in QuickBooks Software for Windows Desktop. The main focus of this guide is on how to use the features in QuickBooks Premier and Accountant, but most exercises can be completed using QuickBooks Pro. This guide does not cover how to use the features in QuickBooks Online or QuickBooks Pro for Mac.

While this guide does not specifically address how to use QuickBooks Enterprise Solutions, many of the procedures described in the guide will work with Enterprise Solutions editions. If you restore the exercise file using a QuickBooks Enterprise Solutions product, QuickBooks walks you through the file update process that is necessary for Enterprise Solutions to be able to read the file.

The step-by-step instructions and screen captures in this guide were created with QuickBooks Accountant 2014. Your screens may differ, and some instructions may vary slightly, if you are using a different edition.

Using This Book

Throughout this book, you will find tips on how to set up and use QuickBooks so that you and your company have the information you need to make business decisions.

Each chapter covers how to manage a general part of your business. To allow you to learn the chapters in any order, each chapter uses a separate QuickBooks data file that you can use with QuickBooks to complete the practice lessons.

Academy Photography, Inc. is the model company used throughout the chapters. By performing the in-chapter practices, students gain hands-on experience with the topics discussed in the chapter, which are based on the day-to-day operations of this small corporation.

Each chapter is designed to aid understanding by providing an overview of topics, numerous hands-on tutorial practices, key terms, the "accounting behind the scenes," and many extra notes. The illustrated text includes step-by-step instructions with hands-on computer exercises to provide you with practical experience.

The end-of-chapter applications include comprehension questions, multiple choice questions, completion sentences, and real-world problems that require the student to perform tasks with the software.

Each chapter also includes a section titled QuickBooks and Beyond. This is an excerpt from a blog post available on the Sleeter Group's blog (www.sleeter.com/blog) which is relevant to that chapter. Topics range from how to handle specific QuickBooks issues to reviews of third-party add-ons that can enhance a company's accounting. Each QuickBooks and Beyond section includes an explanation of new terminology and questions to help you evaluate how you would use this information in your own company or workplace.

The final two chapters of this book are business simulations. They consist of summary problems covering topics culled from all the chapters in this book.

From using this book you will gain confidence in every aspect of QuickBooks by trying out each feature as you complete problems and simulations of a "real" business. You will want to keep this book for reference for years to come.

Integrating QuickBooks with other products

If you plan to use the Microsoft Office integration features available in QuickBooks, such as exporting to Excel, you will need to have Microsoft® Office installed on your system.

Using QuickBooks Student Trial

QuickBooks Accountant 2014 Student Trial is a full-featured version of QuickBooks that is included with this guide. You can install it on your computer and use it to complete the exercises in this guide and to practice using QuickBooks.

QuickBooks Accountant can "toggle" to other versions of QuickBooks, including QuickBooks Premier, Pro and Industry editions. The trial software can be used to explore any of these versions of QuickBooks.

To install QuickBooks Accountant 2014, insert the software CD into your computer and follow the on-screen instructions. You will be required to register this copy of QuickBooks using the Product Number and License Number printed on the yellow sticker that is adhered to the software sleeve.

If you would rather download the software, visit www.quickbooks.com/support. Under the *Downloads and Updates* section, select *Premier, Accountant 2014*. You can use the same license information attached to the CD for the downloaded software.

You can use this product for 140 days after installation.

About the exercise files

Exercise files are used with the chapters and problems throughout this book. For each lesson and problem in this guide, you'll restore a copy of the exercise file named in the beginning of the section, and use that file to complete the lesson. This means that at the start of each lesson, you'll be restoring a new file. It is very important to be in the correct file to ensure that your screen will match the book's screenshots.

Installing the exercise files

The exercise files for the chapters and problems are available at www.sleeter.com/student. To install the files on your hard drive, follow these steps:

Step 1. Go to www.sleeter.com/student.

Step 2. Find this book's title and click the link to download the exercise files. You will be asked to create an account or, if you have an account on sleeter.com, to login.

If you do not see this book's title, follow the onscreen directions.

Step 3. Once you have downloaded *QuickBooks_2014_Classroom_Files.exe*, open the file and extract the files to the desired location on your local system.

If you are using a computer in a classroom or lab environment, ask your instructor for the proper location to store your exercise files.

> **Important:**
> The Classroom Files are in QuickBooks Portable File Format. You cannot open these files by double-clicking them. For more on how to begin using these files, see page 9.

Instructor Resources

Instructor resources, including the Instructor's Manual, test banks, solution files and PowerPoints are available at www.sleeter.com/downloads. You must be a verified instructor with an accredited school to access these files. If you do not already have an instructor login, please contact info@sleeter.com.

Restoring exercise files

Each chapter uses a separate practice file (e.g., Intro-14.QBW) for performing the in-chapter practices. In order to open this file, you must "restore" it as described in the first chapter (see page 9).

In the beginning of each chapter, the *Restore This File* instruction (see example below) instructs you to restore the practice file for that chapter to use with the computer practice lessons.

Example *Restore this file* instruction:

> **Restore this File:**
> This chapter uses XXXXXXXXXXX-14.QBW. To open this file, restore the XXXXXXXXXXX-14.QBM file to your hard disk. See page 9 for instructions on restoring files.

The lessons are identified throughout the book with the words **COMPUTER PRACTICE**.

In some cases, concepts are presented in step form, but are not intended to be performed in your data file. In this case, you'll see a note at the top of the section that says:

> **DO NOT PERFORM THESE STEPS NOW. THEY ARE FOR REFERENCE ONLY.**

For these sections, you should look through and understand the material, but you should not enter any of the data in your practice file.

Certification

This book is excellent preparation for the QuickBooks User Certification Exam. This certification validates your QuickBooks knowledge. After successfully completing the exam, you will become an Intuit QuickBooks Certified User. For more information and for locations of testing centers, visit http://www.certiport.com/quickbooks.

Acknowledgements

I'd like to extend my heartfelt thanks to the co-authors, consultants, copy editors and contributors who have worked on all of our college textbooks over the years. Many people have put their head and their heart into each edition. All of you have improved and enhanced this textbook and I offer my gratitude.

This year's update was managed by The Sleeter Group's Director of Educational Products, Deborah Pembrook. Updating this textbook is a labor of love for Deborah and I hope you see this reflected on the following pages.

My sincere thanks also goes to David Brewster, Pat Carson, Ellen Orr, Joy Prado who all contributed to this book. Thank you for being such valued part of bringing this book into being.

We hope you enjoy *QuickBooks Fundamentals*.

Doug Sleeter
Pleasanton, CA
January, 2014

Chapter 1
Introducing QuickBooks

Topics

In this chapter, you will learn about the following topics:
- The QuickBooks Product Line (page 1)
- Accounting 101 (page 2)
- QuickBooks Files (page 5)
- Opening Portable Company Files (page 9)
- Restoring Backup Files (page 13)
- Entering Transactions in QuickBooks (page 20)
- QuickBooks User Interface Features (page 17)
- QuickBooks Help (page 25)

QuickBooks is one of the most powerful tools you will use in managing your business. QuickBooks isn't just a robust bookkeeping program, QuickBooks is a *management tool*. When set up and used properly, QuickBooks allows you to track and manage income, expenses, bank accounts, receivables, inventory, job costs, fixed assets, payables, loans, payroll, billable time, and equity in your company. It also provides you with detailed reports that are essential to making good business decisions.

QuickBooks helps small business owners run their businesses efficiently without worrying about the debits and credits of accounting entries. However, to use QuickBooks effectively, you still need to understand how QuickBooks is structured, how its files work, how to navigate in the system to do tasks, and how to retrieve information about your business. In this chapter you'll learn some of the basics of the QuickBooks program and then you will explore the world of accounting.

The QuickBooks Product Line

The QuickBooks family of products is designed to be easy to use, while providing a comprehensive set of accounting tools including: general ledger, inventory, accounts receivable, accounts payable, sales tax, and financial reporting. In addition, a variety of optional, fee-based payroll services, merchant account services, and other add-on products integrate with the QuickBooks software.

QuickBooks Editions

The QuickBooks product line includes several separate product editions: *QuickBooks Online, QuickBooks Pro, QuickBooks Premier, QuickBooks Accountant* and *QuickBooks Enterprise Solutions*. The *Premier* and *Enterprise Solutions* editions are further broken down into six industry-specific editions for *General Business, Contractors, Manufacturers/Wholesalers, Nonprofit Organizations, Professional Services,* and *Retailers*. All editions of QuickBooks support multiple users, however, each user must have the same version of QuickBooks to access the file.

This book covers the features and usage of *QuickBooks Pro, Premier (non-industry specific)*, and *Accountant*, since most small businesses will use one of these editions. Also, once you learn how to use one of these editions, you'll be prepared to use *any* of the other editions, with the exception of the online edition. The online edition is a web-based software product, with different, yet similar features to the editions covered in this book. For a comparison of all editions and options, see www.quickbooks.com.

QuickBooks Releases

Occasionally, errors are found in the QuickBooks software after the product is released for sale. As errors are discovered, Intuit fixes the problem and provides program "patches" via the Internet. Each patch increases the **Release Level** of the QuickBooks application. To see what release level of the software you have, press **Ctrl+1** (or **F2**) while QuickBooks is running. At the top of the window, you will see the QuickBooks product information including the release level.

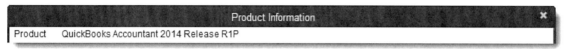

Figure 1-1 Product information window showing version and release

This book is based on QuickBooks Accountant 2014 release R1P. If you have a newer (higher) release, you may see some slight differences compared to the screens in this book, but most likely you won't see any differences.

To patch your software with the latest maintenance release, download this release by selecting the *Help* menu and then selecting **Update QuickBooks**. Follow the instructions on these screens to download and install maintenance releases in QuickBooks via the Internet.

Accounting 101

Having a basic background in the accounting process will help you learn QuickBooks and run your business. In this section, we look at some basic accounting concepts and how they relate to QuickBooks.

Accounting's Focus

Accounting's primary concern is the accurate recording and categorizing of transactions so that you can produce reports that accurately portray the financial health of your organization. Put another way, accounting's focus is on whether your organization is succeeding and how well it is succeeding.

The purpose of accounting is to serve management, investors, creditors, and government agencies. Accounting reports allow any of these groups to assess the financial position of the organization relative to its debts (liabilities), its capabilities to satisfy those debts and continue operations (assets), and the difference between them (net worth or equity).

The fundamental equation (called the *Accounting Equation*) that governs all accounting is:

Assets = Liabilities + Equity, or Equity = Assets - Liabilities.

Accounts, Accounts, Everywhere Accounts

Many factors go into making an organization work. Money and value are attached to everything that is associated with operating a company — cash, equipment, rent, utilities, wages, raw materials, merchandise, and so on. For an organization to understand its financial position, business transactions need to be recorded, summarized, balanced, and presented in reports according to the rules of accounting.

Business transactions (e.g., sales, purchases, operating expense payments) are recorded in several types of *ledgers*, called accounts. The summary of all transactions in all ledgers for a company is called the *General Ledger*. A listing of every account in the General Ledger is called the *Chart of Accounts*.

Each account summarizes transactions that increase or decrease the *equity* in your organization. The figure below shows a general picture of the effect your accounts have on the equity of your organization. Some accounts (those on the left) increase equity when they are increased, while others (those on the right) decrease equity when they are increased.

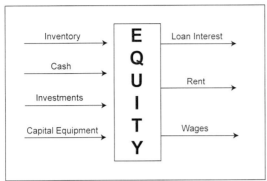

So let's return to the Accounting Equation. To understand the accounting equation, consider the following statement. **Everything a company owns was purchased by funds from creditors or by the owner's stake in the company.**

Account Types and Financial Reports

Each account in the general ledger has a type, which describes what kind of business transaction is stored in that account. There are primarily five types of accounts: asset, liability, equity, income, and expense. Assets, liabilities, and equity accounts are associated with the **Balance Sheet** report which is used to analyze the net worth of a business. The income and expense accounts are associated with the **Profit and Loss** report (also called Income Statement) which is used to analyze the operating profit or loss for a business over a specific time range (month, quarter, year, etc.).

The Balance Sheet report preserves the fundamental accounting equation - **Total assets always equal the total liabilities plus equity,** between the accounts. This means that the total of the assets (which represent what the company "owns") is always equal to the sum of the liabilities (representing what the company owes) plus the equity (representing the owner's interest in the company). Although income and expense accounts are not directly shown in the accounting equation, they do affect this equation via the equity account as shown below.

The income and expenses are tracked throughout the year as business transactions occur and are totaled at the end of the year to calculate Net Income (or Loss). **Net income (total revenues minus total expenses) increases the owner's equity in the business, and net loss (when expenses exceed revenues) decreases the owner's equity in the business.** Thus the Income and Expense accounts indirectly affect the Equity component of the Accounting Equation of Assets = Liabilities + Equity, where **Equity increases or decreases each year depending on whether the year's income exceeds expenses or not.**

At the end of the year, the balance of each income and expense account is reset to zero so these accounts can track the next year's transactions.

Double-Entry Accounting

Double-entry accounting is the technique that makes the Accounting Equation work. It divides each account into two sides. One side is a record of transactions that increase the account and the other side is a record of all transactions that decrease the account. One side (the left side) is for debits, and the other (the right side) is for credits. Depending on the type of account, a debit might increase the account or decrease it. The same is true of credits. Therefore, debits are not always bad and credits are not always good. They are just part of the system of accounting. However, the rule of double-entry accounting is that **total debits must always equal total credits.** Every transaction creates a debit in one or more accounts and a credit in one or more accounts. If the debits and credits for any transaction are not equal, the transaction has an error or is incomplete.

Accounting Behind the Scenes

Recording and categorizing all of your business transactions into the proper accounts, summarizing and adjusting them, and then preparing financial statements *can be an enormous, labor-intensive task* without the help of a computer and software. This is where QuickBooks comes in. **QuickBooks focuses on ease of use and hiding accounting details.** To make all this possible, QuickBooks uses components like accounts, items, forms, registers, and lists, which are discussed later in the chapter. Familiar-looking forms such as invoices, checks, and bills are used for data entry. As you enter data in forms, QuickBooks handles the accounting entries for you. Thus business owners can use QuickBooks to efficiently run a business without getting bogged down with the debits and credits of accounting entries.

QuickBooks also handles double-entry for you. Every transaction you enter in the program automatically becomes a debit to one or more accounts and a credit to one or more other accounts, and QuickBooks won't let you record the transaction until the total of the debits equals the total of the credits. This means you can create reports that show the transactions in the full double-entry accounting format whenever you need them, allowing you to focus on the business transaction rather than the debits and credits in the General Ledger.

Cash or accrual method, as discussed in the next section, is handled in QuickBooks as a simple reporting option. You can create reports for either cash or accrual basis regardless of the method you use for taxes.

As the book introduces new transaction types (e.g., Invoices, Bills, or Checks), the text will include a section called "The accounting behind the scenes." For example, when you first learn about invoices you will see the following message:

> **The accounting behind the scenes:**
> When you create an **Invoice**, QuickBooks increases (with a debit) **Accounts Receivable** and increases (with a credit) the appropriate **income** account. If applicable, **Invoices** and **Sales Receipts** also increase (with a credit) the sales tax liability account.

Letting QuickBooks handle the accounting behind the scenes means you can focus on your organization and identify the important factors that will help you succeed. Once you identify these factors, you can use QuickBooks to monitor them and provide information that will guide you in managing your operations.

Accounting for the Future: Cash or Accrual?

Another critical aspect of accounting is managing for the future. Many times, your organization will have assets and liabilities that represent money owed to the company, or owed to others by the company, but are not yet due. For example, you may have sold something to a customer and sent an invoice, but the payment has not been received. In this case, you have an outstanding *receivable*. Similarly, you may have a bill for insurance that is not yet due. In this case, you have an outstanding *payable*.

An accounting system that uses the *accrual basis* method of accounting tracks these receivables and payables and uses them to evaluate a company's financial position. The *accrual basis* method specifies that revenues and expenses are *recognized* in the period in which the transactions occur, rather than in the period in which cash changes hands. So to help you manage the future and to more accurately reflect the true profitability of the business in each period, assets, liabilities, income, and expenses are entered when you know about them, and they are used to identify what you need on hand to meet both current, and known, future obligations.

In the *cash basis* method, revenues and expenses are not *recognized* until cash changes hands. So revenue is recognized when the customer pays, and an expense is recognized when you pay the bill for the expense. In most cash basis systems, you must use an outside system to track open invoices and unpaid bills, which means you cannot view both cash and accrual reports without going to several places to find information. However, in QuickBooks, you can record transactions such as invoices and bills to facilitate *accrual basis* reporting, and you can create *cash basis* reports that remove the receivables and payables with the same system.

Although certain types of organizations can use the cash basis method of accounting (many are not allowed to do so under IRS regulations), the accrual method provides the most accurate picture for managing your organization. You should check with your tax accountant to determine which accounting method — cash or accrual — is best for you.

Academy Photography

Throughout this book, you will see references to a fictitious company called Academy Photography. Academy Photography is a photography studio that also sells camera equipment. This company uses QuickBooks for its accounting and business management. Academy Photography may not be exactly like your business; however, the examples in this text that focus on Academy Photography are generic enough to guide you on your own use of QuickBooks.

Academy Photography has two locations, one in San Jose and another in Walnut Creek. In order for management to separately track revenue and expenses for each store, Academy Photography uses **Classes** in QuickBooks. As you proceed through the book, you'll see how each transaction (bill, check, invoice, etc.) is tagged with what *Class* it belongs to, so that later you can create reports like Profit & Loss by Class. Classes can be used to separately track departments, profit centers, store locations, or funds in any business.

Academy Photography also needs to separately track revenue and expenses for each job it performs. When a customer orders a photo shoot, Academy Photography needs to track all of the revenue and expenses specifically related to that job so it can look back and see how profitable the job was. This concept is called *job costing*, and many different businesses need to track jobs in similar ways.

As you think through the examples with Academy Photography, ask yourself what parallels you see to your own organization. Certainly, areas such as salaries, supplies, equipment, and others will be appropriate for your setup, but the names and specifics of the accounts, items, lists, and forms will probably be different.

QuickBooks Files

Before using QuickBooks, it is important for you to understand how QuickBooks files are structured and used. QuickBooks has three primary types of files described below. All file types can be opened using the *Open or Restore Company* option from the *File* menu.

1. *Working Data Files)* – These files are used to enter transactions and create reports. *(File Extension .QBW)*
2. *Portable Company Files* – These files are a compact version of the company data files and are used to transport the file between computers. These files should never be used to back up your QuickBooks data. These files must be "Restored" to a working data file to be used. *(File Extension .QBM)*
3. *Backup Files* – These files are a compressed version of the company data files and are used as backup to safeguard the information. These files cannot be used directly within QuickBooks and must be "Restored" to working data file format. *(File Extension .QBB)*

This means, if you name your company file ABC, QuickBooks will store the working data file as "ABC.QBW." When you back up your company file using the QuickBooks Backup function, QuickBooks will store your backup file with the name "ABC.QBB." If you create a portable data file using the QuickBooks Portable file creation function, the portable file "ABC.QBM" will be created and stored on the disk.

In addition to the Backup and Restore process, which moves the complete QuickBooks file between computers, QuickBooks also has a feature called the Accountant's Copy. This feature enables an accounting professional to review and make corrections to a special copy of the client's company file while the client continues to work. Then the client can *merge* the accountant's changes back into the original file. See the QuickBooks Help Index for information on this feature.

> **Important:**
> Each file type has a specific purpose and should be used accordingly. Working data files are used to enter data and run reports, backup files are used to safeguard the data, and portable files are compressed files used to transport data via the Internet where smaller files transfer faster.

Creating a New File

There are four ways to create a new QuickBooks file, *Express Start, Detailed Start, Company Based on an Existing Company,* and *Conversion from Other Accounting Software*. Although it is possible to create a QuickBooks file relatively quickly using *Express Start*, we recommend utilizing a 12-Step process for creating a file to properly set up accounts and account balances. We have placed the chapter that explains file setup later in the book so you will be able to utilize knowledge gained in earlier chapters. You can learn more about file setup in our File Setup chapter starting on page 233.

Opening a QuickBooks Sample File

For learning purposes, QuickBooks provides sample data files that allow you to explore the program. To open a sample data file, follow these steps:

COMPUTER PRACTICE

Step 1.   Launch the QuickBooks program by double-clicking the icon on your desktop or selecting it from the Windows Start menu.

Step 2.   When QuickBooks opens, you will either see the *No Company Open* window (Figure 1-2) or the *last working data file* used.

No Company Open window is displayed if you are opening QuickBooks for the first time or if you closed the working data file *before* exiting in your last session. By default, the last working data file used will open, if you closed the QuickBooks *program* before closing the *file*.

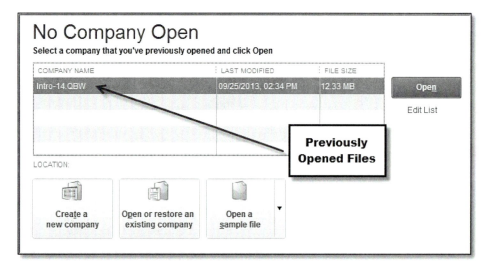

Figure 1-2 No Company Open window

Introducing QuickBooks - QuickBooks Files

Step 3.   If you don't see the *No Company Open* window (Figure 1-2), select the **File** menu, and then select **Close Company**. Click **No** if you are prompted to back up your file.

Step 4.   Click **Open a Sample file** button and select *Sample product-based business* from the list. The selected sample file will open with the *QuickBooks Information* screen (see Figure 1-3).

Step 5.   Click **OK** to continue.

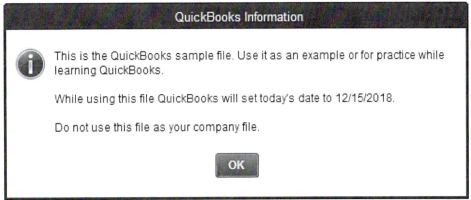

Figure 1-3 Sample File Information Screen

Step 6.   The sample file you selected will open. If you see the *Accountant Center* or the *External Accountant* message, uncheck the box that says **Show window when opening a company file** and close the window by clicking the X in the top right corner of the *Accountant Center*.

Opening Other QuickBooks Data Files

If you want to open a QuickBooks company file other than the sample data files, follow the steps below. We will not complete these steps now, but will use a restored portable file in the next section.

> DO NOT PERFORM THESE STEPS. THEY ARE FOR REFERENCE ONLY.

1. Launch the QuickBooks program by double-clicking the icon on your desktop or selecting it from the Windows Start menu. When QuickBooks opens, it launches the data file you previously had open when you last exited the program, unless you specifically closed the data file before exiting.

2. To open a different file, select the **File** menu and then select **Open or Restore Company** (see Figure 1-4).

Figure 1-4 File menu

3. In the *Open or Restore Company* window, select **Open a company file** and click **Next**.

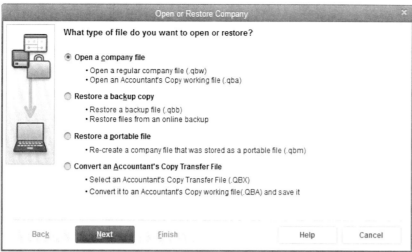

Figure 1-5 Open or Restore Company

4. Set the *Look in* field to the folder on your hard disk where you store your QuickBooks file (see Figure 1-6).

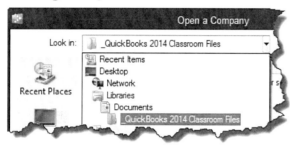

Figure 1-6 Selecting the folder where the QuickBooks files are stored

5. Select the file from the list of QuickBooks files (see Figure 1-7). Then click **Open**.

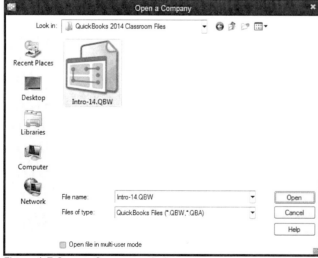

Figure 1-7 Open a Company window

> **Note:** When you open a data file, depending on today's date, you may see one or more "Alerts" for learning to process credit cards, pay taxes, or similar activities. Click Mark as Done when you see these alerts.

Your company file will open, and you'll be ready to work with QuickBooks.

Closing QuickBooks Files

Step 1. Close the company data file by selecting **Close Company** from the *File* menu (see Figure 1-8). If you skip this step, this data file will open automatically the next time you start the QuickBooks program.

Figure 1-8 Close Company File option

Opening Multiple Files

It is possible to open two company files at the same time if you are using QuickBooks Accountant or Enterprise Solution, however, the activities that can be performed in the second file are very limited. We recommend you always close the file before opening or restoring a different file.

Closing the QuickBooks Program

Just as with any other Windows program, you can close the QuickBooks program by clicking the close button (the red *X*) at the upper right hand corner of the QuickBooks window, or by selecting **Exit** from the *File* menu. The *Exiting QuickBooks* window will appear to confirm that you want to exit the QuickBooks program, as opposed to closing a window in QuickBooks. You can disable this message by checking the box next to Do *not display this message in the future* (see Figure 1-9).

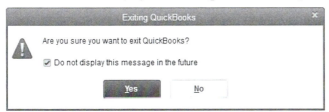

Figure 1-9 Exiting QuickBooks window

Opening Portable Company Files

Portable Company Files are compact company data files that can be easily transported. The exercise files that accompany this book are Portable Company Files. You will need to open these exercise files at the start of each chapter and each problem.

> Note:
> When you move a data file from one computer (computer A) to another (computer B), any data you enter on computer B will cause the file on the computer A to become "obsolete." Take care to make sure you are always working in the true, active data file.

COMPUTER PRACTICE

To open portable files follow the steps below.

Step 1. Select the **Open or Restore Company** option from the *File* menu (see Figure 1-10).

Step 2. QuickBooks displays the *Open or Restore Company* window. Select **Restore a portable file (.QBM)** and click **Next**.

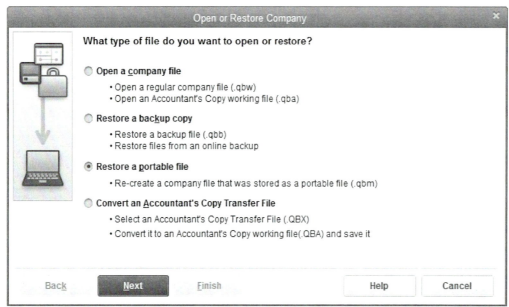

Figure 1-10 Open or Restore Company window

Step 3. QuickBooks displays the *Open Portable Company File* window (see Figure 1-11). Navigate to the location of your exercise files. You may need to ask your instructor if you do not know this location. Once you are viewing the contents of the correct folder, select **Intro-14.QBM** and click **Open**.

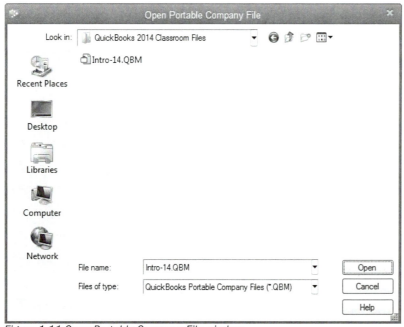

Figure 1-11 Open Portable Company File window

Step 4. Next you will need to tell QuickBooks where to save the working file that will be created from the portable file (see Figure 1-12). Click **Next** in the *Open or Restore Company* window to continue.

Introducing QuickBooks - Opening Portable Company Files

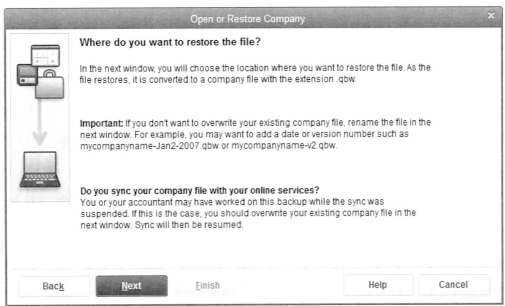

Figure 1-12 Open or Restore Company Location

Step 5. The *Save Company File as* window displays (see Figure 1-13). Ask your instructor or choose a location to save the file. When you have navigated to the appropriate folder, click **Save**.

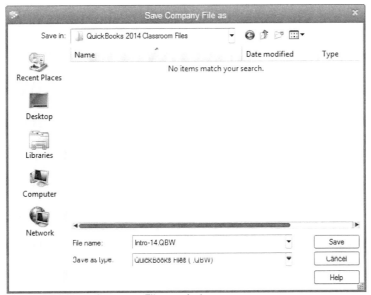

Figure 1-13 Save Company File as window

Step 6. If asked to update your company files, click **Yes**.

Step 7. Once the Intro-14.QBW company file finishes opening, you will see the Home page.

Creating Portable Company Files

Although we will not create one now, you can also create a Portable file using the following steps.

> DO NOT PERFORM THESE STEPS. THEY ARE FOR REFERENCE ONLY.

1. Select the **Create Copy** option from the *File* menu (see Figure 1-14).

Figure 1-14 Create Copy

2. The *Save Copy or Backup* window displays. Select the **Portable company file** option and click **Next**.

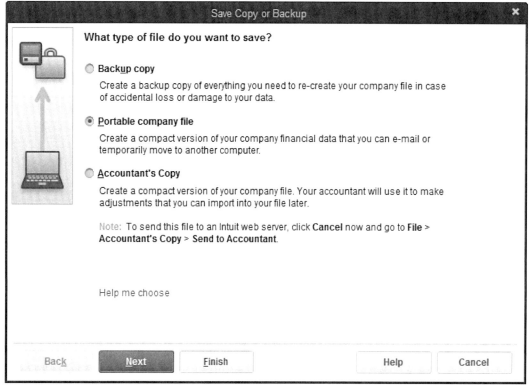

Figure 1-15 Save Copy or Backup window

3. The *Save Portable Company File* window appears. The default file name in the *File name* field is the same as the working file name with "(Portable)" added to the end. Navigate to the student file location and click **Save**.

4. The message shown in Figure 1-16 will appear before the portable file is created. Click **OK** to continue.

Introducing QuickBooks - Restoring Backup Files

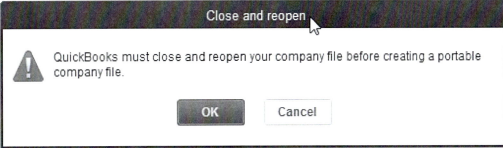

Figure 1-16 Message for creating portable company file

5. QuickBooks displays the *QuickBooks Information* dialog box (see Figure 1-17). Click **OK** to return to the working data file.

Figure 1-17 Message that the Portable File has been successfully created

Restoring Backup Files

When working with important financial information, creating backup files is a crucial safeguard against data loss. Every business should conduct regular backups of company information. QuickBooks has useful tools to automate this process.

In the event of an emergency, you may need to restore lost or damaged data. For example, if your computer's hard drive fails, you can restore your backup onto another computer and continue to work.

> Note:
> Portable files should never be used as a substitute for backup files. Backup files are larger than portable files and hold more information about the company.

Backing up Your Data File

Backing up your data is one of the most important safeguards you have to ensure the safety of your data.

> **DO NOT PERFORM THESE STEPS. THEY ARE FOR REFERENCE ONLY.**

1. To back up your company file, select **Create Copy** from the *File* menu.
2. Choose **Backup copy** from the *Save Copy or Backup* window (see Figure 1-18). Click **Next**.
3. You are given the option to save the backup to a local area, such as a removable hard disk, or an online backup using a fee-based service available from Intuit. Online backup is a good option for many companies.

   Choose **Local backup** and click **Next**.

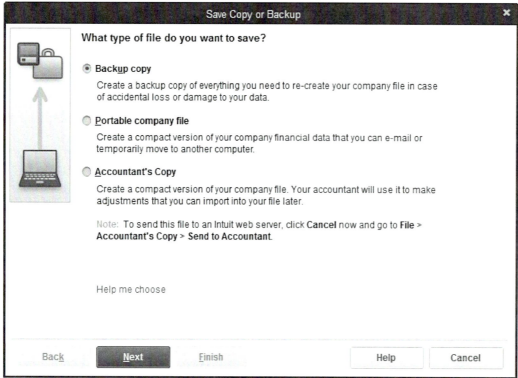

Figure 1-18 Save Copy or Backup window

4. The *Backup Options* window is displayed (see Figure 1-19). Under the *Local backup only* section, click the Browse button.

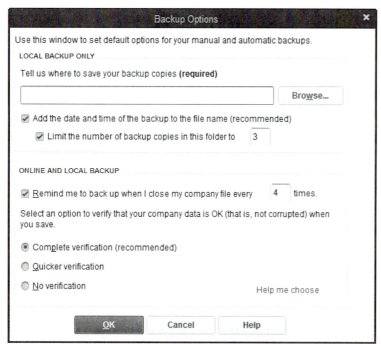

Figure 1-19 Backup Options window

5. Select the folder where you want to store your backup file (see Figure 1-20). You should store the backup files in a safe location, preferably on a different drive than your working data file. That way, if the drive with the working file is damaged, the backup will still be available.

Figure 1-20 Backup options Browse for Folder window

6. When finished, click OK.
7. The *Save Copy or Backup* window is displayed (see Figure 1-21). You can save a backup now, schedule future backups, or both. Select **Only schedule future backups** and click **Next**.

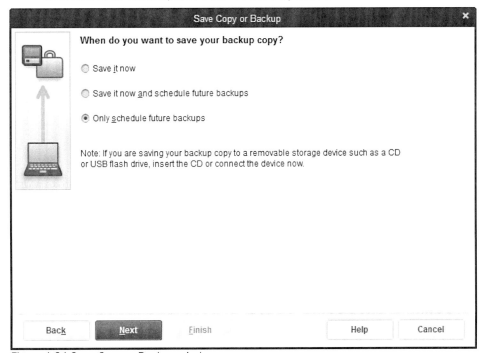

Figure 1-21 Save Copy or Backup window

8. In the *Save Copy or Backup* window, select **New** under the *Schedule Backup* area.

Figure 1-22 Save Copy or Backup window

9. The Schedule Backup window appears (see Figure 1-23). Enter a descriptive name for the backup, the location of the folder to contain the backups, and the time when the backup file will be created.

Figure 1-23 Schedule Backup window

10. When finished, click **OK** to close the *Schedule Backup* window.
11. The *Store Windows Password* window opens. Enter your Windows username and password and click **OK**.
12. Click **Finish** to close the *Schedule Backup* window.
13. If necessary, click **No, Thanks** for the offer to try Online Backup.

Restoring a Backup File

To restore a QuickBooks backup file, follow these steps.

Introducing QuickBooks - QuickBooks User Interface Features

> Do Not Perform These Steps. They Are For Reference Only.

1. Select the **File** menu and then select **Open or Restore Company**.
2. Choose **Restore a backup copy** from the *Open or Restore Company* window.
3. In the *Open or Restore Company* window you can specify whether the file is stored locally or through Intuit's fee-based *Online Backup* service. Choose **Local backup** and click **Next**.
4. The *Open Backup Copy* window allows you to specify where the backup file is locate. Navigate to the folder that contains the file, select it and click **Open**.
5. The *Open or Restore Company* window displays. Click **Next**.
6. The *Save Company File as* window allows you to specify where to restore the working files. Navigate to the appropriate folder and click **Save**. QuickBooks will then restore your backup file in the folder you specified. When QuickBooks restores the file, it creates a **.QBW** file.
7. If you receive the warning message shown in Figure 1-24, it means that QuickBooks is attempting to overwrite an existing file on your computer. If this is your intention, click **Yes**. You will be asked to confirm the deletion. If you do not intend to replace an existing file, click **No** and change the name of the restored file.

Figure 1-24 Restore To warning

> **Tip:** If you are not sure if you should replace a file, change the name of the restoring file slightly. For example *Intro-14 (version 2).QBW* would keep the file from being overwritten and indicate to users the most recent version.

8. After completion, a window displays that the new file has been successfully restored (see Figure 1-25).

Figure 1-25 After restoring backup file

> **Note:** When you restore a data file, depending on today's date, you may see one or more "Alerts" for learning to process credit cards, pay taxes, or similar activities. Click *Mark as Done* when you see these alerts.

QuickBooks User Interface Features

QuickBooks provides a number of shortcuts and aids that assist the user in entering information and transactions. You should become familiar with these features so you can get to a task quickly. There are various methods of accessing the data entry windows: the **Home** page, **Snapshots**, **Menus**, **QuickBooks Centers**, **Icon Bar**, and **Shortcut Keys**.

Home Page

As soon as you open a company file, QuickBooks displays the *Home* page (Figure 1-26). The *Home* page is broken into five sections – each dealing with a separate functional area of a business. These areas are: Vendors, Customers, Employees, Company, and Banking. Each area has icons to facilitate easy access to QuickBooks tasks. The *Home* page also displays a flow diagram showing the interdependency between tasks.

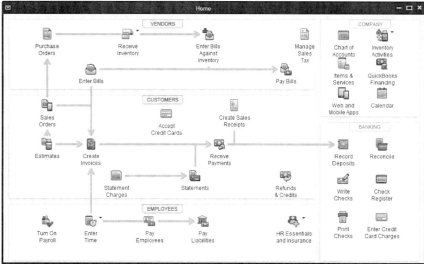

Figure 1-26 QuickBooks Accountant 2014 Home page

To start a task, just click on its related icon on the *Home* page. If you close the *Home* page, it can be opened by clicking on the **Home** icon on the Icon bar.

Centers

Centers are organized to give pertinent information in one place. There are several Centers for specific relationships and tasks.

Customer, Vendor, and Employee Centers are very important since they provide the only way to access a list of all your customers, vendors, and employees. These three lists are referred to as the *Center-based Lists*. These Centers summarize general information and transactions in the same area. For example, the Customer Center shows the customer balance, their general information, and all transactions for each customer (see Figure 1-27).

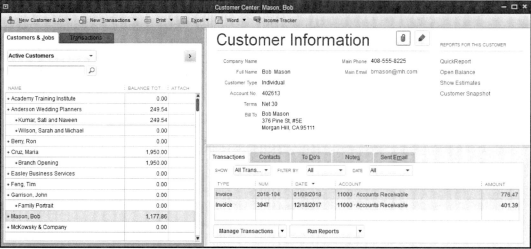

Figure 1-27 Customer Center

Introducing QuickBooks - QuickBooks User Interface Features   **19**

Other Centers include the *App Center*, *Bank Feeds Center*, *Report Center,* and *Doc Center*. These Centers will be addressed later in this book.

Snapshots

The *Snapshots* is a single screen summary of different aspects of a company. Charts such as *Income and Expense Trends*, *Previous Year Income Comparison,* and *Expense Breakdown* are displayed along with important lists such as *Account Balances* and *Customers Who Owe Money*. The Snapshots can be easily customized to show the information that is of most interest to you and your company.

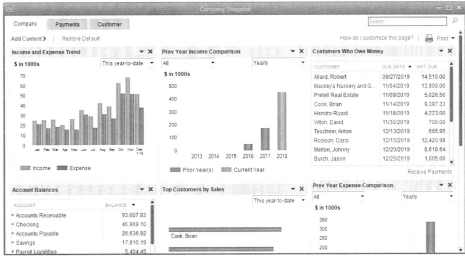
Figure 1-28 Snapshots - your screen may vary

Icon Bar

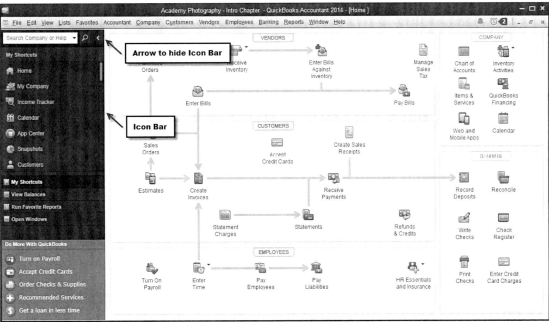
Figure 1-29 Icon Bar

The QuickBooks Icon Bar allows you to select activities and available services by clicking icons on the bar (see Figure 1-29). For example, you can open the Home page by clicking **Home** on the Icon Bar.

Calendar

You can view transactions on a *Calendar*. The calendar displays transaction on the *Entered* date and the *Due* date.

> **Note:**
> The *Entered* date is not literally the date when the transaction is entered into QuickBooks. It is the transaction date that is input on the transaction form. If you create an invoice on January 5th, 2018 and enter the date 01/06/2018 in the date field, the invoice will show on January 6th, 2018 on the Calendar.

Figure 1-30 QuickBooks Calendar- your screen may vary

COMPUTER PRACTICE

Step 1. Click the Calendar icon on the Company section of the Home page.

Step 2. The Calendar window opens (see Figure 1-30). When finished, close the Calendar window.

QuickBooks Mobile

You can download a mobile app called *QuickBooks for Windows* for a smartphone that enables you to use several QuickBooks features when you are not at your desktop computer. Features include accessing your customers' contact information as well as creating *Estimates*, *Invoices* and *Sales Receipts*. As of this printing, QuickBooks Mobile is available for iPhones, iPads, and Android devices and requires a paid QuickBooks Mobile Subscription.

> **Note:**
> There are two different QuickBooks mobile apps, *QuickBooks for Windows*, a companion to the QuickBooks desktop application discussed in this book and *QuickBooks Online*, which is a web based application. This book does not cover QuickBooks Online.

Entering Transactions in QuickBooks

Whenever you buy or sell products or services, pay a bill, make a deposit at the bank, or transfer money, you need to enter a transaction into QuickBooks.

Forms

In QuickBooks, transactions are created by filling out familiar-looking forms such as invoices, bills, and checks. When you finish filling out a form, QuickBooks automatically records the accounting entries behind the scenes. Most forms in QuickBooks have drop-down lists to allow you to pick from a list instead of spelling the name of a customer, vendor, item, or account.

COMPUTER PRACTICE

Step 1. Click the **Enter Bills** icon on the *Home page* Vendors section (see Figure 1-31).

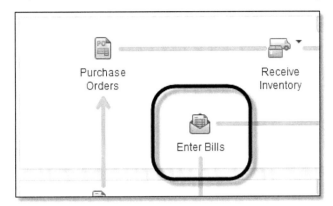

Figure 1-31 Enter Bills on the Home page

Step 2. Click the **Previous** button in the upper left corner of the *Enter Bills* window until you see the previously entered bills in Figure 1-32.

Step 3. Click the down arrow next to the vendor field to see the dropdown list for vendors.

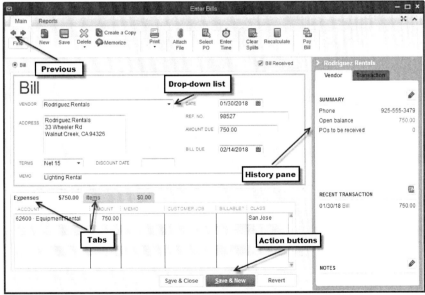

Figure 1-32 Bill form

Step 4. Click the calendar icon next to the date to see the calendar pop-up menu.

Step 5. When finished exploring, click the **Revert** button which will return the transaction to the last saved state.

Step 6. Close the Enter Bills window.

By using forms to enter transactions, you provide QuickBooks with *all of the details* of each transaction. For example, by using the Enter Bills form in Figure 1-32, QuickBooks will track the vendor balance, the due date of the bill, the discount terms, and the debits and credits in the General Ledger. This is a good example of how QuickBooks handles the accounting behind the scenes, and also provides management information beyond just the accounting entries.

Lists

Lists are one of the most important building blocks of QuickBooks. Lists store information that is used again and again to fill out forms. For example, when you set up a customer, including their name, address and other details, QuickBooks can use the information to automatically fill out an invoice. Similarly, when an Item is set up, QuickBooks can automatically fill in the Item's description, price, and associated account information. This helps speed up data entry and reduce errors.

> **Note:**
> There are two kinds of lists — **menu-based** and **center-based**. Menu-based lists are accessible through the *Lists* menu and include the *Item* list and *Terms* lists. Center-based lists include the *Customer Center* and *Vendor Center*, discussed on page 18.

Lists can be viewed by selecting an icon from the *Home* page (for example, the *Items & Services* button), choosing a menu option from the *Lists* menu, or viewing a list through one of the various QuickBooks Centers.

Accounts

QuickBooks provides the means to efficiently track all of your business transactions by categorizing them into *accounts*. The **Chart of Accounts** is the list of these accounts.

COMPUTER PRACTICE

Step 1.　To display the Chart of Accounts, click the *Chart of Accounts* icon on the *Home* page. Alternatively, you could select **Chart of Accounts** from the *List* menu, or press **Ctrl+A**.

Step 2.　Scroll through the list. Leave the *Chart of Accounts* open for the next exercise.

By default, the Chart of Accounts is sorted *by account number* within each account type (see Figure 1-33). The *Name* column shows the account names that you assign; the *Type* column shows their account type; the *Balance Total* column shows the balance for asset, liability, and equity accounts (except Retained Earnings), and the ***Attach*** column shows if there are attached documents.

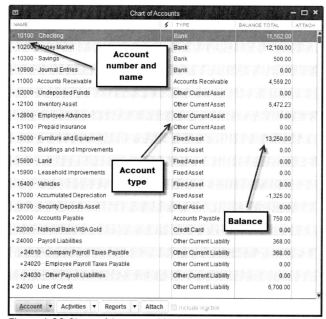

Figure 1-33 Chart of Accounts List

Registers

Each asset, liability, and equity account (except Retained Earnings) has a *register* (see page 2 for more information on these account types). Registers allow you to view and edit transactions in a single window. Income and expense accounts do not have registers; rather, their transactions must be viewed in a report.

COMPUTER PRACTICE

Step 1. To open the *Checking* account register, double-click on **10100 Checking** in the *Chart of Accounts* list.

Step 2. The **Checking** register opens (see Figure 1-34). Scroll through the register.

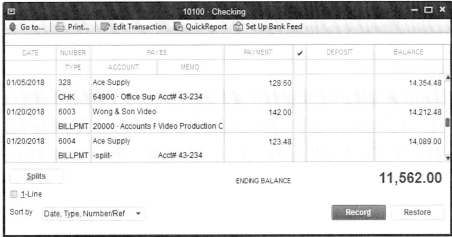

Figure 1-34 Checking account register

Step 3. Close the Checking account register by clicking the close button in the upper right corner.

Step 4. Double click the **40000 Services** account. You may need to scroll down. This is an *Income* account.

Step 5. Instead of opening a register, QuickBooks opens a report (see Figure 1-35).

Step 6. If necessary, change the *Date* field to **All**.

Step 7. Close the report.

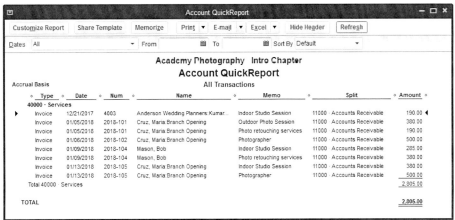

Figure 1-35 Services Account QuickReport – your screen may vary

Step 8. Close the Chart of Accounts.

Items

Items are used to track products and services. Since every business has its own unique set of products and services, QuickBooks can be customized by creating Items for each service or product your company buys or sells. For more detail on Items and the different Item Types, see page 294.

When you define Items, you associate Item names with Accounts in the Chart of Accounts. This association between Item names and Accounts is the "magic" that allows QuickBooks to automatically create the accounting entries behind each transaction.

For example, Figure 1-37 displays the *Item* list. The Item, **Camera SR32**, is associated, or linked, to the **Sales** account in the Chart of Accounts. Every time the **Camera SR32** Item is entered on an invoice, the dollar amount actually affects the **Sales** account in the Chart of Accounts.

Items are necessary because to use a sales form in QuickBooks (e.g., invoices and sales receipts), you must use Items. On an invoice, for example, every line item will have a QuickBooks Item which may represent products, services, discounts, or sales tax.

COMPUTER PRACTICE

Step 1. To see what Items are available in the file, click the **Item & Services** icon on the *Home page in the company section* (see Figure 1-36). Alternatively, you could select **Item List** from the *Lists* menu.

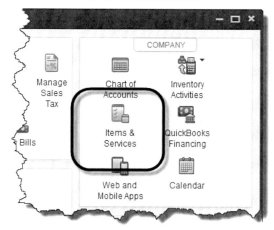

Figure 1-36 Items & Services button on Home page

Step 2. Figure 1-37 shows the *Item* list. Double click the **Camera SR32** item.

NAME	DESCRIPTION	TYPE	ACCOUNT	TOTAL QUANTITY	ON SALE	PRICE	ATTA
Indoor Photo Session	Indoor Studio Session	Service	40000 · Services			95.00	
Outdoor Photo Session	Outdoor Photo Session	Service	40000 · Services			95.00	
Photographer	Photographer	Service	40000 · Services			125.00	
Retouching	Photo retouching services	Service	40000 · Services			95.00	
Camera SR32	Supra Digital Camera SR32	Inventory Part	45000 · Sales	9	0	695.99	
Case	Camera and Lens High Impact Case	Inventory Part	45000 · Sales	24	0	79.99	
Frame 5x7	Picture Frame - 5' x 7' Metal Frame	Inventory Part	45000 · Sales	22	0	5.99	
Lens	Supra Zoom Lens	Inventory Part	45000 · Sales	7	0	324.99	
Photo Paper	Standard Photo Paper, Glossy, 8.5"x11", 7 Mil, Pa...	Non-inventory Part	45000 · Sales			12.36	
Premium Photo Package	Premium Package of Photography from Session	Non-inventory Part	45000 · Sales			85.00	
Standard Photo Package	Standard Package of Photography from Session	Non-inventory Part	45000 · Sales			55.00	
Bad Debt	Bad Debt - Write off	Other Charge	60300 · Bad Debts			0.00	
Bounce Chg	Return Check Fee	Other Charge	45000 · Sales			0.00	
Contra Costa	Contra Costa County Sales Tax	Sales Tax Item	25500 · Sales Tax Payable			8.25%	
Out of State	Out-of-state sale, exempt from sales tax	Sales Tax Item	25500 · Sales Tax Payable			0.0%	
Santa Clara	Santa Clara County Sales Tax	Sales Tax Item	25500 · Sales Tax Payable			8.25%	

Figure 1-37 Item List

Step 3. If the New Feature window opens, click **OK**.

Step 4. The *Edit Item* window opens (see Figure 1-38). Notice this item is linked to the Sales account. Every time this item is entered on an invoice, it changes the **Sales** account.

Step 5. Close the *Edit Item* and *Item List* windows.

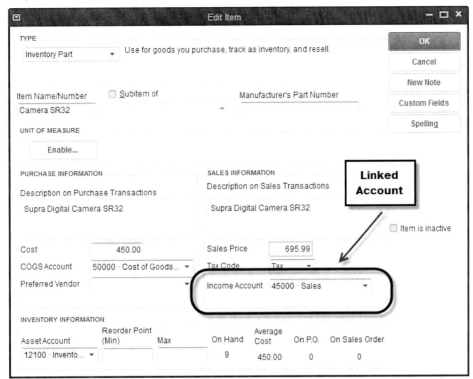

Figure 1-38 Camera SR32 Edit Item window – your screen may vary

QuickBooks Help

Support Resources

QuickBooks provides a variety of support resources that assist in using the program. Some of these resources are on the Internet and others are stored in help files locally along with the QuickBooks software on your computer. To access the support resources, select the *Help* menu and then select **QuickBooks Help**. QuickBooks will display answers to problems you might be having based on your recent activity. You can also enter a question and QuickBooks will search its Help Content and the Online Community for related answers.

QuickBooks Learning Center

As you begin using QuickBooks, the first thing you see is the QuickBooks Learning Center (see Figure 1-39). This center provides interactive tutorials to help users learn how to use QuickBooks in common business scenarios. If you have deactivated the Learning Center so that it does not start once the program is launched, you can always access it by selecting **Learning Center Tutorials** from the *Help* menu.

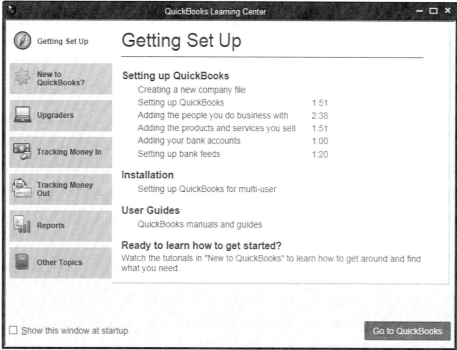
Figure1- 1-39 QuickBooks Help Menu

Certified QuickBooks ProAdvisors

Certified QuickBooks ProAdvisors are independent consultants, accountants, bookkeepers, and educators who are proficient in QuickBooks and who can offer guidance to small businesses in various areas of business accounting. To find a Certified ProAdvisor, select **Find a Local QuickBooks Expert** from the *Help* menu.

Another source of highly qualified advisors, certified by the author of this book can be found at The Sleeter Group's web site at www.sleeter.com.

Review Questions

Comprehension Questions

1. Explain the difference between a QuickBooks working data file, a QuickBooks backup file and a QuickBooks portable file. How can you differentiate between the three types of files on your hard disk?

2. What is the main reason for creating portable files?

3. Explain the importance of the QuickBooks Home page.

4. Explain why it is important to enter transactions in QuickBooks using Forms rather than accounting entries.

5. Describe the primary purpose of accounting in business.

Multiple Choice

Select the best answer(s) for each of the following:

1. The fundamental accounting equation that governs all accounting is:
    a) Net income = Revenue - expenses.
    b) Assets + Liabilities = Equity.
    c) Assets = Liabilities + Equity.
    d) Assets = Liabilities - Equity.

2. Which of the following statements is true?
    a) Debits are bad because they reduce income.
    b) Equity is increased by a net loss.
    c) Debits - credits = 0.
    d) Assets are increased with a credit entry.

3. Under accrual accounting:
    a) A sale is not recorded until the customer pays the bill.
    b) Income and expenses are recognized when transactions occur.
    c) An expense is not recorded until you write the check.
    d) You must maintain two separate accounting systems.

4. QuickBooks is:
    a) A job costing system.
    b) A payroll system.
    c) A double-entry accounting system.
    d) All of the above.

5. Which is not a method of accessing the data entry screens?
    a) Menus
    b) Home page
    c) Icon bar
    d) Data entry button

Completion Statements

1. As you enter data in familiar-looking _____, QuickBooks handles the _____ entries for you.

2. You should _____ your data file regularly because it is one of the most important safeguards you can do to ensure the safety of your data.

3. When you open your working data file, QuickBooks displays the _____ _____. This page is broken into five sections – each dealing with a separate functional area of a business.

4. _____ are used in QuickBooks Sales forms and represent what the company buys and sells.

5. A list which shows all the accounts in your working data file is called the _____ __ _____.

Introduction Problem 1

> Restore the Intro-14Problem1.QBM file.

1. Select **Customers** from the QuickBooks *Icon* Bar. This will display the *Customer Center*.
   a) What is the first customer listed on the left of the Customer Center? *AAA Services*

   > **Note:**
   > The answer to this first question is **AAA Services**. If you don't see AAA Services in the *Customer Center*, make sure to restore *Intro-14Problem1.QBM* as directed in the box above. *This book uses specific files for each chapter and each problem. If you don't restore the correct file, you will have trouble completing the exercises.*

   b) In the Customers & Jobs Center, single click on **Miranda's Corner**. What is Miranda's Corner's balance? *$3575.00*
   c) Click the *Date* dropdown list above the transaction listing in the right-hand panel and scroll up to the top of the list to select **All**. How many transactions do you see and of what type? *0 None*
   d) Close the Customer Center.

2. From the *Home Page*, click the **Enter Bills** icon. The *Enter Bills* window opens.
   a) Click the previous button in the upper left corner. What is the name of the Vendor displayed on this Bill? *Sinclair Insurance*
   b) What is the amount of this bill? *$400.00*

3. From the *Home* page, click the **Chart of Accounts** icon to display the Chart of Accounts.
   a) What type of account is the **Checking** Account? *Bank*
   b) How many total accounts are there of this same type? *4*
   c) What is the Balance Total for the National Bank VISA Gold Credit Card account? *$600.00*

Introduction Problem 2 (Advanced)

> Restore the Intro-14Problem2.QBM file.

1. Select **Customers** from the QuickBooks *Icon* Bar. This will display the *Customer Center*.
   a) What is the first customer listed on the left of the Customer Center?

   > **Note:**
   > The answer to this first question is **ABC International**. If you don't see ABC International in the *Customer Center*, make sure to restore *Intro-14Problem2.QBM* as directed in the box above. *This book uses specific files for each chapter and each problem. If you don't restore the correct file, you will have trouble completing the exercises.*

   b) In the Customers & Jobs Center, single click on **Anderson Wedding Planners: Kumar, Sati and Naveen**. What is Anderson Wedding Planners' balance?
   c) Click the *Date* dropdown list above the transaction listing in the right-hand panel and scroll up to the top of the list to select **All**. How many transactions do you see and of what type?
   d) Close the Customer Center.

Introducing QuickBooks - Introduction Problem 2 (Advanced)   **29**

2. Select **Vendors** from the QuickBooks *Icon* Bar. This displays the *Vendor Center*.
    a) Double-click *Rodriguez Rentals*. This opens the *Edit Vendor* window. What is the Address? Close the *Edit Vendor* window.
    b) What is the amount of Bill number 5055 to *Sinclair Insurance*? (You may need to set the *Date* to **All** as in Step 1.)
    c) Close the Vendor Center.

3. From the *Home* page, click the **Chart of Accounts** icon to display the Chart of Accounts.
    a) What type of account is the **Furniture and Equipment** Account?
    b) How many accounts of type **Bank** are in the Chart of Accounts?
    c) How many accounts of type **Fixed Asset** are in the Chart of Accounts?

4. While still in the **Chart of Accounts**, Double-click the **Checking** account on the Chart of Accounts list. This will open the register for Checking account.
    a) Who was the payee for the check on 2/11/2018?
    b) What was the amount of the check?
    c) Close the checking account register and Chart of Accounts list.

5. Click the **Create Invoices** icon on the *Home page*, and then click on the **Previous** arrow (top left).
    a) What is the Invoice Date?
    b) How many different Items are listed in this invoice?
    c) Close the invoice.

6. Select the **Chart of Accounts** option from the *Lists* menu. Double-click on the **Checking** account.
    a) Which vendor was paid by the last bill payment in the register?
    b) What is the amount of the last bill payment in the register?
    c) Close the **Checking** register and close the **Chart of Accounts** list.

7. Click the **Write Checks** icon on the *Home* page and follow these steps:
    a) Click on the *Calendar* icon immediately to the right of the *Date* field. Select **tomorrow's date** in the *Date* field and press **Tab**.
    b) In the Pay to the Order of field, enter *Parker, William S., CPA*. Press **Tab**.
    c) Enter *80.00* in the *Amount* field and press **Tab**.
    d) Click in the **Print Later** check box at the top of the window.
    e) What is the city displayed in the Address field on the check for *Parker, William S., CPA*?
    f) Click **Clear** and then close the check window.

8. Select the **Chart of Accounts** option from the *Lists* menu and double-click on **Accounts Receivable**.
    a) What is the ending balance in the account?
    b) Who was the customer on the last transaction in the register?
    c) Close the register and the Chart of Accounts.

9. Click the **Check Register** button on the Home page.
    a) Select **10100 – Checking** from the *Use Register* dialog box.
    b) What is the ending balance in the checking register?
    c) Close the Checking Register.

10. Close the working data file Intro-14Problem2.QBW.

QUICKBOOKS AND BEYOND – *TAKE THE NEXT STEP WITH THE SLEETER GROUP BLOG*

QuickBooks and Beyond, The Sleeter Group's blog (www.sleeter.com/blog) offers innovative and up-to-date news on small business accounting technology. It goes beyond the QuickBooks material covered in this textbook. You will find blog posts that range from how to handle specific QuickBooks issues to cloud-based accounting tools. Each chapter includes an excerpt and reference to a relevant blog post, including an explanation of new terminology you might encounter and questions to help you evaluate how you would use this information in your own company or workplace.

"From Click to Cart: A Holiday Survival Guide for Small Business Retailers"

The holidays can be the most wonderful time of the year for retailers of all sizes and specialties. With gift purchases representing more than 47% of total holiday sales and with as much as 40% of annual sales occurring in the last two months of the year for some businesses, retailers need to gear up for the season and look for new ways to streamline operations. A solid holiday plan will attract new and repeat customers, allowing businesses to enjoy strong holiday sales and to continue the trend throughout the year.

In this *QuickBooks and Beyond* section, Fred Lizza covers what your company can do to prepare for the holiday season. Read the full post at www.sleeter.com/blog/?p=4912.

New Terminology

SEO – Search Engine Optimization, or a process of making your website or web store prominent on search engines, such as Google.

HTML 5 – The fifth and most recent revision of a markup language used for structuring and presenting content on the World Wide Web. Acronym stands for Hypertext Markup Language.

Rich Media – Interactive multimedia, or media that uses a combination of different content forms.

Putting New Knowledge to Use

1. Is the end of the year a busy season for your business or workplace? If not, are there other busy seasons you need to prepare for?

Chapter 2
The Sales Process

Topics

In this chapter, you will learn about the following topics:
- Tracking Company Sales (page 31)
- Setting Up Customers (page 35)
- Job Costing (page 40)
- Recording Sales (page 41)
- Receiving Payments from Customers (page 53)
- Making Bank Deposits (page 61)
- Income Tracker (page 68)

> **Restore this File:**
> This chapter uses Sales-14.QBW. To open this file, restore the Sales-14.QBM file to your hard disk. See page 9 for instructions on restoring files.
>
> **Note:** When you restore a data file, depending on today's date, you may see one or more "Alerts" for learning to process credit cards, pay taxes, or similar activities. Click Mark as Done when you see these alerts.

In this chapter, you will learn how QuickBooks can help you record and track revenues in your business.

Each time you sell products or services, you will record the transaction using one of QuickBooks' forms. When you fill out a QuickBooks **Invoice** or **Sales Receipt**, QuickBooks tracks the detail of each sale, allowing you to create reports about your sales.

Tracking Company Sales

Sales are recorded two different ways, either with a *Sales Receipt* when the customer pays at the time of sale or service (called *cash customers*), or an *Invoice* when the customer pays after the sale or service (*credit customers*). Transactions with cash customers follow a specific process. At the time of sale, a Sales Receipt is issued, and then a deposit is recorded. This process is displayed graphically on the Home Page (Figure 2-1). A Sales Receipt records both the items sold and the amount received. Then the funds are deposited.

> **Note:**
> Payment with a credit card is received immediately, therefore a customer who pays at the time of sale with a credit card is a cash customer.

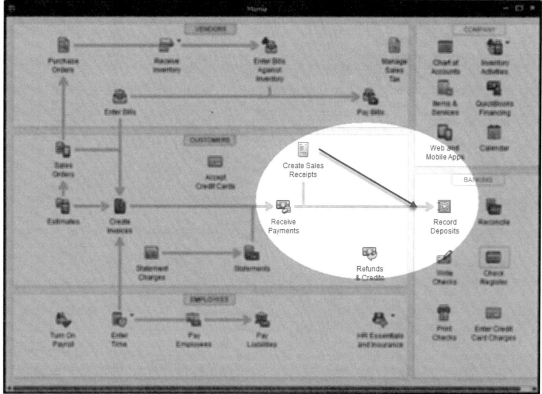

Figure 2-1 Payment with Cash Sale Workflow

When working with a credit customer, the sales process has a different workflow. Often, the first step is to create an Invoice. The payment is received and the amount is applied to the Invoice. Then a deposit is recorded. This process is displayed in Figure 2-2.

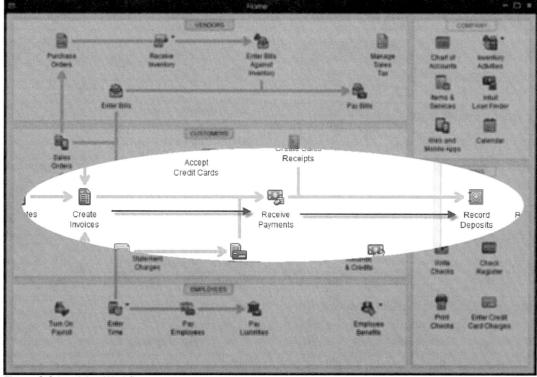

Figure 2-2 Invoicing Workflow

Table 2-1 provides more details about the cash and credit customer sales processes. In this table, you can see how to record business transactions for cash and credit customers. In addition, the table shows the *accounting behind the scenes* of each transaction. As discussed on page 4, the accounting behind the scenes is critical to your understanding of how QuickBooks converts the information on forms (Invoices, Sales Receipts, etc.) into accounting entries.

Each row in the table represents a business transaction you might enter as you proceed through the sales process.

Business Transaction	Cash Customers (Pay at time of sale)		Credit Customers (Pay after the sale date)	
	QuickBooks Transaction	Accounting Entry	QuickBooks Transaction	Accounting Entry
Estimate (Optional)	Not Usually Used		Estimates	Non-posting entry used to record estimates (bids) for Customers or Jobs
Sales Order (Optional)	Not Usually Used		Sales Orders	Non-posting entry used to record customer orders
Recording a Sale	Create Sales Receipts	Increase (debit) Undeposited Funds, increase (credit) *income* account	Create Invoices	Increase (debit) Accounts Receivable, increase (credit) *income* account
Receiving Money in Payment of an Invoice	No additional action is required on the sales form.		Receive Payments	Increase (debit) Undeposited Funds, decrease (credit) Accounts Receivable
Depositing Money in the Bank	Record Deposits	Decrease (credit) Undeposited Funds, increase (debit) *bank* account	Record Deposits	Decrease (credit) Undeposited Funds, increase (debit) *bank* account

Table 2-1 Steps in the sales process

The *Sales Receipt* form records the details of who you sold to and what you sold and then uses, by default, a special account called **Undeposited Funds**. This account is an *Other Current Asset* account, and it can be thought of as a drawer where you keep your checks and other deposits before depositing in the bank. See page 45 for more information on **Undeposited Funds**.

> **The accounting behind the scenes:**
> When you create a **Sales Receipt**, QuickBooks increases (with a debit) **a bank account or Undeposited Funds**, and increases (with a credit) the appropriate *income* account. If applicable, **Sales Receipts** also increase (with a credit) the sales tax liability account. If the sale includes an Inventory Item, it also decreases (credits) the Inventory asset and increases (debits) the Cost of Goods Sold account.

For credit customers, the sales process usually starts with creating an **Invoice**. The **Invoice** form records the details of who you sold to and what you sold.

> **The accounting behind the scenes:**
> When you create an **Invoice**, QuickBooks increases (with a debit) **Accounts Receivable** and increases (with a credit) the appropriate *income* account. If applicable, **Invoices** also increase (with a credit) the sales tax liability account. If the sale includes an Inventory Item, it also decreases (credits) the Inventory asset and increases (debits) the Cost of Goods Sold account.

When you receive money from your credit customers, use the **Receive Payments** function to record the receipt. If you have created an *Invoice*, you must accept payment through this process to close the *Invoice*.

> **The accounting behind the scenes:**
> When you record a received **Payment**, QuickBooks increases (with a debit) **Undeposited Funds** or a bank account, and decreases (with a credit) **Accounts Receivable**.

Whether you posted to Undeposited Funds through a **Sales Receipt** or a **Payment**, the last step in the process is to make a **Deposit** to your bank account. This step is the same for both cash and credit customers. Use the **Make Deposits** function to record the deposit to your bank account.

If you prepare estimates (sometimes called bids) for Customers or Jobs, you can create an **Estimate** to track the details of what the sale will include. Estimates are provided to customers to help them decide on their purchases, products or services. QuickBooks does not post **Estimates** to the **General Ledger**, but it helps you track the estimate until the job is complete. QuickBooks also provides reports that help you compare estimated vs. actual revenues and costs.

> **The accounting behind the scenes:**
> When you create an **Estimate**, QuickBooks records the estimate, but there is no accounting entry made. **Estimates** are "non-posting" entries.

If you use sales orders in your business, you can use a **Sales Order** form to track the details of what the sale will include. For example, if you order goods you currently have out of stock for a specific customer, you could create a **Sales Order** to track the Customer's order. **Sales Orders** are very similar to **Estimates** because they are both non-posting entries, and they both help you track future sales. QuickBooks does not post **Sales Orders** to the **General Ledger**, but it helps you track your orders until they are shipped to the customer. **Sales Orders** are only available in QuickBooks Premier, Accountant and Enterprise Solutions.

> **The accounting behind the scenes:**
> When you create a **Sales Order**, QuickBooks records the sales order, but there is no accounting entry made. **Sales Orders** are "non-posting" entries.

In the following sections, you will learn about each step of the payment at the time of sale and invoicing workflows.

The Sales Process - Setting Up Customers

Setting Up Customers

For each of your customers, create a record in the **Customers & Jobs** list of the *Customer Center*. Academy Photography has a new credit customer – Dr. Tim Feng. To add this new customer, follow these steps:

COMPUTER PRACTICE

Step 1. Select the **Customers** button from the *Icon bar*.

Step 2. To add a new customer, select **New Customer** from the **New Customer & Job** drop-down menu (see Figure 2-3).

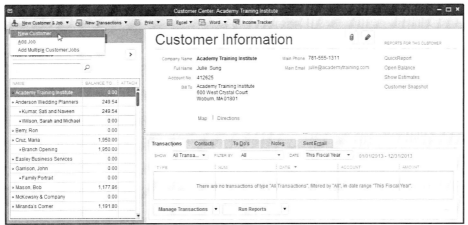

Figure 2-3 Adding a new customer record

Step 3. Enter *Feng, Tim* in the *Customer Name* field (see Figure 2-4) and then press **Tab**.

Step 4. Press **Tab** twice to skip the *Opening Balance* and *as of* fields. Since you will not enter an amount in the *Opening Balance* field, there is no need to change the *as of* date.

Figure 2-4 New Customer window

> **Important Tip:**
> It is best NOT to use the *Opening Balance* field in the customer record. When you enter an opening balance for a customer in the *Opening Balance* field, QuickBooks creates a new account in your Chart of Accounts called Uncategorized Income. Then, it creates an **Invoice** that increases (debits) **Accounts Receivable** and increases (credits) **Uncategorized Income**.
>
> It is preferable to enter the actual open *Invoices* for each customer when you set up your company file. That way, you will have all of the details of which Invoice is open, and what Items were sold on the open Invoices. When you use Invoices, the actual income accounts will be used instead of **Uncategorized Income**.

Step 5.   Because this customer is an individual (i.e., not a company), press **Tab** to skip the *Company Name* field.

Step 6.   Continue entering information in the rest of the fields using the data in Table 2-2. You do not need to enter anything in the fields not included below.

Field	Data
Mr./Mrs.	Dr.
First Name	Tim
M.I.	S.
Last Name	Feng
Job Title	Owner
Main Phone	408-555-8297
Main Email	drf@df.biz
Invoice/Bill To Address **Hint:** Press **Enter** to move to a new line in this field.	Tim S. Feng 300 Main St., Suite 3 San Jose, CA 95111
Ship To	Click >>**Copy**>>. This displays the *Add Shipping Address Information* window (see Figure 2-5). Type *Office* in the Address Name field and click **OK**. In QuickBooks, you can select multiple Ship To addresses for your customers.

Table 2-2 Data to complete the Address Info tab

Figure 2-5 Add Ship To Address Information window

Figure 2-6 shows the finished Address Info section of the customer record. Verify that your screen matches Figure 2-6.

The Sales Process - Setting Up Customers   **37**

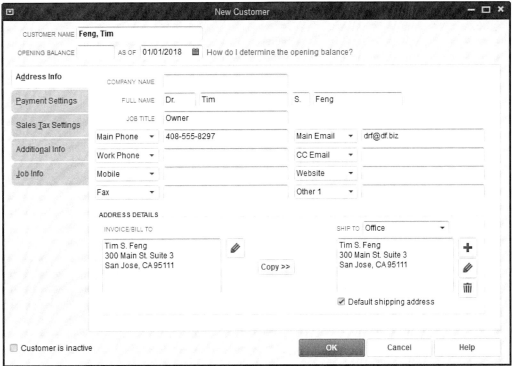

Figure 2-6 Completed Address Info tab

> **Tip:**
> There are four name lists in QuickBooks: **Vendor, Customer:Job, Employee,** and **Other Names**. After you enter a name in the *Customer Name* field of the *New Customer* window, you cannot use that name in any of the other three lists in QuickBooks.
>
> **When Customers are Vendors:**
> When you sell to and purchase from the same company, you'll need to create two records – one in the Vendor List and one in the Customer:Job list. Make the two names slightly different. For example, you could enter Feng, Tim-C in the *New Customer* window and Feng, Tim-V in the *New Vendor* window. The vendor and customer records for Tim Feng can contain the same contact information.

Step 7.   Click the **Payment Settings** tab on the left of the *New Customer* window to continue entering information about this customer as shown in Figure 2-7.

Step 8.   Enter *3543* in the *Account No.* field to assign a customer number by which you can sort or filter reports. Press **Tab**.

Step 9.   Enter *5,000.00* in the *Credit Limit* field and press **Tab**.

QuickBooks will warn you if you record an Invoice to this customer when the balance due (plus the current sale) exceeds the credit limit. Even though QuickBooks warns you, you'll still be able to record the Invoice.

Step 10.   Select **Net 30** from the *Payment Terms* drop-down list as the terms for this customer and then press **Tab**.

QuickBooks is *terms smart*. For example, if you enter terms of 2% 10 Net 30 and a customer pays within 10 days, QuickBooks will automatically calculate a 2% discount. For more information about setting up your Terms list, see page 300.

Figure 2-7 Completed Payment Settings tab

Step 11. Select **Commercial** from the *Price Level* drop-down list. See page 302 for information on setting up and using price levels. Press **Tab**.

Step 12. Leave the default setting of **None** in the *Preferred Delivery Method* field and **Follow Company Default** in the *Add Online Payment Link to Invoices* field.

You would use the *Preferred Delivery Method* field if you plan to email Invoices to a customer on a regular basis or if you plan to use QuickBooks' Invoice printing and mailing service.

> **Note:**
> For more information on the QuickBooks invoice payment and mailing service, select the **Help** menu and then select **Add QuickBooks Services**. You will then be directed online to the Intuit website. Scroll down and click on the **QuickBooks Billing Solutions** link under the *Financial Services* section. Additional transaction fees apply for this service.

Step 13. Select **Visa** from the *Preferred Payment Method* drop-down list and then press **Tab**. When you set the fields on this window, you won't have to enter the credit card information each time you receive money from the customer.

> **Tip:**
> If more than one person accesses your QuickBooks file, set up a separate user name and password for each additional user. When you set up a user, you can restrict him or her from accessing *Sensitive Accounting Activities*. This will prevent the additional user from seeing the customer's credit card number. See page 270 for more information about setting up user names and passwords.

Step 14. Enter the remaining data as shown in Figure 2-7 in the *Credit Card Information* section. Some of the fields will auto-populate as you tab into those fields. You may overwrite the auto-populated values if needed.

If you use the QuickBooks merchant account service, enter the default credit card

The Sales Process - Setting Up Customers

number in the *Preferred Payment Method* area. This sets defaults on sales transactions for this customer.

> **Note:**
> If you track multiple jobs for each customer, it is best NOT to enter job information on the *Job Info* tab of the main customer record. If you want to track jobs for this customer, you can create separate job records in the **Customers & Jobs** list.

Step 15. Click the **Sales Tax Settings** tab in the *New Customer* window (see Figure 2-8).

Step 16. Press **Tab** to accept the **Tax** default **Sales Tax Code** in the *Tax Code* field.

Sales Tax Codes serve two purposes. First, they determine the default taxable status of a customer, item, or sale. Second, they are used to identify the type of tax exemption. For complete information on sales tax codes, see page 91.

Step 17. Set the *Tax Item* field to **Santa Clara**. This indicates which sales tax rate to charge and which agency collects the tax. Press **Tab** when finished.

> **Tip:**
> In most states, you charge sales tax based on the delivery point of the shipment. Therefore, the **Sales Tax Item** should be chosen to match the tax charged in the county (or tax location) of the *Ship To* address on the *Address Info* tab.

Step 18. Leave the *Resale No.* field blank.

If the customer is a reseller, you would enter his or her reseller number.

Figure 2-8 Completed Sales Tax tab

Step 19. Select the **Additional Info** tab in the *New Customer* window (see Figure 2-9).

Step 20. Select **Business** from the *Customer Type* drop-down list and then press **Tab**.

QuickBooks allows you to group your customers into common types. By grouping your customers into types, you'll be able to create reports that focus on one or more types. For example, if you create two types of customers, Residential and Business, you are able to tag each customer with a type. Then you can create reports, statements, or mailing labels for all customers of a certain type.

Step 21. Select **MM** or Mike Mazuki in the *Rep* drop-down list and then press **Tab**.

The *Rep* field can contain the initials of one of your employees or vendors. Use this field to assign a sales rep to this customer. If you use the *Rep* field, you can create reports (e.g., Sales by Rep report) that provide the sales information you need to pay commissions. Each sales form (**Invoice** or **Sales Receipt**) can have a different name in the *Rep* field.

Step 22. Enter *Santa Clara* in the *County* field.

The **Define Fields** button on the **Additional Information** tab allows you to define **Custom Fields** to track more information about your customers. For more information on setting up and using custom fields, see page 304.

Figure 2-9 Completed Additional Info tab

Step 23. Click **OK** to save and close the *New Customer* window.

> Note:
> If you see an error message when saving the Feng, Tim customer (see Figure 2-10), you may not be in the correct exercise file. Make sure you restore the correct file at the start of each chapter and problem, otherwise your exercises may not match the activities in this book. For this chapter, you should be using Sales-14.QBW. For instructions on restoring portable files, please see page 9.

Figure 2-10 Error Message when saving a Name that already exists

Step 24. Close the Customer Center by clicking the close button on the *Customer Center* window or by pressing the **Esc** key.

Job Costing

Each customer listed in the *Customer Center* can have one or more jobs. Setting up *Jobs* for *Customers* helps you track income and expenses by job and therefore create reports showing detailed or summarized information about each job. This is particularly important for some industries, such as construction.

To create a job for an existing customer record, open the *Customer Center*, then select the customer, and then select **Add Job** from the **New Customer & Job** drop down menu. You don't need to do this now, because the sample data file already has Jobs set up.

Figure 2-11 Adding a Job to an existing customer record

> **Key Term:**
> Tracking income and expenses separately for each Job is known as *Job Costing*. If your company needs to track job costs, make sure you include the Job name on each income and expense transaction as these transactions are entered.

In the **Name** column of the *Customers & Jobs* list, Jobs are slightly indented under the Customer name.

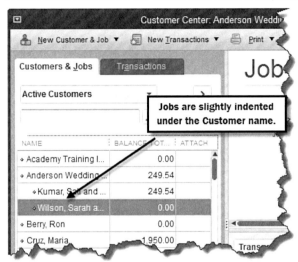

Figure 2-12 Customers & Jobs list

> **Did You Know?**
> To *Quick Add* a **Job** for a **Customer** on an Invoice or Sales Receipt, enter the Customer's name followed by a colon (the Customer name must already exist in the Customer list first). After the colon, enter the name of the job. QuickBooks will then prompt you to either *Quick Add* or *Set Up* the Job. If the *Customer* record already includes job information on its Job tab, you won't be able to use *Quick Add* to create a Job for the customer. In this case, you will need to create the job in the **Customers & Jobs** list before you begin entering sales.

Recording Sales

Now that you've set up your *Customers*, you're ready to begin entering sales. We will look at the *Sales Receipts* form first. Use this form when you receive a cash, check, or credit card payment at the time of the sale. We will also look at the *Invoice*, the other way to enter sales. Use this form when you record credit sales to customers.

Entering Sales Receipts

When customers pay at the time of the sale by cash, check, or credit card, create a **Sales Receipt** transaction.

COMPUTER PRACTICE

Step 1. Click the **Create Sales Receipts** icon in the *Customers* section on the *Home* page (see Figure 2-13). This opens the *Enter Sales Receipts* window (see Figure 2-14).

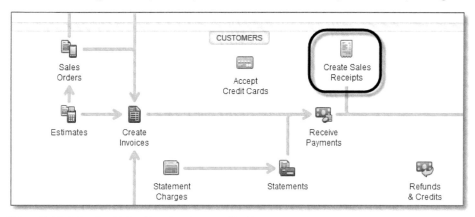

Figure 2-13 Selecting Sales Receipts icon on the Home page

Step 2. Enter *Perez, Jerry* in the *Customer:Job* field and press **Tab**.

> **Note:**
> Many forms display Customer Summary information in the *History Pane* on the right side of the form, which includes two tabs – one for *Customer* (also called *Name*) information and the other for *Transaction* information. Jerry Perez is a new Customer and therefore does not have any information or history to display.

Step 3. When the *Customer:Job Not Found* warning window appears (see Figure 2-15), click **Quick Add** to add this new customer to the *Customer:Job* list. If you choose this option, you can edit the customer record later to add more details.

Figure 2-14 Sales Receipt form

> **Note:**
> **Quick Add** works on all your lists. Whenever you type a new name into any field on any form, QuickBooks prompts you to **Quick Add, Set Up,** or **Cancel** the name.
>
> **Tip:**
> If your customer is an individual (i.e., not a business), it's a good idea to enter the customer's last name first. This way, your **Customer:Job** list sorts by last name so it will be easier to find names in the list.

Figure 2-15 Use Quick Add to add new customers

Step 4. Enter *San Jose* in the *Class* field and then press **Tab**.

QuickBooks uses Classes to separately track income and expenses for departments, functions, activities, locations, or profit centers. For more information on classes, see page 112. Note that if the Class has already been set up, it will appear in that field as you type it or in the drop-down menu.

Step 5. In the *Template* field, **Custom Sales Receipt** is already selected. Press **Tab**.

You can create your own custom forms, as you'll learn in the section beginning on page 305.

Step 6. Enter *01/25/2018* in the *Date* field and then press **Tab** (see Figure 2-16).

> **Did You Know?**
> Whenever you enter a date in QuickBooks, you can use any of several shortcut keys to quickly change the date. For example, if you want to change the date to the first day of the year, press **y**. "Y" is the first letter of the word "year," so it's easy to remember this shortcut. The same works for the end of the year. Press **r** since that's the last letter of the word "year." The same works for "month" (**m** and **h**) and "week" (**w** and **k**). You can also use the + and - keys to move the date one day forward or back. All of these shortcuts will be relative to the date already entered in the date field. Finally, press **t** for "today" or the system date.

Step 7. Enter *2018-1* in the *Sale No.* field.

The first time you enter a *Sales Receipt*, enter any number you want in the *Sale No.* field. QuickBooks will automatically number future Sales Receipts incrementally. You can change or reset the numbering at any time by overriding the *Sale No.* on a Sales Receipt.

Step 8. Press **Tab** to skip the *Sold To* field.

QuickBooks automatically fills in this field, using the information in the *Invoice/Bill To* field of the customer record. Since you used *Quick Add* to add this customer, there is no address information. You could enter an address in the *Sold To* field by entering it directly on the sales form. When you record the Sales Receipt, QuickBooks will give you the option of adding the address in the *Invoice/Bill To* field of the customer record.

Step 9. Enter *3612* in the *Check No.* field and then press **Tab**.

The number you enter here shows up on your printed deposit slips. If you were receiving a cash or credit card payment, you would leave this field blank.

Step 10. Select **Check** from the *Payment Method* drop-down list (or start typing the word *Check*) and then press **Tab**.

If you wanted to add a new payment method, you would enter the new method in this field. QuickBooks would prompt you to either *Quick Add* or *Set Up* the new *Payment Method*.

Step 11. Select **Indoor Photo Session** from the *Item* drop-down list and then press **Tab**.

Step 12. Press **Tab** to accept the default description *Indoor Studio Session* in the *Description* column.

As soon as you enter an Item, QuickBooks enters the description, rate, and sales tax code using data from the Item that has already been set up.

Step 13. In the *Tax* column, the *SRV* sales tax code is already selected. Press **Tab**.

Step 14. Enter *1* in the *Qty.* (quantity) column and then press **Tab**.

Step 15. Leave the default rate at *95.00* in the *Rate* column and then press **Tab**.

Step 16. Press **Tab** to accept the calculated amount in the *Amount* column.

After you enter the rate and press **Tab**, QuickBooks calculates the amount by multiplying the quantity by the rate. If you override the *Amount* field, QuickBooks calculates a new rate by dividing the amount by the quantity.

Step 17. Select **Premium Photo Package** from the *Item* drop-down list and then press **Tab** three times.

Step 18. Enter *2* in the *Qty* column and press **Tab.**

Step 19. Press **Tab** to accept the default rate of *85.00*.

You can override this amount directly on the Sales Receipt if necessary. As with the line above, QuickBooks calculates the total in the *Amount* column and QuickBooks uses the default sales tax code *Tax,* which is set up for the *Premium Photo Package* Item.

Step 20. Select **Thank you for your business.** from the *Customer Message* drop-down list.

You can enter a message in the *Customer Message* field that will show on the printed *Sales Receipt*. This is typically a thank you message, but it can be whatever you want. If you type in a new message, *Quick Add* will prompt you to add your new message to the *Customer Message* list. If you want to edit an existing Customer Message, or if you want to remove a Customer Message from the list, select the *Lists* menu, then select *Customer & Vendor Profile Lists*, and then select *Customer Message List*.

Step 21. Press **Tab** and enter *Santa Clara* in the *Tax* field, then **Tab** again to advance to the *Memo* field.

The Sales Tax item shown in the *Tax* field determines the rate of tax to be charged on all *Taxable* Items shown on the form. Each line in the body of the Invoice is marked with a Sales Tax Code that determines the taxability or non-taxability of the item on that line (see Figure 2-16).

The Sales Process - Recording Sales

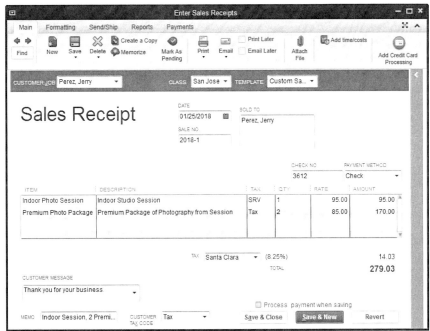

Figure 2-16 Completed Sales Receipt

Step 22. Enter Indoor Session, 2 Premium Packages in the Memo field.

Step 23. Click **Save & Close** to record the sale.

QuickBooks does not record any of the information on any form until you save the transaction by clicking *Save & Close*, *Save & New*, *Previous*, or *Next*.

> **Note:**
> If you prefer to use your keyboard over the mouse, you can use the *Alt* key in combination with other keys to execute commands. QuickBooks will tell you which key can be used in connection with the *Alt* key by underlining the letter in the command. For example, in the Sales Receipt window, the S is underlined on the *Save & New* button. You can save the receipt and move to a new Sales Receipt window by pressing the **Alt** key with the **S**.

Step 24. QuickBooks displays the *Information Changed* dialog box (see Figure 2-17). This dialog box appears because you added the *Class* and *Tax Item* fields after creating the Customer using *QuickAdd*. Click the **Yes** button.

Figure 2-17 Information Changed dialog box

Undeposited Funds

The **Undeposited Funds** account is a special account that is automatically created by QuickBooks. The account works as a temporary holding account where QuickBooks tracks monies received from customers before the money is deposited in a bank account.

As illustrated in Figure 2-18, as you record Payments and Sales Receipts, QuickBooks gives you a choice between (Option 1) grouping all receipts into the **Undeposited Funds** account or (Option 2) immediately depositing the funds to one of your bank accounts.

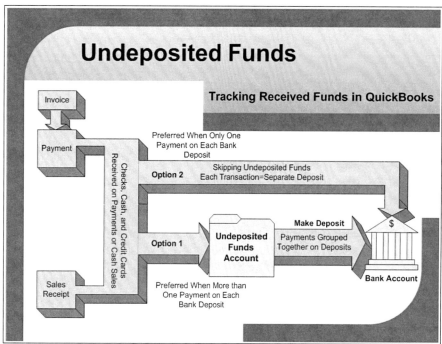

*Figure 2-18 All funds from sales transactions go through **Undeposited Funds** or directly to a bank account.*

There is a tradeoff here. When you use the **Undeposited Funds** account, you have to create a separate transaction (an additional step) to actually deposit money into a bank account. At first that might seem like extra work. However, when you skip the **Undeposited Funds** account, each sales transaction creates a separate deposit in your bank account.

Since it is most common to have multiple sales transactions per bank deposit, QuickBooks has a default preference setting that makes all Payments and Sales Receipts affect the balance in the **Undeposited Funds** account. Then when you actually make a deposit at the bank, you record a single deposit transaction in QuickBooks that empties the **Undeposited Funds** account into the bank account. This method makes it much easier to reconcile the bank account at the end of each month because the deposits on the bank statement will match the deposits in your QuickBooks bank account. Unless you only make one sale each day and your deposits include only the funds from that single sale, you will want to keep this default preference.

COMPUTER PRACTICE

You can modify the **Undeposited Funds** preference by following these steps:

Step 1.   Select the *Edit* menu and then select **Preferences**.

Step 2.   Select **Payments** on the left side of the *Preferences* window.

Step 3.   In the **Company Preferences** tab, the box next to **Use Undeposited Funds as a default deposit to account** is checked (see Figure 2-19).

> **Note:**
> Entering the spacebar on the keyboard when a checkbox is selected will either check or uncheck that checkbox.

Step 4.   If you prefer to deposit payments individually, uncheck the box next to **Use Undeposited Funds as a default deposit to account**. You will then have the option to select an account to deposit to in the *Sales Receipt* and *Receive Payment* windows.

Step 5.   Click **Cancel** to leave default setting for the use of **Undeposited Funds**.

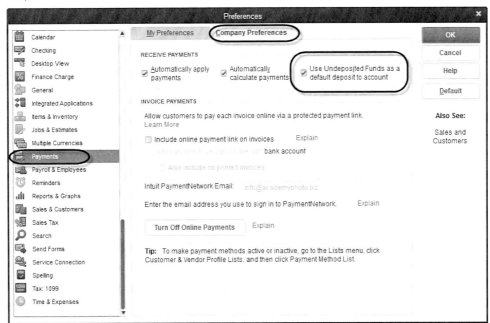

*Figure 2-19 Preference for Payments to go to **Undeposited Funds** or another account*

When this preference is off (see Figure 2-20), QuickBooks displays the **Deposit To** field on the **Receive Payments** and **Enter Sales Receipt** windows (see Figure 2-21).

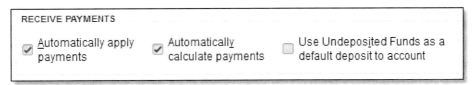

*Figure 2-20 Setting for **Undeposited Funds** on Company Preferences for Payments*

You must choose a destination account for the transaction from the *Deposit to* drop-down list.

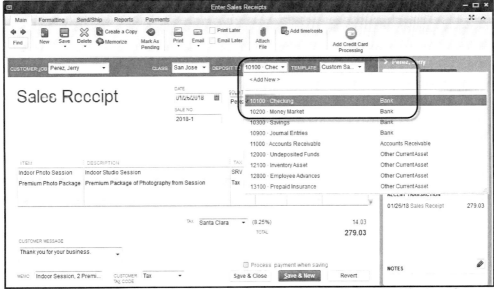

*Figure 2-21 The **Deposit To** field shows on Sales Receipts when the Undeposited Funds preference is off.*

Creating Invoices

Invoices are very similar to Sales Receipts. The only difference is that Invoices increase Accounts Receivable while Sales Receipts increase Undeposited Funds (or the specified bank account). You should use Invoices to record sales to your credit customers.

COMPUTER PRACTICE

To create an Invoice, follow these steps:

Step 1. From the *Customer Center* select **Mason, Bob** from the *Customers & Jobs* list. Then select **Invoices** from the *New Transactions* drop-down list.

Alternatively, click the **Create Invoices** icon on the *Home page* and select **Mason, Bob** from the *Customer:Job* drop-down list. Press **Tab** (see Figure 2-22).

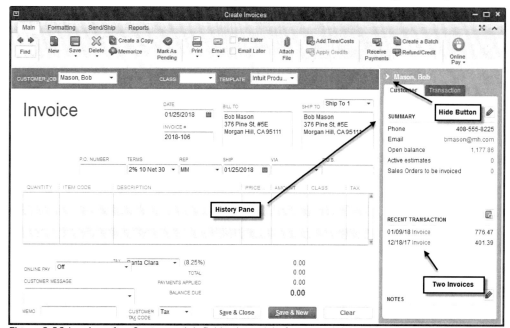

Figure 2-22 Invoice after Customer:Job field selected, before remaining data entered.

> **Did You Know?**
> When you type the first few characters of any field that has a list behind it, QuickBooks completes the field using a feature called *QuickFill*. QuickFill uses the first few characters you type to find the name in the list. If the name does not come up right away, keep typing until the correct name appears.

Step 2. Notice that Bob Mason has two open invoices listed in the *History Pane*.

The *History Pane* displays recent transactions and notes about a customer or a transaction on *Invoices* and *Sales Receipts*.

Step 3. Click the **Hide** button to hide the *History Pane*. The Hide button is a right facing triangle on the top left edge of the *History Pane* (see Figure 2-22).

Step 4. Click in the **Class** field. Enter an *s* in the *Class* field. QuickBooks will QuickFill the field with the full word *San Jose*. Then press **Tab**.

Step 5. In the *Template* field, select **Academy Photo Service Invoice**. Press **Tab**.

Step 6. Enter *01/26/2018* in the *Date* field and then press **Tab**.

Step 7. Leave *2018-106* in the *Invoice #* field and then press **Tab**.

The Sales Process - Recording Sales   **49**

>   The first time you enter an Invoice, enter any number you want in the *Invoice #* field.
>   QuickBooks will automatically number future Invoices incrementally. You can change or
>   reset the numbering at any time by overriding the number on a future Invoice.

Step 8.   Press **Tab** to accept the default information in the *Bill To* field.

>   QuickBooks automatically enters the address in this field, using the information in the
>   *Invoice/Bill To* field of the customer record. If necessary, change the *Bill To* address by
>   typing over the existing data.

Step 9.   Leave the *P.O. Number* field blank and then press **Tab**.

>   The P.O. (purchase order) number helps the customer identify your Invoice. When your
>   customers use purchase orders, make sure you enter their P.O. numbers on Invoices you
>   create for them.

> **Warning:**
> Make sure you enter the P.O. number if your customer uses purchase orders. Some
> customers may reject Invoices that do not reference a P.O. number.

Step 10.   In the *TERMS* field, *2% 10 Net 30* is already selected. Press **Tab** to proceed to the next
            field.

>   The *TERMS* field on the *Invoice* indicates the due date for the *Invoice* and how long your
>   customer can take to pay you. The entry in this field determines how this Invoice is
>   reported on Customers & Receivables reports such as the *A/R Aging Summary* and the
>   *Collections Report*. To learn more about the *Terms List*, and how to set up terms, see
>   page 300.

Step 11.   Enter the sale of 2 Hours for an Indoor Photo Session and 1 Standard Photo Package into
            the body of the *Invoice* as shown in Figure 2-23.

Step 12.   Select **Thank you for your business** from the *Customer Message* drop-down list and then
            press **Tab**.

Step 13.   **Santa Clara** in the *Tax* field is already selected. Press **Tab**.

>   As with Sales Receipts, QuickBooks selects the *Sales Tax Item* based on the defaults in
>   *Sales Tax Preferences* or in the Customer's record.

Step 14.   Enter *2 Hr Indoor Session, 1 Standard Package* in the *Memo* field at the bottom of the
            form.

> **Tip:**
> If you intend to send statements to your customers, the *Memo* field is extremely
> important. QuickBooks allows you to show line item detail from your customer's Invoices.
> However, if you want your statements to be more concise, you can choose not to show
> the line item detail and show the text from the *Memo* field instead. The text from the
> *Memo* field will show along with the information in the *Invoice #,* and *Date* fields. The
> customer's statement will also show a three-letter code "INV" representing the Invoice
> transaction. Therefore, it is best to include information about the products or services you
> sold to the customer in the *Memo* field.

Step 15.   Compare your screen with the Invoice shown in Figure 2-23. If you see any errors, correct
            them. Otherwise, click **Save & Close** to record the Invoice.

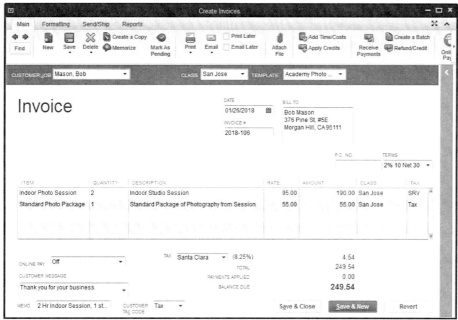

Figure 2-23 Completed Invoice

QuickBooks automatically tracks all of the accounting details behind this transaction so that all of your reports will immediately reflect the sale. For example, the Open Invoices report, the Profit & Loss Standard report, and the Balance Sheet Standard report will all change when you record this Invoice.

Adding Calculating Items to an Invoice

On the next Invoice, you'll learn how to include discounts and subtotals on an **Invoice**. Discounts and subtotals are called *Calculating Items*.

> **Key Term:**
> *Calculating Items* use the amount of the preceding line to calculate their amount. For example, if you enter 10% in the Discount item setup window and then enter the Discount item on an Invoice, QuickBooks will multiply the line just above the Discount item by 10% and enter that number, as a negative, in the **Amount** column for the discount line.

COMPUTER PRACTICE

To create an Invoice with a calculating item, follow these steps:

Step 1. From the *Customer Center* select the **Branch Opening** job for Cruz, Maria from the *Customers & Jobs* list.

Step 2. Select **Invoices** from the *New Transactions* drop-down list; or, press Ctrl+ I.

Step 3. The Branch Opening job for Cruz, Maria is already selected. Press **Tab**.

Step 4. Enter *Walnut Creek* in the *Class* field and then press **Tab**.

Step 5. Select the Academy Photo Service Invoice template in the *Template* drop-down list is already selected. Press **Tab**.

Step 6. *1/26/2018* is already entered in the *Date* field. Press **Tab**.

Step 7. Notice the *INVOICE #* is automatically entered for you with the next Invoice number (i.e., **2018-107**). Press **Tab** to skip to the next field.

Step 8. Press **Tab** to skip the *Bill To* field.

Step 9. Press Tab twice to skip the *P.O. No. and the Terms* fields.

Step 10. Enter the two items shown in Table 2-3 in the body of the **Invoice**.

The Sales Process - Recording Sales

Item	Description	Qty	Rate	Amount
Camera SR32	Supra Digital Camera SR32	4	695.99	2,783.96
Lens	Supra Zoom Lens	1	324.99	324.99

Table 2-3 Data for use in the Invoice

Step 11. On the third line of the body of the Invoice, in the **Item** column, enter *Subtotal* to sum the previous two item lines, and press **Tab** twice.

Notice that QuickBooks automatically calculates the sum of the first two lines on the Invoice.

Step 12. Enter *Disc 10%* in the **Item** column and press **Tab**.

The *Disc 10%* Item is a special Calculating Item that calculates a percentage of the preceding line on sales forms. Since it is a **Discount Item**, QuickBooks performs the calculation and enters a negative amount for your discount. This subtracts the discount from the total of the Invoice and adjusts sales tax accordingly.

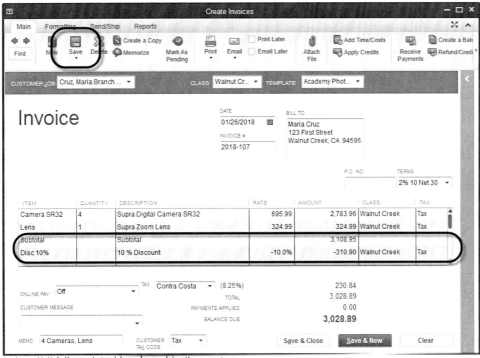

Figure 2-24 Completed Invoice with discount

> **Did You Know?**
> You can insert or delete lines on an Invoice (or any other form). To insert a line between two existing lines, click on the line that you want to move down and press Ctrl+Insert (or select the **Edit** menu, and then select **Insert Line**). To delete a line, click on the line you want to delete and press Ctrl+Delete (or select the **Edit** menu, and then select **Delete Line**).

Step 13. Leave the *Customer Message* field blank.

Step 14. Leave **Contra Costa** in the *Tax* field. Also leave **Tax** in the *Customer Tax Code* field.

Step 15. Enter *4 Cameras, Lens* in the *Memo* field.

Step 16. Verify that your screen matches Figure 2-24. To save the Invoice, click **Save** in the *Main* tab at the top of the *Invoice*. Leave this window open for the next Computer Exercise.

Figure 2-25 Recording Transaction window warns you about the customer's credit limit

Step 17. If you see the *Recording Transaction* warning about Maria Cruz exceeding her credit limit (Figure 2-25), click **Yes**.

Open Invoices Report

Now that you've entered Invoices for your customers, QuickBooks' reports reflect the Invoices that are "open" and the "age" of each Invoice. The Open Invoices report is shown in Figure 2-27.

COMPUTER PRACTICE

Step 1. Select the **Reports** tab at the top of the invoice, and click on **View Open Invoices** icon, as shown in Figure 2-26. Or, alternatively, select the **Reports** menu, select **Customers & Receivables**, and then select **Open Invoices**.

Step 2. Set the *Dates* field at the top of the report to *01/31/2018* and then press **Tab**.

Step 3. Verify that your Open Invoices report matches Figure 2-27.

Step 4. Close the report by clicking the X in the upper right corner of the window.

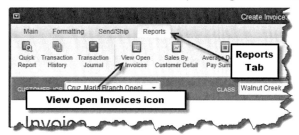

Figure 2-26 View Reports Tab

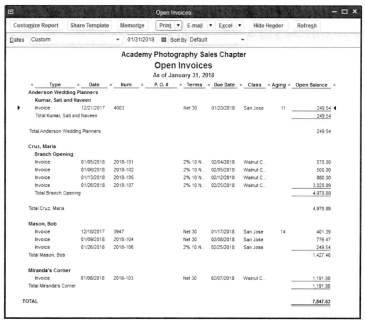

Figure 2-27 Open Invoices report

The Sales Process - Receiving Payments from Customers

Step 5.   If you see a Memorize Report dialog box, click the No button (see Figure 2-28).

Step 6.   Click Save & Close to close the Invoice.

Figure 2-28 Memorized Reports window

> **Did You Know?**
> You can adjust the width of any column on the report by dragging the small diamond at the right of the column title to the left (narrowing the columns) or to the right (widening the columns).

Receiving Payments from Customers

Receiving Payments by Check

To record payments received from your customers and apply the payments to specific Invoices, follow these steps:

COMPUTER PRACTICE

Step 1.   Click **Receive Payments** on the *Home* page.

Step 2.   Select **Mason, Bob** in the *Received From* field of the *Receive Payments* window (see Figure 2-29). Once a customer is selected, the *Customer Payment* window shows the open Invoices for that specific customer. This section shows the dates of the Invoices, along with the Invoice number, original amount, the last date for the prompt payment discount, and the amount due.

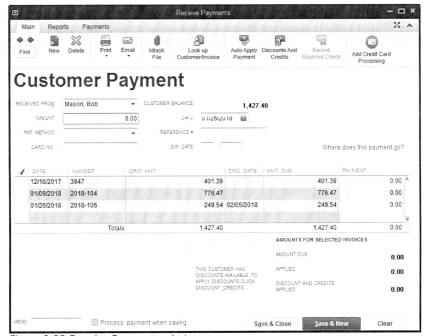

Figure 2-29 Receive Payments window

Step 3.   Enter 401.39 in the *Amount* field and then press **Tab**.

Step 4. Enter *1/27/2018* in the *Date* field and then press **Tab** (see Figure 2-30).
Step 5. Select **Check** from the *Pmt. Method* drop-down list and then press **Tab**.
Step 6. Enter *5256* in the *Check No.* field and then press **Tab**.
Step 7. Confirm that **Invoice #3947** is already checked.

> **Note:**
> **When One Payment Applies to More than One Invoice**
> You can apply one check from a customer to multiple Invoices. When you receive payments, you can override the amounts in the **Payment** column to apply the payment to Invoices in whatever combination is necessary.
>
> **When You Don't Want to Apply the Entire Amount of the Payment**
> If you don't want to apply the entire amount of the customer's check to the Invoice, reduce the amount in the **Payment** column. You can apply the remaining balance of the customer's check to additional Invoices. If you do not, QuickBooks will give you a choice to either hold the remaining balance as a credit for the customer or refund the amount to the customer.

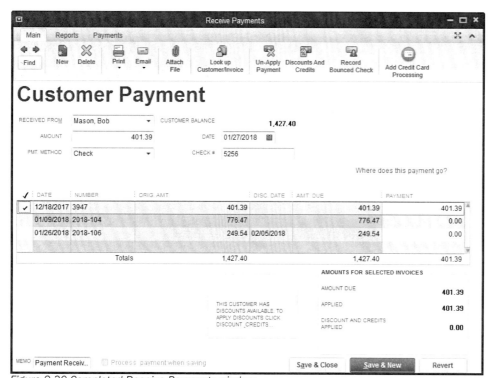

Figure 2-30 Completed Receive Payments window

Step 8. Verify that the **Amount Due** and **Payment** columns for the selected invoice both show $*401.39*.

The checkmark to the left of the **Date** column indicates the Invoice to which QuickBooks will apply the payment. QuickBooks automatically selected this Invoice because the amount of the customer's check is the same as the unpaid amount of the Invoice (see page 57). If applicable, you can deselect the Invoice by clicking on the checkmark. You can then select another Invoice from the list.

Step 9. Enter *Payment Received - Invoice #3947* in the *Memo* field and then press **Tab**.

When entering a memo, type *Payment Received* followed by the Invoice number. Memos do not affect the application of payments to specific Invoices, but they are helpful in two very important ways. First, if you send your customers statements, only the information in the *Check #, Date,* and *Memo* fields will show on statements, along with a three-letter code (PMT), representing the Payment transaction. Also, if you ever have to go back to the transaction and verify that you've applied the payment to the correct Invoice(s), you'll be able to look at the *Memo* field to see the Invoice(s) to which you *should* have applied the payments.

Step 10. Verify that your screen matches Figure 2-30. If you see errors, correct them.

Step 11. Click **Save & Close** to record the Payment transaction.

Handling Partial Payments

In the last example, Bob Mason paid Invoice #3947 in full. However, if a customer pays only a portion of an Invoice, you should record the payment just as you did in the last example except that the amount would be less than the full amount due on any of the open Invoices. Apply the payment to the appropriate Invoice. QuickBooks will give the option to either leave the Invoice open or write off the unpaid amount. By clicking the *View Customer Contact Information* button, QuickBooks displays the *Edit Customer* window that allows you to see the customer's contact information. This is helpful if you need to contact the customer to ask a question about the partial payment (see Figure 2-31).

Figure 2-31 Partial Payment of Invoice

If you chose to leave the underpayment, the next time you use the **Receive Payments** function for that customer, the Invoice will show the remaining amount due. You can record additional payments to the Invoice in the same way as before.

Receiving Payments by Credit Card

The next example shows that Maria Cruz paid off the amount owing on the Branch Opening job. Maria Cruz used a credit card to pay her invoices, so this example shows how to receive credit card payments.

COMPUTER PRACTICE

Step 1. From the *Customer Center* select the **Cruz, Maria:Branch Opening** job from the *Customers & Jobs* list. Select **Receive Payments** from the *New Transactions* drop-down list.

Step 2. Enter data into the *Amount,* and *Date* fields as shown in Figure 2-32.

Step 3. Enter *American Express* in the *Pmt. Method* field and then press **Tab**.

Step 4. Leave the *Reference#* field blank. Press **Tab**.

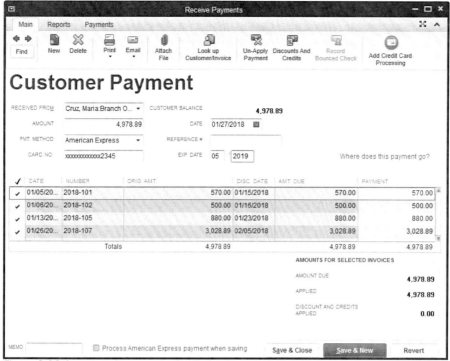

Figure 2-32 Customer Payment by Credit Card

Step 5. Enter *1234-123456-12345* in the *Card No.* field. Press **Tab**.

QuickBooks shows the credit card number with some x's for security purposes.

Step 6. In the *Exp. Date* field, enter *05,* then press **Tab** and enter *2019*.

Step 7. Verify that your screen matches Figure 2-32 and click **Save & Close**. If the Merchant Account Service Message appears, click the **Not Now** button.

> Note:
> If you want to keep a record of the customer's credit card information, including card number, expiration date, billing address and billing zip code, enter credit card information into the *Payment Info* tab of the Customer or Job record before you process the payment through the Receive Payments window. When you enter the customer or job name, QuickBooks will enter the credit card information automatically.

Where Do the Payments Go?

Recall the earlier discussion about **Undeposited Funds** beginning on page 45. Unless you turned off "Use **Undeposited Funds** as a default deposit to account" preference, QuickBooks does not increase your bank balance when you receive payments. Instead, when you record a payment transaction as shown above, QuickBooks reduces the balance in **Accounts Receivable** and increases the balance in **Undeposited Funds**. In order to have your payments show up in your bank account (and reduce **Undeposited Funds**), you must **Make Deposits.** See the section called *Making Bank Deposits* beginning on page 61.

> The accounting behind the scenes:
> Payments increase (debit) **Undeposited Funds** (or a bank/other current asset account) and decrease (credit) **Accounts Receivable**.

Preferences for Applying Payments

As soon as you enter the customer name at the top of the *Receive Payments* window and press **Tab**, QuickBooks displays all of the open Invoices for that customer in the lower section of the window. See Figure 2-33.

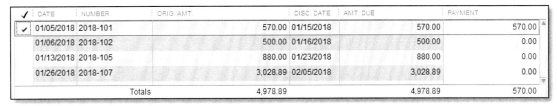

Figure 2-33 Payment automatically applied to the oldest Invoice

Then, when you enter the payment amount, QuickBooks looks at all of the open Invoices for that customer. If it finds an amount due on an open Invoice that is the exact amount of the payment, it matches the payment with that Invoice. If there is no such match, it applies the payment to the *oldest* Invoice first and continues applying to the next oldest until the payment is completely applied. If this auto application of payments results in a partially paid Invoice, QuickBooks holds the balance on that Invoice open for the unpaid amount. This is a feature called *Automatically Apply Payments*.

If you select an *Invoice* in the *Receive Payments* form before entering an *Amount*, QuickBooks calculates the sum of the selected Invoice(s) and enters that sum into the *Amount* field. This feature is called *Automatically Calculate Payments*.

COMPUTER PRACTICE

To modify the Automatically Apply Payments and Automatically Calculate Payments settings, change the Company Preferences for Payments.

Follow these steps:

Step 1. Select the *Edit* menu and then select **Preferences** (see Figure 2-34).

Step 2. Select the **Payments** icon from the preference category in the list on the left. Then click the **Company Preferences** tab.

Step 3. Check or uncheck the *Automatically apply payments* box to change it. For now, leave it checked.

With this feature disabled, in the Receive Payments window you will have to click Auto Apply Payment for each payment you process, or you will have to manually apply payments to Invoices by clicking in the column to the left of the Invoice and modifying the amount in the Payment column as necessary.

Step 4. You can change the *Automatically calculate payments* box by checking or unchecking it. For now, leave it checked.

When this preference is on, QuickBooks will automatically calculate the payment received from the customer in the Amount field of the Receive Payments window as you select the Invoices. When this preference is off, QuickBooks does not automatically calculate payments.

Step 5. Click OK.

Figure 2-34 Payment Company Preferences

Recording Customer Discounts

What if your customer takes advantage of the discount you offer on your Invoice? In the next example, the payment you receive is less than the face amount of the Invoice because the customer took advantage of the 2% 10 Net 30 discount terms that Academy Photography offers.

COMPUTER PRACTICE

Follow these steps to record a payment on which the customer took a discount:

Step 1. From the *Customer Center* select **Mason, Bob** from the *Customers & Jobs* list. Then select **Receive Payments** from the *New Transactions* drop-down list.

Step 2. Enter all the customer payment information as shown in Figure 2-35. The customer is paying for Invoice #2018-106 after taking the discount allowed by the terms.

Figure 2-35 Top portion of the Receive Payments window

Step 3. The bottom portion of the *Receive Payments* window (see Figure 2-36) displays the open Invoices for this customer. If the customer is eligible for discounts, a message will appear as shown just below the open Invoices. The **Disc. Date** column shows the date through which the customer is eligible to take a discount.

If the amount paid is not an exact match with any Invoice balance, QuickBooks will automatically apply the payment to the oldest Invoices. Here, Invoice #2018-104 is automatically selected since the amount $244.55 does not match any open invoices. The underpayment is also displayed. We'll fix this in the next step.

The Sales Process - Receiving Payments from Customers

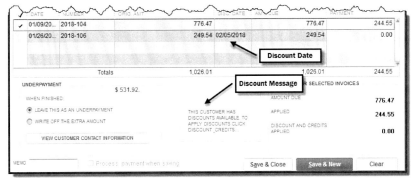

Figure 2-36 Bottom portion shows discount and credit information box, Invoice selected and Underpayment

> **Note:**
> In the *Receive Payments* window the Underpayment amount is displayed with options to **Leave this as an underpayment** or **Write off the extra amount**. These options are displayed when the payment is less than the amount due on the selected Invoices. Similarly, Overpayment amounts are displayed with options to **Leave the credit to be used later** or **Refund the amount to the customer** when the payment is more than the amount due on the selected Invoices.
>
> **Tip:**
> If the payment amount doesn't add up exactly to the discounted amount, you'll need to make a choice. If the payment is too high, you could reduce the amount of the discount by lowering the amount in the *Discounts and Credits* window. If the payment is too low, you could raise the amount in the *Discounts and Credits* window. If the payment amount is significantly different, you can apply the amount of the payment and then send a Statement to the customer showing the balance due (if the payment is too low) or send a refund to the customer (if the payment is too high).

Step 4. Click in the column to the left of Invoice **#2018-104** to uncheck it and then click to check Invoice **#2018-106** (see Figure 2-37). This moves the payment so that it now applies to Invoice #2018-106. Make sure to uncheck #2018-104 before checking #2018-106, or you will see a Warning message.

Figure 2-37 Payment is now applied to the correct Invoice

Step 5. Since the customer took advantage of the 2% 10 Net 30 terms that Academy Photography offered him, you'll need to reduce the amount due by 2%. To apply the discount to this Invoice, click **Discount and Credits** button at the top of the *Receive Payments* window.

Step 6. QuickBooks calculates and enters a suggested discount based on the terms on the customer's Invoice as shown in Figure 2-38. You can override this amount if necessary. Press **Tab**.

Figure 2-38 Discounts and Credits window

Step 7. Select **46000 Sales Discounts** in *the Discount Account* field. Press **Tab**.

The *Discount Account* field is where you assign an account that tracks the discounts you give to your customers.

Step 8. Enter *San Jose* in the *Discount Class* field and then click **Done**.

Since Academy Photography uses class tracking, you will need to enter the appropriate class in this field. If you do not classify this transaction, QuickBooks will display the amount in an *Unclassified* column on the **Profit & Loss by Class** report. Refer to the Invoice you are discounting to determine the Class. Academy Photography used the *San Jose* Class when recording Invoice 2018-106.

After recording the discount, the *Receive Payments* window reflects Total Discount and Credits Applied at the bottom of the Receive Payments window.

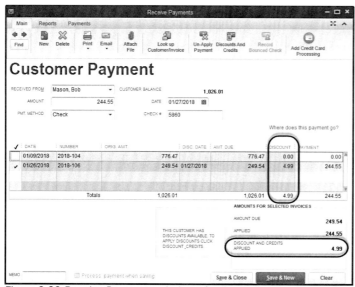

Figure 2-39 Receive Payments window after (recording the discount)

Step 9. Verify that your screen matches Figure 2-39.

Step 10. Click **Save & Close** to record the transaction.

Step 11. Close the Customer Center.

Making Bank Deposits

As you record payments from customers using the *Enter Sales Receipts* and *Receive Payments* windows, by default these payments are posted to a special QuickBooks account called **Undeposited Funds**. To deposit these payments into your bank account, you will need to record a *Deposit* transaction. Deposit transactions move money from the **Undeposited Funds** account to the appropriate bank account. As you will see in this section, QuickBooks provides a special window (the *Payments to Deposit* window) to help you identify which payments are included on each deposit.

Since you will probably receive payments from your customers in several different ways (checks, cash, and credit cards), record deposits of each payment type separately. This way, your deposits in QuickBooks will match how your bank posts these transaction. This will make bank reconciliations much easier. Start with the checks and cash, followed by the VISA, MasterCard and Discover receipts and then the American Express receipts.

Depositing Checks and Cash

COMPUTER PRACTICE

To enter a deposit, follow these steps:

Step 1. From the *Home* page select **Record Deposits**.

Since you have payments stored in the **Undeposited Funds** account, QuickBooks displays the *Payments to Deposit* window (see Figure 2-40).

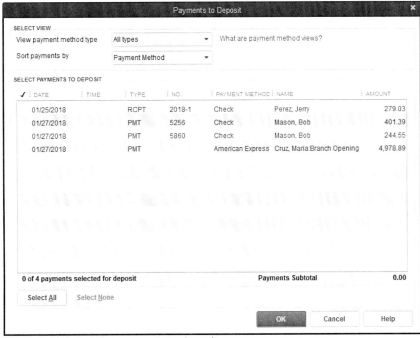

Figure 2-40 *Select the payments to deposit*

Step 2. Select **Cash and Check** from the *View Payment Method Type* drop-down list (see Figure 2-41).

Since the checks and cash you deposit in your bank account will post to your account separately from credit card receipts, it is best to filter the report by payment type and then create a separate deposit for each payment type. Depending on your merchant service, you will probably need to create a single deposit for your VISA, MasterCard and Discover receipts. Most merchant services combine MasterCard, VISA and Discover receipts when they credit your bank account.

> **Tip:**
> Since you can filter the *Payments to Deposit* window by only one payment method at a time, using a single *Payment Method* for *Checks* and *Cash* will allow you to filter for both payment methods on this window. Depending on your merchant service, you may want to create a single *Payment Method* for MasterCard, VISA and Discover as well. To edit *Payment Methods* select the *Lists* menu, then select *Customer & Vendor Profile Lists*, and then select *Payment Methods List*. Once the *Payment Method List* window opens, select the Payment Method and select *Edit Payment Method* from the *Payment Method* menu.

Figure 2-41 Cash and Check payments

Step 3.   Click **Select All** to select all of the cash and check deposits. See Figure 2-42. Click **OK**. A checkmark in the column on the left indicates that QuickBooks will include the payment in the deposit.

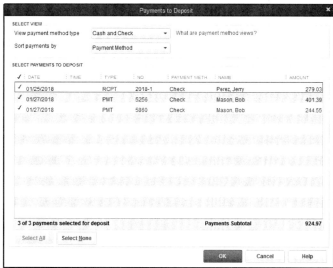

Figure 2-42 Select the payments to deposit

Step 4.   In the *Make Deposits* window, the **Checking** account is already selected in the *Deposit To* field (see Figure 2-43). The payments will be deposited to this bank account. Press **Tab**.

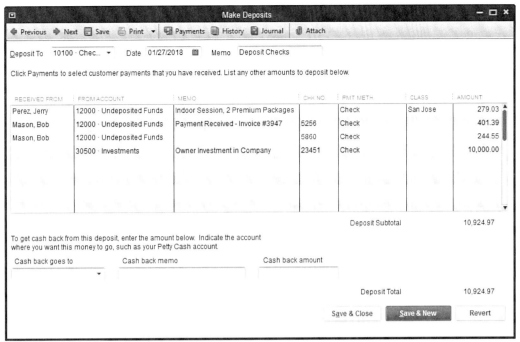

Figure 2-43 Make Deposits window

Step 5. Enter *01/27/2018* if it does not already display in the *Date* field and press **Tab**.

Step 6. Enter **Deposit Checks** in the *Memo* field and press **Tab**.

Step 7. On this deposit, we will add a non-sales-related item. Occasionally, you will have deposits that are not linked to other transactions in QuickBooks, which can be entered directly in the *Deposit* window. Complete the following steps::

   a) On the first blank line, enter **Investments** in the *From Account* column and press **Tab**. The *From Account* column on the *Make Deposits* window shows the account that the deposit is coming "from."

   b) Enter **Owner Investment in Company** in the *Memo* column and press **Tab**.

   c) Enter *23451* in the *Chk No.* column and press **Tab**.

   d) Enter **Check** in the *Pmt Meth.* column and press **Tab**.

   e) Press **Tab** to skip the *Class* column.

   f) Enter *10,000.00* in the *Amount* column.

Step 8. If you wish to print the deposit slip, click **Print** on the *Make Deposits* window. Click **Save & Close** to record the deposit.

> **The accounting behind the scenes:**
> In the deposit transaction (Figure 2-43) the checking account will increase (with a debit) by the total deposit ($10,924.97). All of the customer checks are coming from the **Undeposited Funds** account, and the owner investment is coming from the **Investments** account. The customer checks will decrease (credit) the balance in **Undeposited Funds** and the loan from the owner will increase (credit) the balance in the **Investments** account.

Holding Cash Back from Deposits

If you hold cash back when you make your deposits to the bank, fill in the bottom part of the deposit slip indicating the account to which you want to post the cash (see Figure 2-44).

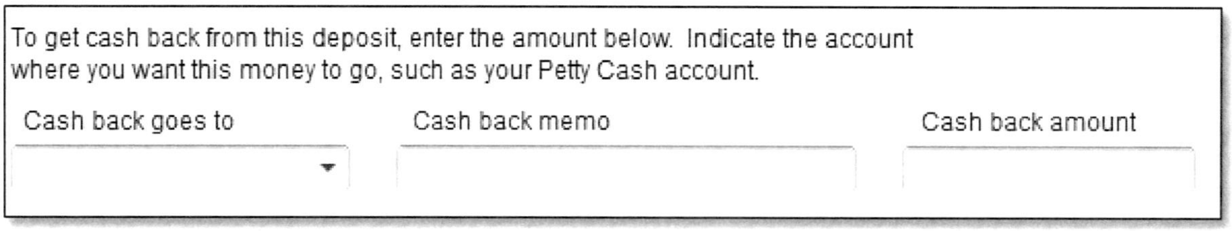

```
To get cash back from this deposit, enter the amount below. Indicate the account
where you want this money to go, such as your Petty Cash account.

Cash back goes to          Cash back memo                    Cash back amount
```

Figure 2-44 The bottom of the deposit slip deals with cash back

There are two ways you might use the cash back section of the deposit:

1. If you're splitting the deposit between two different bank accounts, you could enter the other bank account and amount here. For example, if you send part of the funds from the deposit to the Money Market account, you could enter *Money Market* in the *Cash back goes to* field and the amount in the *Cash back amount* field.

2. If you routinely hold back funds from your deposits and use them for several different purchases, you may want to set up a new QuickBooks bank account called **Petty Cash** and enter that account in the *Cash back goes to* field. The Petty Cash account is not really a bank account, but it's an account where you can track all your cash expenditures.

> **Tip:**
> It's not a good idea to hold cash back from deposits as "pocket money." If your business is a Sole Proprietorship, it's better to write a separate check (or ATM withdrawal) and then code it to **Owner's Draw**. This is a much cleaner way to track the money you take out for personal use. Discuss this with your QuickBooks ProAdvisor, or with your accountant.

Printing Deposit Slips

QuickBooks can print deposit slips on preprinted deposit slips.

> **DO NOT PERFORM THESE STEPS. THEY ARE FOR REFERENCE ONLY.**

To print on preprinted deposit slips, follow these steps:

1. Display the most recent deposit transaction by selecting the *Banking* menu and then selecting **Make Deposits.**

   Click **Cancel** if you see the *Payments to Deposit* window. Then click the **Previous** button on the *Make Deposits* window. Alternatively, you could double-click the deposit transaction from the checking account register window.

2. Click **Print** on the *Make Deposits* window (see Figure 2-45).

3. Select **Deposit slip and deposit summary** on the window shown in Figure 2-46 and click **OK**.

   Normally, you would load the preprinted deposit slips into the printer before printing. However, if you do not have a deposit slip print the deposit on blank paper.

The Sales Process - Making Bank Deposits

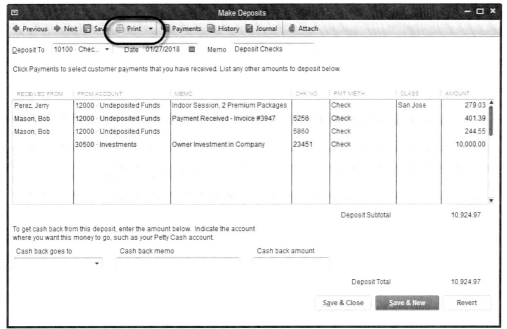

Figure 2-45 Printing a deposit

Figure 2-46 Print Deposit window for deposit slips

4. Check the settings on the Print Lists window shown in Figure 2-47.

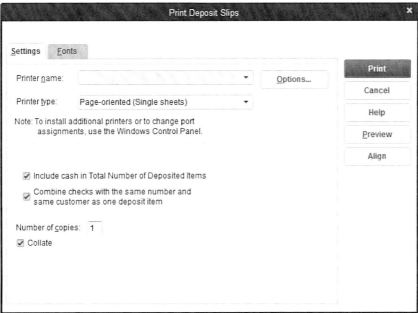

Figure 2-47 Settings on the Print Deposit Slips window

5. Select your printer in the *Printer name* field.
6. Click **Print** to print the deposit slip (see Figure 2-48).
7. Click **Save & Close** to save the Deposit.

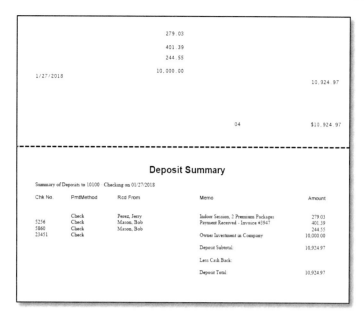

Figure 2-48 Deposit slip and deposit summary

Depositing Credit Card Payments

As mentioned previously, to ensure that your bank reconciliations go smoothly, you should always deposit your checks and cash separately from your credit card payments.

COMPUTER PRACTICE

Step 1.   Select the **Banking** menu, and then select **Make Deposits**. The *Payments to Deposit* window opens.

Step 2.   Click in the left column on the line to select the American Express receipt (see Figure 2-49). Then click **OK**. The *Make Deposits* window opens.

Figure 2-49 Payments to Deposit window

Step 3.   The **Checking** account is already selected in the *Deposit To* field. Press **Tab**.

Step 4.   Enter *01/27/2018* if it is not already entered in the *Date* field. Press **Tab**.

Step 5.   Enter *Deposit American Exp* in the *Memo* field.

As stated earlier, make sure you group together receipts in a way that agrees with the actual deposits made to your bank. This is a critical step in making your bank reconciliation process go smoothly.

Step 6.   On the first blank line of the deposit slip, enter *Bankcard Fees* in the **From Account** column and then press **Tab**.

The Sales Process - Making Bank Deposits

You only need to create this line if your credit card processing company (or your bank) charges a discount fee on each credit card deposit rather than monthly.

Step 7. Enter *Discount Fee* in the **Memo** column and then press **Tab**.

Step 8. Press **Tab** to skip the **Chk No.** column.

Step 9. Enter *American Express* in the **Pmt Method** column and then press **Tab**.

Step 10. Enter *Walnut Creek* in the *Class* column and then press **Tab**.

Step 11. You can use the QuickMath feature to enter the discount fee directly on the **Make Deposits** window. Enter *4978.89 * -.02* in the *Amount* column and press **Enter**.

QuickMath is a feature that helps you add, subtract, multiply, or divide in any QuickBooks Amount field. When you enter the first number (4978.89), it shows normally in the *Amount* column. Then when you enter the * (asterisk key or Shift+8), QuickMath shows a small adding machine tape on your screen (see Figure 2-50). Continue typing your formula for recording the discount fee. If the discount is 2%, enter *-.02* (minus point zero two) and press *Enter*. The result of the calculation shows in the *Amount* column (-99.58). **The minus sign makes the result a negative number and reduces the amount of your deposit.** This also increases (debits) your **Bankcard Fees** expense account.

Step 12. Press **Tab** to have the total of the deposit updated automatically.

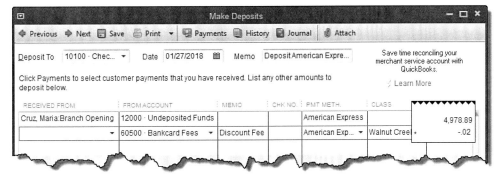

Figure 2-50 QuickMath makes an adding machine tape appear

Step 13. Verify that your screen matches Figure 2-51. Click **Save & Close**.

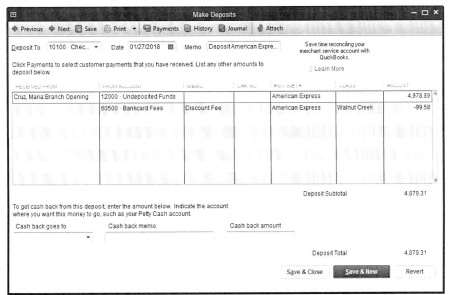

Figure 2-51 Make Deposits window after a credit card deposit

Now that you have entered your deposits, the checking account register shows each deposit and the updated balance in the account.

COMPUTER PRACTICE

To see the detail of a deposit, follow these steps:

Step 1.   Click the **Chart of Accounts** icon on the *Home* page.

Step 2.   Double-click on the **Checking** account in the *Chart of Accounts* window.

Step 3.   Scroll up until you see the two deposit transactions shown in Figure 2-52.

Step 4.   Close the *Checking* register and *Chart of Accounts*.

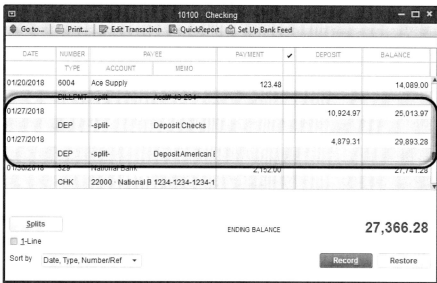

Figure 2-52 Checking register after entering deposits

Income Tracker

New with QuickBooks 2014, the **Income Tracker** provides you with a fast way to see the status of your unbilled and unpaid sales transactions all from one location. It also provides features to improve billing/collections as well as create new sales transactions. You can access the **Income Tracker** from the icon in the *Customer Center* (see Figure 2-53). Alternatively, use the *Customer Menu* or the Icon Bar.

Figure 2-53 Income Tracker icon in Customer Center

From the **Income Tracker** you can:

- See all of your unbilled and unpaid sales transactions
- Select just one category by clicking on the colored bar or using filters
- Right click on any sales transaction for options to view or edit that transaction, *Customer*, or *Job*
- Print or send a copy of a sales transaction by email
- Convert an *Estimate* or *Sales Order* into an *Invoice*
- Sort the list by clicking on any column heading

The Sales Process - Income Tracker

- Print a group of sales transactions in a batch
- Create new *Customer* transactions

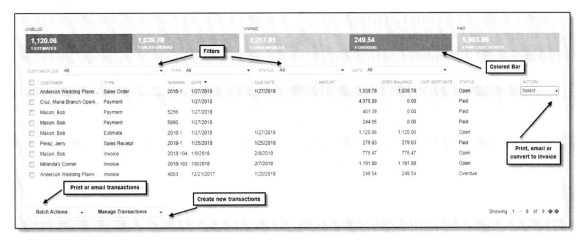

Figure 2-54 Income Tracker. Your screen may vary

COMPUTER PRACTICE

To use the **Income Tracker** to process a transaction:

Step 1. Click the **Income Tracker** icon on the *Icon Bar* (Figure 2-55).

Figure 2-55 Income Tracker on Icon Bar

Step 2. Check **Miranda's Corner**, on the left side of the **Income Tracker.**

Step 3. Click on the drop-down arrow in the *Action* column for **Miranda's** Corner, and choose **Receive Payment.**

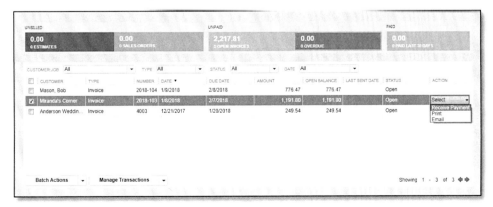

Figure 2-56 Receive Payment in Income Tracker

Step 4. **Receive Payment** for $1,191.80.

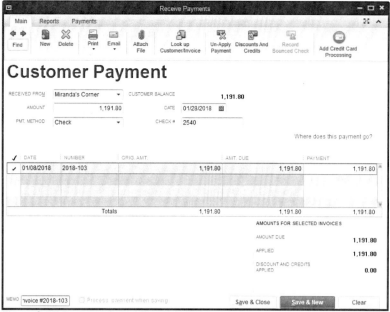
Figure 2-57 Payment from Miranda's Corner

Step 5. Verify that your screen matches Figure 2-57.
Step 6. Click **Save & Close** to record the transaction.
Step 7. Close **Income Tracker.**

Review Questions

Comprehension Questions

1. When you make a sale to a customer who pays at the time of the sale, either by check or by credit card, which type of form should you use in QuickBooks to record the transaction?
2. Explain how the **Undeposited Funds** account works and why it is best to use the option, **Use Undeposited Funds as a default deposit to account**, as a *Payments* preference.
3. How does the *Automatically Apply Payments* feature work?
4. How does the *Automatically Calculate Payments* feature work?

Multiple Choice

Select the best answer(s) for each of the following:

1. In the *New Customer* window, you find everything except:
    a) Customer Name.
    b) Customer Invoice/Bill To and Ship To address.
    c) Customer active/inactive status.
    d) Year-to-date sales information.

2. You should record a Sales Receipt when the customer pays:
   a) By cash, check, or credit card at the time of sale.
   b) By cash, check, or credit card at the end of the month.
   c) Sales tax on the purchase.
   d) For the order upon receipt of Invoice.

3. Which statement is false?
   a) Invoices are very similar to the Sales Receipt form.
   b) Invoices decrease Accounts Receivable.
   c) Sales Receipts have no effect on Accounts Receivables.
   d) Invoices should be created when customers are going to pay after the date of the initial sale.

4. You may specify payment Terms on the *New Customer* window; however:
   a) The payment Terms will only show on Sales Receipt transactions.
   b) The Terms can only be changed once a year.
   c) The sales representative must be informed.
   d) You are also permitted to override the Terms on each sale.

5. Your company has just accepted a payment for an Invoice. What should you do in QuickBooks to record this payment?
   a) Open the Invoice by clicking the **Invoices** icon on the *Home* page.
   b) Create a Sales Receipt by clicking the **Sales Receipt** icon on the *Home* page.
   c) Make a deposit by clicking the **Record Deposits** icon on the *Home* page.
   d) Receive the payment by clicking the **Receive Payments** icon on the *Home* page.

6. Which statement is false?
   a) Many customers reject Invoices that do not reference a P.O. (purchase order) number.
   b) The P.O. number helps the customer identify your Invoice.
   c) The P.O. number is required on all Invoices.
   d) The P.O. number is generated by the customer's accounting system.

7. To record a deposit in QuickBooks:
   a) Make a separate deposit that includes both Checks and Cash receipts.
   b) Make a separate deposit that includes both VISA and MasterCard receipts.
   c) Make a separate deposit that includes American Express receipts.
   d) All of the above.

8. Your company has just received an order from a customer who will pay within 30 days. How should you record this transaction in QuickBooks?
   a) Open the invoice by clicking the *Invoices* button on the *Home* page.
   b) Create a sales receipt by clicking the *Sales Receipt* button on the *Home* page.
   c) Make a deposit by clicking the *Record Deposits* button on the *Home* page.
   d) Receive the payment by clicking the *Receive Payment* button on the *Home* page.

9. When you make a deposit, all of the following are true except:
   a) You must print a deposit slip in order to process a deposit.
   b) A "Make Deposit" transaction typically transfers money from **Undeposited Funds** into your bank account.
   c) You should separate your deposits by payment type.
   d) You should create deposits so that they match exactly with the deposits on your bank statement.

10. Which item is false regarding calculating items?
    a) Calculating items can be used on invoices, sales receipts, and credit memos.
    b) A calculating item calculates based upon the amount of the line directly above it.
    c) A discount item is a calculating item.
    d) An item of type *service charge* is a calculating item.

11. When creating a customer record, which statement is false:
    a) After you enter a name in the *Customer Name* field of the *New Customer* window, you cannot use that name in any of the other name lists in QuickBooks.
    b) The credit limit can be added in the new customer window.
    c) A sales rep must be selected when creating a new customer.
    d) When you sell to and purchase from the same company, you should create two records, one in the Vendor List, and one in the Customer: Job List.

12. When receiving payments from customers to whom you have sent invoices, you must:
    a) Receive the payment in full. Partial payments cannot be accepted in QuickBooks.
    b) Enter them directly into the checking account register.
    c) Enter the payment into the receive payments window and check off the appropriate invoice(s) to which the payment applies.
    d) Delete the invoice so it does not show on the customer's open records.

13. You need to calculate the amount of a bankcard fee by multiplying the amount of the received payments by -1%. What useful QuickBooks feature could you use?
    a) Calculating Items
    b) QuickMath
    c) QuickAdd
    d) The *Fees* button on the bottom of the *Make Deposit* window

14. The Undeposited Funds account tracks
    a) Bad debts.
    b) Funds that have been received but not deposited.
    c) Funds that have not been received or deposited.
    d) All company sales from the point an invoice is created until it is deposited in the bank.

15. After entering an existing customer in the *Customer:Job* field of an invoice, a *Customer:Job Not Found* dialog box opens to say the customer is not on the *Customer List*. What should you do?
    a) Click the *Quick Add* button to add the customer to the *Customer List*.
    b) Click the *Set Up* button to enter the customer's information in a *New Customer* window.
    c) Click *Cancel* to check the name you entered in the *Customer:Job* field for typos or other errors.
    d) None of the above.

Completion Statements

1. A new customer can be added to the customer list "on the fly" by clicking _____ _____ after entering a new customer name on a sales form.

2. When you create a Sales Receipt, QuickBooks increases (with a debit) a(n) _____ account or the _____ _____ account.

3. Discounts and subtotals are called _____ Items.

4. Receiving payments reduces the balance in _____ _____ and increases the balance in the **Undeposited Funds** or a bank account.

5. _____ _____ helps you add, subtract, multiply or divide numbers in an *Amount* field.

Sales Problem 1

> Restore the Sales-14Problem1.QBM file.

1. Enter your own name and address information into the Customer Center List. Then print the Customer List by selecting the *Reports* menu, **List**, and then **Customer Contact List.**

2. Enter a Sales Receipt using the data in Table 2-6. The payment will be automatically grouped with other payments in **Undeposited Funds** account. You'll need to create the customer record using Quick Add, or by setting it up in the list before adding the sale. Print the sale on blank paper.

Field	Data
Customer Name	Stein, Kim
Class	Walnut Creek
Date	01/20/2018
Sale No.	2018-1
Sold To	Kim Stein 955 Swenton Rd. Walnut Creek, CA 94599
Check No	477
Payment Method	Check
Item	Camera SR32, Qty 2
Sales Tax	Contra Costa (8.25%) – Auto Calculates
Customer Tax Code	Tax
Memo	2 Cameras

Table 2-4 Use this data for a Sales Receipt in Step 2

3. Enter an Invoice using the data in the table below. Print the Invoice on blank paper.

Field	Data
Customer Name	Berry, Ron
Class	Walnut Creek
Custom Template	Academy Photo Service Invoice
Date	01/24/2018
Invoice #	2018-106
Bill To	Ron Berry 345 Cherry Lane Walnut Creek, CA 94599
PO No.	842-5022
Terms	Net 30
Item	Indoor Photo Session, Qty 6, $95/hour (SRV tax code)
Item	Retouching, Qty 3 (hrs), $95/hour (SRV tax code)
Sales Tax	Contra Costa (8.25%) – Auto Calculates
Memo	6 Hour Session, 3 Hour Retouching

Table 2-5 Use this data for an Invoice in Step 3

4. Record a payment dated *2/8/2018* for the full amount from *Berry, Ron* (check #9951123) and apply it to Invoice **2018-106**.

5. Deposit everything from the **Undeposited Funds** account into the **Checking** account on **2/9/2018**. Print **Deposit Slip and Deposit Summary** onto blank paper.

Sales Problem 2 (Advanced)

APPLYING YOUR KNOWLEDGE

> Restore the Sales-14Problem2.QBM file.

1. Enter your own name and address information into the Customer Center List. Then print the Customer List by selecting the *Reports* menu, **List**, and then **Customer Contact List**.

2. Enter a Sales Receipt using the data in Table 2-6. The payment will be automatically grouped with other payments in **Undeposited Funds** account. You'll need to create the customer record using Quick Add, or by setting it up in the Customer Center before adding the sale. Print the sale on blank paper.

Field	Data
Customer Name	Horwitz, Daniel
Class	Walnut Creek
Date	01/29/2018
Sale No.	2018-1
Sold To	Daniel Horwitz 1695 Blue Sky Pkwy Walnut Creek, CA 94599
Check No	477
Payment Method	Check
Item	Camera SR32, Qty 2, $695.99
Item	Case, Qty 1, $79.99
Sales Tax	Contra Costa (8.25%) – Auto Calculates
Customer Tax Code	Tax
Memo	2 Cameras, Case

Table 2-6 Use this data for a Sales Receipt in Step 2

3. Enter an Invoice using the data in the table below. Print the Invoice on blank paper.

The Sales Process - Sales Problem 2 (Advanced)

Field	Data
Customer Name	Pelligrini, George: 1254 Wilkes Rd.
Class	San Jose
Custom Template	Academy Photo Service Invoice
Date	01/31/2018
Invoice #	2018-106
Bill To	*Pelligrini Builders* *222 Santana Ave.* *Los Gatos, CA 94482*
PO No.	8324
Terms	Net 30
Item	Indoor Photo Session, Qty 4, $95/hour (SRV tax code)
Item	Retouching, Qty 4 (hrs), $95/hour (SRV tax code)
Sales Tax	Santa Clara (8.25%) – Auto Calculates
Memo	4 Hour Session, 4 Hour Retouching

Table 2-7 Use this data for an Invoice in Step 3

4. Enter a second Invoice using the data in the table below. Print the Invoice on blank paper. You will need to add this customer either through *Quick Add* or entering the customer information in the *Customer Center*.

Field	Data
Customer Name	Fuller, Nathan
Class	San Jose
Custom Template	Academy Photo Service Invoice
Date	01/31/2018
Invoice #	2018-107
Bill To	Nathan Fuller 99050 Market St. Santa Clara, CA 95111
PO Number	736555
Terms	2% 10 Net 30
Item	Indoor Photo Session, Qty 3, $95/hour (SRV tax code)
Sales Tax	Santa Clara (8.25%) – Auto Calculates
Memo	3 Hour Session

Table 2-8 Use this data for an Invoice in Step 4.

5. Record a payment dated *2/15/2018* for *$285.00* from Nathan Fuller (check #5342) and apply it to Invoice **2018-107**.

6. On *2/15/2018,* you received a partial payment from George Pelligrini for the *1254 Wilkes Rd.* Job for $400. American Express payment, card #4321-654321-54321, expires in 5/2019.

7. On *2/15/2018*, deposit everything from the **Undeposited Funds** account using the following:

a) Deposit Cash and Check payments together (Memo: Deposit Checks). Print **Deposit Slip and Deposit Summary** onto blank paper.

b) Deposit American Express payments separately (Memo: Deposit American Express). Record a 2% bankcard discount fee (use QuickMath to calculate) on the credit card deposit. Use the following data: Account - Bankcard Fee, Payment Method - American Express, Memo-2% Discount Fee. This amount should be a negative number. Print **Deposit Summary Only** onto blank paper.

QUICKBOOKS AND BEYOND – *TAKE THE NEXT STEP WITH THE SLEETER GROUP BLOG*

"How to Integrate PayPal into QuickBooks"

Seth David writes, "PayPal has been around for a long time and to be honest, I don't think they really care about integrating with QuickBooks. They are the payment method of choice for many people on the Internet. They are trusted because they are reliable. Perfect? No, but all in all, reliable. So how do we get transactions from PayPal into QuickBooks?"

In this *QuickBooks and Beyond* section, video blogger Seth David discusses receiving payment from customers via PayPal. Read the full post at www.sleeter.com/blog/?p=8644.

New Terminology

Merchant Processing – Usually refers to credit card payment processing but can also refer to other financial services for businesses.

Payment Gateway – Authorizes credit card payment for retailers and facilitates secure transfer of information between the payment portal (such as e-commerce website or magnetic strip) and the acquiring bank.

IIF File – A file format used to import and export QuickBooks data. Acronym stands for Intuit Interchange Format.

Putting New Knowledge to Use

1. How does your company or workplace accept payment?
2. What is the most efficient way to bring payment information into your QuickBooks file?

Chapter 3
Additional Customer Transactions

Topics

In this chapter, you will learn about the following topics:

- Recording Customer Returns and Credits (page 77)
- Writing Off a Bad Debt (page 84)
- Creating Customer Statements (page 89)
- Collecting Sales Tax (page 91)
- Creating Sales Reports (page 97)

> **Restore this File:**
> This chapter uses Customers-14.QBW. To open this file, restore the Customers-14.QBM file to your hard disk. See page 9 for instructions on restoring files.

In the last chapter, you learned about sales forms and the accounts receivable process. In this chapter, you will learn how QuickBooks records customer returns and refunds, creates customer *Statements*, and processes sales reports.

Recording Customer Returns and Credits

To record customer returns or credits, use QuickBooks *Credit Memos*. *Credit Memos* can be used in the following situations:

- To record the cancellation of an order that has already been invoiced.
- To record a return of merchandise from a customer.
- To record a credit-on-account for a customer.
- To record the first step of making a refund to a customer.

> **Key Term:**
> *Credit Memos* are sales forms that reduce the amount owed to your company by a customer.
>
> **The accounting behind the scenes:**
> *Credit Memos* reduce (credit) Accounts Receivable and reduce (debit) Income and, in some cases, Sales Tax Payable.

When you create a *Credit Memo* in QuickBooks, you must apply the credit to one or more *Invoices*, or use it to give a refund to the customer.

Refunding Customers

There are several situations when you may need to issue a refund to a customer:

1. When a customer pays for merchandise and then returns the merchandise.
2. When a customer requests a discount or refund on merchandise or services for which she has already paid.
3. When a customer overpays an *Invoice* and requests a refund.

If the customer paid with cash or check, you should issue a refund check. If the customer paid with a credit card, you should credit the customer's credit card.

COMPUTER PRACTICE

The first step in issuing a customer refund is to create a *Credit Memo* showing the detail of what is being refunded. Typically, the detail will include the products and/or services returned or discounted.

Bob Mason paid for but didn't use one hour of a photo session. In this exercise, you will create a *Credit Memo* directly from an *Invoice*. This has the advantage of including the details of the *Invoice* in the *Credit Memo*. Later, you will see other ways to create a *Credit Memo*, such as directly from the *Home* page.

Step 1. Click **Customers** in the *Icon* bar to open the *Customer Center*.

Step 2. Select **Mason, Bob** from the *Customer Center* list.

Step 3. If necessary, choose **All** from the *Date* field in the list of transactions in the *Customer Center*. From the list of transactions displayed, double click on Invoice #2018-106. This will open the *Invoice*.

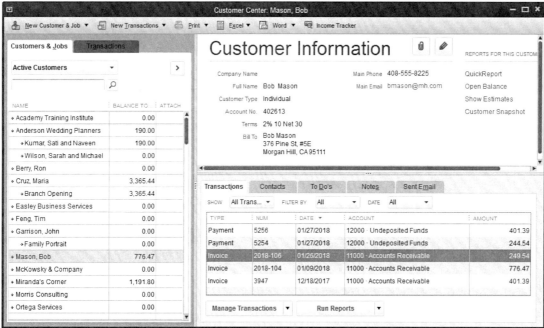

Figure 3-1 Opening Invoice from Customer Center

Step 4. Click the **Refund/Credit** button at the top of the *Create Invoices* window (see Figure 3-2).

Figure 3-2 Refund/Credit button in Create Invoices window

Step 5. A *Credit Memo* opens with the information from the previous *Invoice* (see Figure 3-3).

Credit Memos look similar to *Invoices*, but they perform the opposite function. That is, a *Credit Memo* reduces (debits) Sales, reduces (credits) Accounts Receivable, and in some cases reduces Sales Tax Payable. If Inventory is involved, a *Credit Memo* increases (debits) the Inventory asset and reduces (credits) the Cost of Goods Sold account.

Step 6. Press **Tab** to move to the *Date* field and enter *2/15/2018*. Press **Tab**.

Step 7. Enter *2018-106C* in the *Credit No.* field. Press **Tab** three times.

This credit transaction is included on statements and customer reports, so using the *Invoice* number followed by a "C" in the *Credit No.* field helps identify which *Invoice* this *Credit Memo* should apply to.

Step 8. Leave *Indoor Photo Session* in the *Item* field and tab to the *Qty* field. Change the *Qty* to *1*. Press **Tab** three times.

Step 9. Press **Ctrl+Delete** to remove the line that contains the *Standard Photo Package* from the *Credit Memo*.

Step 10. Enter *Refunded 1 Hr Indoor Photo Session* to the *Memo* field.

Step 11. Make sure your screen matches Figure 3-3. When done press **Save & Close**.

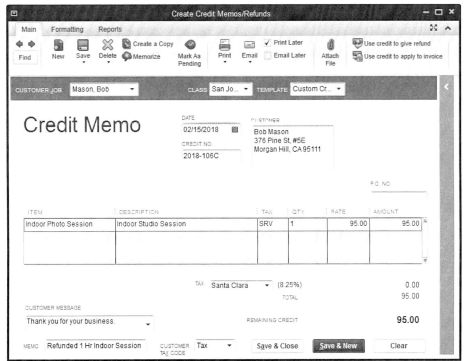

Figure 3-3 Use this data for the Credit Memo for Bob Mason

Step 12. After you save the *Credit Memo*, QuickBooks displays the *Available Credits* window (see Figure 3-4). Select **Give a Refund** and click **OK**.

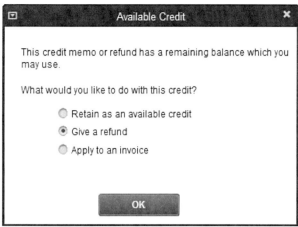

Figure 3-4 Give a refund option in Available Credit window

Step 13. QuickBooks opens the *Issue a Refund* window (see Figure 3-5). Most of the information is already filled in. Enter **Refunded - 1 Hr Photo Session** in the *Memo* field. Click **OK** to record the refund check.

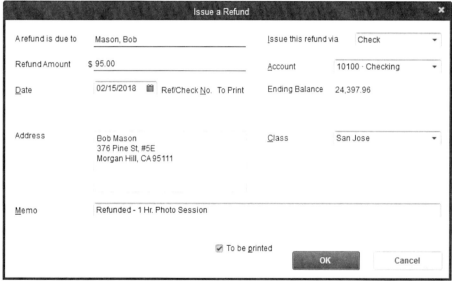

Figure 3-5 Issue a Refund for Photo Session

Step 14. When you click **OK**, QuickBooks creates the refund check in the checking account and records the *Credit Memo*.

Step 15. To redisplay the *Credit Memo*, double click it in the *Customer Center* (see Figure 3-6).

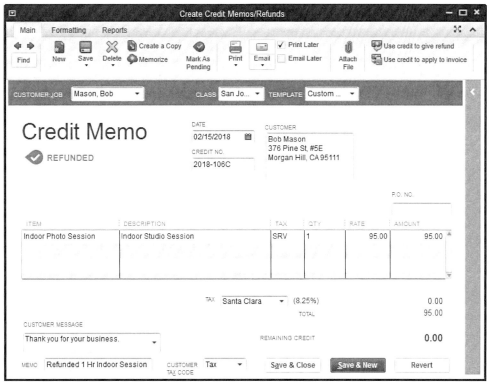

Figure 3-6 Credit Memo after the refund

Step 16.   Close the *Credit Memo* window. Close the *Invoice* window.

Step 17.   Although you will not do it now, this is when you would print the refund check.

Refunding Credit Cards

> **Note:**
> To process a credit card refund using QuickBooks Merchant Account Services, click the **Process credit card refund when saving** field that will display at the bottom of the *Issue a Refund* window. See the onscreen help for more information.

The process for refunding a customer's credit card is similar to the last example on refunding by check, except while check refunds allow you to write a physical check to refund the customer, credit card refunds are held in the Undeposited Funds account and processed in a "batch" each day.

> **DO NOT PERFORM THESE STEPS. THEY ARE FOR REFERENCE ONLY.**

1. To give a customer a credit card refund, begin by creating a Credit Memo. In this example, Maria Cruz: Branch Opening has been given a $190.00 refund for an Indoor Photo Session.
2. Select **Refunds & Credits** from the *Home* page.
3. Fill in the *Credit Memo*, such as the one displayed in Figure 3-7.

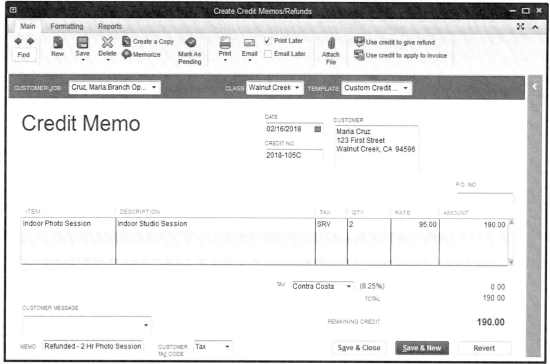

Figure 3-7 Maria Cruz Credit Memo for the credit card refund

4. Click **Save & Close** to save the *Credit Memo*.
5. Select **Give a refund** in the *Available Credit* window and click **OK** (see Figure 3-8).

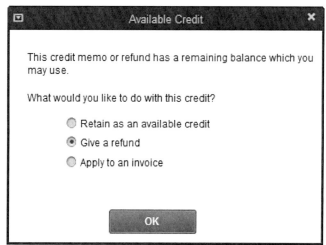

Figure 3-8 Available Credit window

6. In the *Issue a Refund* window, fill in the needed information as shown in Figure 3-9. Then click **OK**.

Additional Customer Transactions - Recording Customer Returns and Credits   **83**

Figure 3-9 Issue a Refund window

> **The Accounting Behind the Scenes**
> Creating a Credit Memo and issuing a refund in this example decreases (or debits) the income account associated with the item on the Credit Memo (i.e. Services) and decreases (or credits) the Undeposited Funds account.

7. To record the credit card refund into the bank account, select **Make Deposits** from the *Banking* menu. Click on the credit card refund in the *Select Payments to Deposit* section and click **OK**.

Figure 3-10 Payments to Deposit window with credit card refund

8. In the *Make Deposits* window, check to make sure your screen matches Figure 3-11.
9. Click **Save & Close**.

Figure 3-11 Make Deposits window

This example assumes that your merchant account service does not deduct a discount fee from each transaction. If your credit card company processes merchant discount fees with each transaction, you will need to calculate the discount in the **Checking** account line and add a **Bankcard fees** account line recorded as a negative amount.

1. Re-display the original *Credit Memo*. Notice that the REFUNDED stamp along the form confirms that the refund has been processed in QuickBooks.

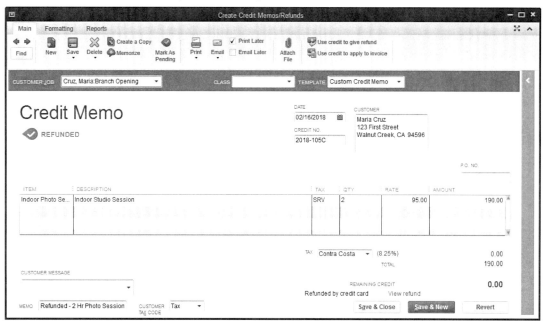

Figure 3-12 Credit Memo showing completed refund process

> **Did You Know?**
> Merchant services companies normally charge two types of fees for processing credit cards: a *transaction* fee and a *discount* fee. A **transaction** fee is a standard fee for each credit card transaction, regardless if it is a sale or refund. A **discount** fee is a percentage charge based on the transaction amount. Some merchant services companies only charge a discount fee for credit card sales. Other companies, however, charge a discount fee for both credit card sales and refunds. Intuit's QuickBooks Merchant Account Services for credit card processing currently charges a discount fee for both sales and refunds.

Writing Off a Bad Debt

If an *Invoice* becomes uncollectible, you'll need to write off the debt. If you use the cash basis of accounting, the uncollectible *Invoice* has not yet been recognized as income on your *Profit & Loss* report, and therefore, you *could* simply delete the *Invoice* to remove it from your records. However, good accounting practice dictates that you enter a new entry to credit the customer balance and reverse the sale (and the sales tax if appropriate).

To properly write off the bad debt, use a *Credit Memo* and a *Bad Debt* Item as shown in the following practice. In the "Customizing QuickBooks" chapter, you'll learn more about Items, but for now, we'll set up a *Bad Debt* Item in the sample file.

COMPUTER PRACTICE

Step 1. From the *List* menu select **Item List.**

Step 2. Press **Ctrl+N** to display the *New Item* window.

Step 3. Create an *Other Charge* Item called **Bad Debt** as shown in Figure 3-13. Link the *Bad Debt* Item to the Bad Debts expense account. Click **OK.**

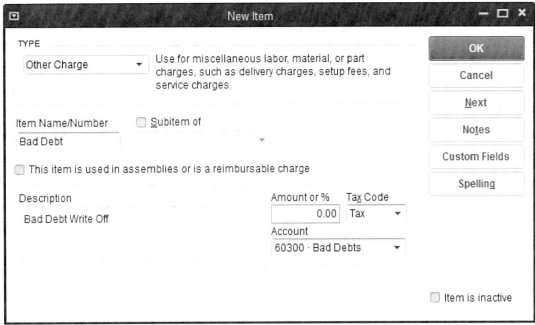

Figure 3-13 Bad Debt Other Charge Item

Step 4. Close the *Item List*.

Step 5. From the *Home* page select **Refunds & Credits**. This opens a *Credit Memo*. Alternatively, you could open the *Invoice* and create a *Credit Memo* from the *Refund/Credit* button.

Figure 3-14 Write off a bad debt with a Credit Memo

Step 6. Fill out the **Credit Memo** as shown in Figure 3-14. Choose *Anderson Wedding Planners: Kumar, Sati and Naveen* in the *Customer:Job* field. Because you are writing off a non-taxed item, set the *Tax* column to **SRV**.

Step 7. QuickBooks displays a warning message because *Invoices* and *Credit Memos* normally increase or decrease Income accounts, rather than Expense accounts (see Figure 3-15). Click **OK**.

Figure 3-15 Warning about the Bad Debt Item pointing to an expense account

> **Note:**
> Under many circumstances, your Bad Debt write-off should not affect sales tax. However, if the sale you are writing off does need to affect your sales tax liability, you'll need to use two lines on the credit memo.
>
> On the first line of the *Credit Memo*, use the **Bad Debt** Item and enter the total of all taxable items in the sale (not including the sales tax) in the *Amount* column. Select **Tax** (or the appropriate Code) in the *Tax Code* column. QuickBooks will calculate the sales tax and reduce your liability by that amount.
>
> On the second line, use the same **Bad Debt** Item and enter the total of the non-taxable items from the original *Invoice*, including any shipping or miscellaneous charges (excluding sales tax). Select a non-taxable *Tax Code* for this line.

Step 8. Click **Save & Close** to record the *Credit Memo*. The *Available Credit* window (see Figure 3-16) will be displayed. Select **Apply to an Invoice** option and click **OK**.

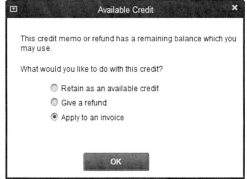
Figure 3-16 Apply to an Invoice option on Available Credit window

> **The accounting behind the scenes:**
> When you use the Bad Debt Item on a *Credit Memo*, the *Credit Memo* decreases (credit) Accounts Receivable and increases (debit) Bad Debts expense.

Applying the Bad Debt Credit Memo to an Open Invoice

COMPUTER PRACTICE

Step 1. The *Apply Credit to Invoices* window is automatically displayed with Invoice #4003 **Check** (✓) column checked (see Figure 3-17).

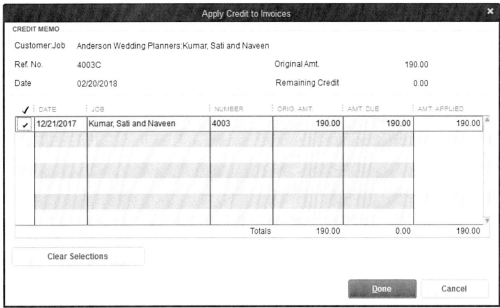

Figure 3-17 Apply Credit to Invoices window

Step 2. Click **Done** to apply the bad debt to the selected *Invoice*.

Create Batch Invoices

Batch Invoices allow you to quickly create invoices for multiple customers, however, the invoices all need to be for the same item at the same price. Companies and nonprofit organizations that offer subscription services or monthly dues or fees can use this feature to invoice all designated customers at one time.

> DO NOT PERFORM THESE STEPS. THEY ARE FOR REFERENCE ONLY.

In this example, Academy Photography will create a *Batch Group* for their Photo Club Members and then create invoices for their monthly dues.

1. Open the **Customers** menu and select **Create Batch Invoices.** The *Batch Invoice* window opens (see Figure 3-18).

    If the *Is your customer info set up correctly?* window displays, click **OK**. QuickBooks uses the terms, sales tax rate and send method set up for each customer to create the invoices so you will need to verify that your settings are correct before you start.

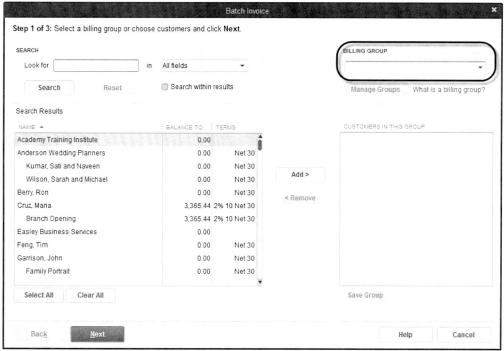

Figure 3-18 Batch Invoice Window

2. Click on the drop down arrow in the *Billing Group* section and select **Add New**.
3. Type *Photo Club* in the name field (see Figure 3-19) and click **Save**.

Figure 3-19 Batch Invoice Group

4. *Double-Click* on **Berry, Ron; Feng, Tim;** and **Mason, Bob** to move them to the column on the right – *Customers in This Group* (see Figure 3-20). This adds these three customers to the Billing Group.

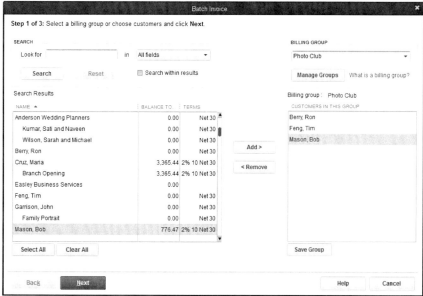

Figure 3-20 Select Customers for Batch Invoice

5. Click **Next**. Click **Yes** if asked to save.
6. Enter the information for the invoice as seen in Figure 3-21. Click **Next**.

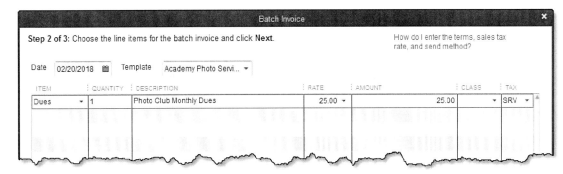

Figure 3-21 Select Items for Batch Invoice

7. QuickBooks shows you a review of the invoices to be created (see Figure 3-22).

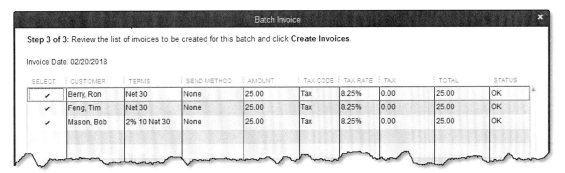

Figure 3-22 Create Batch Invoice

8. You can uncheck the checkmark on the left to skip invoicing a specific customer. When finished reviewing, click **Create Invoices.**
9. You can Print and/or email your invoices or click Close to print/email in a batch later (see Figure 3-23).

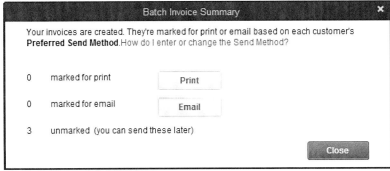

Figure 3-23 Batch Invoice Summary

Creating Customer Statements

QuickBooks Customer *Statements* provide a summary of the activity for an accounts receivable Customer during the period you specify. When you create *Statements*, you can show either all of the Customer's accounts receivable activity or just the transactions that are currently open.

COMPUTER PRACTICE

Step 1. From the *Home* page click the **Statements** icon to open the *Create Statements* window (see Figure 3-24). Alternatively, click **Create Statements** from the *Customers* menu.

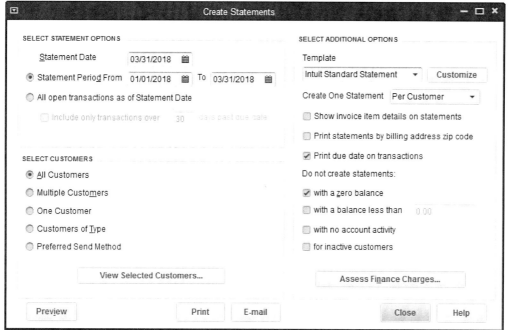

Figure 3-24 Create Statements window

Step 2.   Enter **03/31/2018** in the *Statement Date* field.

Step 3.   Set the *Statement Period From* and *To* fields to *1/1/2018* and *3/31/2018* respectively.

> You need to include a *Statement Date* and a *Statement Period* because the *Statement Date* is the "current" date that will appear on the *Statement*, while *Statement Period* dates include the period for which accounts receivable transactions will show on the *Statement*.

Step 4.   Leave **All Customers** selected in the *Select Customers* section. The options available under *Select Customers* allow you to choose which Statement or Statements to print.

> **Note:**
> If you want to print only the open *Invoices* for each Customer, select **All open transactions as of Statement Date** at the top left of the *Create Statements* window. If you want to show the detail from the *Invoice*, make sure the *Show invoice item details on statements* option is selected.

Step 5.   Leave **Per Customer** selected in the *Create One Statement* drop-down list.

Step 6.   Check the **with a zero balance** box in the *Do not create statements* section.

Step 7.   Click **Preview**.

Step 8.   After previewing the three pages of statements in the *Print Preview* window (see Figure 3-25), click the **Close** button.

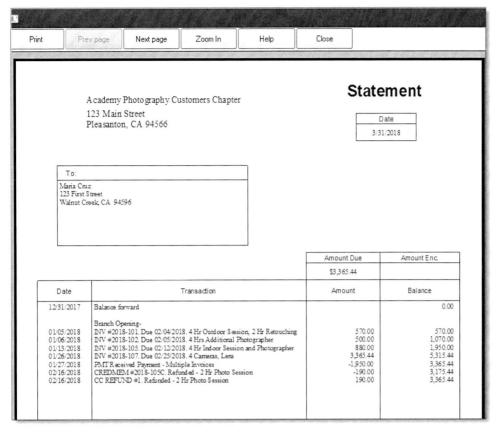

Figure 3-25 Preview your statements before printing

Collecting Sales Tax

If you sell products and certain types of services, chances are you will need to collect and remit sales tax. In many states, aside from the state tax, each county or city may impose an additional tax that businesses are required to track and report.

If you sell non-taxable goods and services, or if you sell to customers that are exempt from paying sales tax, your state will probably require a breakdown of non-taxable sales and the reason sales tax was not imposed.

These differing conditions may not apply in all jurisdictions, but QuickBooks allows you to track sales tax for all of these different situations. If you are not familiar with the sales tax rates or reporting requirements in your area, consult your state agency, your local QuickBooks ProAdvisor, or accountant for guidance.

Setting up Sales Tax

You must set up your **Sales Tax Preferences** before using the Sales Tax feature in QuickBooks.

COMPUTER PRACTICE

Step 1. Click the **Manage Sales Tax** button on the *Home Page*. Or you can choose **Manage Sales Tax** from the *Sales Tax* option on the *Vendors* menu.

Step 2. The *Manage Sales Tax* dialog box will appear (see Figure 3-26).

Step 3. Click the **Sales Tax Preferences** button in the *Get Started* section. Alternatively, you could select **Preferences** from the *Edit* menu, then select the *Sales Tax Company* Preferences.

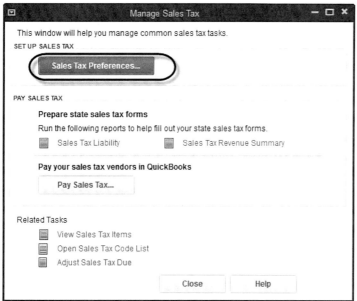

Figure 3-26 The Manage Sales Tax Dialog Box

Step 4. The Sales Tax Company Preferences dialog box appears.

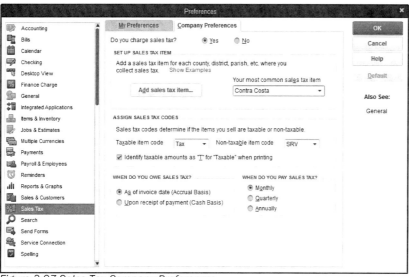

Figure 3-27 Sales Tax Company Preferences

Step 5. Leave **Yes** selected in the *Do you charge sales tax?* section.

Step 6. In the *Set Up Sales Tax Items* section, notice *Out of State* is selected in the *Your most common sales tax item* field. Change this field to **Contra Costa** (see Figure 3-27).

> **Note:**
> The sales tax item listed in the *Your most common sales tax item* field becomes the default sales tax item on new customer records, as well as on *Sales Receipts* and *Invoices*.

Additional Customer Transactions - Collecting Sales Tax

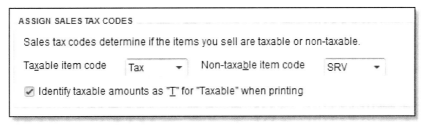

Figure 3-28 Assign Sales Tax Codes area of Sales Tax Company Preferences Window

Step 7. In the *Assign Sales Tax Codes* section, **Tax** is the default code in the *Taxable item code* field and **SRV** is the default for the *Non-taxable item code* field. For more information about *Sales Tax Codes,* see page 94.

Step 8. Review the remaining Preferences. When finished, click **OK** to save your changes and then **Close** to close the *Manage Sales Tax* window.

Sales Tax Items

Sales Tax Items are used on sales forms to calculate the amount of sales tax due on each sale. You can view the *Sales Tax Item* on the bottom of the form, separately from the rest of the *Items* (see Figure 3-29).

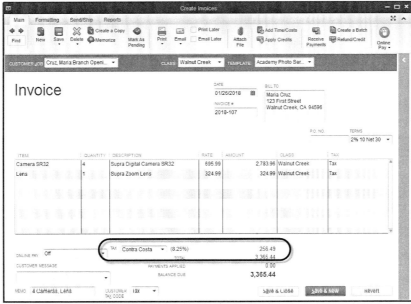

Figure 3-29 Invoice using the Contra Costa Sales Tax Item

To set up your Sales Tax Items, follow these steps:

COMPUTER PRACTICE

Step 1. Select the *Lists* menu and then select **Item List**. Alternatively, click the **Items & Services** icon on the *Home* page.

Step 2. To add a new Item, select the **Item** button at the bottom of the *Item List* and then select **New**.

Step 3. Select **Sales Tax Item** in the *Type* drop-down list and press **Tab**.

Step 4. Enter the *Tax Name, Description, Tax Rate,* and *Tax Agency,* as shown in Figure 3-30. This item will track all sales activity (taxable and nontaxable) for Alameda County and will charge each customer 8.75% in sales tax. The sales taxes collected using the *Alameda Sales Tax Item* will increase the amount due to the *State Board of Equalization.*

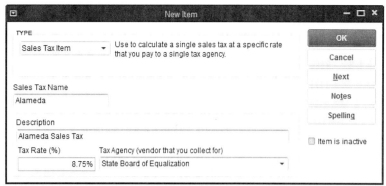

Figure 3-30 Setting up a Sales Tax item

Step 5.   Click **OK** to save the Item.

> **The accounting behind the scenes:**
> **Sales Tax Items** automatically calculate the sales tax on each sales form by applying the sales tax rate to all taxable items on that sale. QuickBooks increases (credits) Sales Tax Payable for the amount of sales tax on the sale. Also, QuickBooks tracks the amount due (debits) by *Tax Agency* in the *Sales Tax Liability* report and in the *Pay Sales Tax* window.

Your sample file includes three additional *Sales Tax Items* for tracking sales in *Contra Costa* and *Santa Clara* counties, as well as *Out of State* sales. After you add the *Alameda Sales Tax Item*, your Item list will look like Figure 3-31.

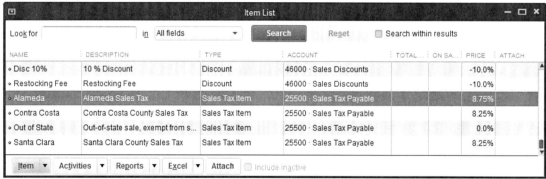

Figure 3-31 Item list scrolled down to Sales Tax Items

> **Note:**
> If you remit sales tax to **only one agency** (e.g., California's State Board of Equalization) but you collect sales tax in several different counties or cities, create a separate *Sales Tax Item* for each taxable location in which you sell products. This allows you to track different sales tax rates for each locale.
>
> **Note:**
> If you pay sales tax to **more than one agency**, you should use *Sales Tax Group*s to combine several different Sales Tax Items into a group tax rate.

Sales Tax Codes

Sales Tax Codes are an additional classification for calculating and reporting sales tax. A Sales Tax Code is assigned to each product or service Item, as well as to each Customer.

Sales Tax Codes serve two purposes. First, Sales Tax Codes indicate whether a specific product or service is taxable or non-taxable. Secondly, Sales Tax Codes categorize revenue based on the reason you charged or did not charge sales tax.

Using Sales Tax Codes on Sales Forms

If you use a taxable *Sales Tax Code* in the *Customer Tax Code* field on sales forms, QuickBooks will apply sales tax (see Figure 3-32). If you use a non-taxable *Sales Tax Code*, QuickBooks will not apply sales tax unless you override the sales tax code (to a taxable code) on one of the lines in the body of the form.

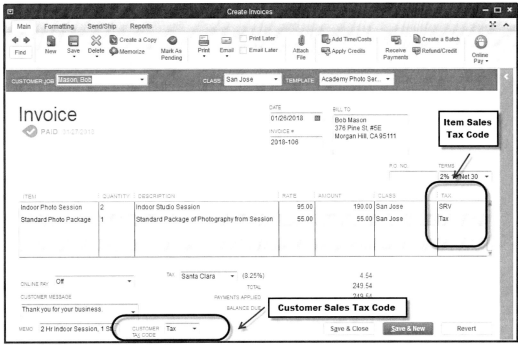

Figure 3-32 Invoice with taxable items

When you set up a Customer record, the *Sales Tax Code* you enter in the Customer record becomes the default in the *Customer Tax Code* field on sales forms.

Similarly, when you set up Items, the *Sales Tax Code* you enter in the *Item* record becomes the default *Tax Code* in the body of sales forms.

You can override the *Sales Tax Code* at the bottom of sales forms by using the *Customer Tax Code* drop-down list, or on each line in the body of the Invoice.

Setting up Sales Tax Codes

COMPUTER PRACTICE

One of your customers, Miranda's Corner, purchases various frames from Academy Photography to resell to her customers, and therefore does not pay sales tax.

Step 1.   From the *Lists* menu select **Sales Tax Code List**. QuickBooks displays the *Sales Tax Code List* window (see Figure 3-33).

Figure 3-33 Sales Tax Code List

Step 2. This file already has five *Sales Tax Codes*. To create a new *Sales Tax Code*, select **New** from the *Sales Tax Code* button at the bottom of the window.

Step 3. Enter the information shown in Figure 3-34. This creates a *Sales Tax Code* for tracking customers who do not pay sales tax because they are resellers.

Figure 3-34 Edit Sales Tax Code window

Step 4. Click OK to save this Sales Tax Code.
Step 5. Close the Sales Tax Code List window.
Step 6. Open the *Customer Center*. Double click **Miranda's Corner** in the *Customer Center*.
Step 7. In the *Edit Customer* window, click on the **Sales Tax Settings** tab.
Step 8. Enter **RSR** from the *Tax Code* field in the *Sales Tax Information* section (see Figure 3-35).

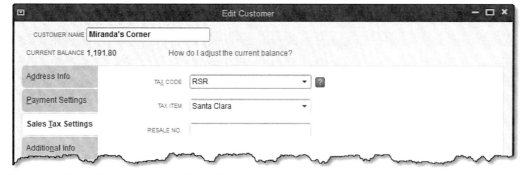

Figure 3-35 Changing the Customer Sales Tax Code

Step 9. Click **OK** to close the *Edit Customer* window. Close the *Customer Center*.

Calculating Sales Tax on Sales Forms

When you properly set up your QuickBooks *Items*, *Customers*, *Sales Tax Codes,* and *Preferences*, QuickBooks automatically calculates and tracks sales tax on each sale.

As illustrated in Figure 3-36 and detailed in the steps above, each line on a sale shows a separate *Item* that is taxed according to the combination of how the *Item*, *Tax Code*, and *Customer* are set up. Only taxable customers will be charged sales tax. If the customer is taxable, then the sum of the *Taxable Items* is multiplied by the Sales Tax Rate. In the example below, the customer is taxable. The only taxable *Item* on the *Invoice* is the *Standard Photo Package*, so the *Amount* of the *Standard Photo Package* ($55.00) is multiplied by the rate for Santa Clara County (8.25%) for a resulting sales tax of $4.54.

If necessary, you can override the *Tax Code* on each line of the sales form or at the bottom of the form. The *Tax Item*, which can also be overridden, determines the rate to charge on the sum of all taxable line items on the sale.

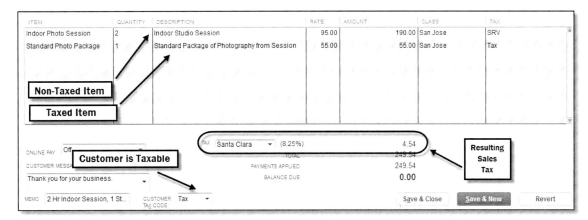

Figure 3-36 Calculating Sales Tax in QuickBooks

For more on paying the collected sales tax, see 146.

Creating Sales Reports

In this section, you'll learn how to create reports that will help you analyze your company's sales.

Customer Open Balance Report

You can create a *Customer Open Balance* report to view the open *Invoices* and the *Credit Memo* for this customer.

Step 1.   If necessary, display the **Customer Center** and then select **Cruz, Maria: Branch Opening** as shown in Figure 3-37.

Step 2.   Under the *Reports for this Job* section, select the **Open Balance** link (see Figure 3-37). You may need to expand the window to see the Reports section.

Additional Customer Transactions - Creating Sales Reports

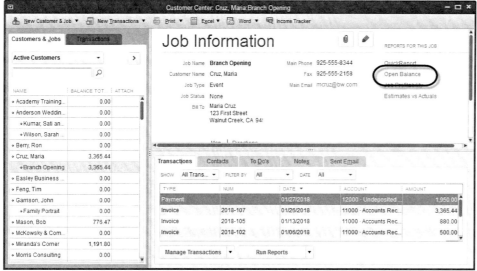

Figure 3-37 Select the job and click the needed report in the Customer Center

Step 3. The *Customer Open Balance* report opens (see Figure 3-38).

Step 4. Click the Close Window button at the top right of the window to close the report or press **Esc** to close the window.

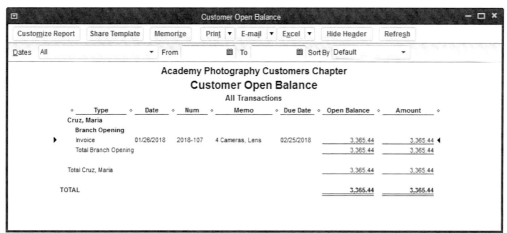

Figure 3-38 Customer Open Balance report

Sales by Customer Summary Report

The *Sales by Customer Summary* report shows how much you have sold to each of your customers over a given date range.

COMPUTER PRACTICE

To create this report, follow these steps:

Step 1. From the *Report Center* select **Sales** from the category list and then double click the **Sales by Customer Summary** report in the *Sales by Customer* section.

Step 2. Enter *01/1/2018* in the *From* date field and then press **Tab**.

Step 3. Enter *2/28/2018* in the *To* date field and then press **Tab**.

Figure 3-39 shows the *Sales by Customer Summary* report for the first two months of 2018.

Step 4. To print the report, click **Print** at the top of the report.

Additional Customer Transactions - Creating Sales Reports

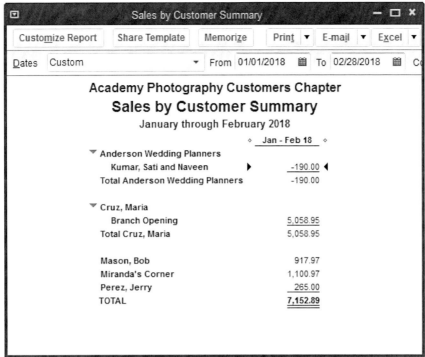

Figure 3-39 Sales by Customer Summary report

Step 5. Close the *Sales by Customer Summary* report. If the *Memorize Report* dialog box opens, click **No** (see Figure 3-40).

Figure 3-40 Memorize Report dialog box

Sales by Item Report

The *Sales by Item* report shows how much you have sold of each Item over a given date range. To create this report, follow these steps:

COMPUTER PRACTICE

Step 1. From the *Report Center* select **Sales** from the category list and then double click the **Sales by Item Summary** sample in the *Sales by Item* section. You may need to scroll down.

Step 2. Enter *1/1/2018* in the *From* date field and then press **Tab**.

Step 3. Enter *2/28/2018* in the *To* date field and then press **Tab**.

Figure 3-41 shows the *Sales by Item Summary* report for the first two months of 2018.

Step 4. To print the report, click **Print** at the top of the report.

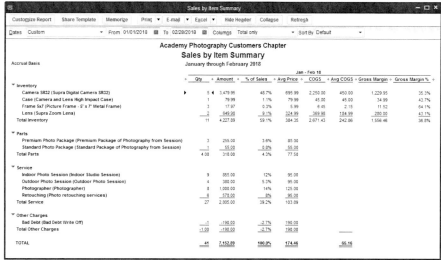

Figure 3-41 Sales by Item Summary report

Step 5. Close the *Sales by Item Summary* report. If the *Memorize Report* window opens, click **No**.

Review Questions

Comprehension Questions

1. When would you choose to give a refund after creating a *Credit Memo*?
2. When would you choose to retain an available credit after creating a *Credit Memo*?

Multiple Choice

Select the best answer(s) for each of the following:

1. Customer *Statements*:
    a) Provide a summary of all accounts receivable activity for a Customer during the period you specify.
    b) Are not available in QuickBooks.
    c) Automatically assess and calculate finance charges for overdue accounts without any user action.
    d) Should only be created and mailed if the Customer's balance is over $500.

2. Which of the following options is not available on the *Available Credit* window?
    a) Give a refund.
    b) Retain as an available credit.
    c) Apply to an *Invoice*.
    d) Use with Receive Payments.

3. What is the best way to write off a bad debt?
    a) Delete the original *Invoice*.
    b) Create a *Credit Memo* using a *Bad Debt* Item and apply the credit to the past due *Invoice*.
    c) Create a *Credit Memo* for the amount of the past due *Invoice* and retain the available credit.
    d) Any of the above.

4. In which of the following situations would you create a *Credit Memo*?
   a) You need to record a cancelled order that has already been invoiced but not paid.
   b) A customer returns merchandise and wants the return credited to a future *Invoice*.
   c) A customer requests a refund.
   d) Any of the above.

5. The *Credit Memo Number* should be
   a) The next number after the *Credit Memo Number* on the last *Credit Memo*.
   b) The next number after the *Invoice Number* on the last *Invoice*, followed by a "C."
   c) Any unique number.
   d) The same number as the *Invoice* to which the *Credit Memo* is linked, followed by a "C."

6. You need to issue a refund to a customer. The customer originally paid with a Visa card. How do you issue the credit?
   a) Pay the refund with your company's credit card.
   b) Pay the refund using any method of payment.
   c) Pay the refund by issuing a refund check.
   d) Pay the refund through the customer's credit card.

7. Your company policy is that each Finance Charge should be at least $5. Where is the best place to set this value in QuickBooks?
   a) Enter a value of at least $5 in the *Finance Charge* field in the *Assess Finance Charges* window.
   b) Enter *$5* in the *Minimum Finance Charge* field in the *Finance Charge Company Preferences* window.
   c) Enter *$5* on the last line of each statement.
   d) Enter *$5* in the *Minimum Finance Charge* field in the *Create Statements* window.

8. Which report would you run to see a summary of income by products and services?
   a) The Sales by Item Summary Report
   b) The Sales by Customer Summary Report
   c) The Customer Open Balance Report
   d) The Revenue by Item Summary Report

9. Which of the following is a way to issue a credit without creating a *Credit Memo*?
   a) Delete an open invoice.
   b) Deposit a check from a customer without receiving a payment.
   c) Receiving a payment from a customer for an amount greater than their Accounts Receivable balance.
   d) You can only issue a credit by creating a *Credit Memo*.

10. Which type of business would most likely use Batch Invoices?
    a) Home Owners Association
    b) Home Builder
    c) Accounting & Tax business
    d) Retail Store

11. A past due invoice contains items that were taxed and items that were not taxed. How would you write off this invoice as a bad debt?
    a) Delete the original invoice.
    b) Delete the taxed items from the original invoice and then delete the entire invoice.
    c) Create a *Credit Memo* with two *Bad Debt* items, the first set to non-taxable with the total of non-taxable items, the second set to taxable with the total of taxable items. Apply this *Credit Memo* to the original invoice.
    d) Create a *Credit Memo* for the taxable amount from the original invoice. Apply the *Credit Memo* to the invoice, and then delete the invoice.

12. Which statement is true?
    a) If you assess Finance Charges for one past due customer, you have to assess them to all past due customers.
    b) You must preview statements before printing them.
    c) Finance Charges are assessed automatically when you create a statement.
    d) You can create a statement for a single customer.

13. After issuing a refund check,
    a) The *Credit Memo* is marked **Refunded** and the *Remaining Credit* field is 0.00
    b) The *Credit Memo* is removed.
    c) The original *Invoice* is marked **Refunded** and the *Remaining Credit* field is 0.00.
    d) The *Total* field on the original invoice is 0.00.

14. Which of the following is true?
    a) You can only apply a *Credit Memo* to an *Invoice* if the *Remaining Credit* amount is equal to the *Amount Due*.
    b) *Credit Memos* are automatically applied to open invoices.
    c) *Credit Memos* look similar to invoices but perform the opposite function, reducing (debiting) Sales accounts and reducing (crediting) Accounts Receivable.
    d) You should not use a *Credit Memo* to write off a bad debt.

15. In which of the following situations would you assess a Finance Charge?
    a) A customer returns merchandise and you want to charge him or her a restocking fee.
    b) You want to write off a bad debt.
    c) A customer's invoice is 60 days past due.
    d) Any of the above.

Completion Statements

1. Regarding Refunds: If the customer paid by _____ or _____, you will need to issue a refund check. If the customer paid with a(n) _____ _____, you will need to credit the customer's credit card account

2. _____ _____ are used to issue refunds or apply credits to existing invoices.

3. You can _____ _____ an uncollectible invoice as a bad debt.

4. When a customer is late paying an invoice, you can assess _____ _____.

5. A customer _____ is a summary of all activity on an account in a specified period.

Customers Problem 1

EXTENDING YOUR KNOWLEDGE

> Restore the Customers-**14Problem1.QBM** file.

1. On Feb.1, 2018, create Invoice #2018-108 to *Feng, Tim*. *Class* is *San Jose*. The customer purchased a 2 hour Indoor Photo Session. Use the *Santa Clara* Tax Item. Print the *Invoice*.

2. Tim Feng only needed a 1 hour Indoor Photo Session. On Feb 5, 2018, create a Credit Memo #2018-108C to write off 1 hour of Indoor Photo Session for Tim Feng. Apply the credit to the open invoice. Print the *Credit Memo*.

3. Print Sales by Customer Summary report for February 2018.

4. Print Sales by Item Summary report for February 2018.

5. Create and print customer *Statements* for the period of February 1, 2018 through February 28, 2018. Print *Statements* for all customers who have a balance due.

Customers Problem 2 (Advanced)

EXTENDING YOUR KNOWLEDGE

> Restore the Customers-**14Problem2.QBM** file.

1. On Feb 7, 2018, create Invoice #2018-108 to Morris Consulting. Use the Walnut Creek class, terms 2% 10, Net 30. (Note: Special terms apply to this *Invoice* only.) The customer purchased a 2 hour Indoor Photo Session ($95 per hour) and 3 hours with a Photographer ($125 per hour). Use the Out of State Sales Tax Item. Print the *Invoice*.

2. On Feb 9, 2018, create Invoice #2018-109 to Easley Business Services. Use the class San Jose. Terms are Net 30. The customer purchased 2 Cameras ($695.99), 2 Lens ($324.99), and 2 Cases ($79.99). Use the Out of State Sales Tax Item. Print the *Invoice*.

3. On Feb 10, 2018, receive check #58621 in the amount of $553.70 from Morris Consulting in full payment of Invoice #2018-108. He took a 2% discount of $11.30. Use the Sales Discount account and the Walnut Creek class.

4. On Feb 15, 2018, Donald Easley of Easley Business Services called and gave his VISA credit card number to pay off the balance on his open Invoices. The payment amount was $2,201.94; VISA #4444-3333-2222-1111; Exp. 05/2018.

5. On Feb 23, 2018, Morris Consulting requested a refund for one hour of Photographer services. Create Credit Memo #2018-108C and use the Walnut Creek class. Issue Morris Consulting a refund check.

6. On Feb 26, 2018, create a Credit Memo to write off Invoice 3696 to Ortega Services. You will need to create a Bad Debt item. Since Invoice 3696 included a taxable item, you will need to mark the Bad Debt item on the *Credit Memo* for the amount $695.99 and mark it as taxable. Use the Walnut Creek class. The entire amount of the write-off is $753.41. Apply the *Credit Memo* to the open *Invoice*.

7. On Feb 27, 2018, receive payment for $1,191.80 from Miranda's Corner in payment of Invoice #2018-103. She uses her VISA card number 7777-8888-9999-0000 expiration date 12/2018, to pay this *Invoice*.

8. On Feb 28, 2018, issue Credit Memo #2018-103C to Miranda's Corner for Invoice #2018-103. The customer returned 1 Camera ($695.99). A 10% restocking fee applies. Use the San Jose class and the Santa Clara County sales tax. Issue a refund to Miranda's Corner's VISA card on Credit Memo #2018-103C. Total refund: $683.81. Print the *Credit Memo* after the refund.

9. Deposit the check in the Undeposited Funds account on 2/28/2018. Total deposit amount is $553.70. Print the Deposit Slip and Deposit Summary.

10. Deposit all VISA receipts on 2/28/18. Record a 2% bankcard discount fee (use QuickMath to calculate) on the credit card deposit. Total deposit amount is $2,655.73. Print the Deposit Summary Only.

11. Print Sales by Customer Summary report for January through February 2018.

12. Print Sales by Item Summary report for January through February 2018.

13. Create and print customer *Statements* for the period of February 1, 2018 through February 28, 2018. Print *Statements* for all customers who have a balance due: one for Anderson Weddings and one for Bob Mason.

QUICKBOOKS AND BEYOND – *TAKE THE NEXT STEP WITH THE SLEETER GROUP BLOG*

"Comparing QuickBooks Desktop with QuickBooks Online"

Charlie Russell blogs, "Intuit is placing an increasing emphasis on QuickBooks Online, but it isn't a product that all accounting professionals are familiar with. Many of us have been working with QuickBooks Desktop (for Windows) for years and that is our comfort zone. Intuit keeps on trying to push us out of that comfort zone. My viewpoint on this is that whether we like it or not, QuickBooks Online is going to be a big player in our future, so we better get to know it! Let's start with a simple comparison of features between the two products."

In this *QuickBooks and Beyond* section, Charlie Russell summarizes the differences between QuickBooks Desktop (which is used in the exercises in this book) and QuickBooks Online, a cloud-based application. This post lists many QuickBooks features that are explained later in the book or that are beyond the scope of this book. If you encounter an unfamiliar feature, continue and you should be able to get an overview of the differences. Read the full post at www.sleeter.com/blog/?p=5725.

New Terminology

QuickBooks Desktop Edition – QuickBooks Pro, Premier, Accountant, or Enterprise editions, designed to be installed on a physical computer. This textbook covers the QuickBooks Desktop Edition.

QuickBooks Online – A cloud-based application created by Intuit, the makers of QuickBooks Desktop Edition. QuickBooks Online is a different application from QuickBooks Desktop Edition.

Putting New Knowledge to Use

1. What are the advantages of using QuickBooks Desktop over QuickBooks Online?
2. What are the advantages of using QuickBooks Online over QuickBooks Desktop?

Chapter 4
Managing Expenses

Topics

In this chapter, you will learn about the following topics:
- Entering Expenses in QuickBooks (page 105)
- Setting Up Vendors (page 108)
- Activating Class Tracking (page 112)
- Tracking Job Costs (page 114)
- Paying Vendors (page 115)
- Printing Checks (page 128)
- Voiding Checks (page 131)
- Applying Vendor Credits (page 133)
- Tracking Company Credit Cards (page 136)
- Paying Sales Tax (page 146)
- Accounts Payable Reports (page 147)

> **Restore this File:**
> This chapter uses Expenses-14.QBW. To open this file, restore the Expenses-14.QBM file to your hard disk. See page 9 for instructions on restoring files.

In this chapter, we will discuss several ways to track your company's expenditures and vendors. We will start by adding vendors to your file, and then discuss several methods of paying them. In addition, this chapter shows you how to track expenses by job.

Entering Expenses in QuickBooks

QuickBooks provides several tools to help you track and manage the expenses in your business. These tools allow you to track your expenses in detail so that you can create extensive reports that help you manage your vendor relationships and control the costs in your business.

The Process of Entering Expenses in QuickBooks

The *Vendors* section of the *Home* page window provides you with a graphical flow of the steps involved in managing vendors, purchases, and payments (see Figure 4-1).

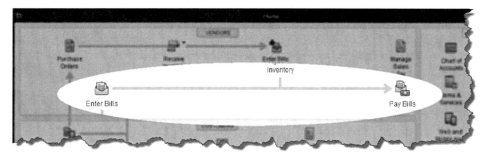

Figure 4-1 QuickBooks Home page

Clicking the *Vendors* icon on the *Home* page or the *Icon Bar* displays the *Vendor Center* (see Figure 4-2). The *Vendor Center* displays information about all of your vendors and their transactions in a single place. You can add a new vendor, add a transaction to an existing vendor, or print the *Vendor List* or *Transaction List*.

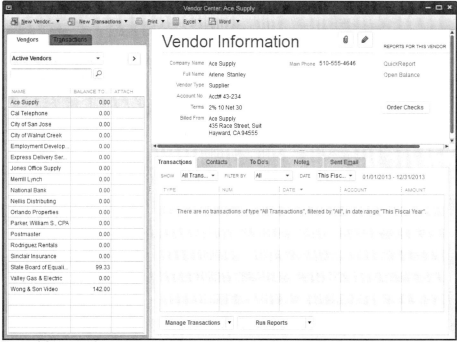

Figure 4-2 Vendor Center

In addition to the *Vendor Center*, the *Banking* section of the *Home* page contains options to help you navigate making deposits, writing checks, opening a check register, and reconciling with the bank statement. Figure 4-3 displays the *Banking* section of the *Home* page.

Figure 4-3 Banking section of the Home page

Table 4-1 shows many of the business transactions that might occur in dealing with vendors to process expenses in QuickBooks.

For illustrative purposes, we have defined two major groups of vendors – cash vendors and credit vendors. Table 4-1 shows how to enter transactions for each of these two groups of Vendors. The table also shows what QuickBooks does "behind the scenes" to record these transactions.

For some vendors, you will decide to track *Bills* and *Bill Payments*. This means the Accounts Payable account will be used to track how much you owe these vendors. We will refer to these as your credit vendors.

With other vendors, you will skip the Accounts Payable account and just write checks or otherwise pay them directly, coding the transactions to the appropriate expense accounts. We will refer to these as your cash vendors. Although you probably will not pay these vendors with actual cash, but with checks or credit cards, we will use the term cash vendor to distinguish them from credit vendors described previously.

Business Transaction	Cash Vendors		Credit Vendors	
	QuickBooks Transaction	Accounting Entry	QuickBooks Transaction	Accounting Entry
Recording a Purchase Order	Not usually used		Purchase Orders	Non-posting entry used to track *Purchase Orders*
Recording a Bill from a Vendor	Not usually used		Enter Bills	Increase (debit) **Expenses**, Increase (credit) **Accounts Payable**
Paying Bills	Write Checks	Increase (debit) **Expense**, Decrease (credit) **Checking**	Pay Bills	Decrease (debit) **Accounts Payable**, Decrease (credit) the **Checking Account**

Table 4-1 Steps for entering expenses

Recording Transactions

The first row in Table 4-1 references *Recording a Purchase Order*. Some vendors require *Purchase Orders* so they can properly process orders. When a *Purchase Order* is recorded, no accounting transaction is entered into QuickBooks; rather, a "memo" entry is made to track the *Purchase Order*. For details on using *Purchase Orders*, refer to our companion textbook *QuickBooks Complete*.

The second row references *Recording a Bill from a Vendor*. When you receive a bill from a vendor, you will record it using the *Enter Bills* window. Then, when it is time to pay your *Bills*, you will use the *Pay Bills* window in QuickBooks to select the *Bills* you want to pay. As shown below in Figure 4-4, both of these commands are available from the *New Transactions* drop-down menu in the Vendor Center.

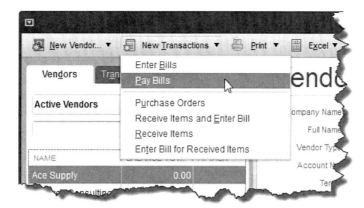

Figure 4-4 New Transactions Menu drop-down list in the Vendor Center

The third row references *Paying Bills*. Sometimes you will need to write a check that is not for the payment of a *Bill*. In that case, you will use the *Write Checks* window. *Write Checks* is accessible by clicking the **Write Checks** icon from the *Home* page, the **Write Checks** option from the *Banking* menu, or by pressing **Ctrl+W**.

Setting Up Vendors

Vendors include every person or company from whom you purchase products or services, including trade vendors, service vendors, and 1099 contract workers. Before you record any transactions to a Vendor in QuickBooks, you must set them up in the *Vendor Center*.

> **Tip:**
> When a vendor is also a customer, you will need to set up two separate records: a vendor record in the *Vendor Center* and a customer record in the *Customer Center*. The customer name must be slightly different from the vendor name. For example, you could enter Boswell Consulting as "Boswell Consulting-V" for the vendor name in the *New Vendor* window, and "Boswell Consulting-C" for the customer name in the *New Customer* window. The contact information for both customer and vendor record can be identical.

To set up a vendor, follow these steps:

COMPUTER PRACTICE

Step 1.   To display the *Vendor Center*, select the **Vendors** icon in the Vendors section of the *Home* page (see Figure 4-5). Alternately, click on the **Vendors** icon on the *Icon Bar*.

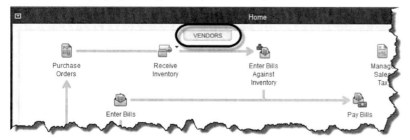

Figure 4-5 Vendors section of the Home page

Step 2.   Click the **New Vendor** button in the *Vendor Center* (see Figure 4-6) and choose **New Vendor** from the popup menu.

Managing Expenses - Setting Up Vendors

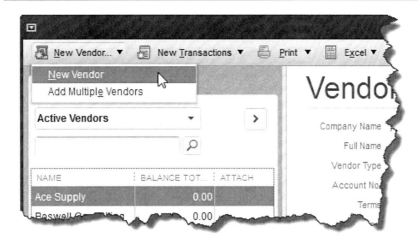

Figure 4-6 Add New Vendor to the Vendor list

Step 3.   The *New Vendor* window displays (see Figure 4-7). Notice there are tabs labeled *Address Info, Payment Settings, Tax Settings, Account Settings* and *Additional Info*.

Figure 4-7 The New Vendor window

Step 4.   Enter *Boswell Consulting* in the *Vendor Name* field and press **Tab**.

> **Tip:**
> The *Vendor List* sorts alphabetically, just like the *Customer List*. Therefore, if your vendor is an individual person, enter the last name first, followed by the first name.

Step 5.   Press **Tab** twice to skip the *Opening Balance* and *as of* fields (see Figure 4-8).

The *Opening Balance* field shows only when you create a new *Vendor* record. You will not see this field when you edit an existing vendor. The date in the *as of* field defaults to the current date. Since you will not enter an amount in the *Opening Balance* field, there is no need to change this date.

> **Important:**
> It is best *not* to use the *Opening Balance* field in the *New Vendor* window. If you *do* enter an opening balance for a vendor in the *Opening Balance* field, QuickBooks creates a *Bill* that increases (credits) Accounts Payable and increases (debits) Uncategorized Expense. Instead, enter each unpaid *Bill* separately after you create the vendor record.

Step 6. Enter *Boswell Consulting* in the *Company Name* field and press **Tab**.

Step 7. Continue entering data in the rest of the fields on the Vendor record, as shown in Figure 4-8. Press **Tab** after each entry.

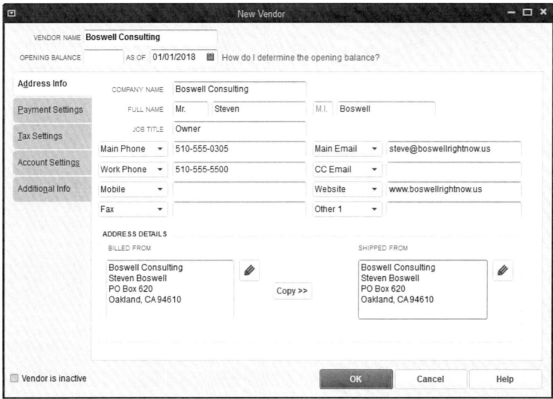

Figure 4-8 New Vendor window after it has been completed

Step 8. Click the **Payment Settings** tab to continue entering information about this vendor (see Figure 4-9).

Figure 4-9 The Payment Settings tab of the New Vendor window

Managing Expenses - Setting Up Vendors **111**

Step 9. Enter *66-112* in the *Account No.* field and press **Tab**.

In this field, you enter the number that your vendor uses to track you as a customer. If your vendor requires you to enter your account number on the checks you send, this is where you enter it. QuickBooks prints the contents of this field on the memo of the check when you pay this vendor's bill.

Step 10. Press **Tab** to leave the *Credit Limit* field blank.

Step 11. Select **2% 10 Net 30** from the *Payment Terms* drop-down list and press **Tab**.

QuickBooks allows you to establish different types of default payment terms, including payment terms to accommodate discounts for early payment. In this example, the terms of 2% 10 Net 30 means that if you pay this vendor within 10 days of the invoice date, you are eligible for a 2% discount. In this field, you can set the payment terms default for this vendor. QuickBooks uses these default terms on all new *Bills* for this vendor. You can override the default terms on each *Bill* as necessary. When you create reports for accounts payable (A/P), QuickBooks takes into account the terms on each *Bill*. To learn more about the *Terms List*, and how to set up terms, see page 300.

Step 12. Choose the **Tax Settings** tab (see Figure 4-10).

Step 13. Enter *123-12-1234* in the *Tax ID* field.

The *Tax ID* field is where you enter the social security or taxpayer identification number of your Form 1099-MISC recipients. QuickBooks prints this number on the Form 1099-MISC at the end of the year.

Step 14. Check the box next to *Vendor eligible for 1099*.

Select this box for all vendors for whom you expect to file a Form 1099-MISC.

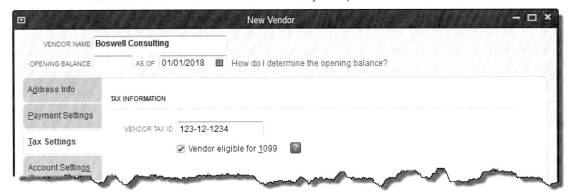

Figure 4-10 The Boswell Consulting Tax Settings tab

Step 15. Click the **Account Settings** tab.

Step 16. Select **Professional Fees** from the first *Tell us which expense account to prefill when you enter bills from this vendor* field (see Figure 4-11). The *Account Prefill* tab allows you to set a default expense account for future transactions with this vendor. This account may be changed as needed whenever you **Enter Bills**.

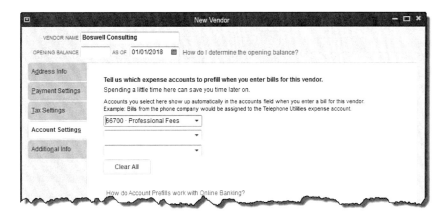

Figure 4-11 The completed Boswell Consulting Account Setting tab

Step 17. Select the **Additional Info** Tab.

Step 18. Select **Consultant** from the *Vendor Type* drop-down list and press **Tab**.

QuickBooks allows you to group your vendors into common types. For example, if you create a *Vendor Type* called Consultant and you tag each of your consultants' vendor records with this type, you could later create a report specific to this *Vendor Type*.

Step 19. Enter *Alameda* in the *County* field and press **Tab**.

The *County* field is a *Custom Field*. The *Define Fields* button in the *New Vendor* window, *Additional Information* tab allows you to define *Custom Fields* to track more information about your vendors. For more information on setting up and using *Custom Fields*, see page 304.

Figure 4-12 Additional Info tab in the New Vendor window

Step 20. Click **OK** to save and close the New Vendor window.

Activating Class Tracking

In QuickBooks, the *Class* field gives you a way to segregate your transactions other than by account name. You can use QuickBooks *Classes* to separate your income and expenses by line of business, department, location, profit center, or any other meaningful breakdown of your business. Alternatively, if your business is a not-for-profit organization, you could use *Classes* to separately track transactions for each program or activity within the organization.

Managing Expenses - Activating Class Tracking

For example, a dentist might classify all income and expenses as relating to either the dentistry or hygiene department. A law firm formed as a partnership might classify all income and expenses according to which partner generated the business. If you use *Classes*, you'll be able to create separate reports for each *Class* of the business. Therefore, the dentist could create separate Profit & Loss reports for the dentistry and hygiene departments, and the law firm could create separate reports for each partner.

In our sample company, Academy Photography uses *Classes* to track income and expenses for each of its stores - San Jose and Walnut Creek.

COMPUTER PRACTICE

Step 1. Select the **Edit** menu, and then select **Preferences**.

Step 2. Select the **Accounting** preference.

Step 3. Select the **Company Preferences** tab, and make sure the box next to *Use class tracking* is checked (see Figure 4-13). When you use *Classes* on each transaction (*Checks*, *Bills*, *Invoices*, etc.), the *Profit & Loss by Class* report shows the income and expenses for each class.

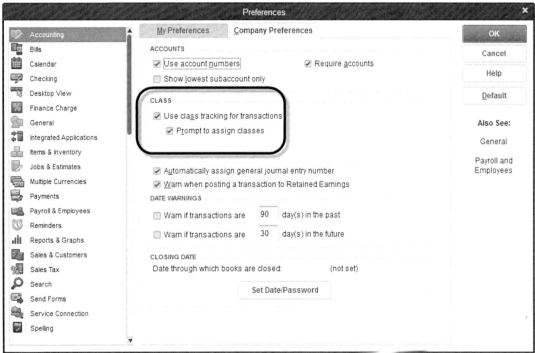

Figure 4-13 Activating class tracking in Accounting preferences

Step 4. The *Prompt to assign classes* field is already checked. Leave the checkmark in this box.

With this setting, QuickBooks prompts you if you fail to assign a *Class* on any line of the transaction.

Step 5. Click **OK**.

Figure 4-14 displays a *Bill* from Wong & Sons Video. The *San Jose* Class is selected in the *Class* column. This tracks the Subcontracted Services Expense to the *San Jose* Class (i.e., the San Jose store) so that the *Profit & Loss by Class* report shows the expense under the column for the *San Jose* Class.

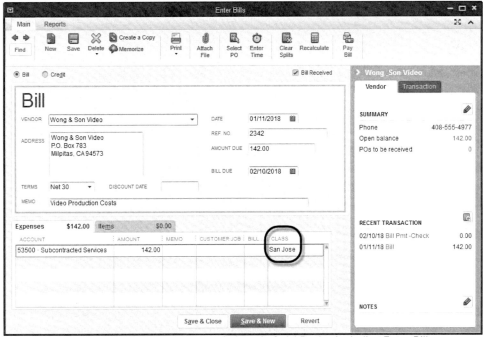

Figure 4-14 The Class field shows on many windows in QuickBooks, including Enter Bills

The *Profit & Loss by Class* report displays the income and expenses for each *Class*. Income and expenses for each Academy Photography store are displayed as separate columns. Note that the *San Jose* column includes the *Subcontracted Services*. For more information about the *Profit & Loss by Class* report, see page 195.

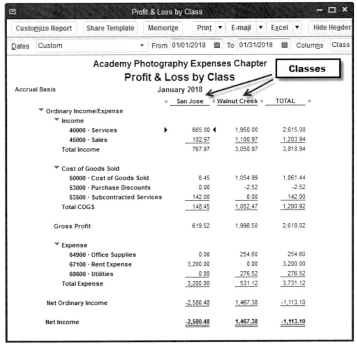

Figure 4-15 Profit & Loss by Class report

Tracking Job Costs

If you want to track the expenses for each *Customer* or *Job* (i.e., track job costs), link each expense with the *Customer* or *Job* to which it applies. In the following sections, you will learn about recording expense transactions in several different situations.

When you record an expense transaction, use the *Customer:Job* column to link each expense account or *Item* with a *Customer* or *Job* (see Figure 4-16).

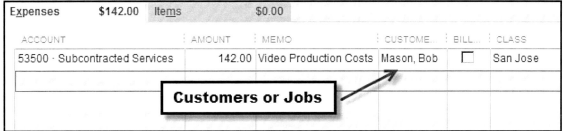

Figure 4-16 Linking expenses to Customers and Jobs (i.e., job costing)

When you track job costs, you can create reports such as the *Profit & Loss by Job* report that shows income and expenses separately for each *Job* (see Figure 4-17). For more information about the *Profit & Loss by Job* report, see page 197.

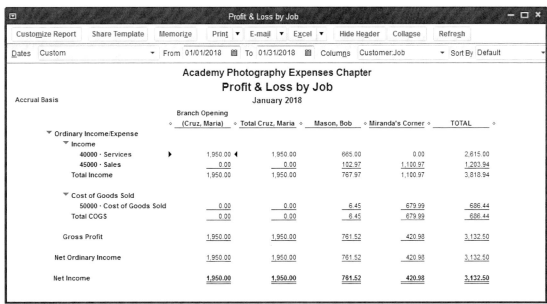

Figure 4-17 Profit & Loss by Job report

Paying Vendors

With QuickBooks, you can pay your vendors in several ways. You can pay by check, credit card, electronic funds transfer, or, though not recommended, cash.

Most of the time, you'll pay your vendors from a checking account, so this section covers three different situations for recording payments out of your checking account. The three situations are:

- Manually writing a check or initiating an electronic funds transfer and recording the transaction in a QuickBooks account register.
- Using the *Write Checks* function to record and print checks.
- Recording accounts payable bills through the *Enter Bills* window and using the *Pay Bills* function to pay these *Bills*.

Using Registers

In this example, you will manually write a check and then record the transaction in the QuickBooks checking account register.

COMPUTER PRACTICE

After you have written a manual check, or made a payment made by electronic funds transfer, you will record the transaction in QuickBooks.

Step 1. Select the **Check Register** icon from the *Home* page. Alternatively, key **Ctrl+R** on your keyboard.

Step 2. In the *Use Register* dialog box, make sure **Checking** displays in the *Select Account* field and click **OK** (see Figure 4-18).

Figure 4-18 Use Register dialog box

Step 3. Enter *02/08/2018* in the first empty line of *Date* column and press **Tab** (see Figure 4-19).

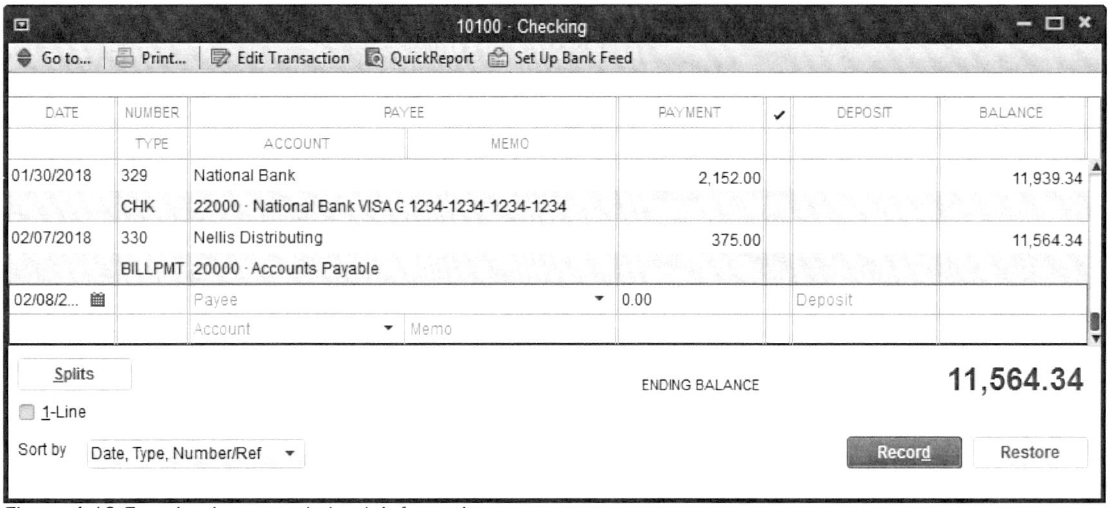

Figure 4-19 Entering in manual check information

Step 4. Enter *331* in the *Number* column and press **Tab**.

If you are entering a previously handwritten check, make sure this number matches the number on the physical check. If you are entering an electronic funds transfer or an ATM withdrawal, enter *EFT* in the check number field. Alternatively, if you are entering a Debit Card transaction, enter *Debit* in the *Number* column.

Step 5. Enter *Bay Office Supply* in the *Payee* column and press **Tab**.

Since *Bay Office Supply* is not in the *Vendor List*, QuickBooks prompts you to *Quick Add* or *Set Up* the vendor (see Figure 4-20). Click **Quick Add** on the *Name Not Found* dialog box.

Managing Expenses - Paying Vendors   **117**

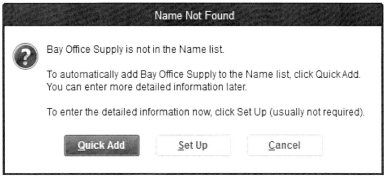
Figure 4-20 Name Not Found dialog box

Step 6. Click **Quick Add** to add this vendor without entering the address and other information to completely set up the vendor. You can always go back later and add the other information by editing the vendor record. In the *Select Name Type* dialog box, the *Vendor* Name Type is selected. Click **OK** to add Bay Office Supply to the *Vendor Center* (see Figure 4-21).

Figure 4-21 Select Name Type options - choose Vendor

Step 7. Enter *128.60* in the *Payment* column and press **Tab**.

Step 8. Enter *Office Supplies* in the *Account* column and press **Tab**.

After you enter the first few characters of the word "*Office*" in the *Account* field, notice that QuickBooks automatically fills in the rest of the field with "Office Supplies." This QuickFill feature helps you to enter data faster.

Step 9. Enter *Printer Paper* in the *Memo* column.

Step 10. Verify that you've entered all of the fields in the transaction correctly, and click **Record** to save the transaction (see Figure 4-22). If the *Set Check Reminder* dialog box opens, click **Cancel**.

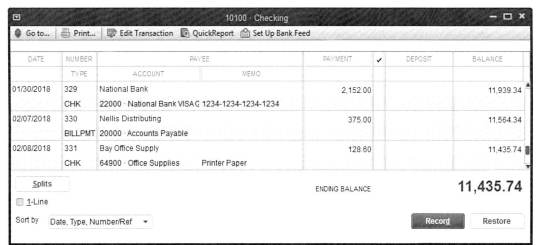
Figure 4-22 Bay Office Supply entry in the Checking register

Notice that QuickBooks automatically updates your account balance after you record the transaction.

Splitting Transactions

Sometimes you will need to split your purchase to more than one account. Let's say that the check you just wrote to Bay Office Supply was actually for the following expenses:

- $100.00 for printer paper, to be used in the San Jose store (*Class*).
- $28.60 for computer cables for the Walnut Creek store (*Class*).

In order to track your printing costs separately from your office supplies, you must *split* the expenses and assign each expense to a separate account.

COMPUTER PRACTICE

Step 1.   With the *Checking* register open, click on check **331** to select it.

Step 2.   Click the **Splits** button as highlighted in Figure 4-23.

QuickBooks displays an area below the check where you can add several lines, memos, and amounts for *splitting* the expenses among multiple accounts.

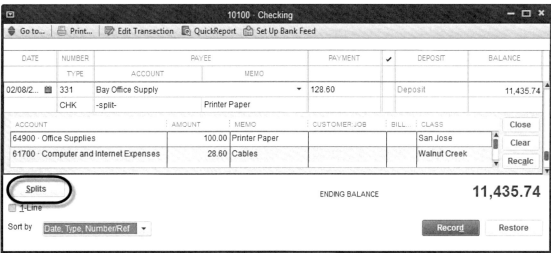

Figure 4-23 Split transaction window

Step 3.   Change the amount on the first line from *128.60* to *100.00*. Then press **Tab**.

Step 4.   Enter *Printer Paper* in the *Memo* column and press **Tab**.

Step 5.   Skip the *Customer:Job* column by pressing **Tab**.

This is the column where you can optionally enter the Customer or Job name where this expense would apply.

Step 6.   Enter *San Jose* in the *Class* column and press **Tab**.

Step 7.   On the second line, enter *Computer and Internet Expenses* in the *Account* column and press **Tab**.

Step 8.   QuickBooks calculates the amount **28.60** in the *Amount* column. This is correct so press **Tab** to leave it and move to the next field.

Step 9.   Enter *Cables* in the *Memo* column and press **Tab**.

Step 10.   Press **Tab** to skip to the **Class** column and enter *Walnut Creek*.

Step 11.   Verify that your screen matches Figure 4-23, and then press **Record**.

Step 12.   QuickBooks displays a dialog box asking if you want to record the changes to the previously recorded transaction. Click **Yes**.

Step 13.   Close the *Checking* register.

Using Write Checks Without Using Accounts Payable

If you are tracking Job costs or *Classes* and are not using the accounts payable feature, it may be best to use the *Write Checks* window instead of the *Register* to record your expenses. If you use *Items* to track purchases and you are not using the accounts payable feature, you *must* use either *Write Checks* or the *Enter Credit Card Charges* window. See page 136 for more information about tracking credit cards.

COMPUTER PRACTICE

Step 1. To display the *Write Checks* window, click on the **Write Checks** icon on the *Home* page. Alternatively, press **Ctrl+W**.

Step 2. Make sure *Checking* is already selected in the *Bank Account* field. Press **Tab**.

Step 3. Enter *T* in the *No.* field and press **Tab**. QuickBooks will automatically fill in *To Print.* Alternately, check the *Print Later* checkbox next to the *Print* Icon at the top of the window.

This indicates that you want QuickBooks to print this check on your printer. When you print the check, QuickBooks will assign the next check number in the sequence of your checks. To enter a manual check, Debit Card or EFT transaction that does not need to be printed, enter *the manual check number or Debit* in the numbers field.

Step 4. Enter *02/08/2018* in the *Date* field. Press **Tab**.

Step 5. Select **Orlando Properties** from the *Pay to the Order of* drop-down list and press **Tab**.

Notice that QuickBooks enters the name and address from the Vendor record as soon as you choose the Vendor name from the list.

Step 6. Enter *3200* in the *$* field and press **Tab**.

Step 7. Press **Tab** to skip the *Address* field.

Step 8. Enter *Rent Expense* in the *Memo* field. Press **Tab**.

Step 9. Enter *Rent Expense* in the *Account* column of the *Expenses* tab if not already selected and press **Tab**.

If necessary, when you enter your own expenses, use the bottom part of the check to split the payment between several different accounts, *Jobs*, and *Classes*.

Step 10. Leave the *Amount* column set to *3,200.00* and press **Tab**.

Step 11. Enter *San Jose Rent* in the *Memo* column, and press **Tab** twice.

Step 12. Enter *San Jose* in the *Class* column and press **Tab**.

Step 13. Verify that your screen matches Figure 4-24. Do not print the check now; we will print it later.

Step 14. Click **Save & Close** to record the transaction.

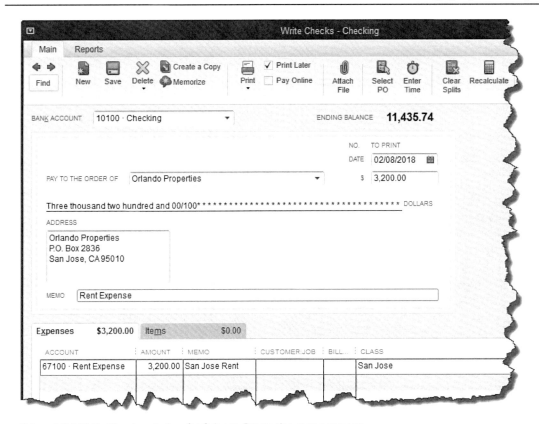

Figure 4-24 Write Checks window for Orlando Properties rent payment

> **Note:**
> In the example above, you recorded the check with a **To Print** status, so that you can print it later, perhaps in a batch with other checks. If you wanted to print the check immediately after you entered it, you would have clicked **Print** at the top of the *Write Checks* window. QuickBooks would ask you to enter the check number.

Managing Accounts Payable

You can also use QuickBooks to track Accounts Payable (A/P). When you receive a bill from a vendor, enter it into QuickBooks using the *Enter Bills* window. Recording a *Bill* allows QuickBooks to track the amount you owe to the vendor along with the detail of what you purchased. For a *Bill* to be considered paid by QuickBooks, you must pay it using the *Pay Bills* window (see 123).

Entering Bills

When a bill arrives from your vendor, enter it into QuickBooks using the *Enter Bills* window.

COMPUTER PRACTICE

Step 1. Select the **Vendors** icon from the *Home* page to display the *Vendor Center*. Select the vendor **Ace Supply**, and then select **Enter Bills** from the *New Transactions* drop-down list (see Figure 4-25). Alternatively, you can click the **Enter Bills** icon on the *Home* page and select **Ace Supply** from the Vendor drop-down field.

Managing Expenses - Paying Vendors   **121**

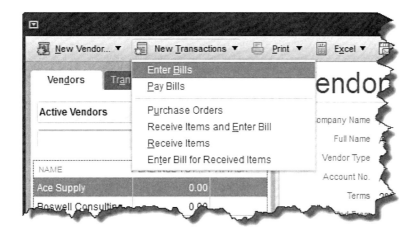

Figure 4-25 Selecting Enter Bills from the New Transaction drop-down list

Step 2. In the *Enter Bills* window, verify that **Ace Supply** is displayed in the *Vendor* field and press **Tab**.

Notice that QuickBooks completes the *Bill Due*, *Terms*, and *Discount Date* fields automatically when you enter the *Vendor* name. QuickBooks uses information from the *Vendor* record to complete these fields. You can override this information if necessary. QuickBooks calculates the *Discount Date* and the *Bill Due* fields by adding the *Terms* information to the date entered in the *Date* field. If the terms do not include a discount, the *Discount Date* will not appear.

Step 3. Enter *02/08/2018* in the *Date* field and press **Tab**.

Step 4. Enter *2085* in the *Ref. No.* field and press **Tab**.

> **Tip:**
> When an A/P transaction increases what is owed, it is called a "bill." However, vendors call them "invoices." Therefore, the *Ref. No.* field on the *Bill* form should match the number on the *Invoice* you received from the vendor. The *Ref. No.* field is important for two reasons. First, it is the number used to identify this *Bill* in the *Pay Bills* window, and second, it is the number that shows on the voucher of the *Bill Payment* check.

Step 5. Enter *360.00* in the *Amount Due* field and press **Tab**.

Step 6. Press **Tab** to skip the *Bill Due* field and to accept the due date that QuickBooks has calculated.

Step 7. Press **Tab** to accept the **2% 10 Net 30** terms already selected.

Step 8. Enter *Photo Materials for Jerry Perez Job* in the Memo field and press Tab.

> **Important:**
> If your vendor requires you to enter your account number on the checks you send, enter it in the *Account No.* field in the *Vendor* record. QuickBooks will print the contents of that field in the *Memo* field on *Bill Payments* to the vendor.

Step 9. Enter *Cost of Goods Sold* in the *Account* column of the *Expenses* tab and press **Tab**.

Step 10. Press **Tab** to accept *360.00* already entered in the *Amount* column.

Step 11. Enter *Photo Materials* in the *Memo* column and press **Tab**.

Step 12. To job cost this purchase, enter *Perez, Jerry* in the *Customer:Job* column and press **Tab**.

Step 13. Leave the *Billable?* field checked. Press **Tab** again and enter *Walnut Creek* in the *Class* column.

Step 14. Verify that your screen matches that shown in Figure 4-26. Click **Save & Close** to record the **Bill**. Close the **Vendor Center** window.

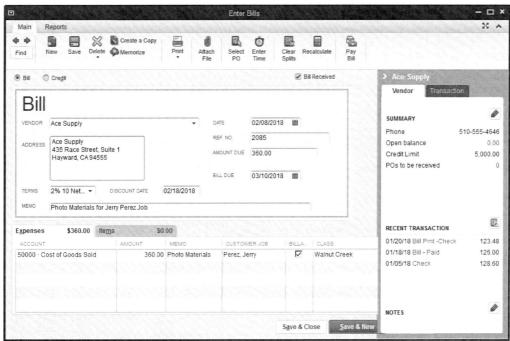

Figure 4-26 Recording Ace Supply bill

Attaching Documents

There are many advantages to storing documents electronically. Going "paperless" increases efficiency and eliminates costly storage.

QuickBooks allows you to attach electronic documents to QuickBooks transactions, such as *Bills*, *Invoices*, and other QuickBooks forms. The attached documents can either be stored on your system for free, or on a secure server managed by Intuit using QuickBooks Document Management for a fee. To attach electronic documentation to a QuickBooks transaction, look for the *Attach* button in the upper section of the transaction window.

Figure 4-27 Attach button in Enter Bills window

The Unpaid Bills Detail Report

To view a list of your unpaid *Bills*, use the *Unpaid Bills Detail* report.

COMPUTER PRACTICE

Step 1. From the *Reports* menu, select **Vendors & Payables** and then select **Unpaid Bills Detail**.

Step 2. Enter *02/10/2018* in the *Date* field and press **Tab**.

Step 3. Verify that your screen matches Figure 4-28. Close the report window. Click **No**, if the *Memorize Report* message appears.

Managing Expenses - Paying Vendors

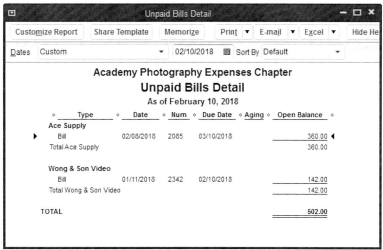

Figure 4-28 Unpaid Bills Detail report

Paying Bills

QuickBooks keeps track of all your bills in the Accounts Payable account. When you pay your bills, you will reduce the balance in Accounts Payable by creating *Bill Payment* checks.

COMPUTER PRACTICE

Step 1. Select the **Vendors** icon from the *Icon Bar* to display the **Vendor Center**. Select **Pay Bills** from the *New Transactions* drop-down list (see Figure 4-29). You *do not* need to select a vendor first. Alternatively, you can click the **Pay Bills** icon on the *Home* page.

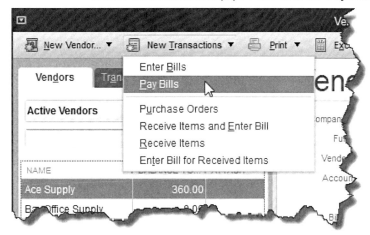

Figure 4-29 Selecting Pay Bills from the New Transactions drop-down list

Step 2. QuickBooks displays the *Pay Bills* window.

Step 3. Click on the radio button *Due on or before* and enter *03/10/2018* in the *Due on or before* date field (see Figure 4-30). QuickBooks allows you to filter the *Pay Bills* window so only the *Bills* due on or before a given date are shown.

> Note:
> The *Due on or before* field applies only to the *Bill* due date. There is no way to show only the *Bills* whose *discounts* expire on or before a certain date. However, you can sort the list of bills by the discount dates in the *Pay Bills* window by selecting **Discount Date** from the *Sort Bills by* drop-down list.

Figure 4-30 Entering the date in the Due on or before field

Step 4. As shown in Figure 4-31, *Filter By* can be set to *All vendors* or you can select to only show a specific vendor. Also, *Due Date* is already selected from the *Sort By* drop-down list. If you have several *Bills* from the same vendor, it is sometimes easier to see all of the *Bills* sorted by *Vendor*. You can also sort the bills by *Discount Date* or *Amount Due*.

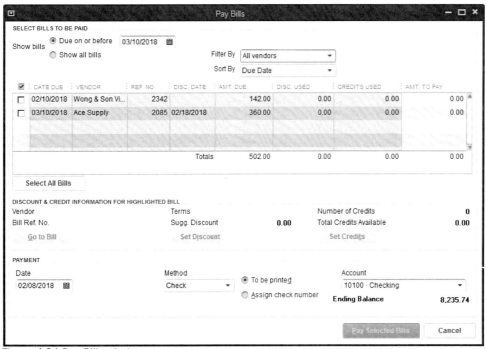

Figure 4-31 Pay Bills window

Step 5. Leave **Check** in the *Method* field selected. Ensure that the *To be printed* radio button is selected.

Step 6. Leave **Checking** in the *Account* field.

> **Note:**
> The *Payment Method* field allows you to choose to pay the bills by check or credit card. If you pay by check, QuickBooks automatically creates a check in your checking account for each bill selected for payment. To pay by credit card, select **Credit Card** and select the name of the credit card you want to use for the *Bill Payments*. QuickBooks will then create a separate credit card charge for each *Bill Payment*.

Step 7. Enter **02/10/2018** in the *Payment Date* field.

Step 8. Click the **Select All Bills** button in the middle to select both *Bills* that are displayed. Alternately, place a checkmark in front of the *Bills* you want to pay.

Managing Expenses - Paying Vendors

> **Tip:**
> If you want to display the original *Bill*, select the *Bill* on the *Pay Bills* window and click **Go to Bill**. This displays the original *Bill* so you can edit it if necessary.
>
> If you want to make a partial payment on a *Bill*, enter only the amount you want to pay in the *Amt. To Pay* column. If you pay less than the full amount due, QuickBooks will track the remaining amount due for that *Bill* in Accounts Payable. The next time you go to the *Pay Bills* window, the partially paid *Bills* will show with the remaining amount due.

Step 9. To record a discount on the Ace Supply *Bill*, click on the *Bill* to select it. The *Discount & Credit Information for Highlighted Bill* section displays the terms and a suggested discount for the *Bill* (see Figure 4-32).

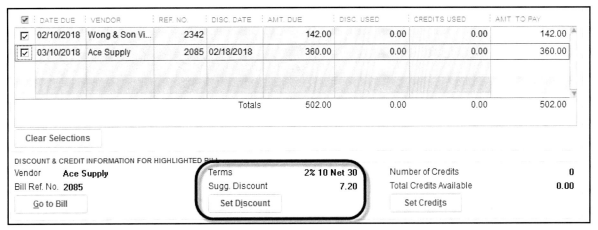

Figure 4-32 Discount section for Ace Supply bill

Step 10. Click **Set Discount**.

In the *Discounts and Credits* window, notice that QuickBooks calculates the discount according to the terms set on the *Bill* (see Figure 4-33). In this case, the terms are *2% 10 Net 30*.

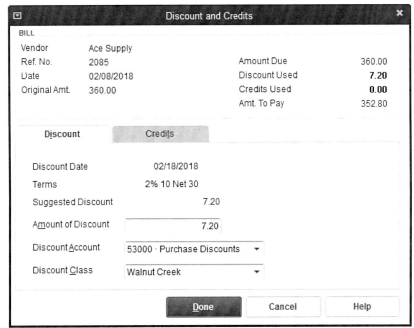

Figure 4-33 Discount and Credits window

Step 11. Select **Purchase Discounts** in the *Discount Account* field to assign this discount to the proper account.

Step 12. Enter *Walnut Creek* in the *Discount Class* field to assign this discount to the proper *Class*.

Refer to the *Bill* to determine the *Class*. The *Bill* being discounted was originally assigned to the *Walnut Creek Class* so the discount should use that class as well.

Step 13. Click **Done**. This returns you to the *Pay Bills* window.

> **Note:**
> In some cases, it is better to use a *Bill Credit* instead of a discount. For example, when you want to associate the discount with a *Job*, or if you want to track discount items, use *Bill Credits* instead of using discounts in the *Pay Bills* process. You can record items, accounts, classes, and job information on the *Bill Credit*, just as you do on *Bills*. Then, in the *Pay Bills* window, click **Set Credits** to apply the *Bill Credit* to the *Bill*. To see how this would work, see the section on *Applying Vendor Credits* beginning on page 133.

Step 14. Verify that your *Pay Bills* window matches that shown in Figure 4-34. Click **Pay Selected Bills** to record the *Bill Payments*.

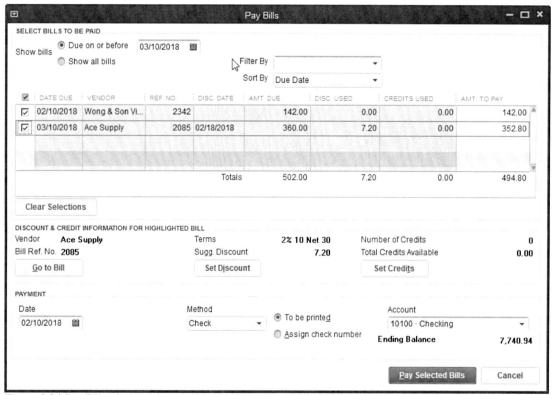

Figure 4-34 Pay Bills window after setting the discount

Step 15. QuickBooks displays a *Payment* Summary dialog box as shown in Figure 4-35. Review the payments and click **Done**.

Step 16. Close all windows except for the *Home* page.

Managing Expenses - Paying Vendors   **127**

Figure 4-35 Payment Summary dialog box

> **Note:**
> If you select more than one *Bill* for the same vendor, QuickBooks combines all of the amounts onto a single *Bill Payment*.

When you use a check to pay *Bills*, QuickBooks records each *Bill Payment* in the *Checking* account register and in the Accounts Payable account register (see Figure 4-36 and Figure 4-37). *Bill Payments* reduce the balance in both the Checking account (credit) and the Accounts Payable account (debit).

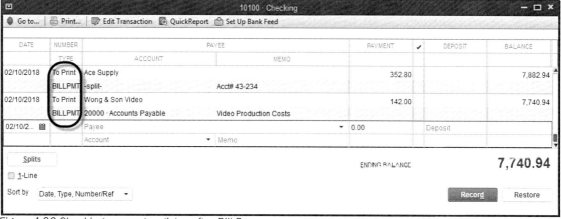

Figure 4-36 Checking account register after Bill Pay

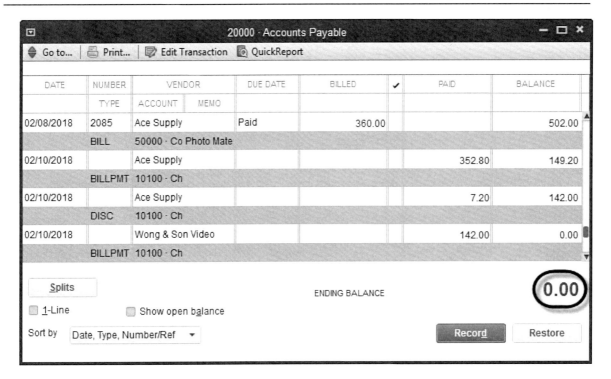

Figure 4-37 Accounts Payable register after Bill Pay

Printing Checks

COMPUTER PRACTICE

You do not need to print each check or *Bill Payment* separately. As you write checks and pay *Bills*, you have the option to record each check with a *Print Later* status. Follow these steps to print checks and *Bill Payments* that you have previously recorded with a *Print Later* status:

Step 1. From the *File* menu, select **Print Forms** and then select **Checks**.

Step 2. **Checking** in the *Bank Account* field is already selected (see Figure 4-38). This is the bank account on which the checks are written. Press **Tab**.

Step 3. Enter *6001* in the *First Check Number* field, if necessary.

The *First Check Number* field is where you set the number of the first check you put in the printer.

> **Note:**
> QuickBooks assigns check numbers when it prints checks. You have the opportunity to set the check number just before you print the checks and after you assign a check number. QuickBooks keeps track of each check it prints and keeps the check number up to date.

Step 4. QuickBooks automatically selects all of the checks for printing. Click **OK**.

To prevent one or more checks from printing, you can click in the left column to remove the checkmark for each check you don't want to print. Since we did not print the rent check, it shows in Figure 4-38 along with the two *Bill Payments*. We will include it here so we can "batch print" all checks together.

Managing Expenses - Printing Checks

Figure 4-38 Select Checks to Print window

Step 5.   When the *Print Checks* window displays, click **Signature** on the right side of the window (see Figure 4-39).

You can automatically print signed checks by uploading a graphic file of a signature during the printing process.

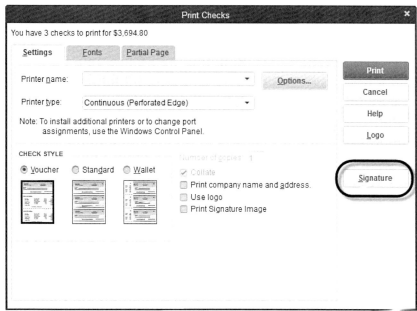

Figure 4-39 Signature Button in Print Checks window

Step 6.   In the *Signature* window, click the **File** button to upload the graphic file (see Figure 4-40).

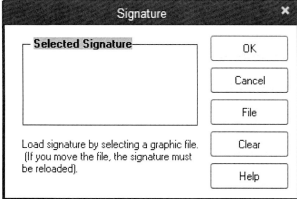

Figure 4-40 Signature window

Step 7.	In the *Open File* window, navigate to where you store your exercise files and open **Sig.png**. This file was included with the portable exercise files.
Step 8.	If QuickBooks displays a warning window, click **OK**. QuickBooks will copy the image file to a new folder called *Expenses-14 – Images*.
Step 9.	The *Signature* window now displays an image of the uploaded signature file (see Figure 4-41). Click **OK**.

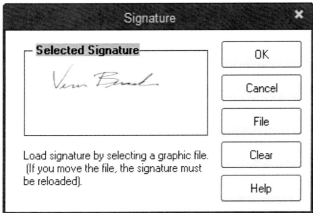

Figure 4-41 Signature window with file uploaded

> **Note:**
> Once you select the signature, QuickBooks will leave the box checked to always print the signature unless you uncheck the *Print Signature Image* shown in Figure 4-42.

Step 10.	Confirm your printer settings on the *Print Checks* window and click **Print** when you are ready to print (see Figure 4-42).

Figure 4-42 Print Checks window

> **Tip:**
> Make sure your checks are oriented correctly in the printer. With some printers, you feed the top of the page in first, and some you feed in bottom first. With some printers, you must insert the check face up, and with others, face down.

Step 11.	When QuickBooks has finished printing the checks, you will see the *Print Checks – Confirmation* dialog box in Figure 4-43.

Managing Expenses - Voiding Checks

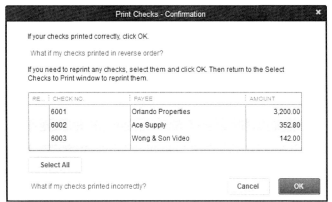

Figure 4-43 Print Checks - Confirmation dialog box

Step 12.   If the *Set Check Reminder* dialog box opens, click **Cancel**.
Step 13.   Click **OK**.

> **Note:**
> If your printer damages your checks and you select checks for reprinting, it is best accounting practice to void each damaged check and re-enter a new check in the bank account register or on the *Write Checks* window.

> **Tip:**
> If you are paying multiple bills on a single check and you want the vendor to be able to identify these bills, you can print a *Bill Payment Stub* by choosing **Bill Payment Stub** from the *Print Forms* submenu on the *File* menu.

Voiding Checks

QuickBooks allows you to keep the information about voided checks so that you retain a record of these checks. It is important to enter each check into your register even if the check is voided. This will prevent gaps in your check number sequence.

> **Did You Know?**
> QuickBooks has a special report called *Missing Checks* that allows you to view all of your checks sorted by check number. The report highlights any gaps in the check number sequence. To view this report, select the **Reports** menu, then select **Banking,** and then select **Missing Checks**.

COMPUTER PRACTICE

Step 1.   Open the **Checking** account register and then select check 6003 by clicking anywhere on that record. You will be able to tell that the record has been selected as it will be outlined in the register.

Step 2.   From the *Edit* menu select **Void Bill Pmt-Check** (see Figure 4-44).

When you void a check, QuickBooks changes the amount to zero, marks the check cleared, and adds VOID to the *Memo* field.

Step 3.   Click **Record** to save your changes.

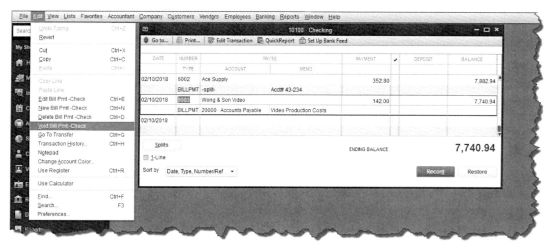

Figure 4-44 Voiding a check from the Edit menu

Since you are voiding a *Bill Payment*, QuickBooks warns you that this change will affect the application of this check to the *Bills* (see Figure 4-45). In other words, voiding a *Bill Payment* will make the *Bill* payable again.

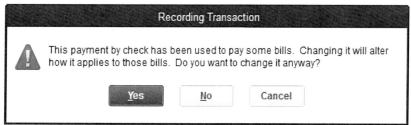

Figure 4-45 Recording Transaction dialog box about voiding BILLPMT check 6003

Step 4.   Click **Yes**.

Notice that the transaction shows as cleared in the register, and that QuickBooks set the amount of the check to zero (see Figure 4-46).

Step 5.   Close all open windows except the *Home* page.

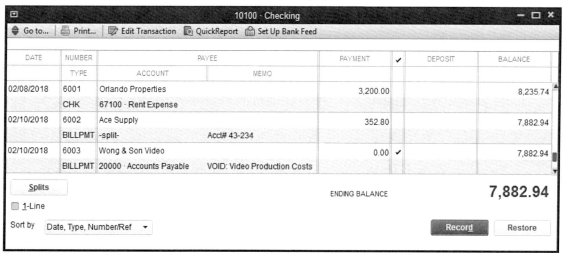

Figure 4-46 Check register after voided transaction

To repay the *Bill*, repeat the bill paying and printing process by following the steps below.

COMPUTER PRACTICE

Step 1.   Select the **Pay Bills** icon on the *Home* page.

Step 2. Complete the *Pay Bills* window for the **Wong & Son Video** *Bill* per the instructions given in the *Paying Bills* section beginning on page 123. Verify that your screen matches Figure 4-47. Set the Payment Date to *02/16/2018*.

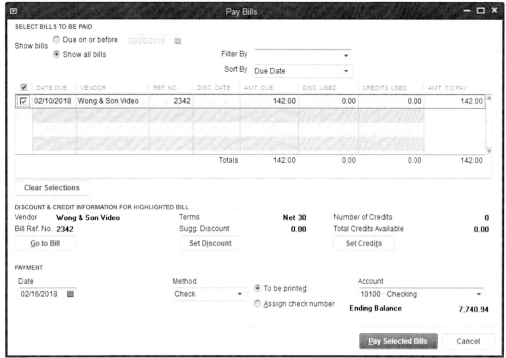

Figure 4-47 Completed Pay Bills window

Step 3. Click **Pay Selected Bills** on the *Pay Bills* window to record the *Bill* payment.

Step 4. Click **Done** on the *Payment Summary* dialog box.

Applying Vendor Credits

When a vendor credits your account, you should record the transaction in the *Enter Bills* window as a *Credit* and apply it to one of your unpaid *Bills*. In some situations, it is best to use a *Bill Credit* instead of the *Discount* window to record certain vendor credits, because the *Discount* window does not allow you to record any of the following information:

- Reference numbers or memos – These may be important for reference later.
- Allocation of the credit to multiple accounts.
- Allocation to *Customers* or *Jobs* – This may be critical in many situations.
- Information using *Items*.

COMPUTER PRACTICE

First, create a *Bill* from Nellis Distributing for Custom Framing Material.

Step 1. Click on the **Enter Bills** icon on the *Home* page.

Step 2. Enter the *Bill* shown in Figure 4-48.

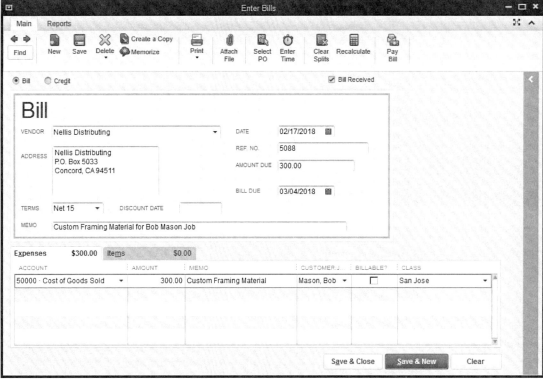

Figure 4-48 Bill from Nellis Distributing for Bob Mason job

Step 3. When you're finished entering the data in Figure 4-48, click **Save & New**.

COMPUTER PRACTICE

Now, enter a Bill Credit.

Step 1. On the next (blank) *Bill* form, select the **Credit** radio button at the top left of the window.

Step 2. Fill in the *Bill Credit* information as shown in Figure 4-49. Click **Save & Close** to record the credit.

Figure 4-49 Creating a Bill Credit

> **The accounting behind the scenes:**
> When you record the **Bill Credit** shown in Figure 4-49, QuickBooks reduces (debits) Accounts Payable and reduces (credits) Purchase Discounts, a Cost of Goods Sold account.

Managing Expenses - Applying Vendor Credits **135**

COMPUTER PRACTICE

Step 1. To apply the *Bill Credit* to a *Bill* for that vendor, select **Pay Bills** from the *Home* page (See Figure 4-50).

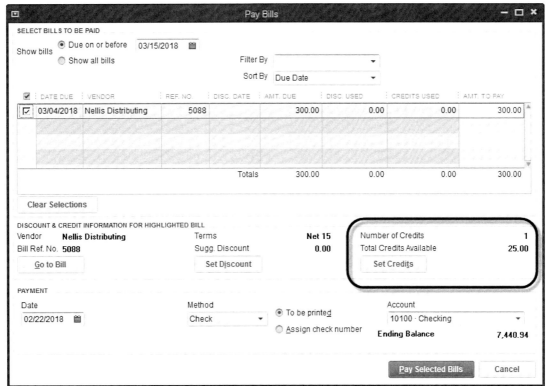

Figure 4-50 Pay Bills window for Nellis Distributing

Step 2. Enter *03/15/2018* in the *Due on or before* field and press **Tab**. If needed, set Filter By to **All Vendors**.

Step 3. Leave **Check** in the *Method* field and **Checking** in the *Account* field. Enter **02/22/2018** in the *Date* field.

> **Important:**
> In order to apply a *Bill Credit*, the vendor name must be the same on both the *Bill* and the *Bill Credit*.

Step 4. Select the unpaid Bill for **Nellis Distributing** as shown in Figure 4-50.

When you select a *Bill* from a vendor for whom one or more unapplied credits exist, QuickBooks displays the total amount of all credits for the vendor in the *Total Credits Available* section. Notice the credit of $25.00 in Figure 4-50 for Nellis Distributing which we created above.

Step 5. Click **Set Credits**.

Figure 4-51 Discount and Credits window to set Bill Credit

In the *Discounts and Credits* window, QuickBooks automatically selected the credits to be applied to the *Bill*. You can override what is shown by deselecting the credit (removing the checkmark), or by entering a different amount in the *Amt. To Use* column.

Step 6.   Leave the credit selected as shown in Figure 4-51 and click **Done**.

QuickBooks has applied the $25.00 credit to Bill #5088 and reduced the amount in the *Amt. To Pay* column to $275.00 (see Figure 4-52).

Figure 4-52 Pay Bills window after Bill Credit has been applied

Step 7.   Click **Pay Selected Bills** to pay the bill.
Step 8.   Click **Done** on the *Payment Summary* dialog box.

> **Note:**
> If you want to apply the credit without paying the *Bill*, reduce the *Amt. To Pay* column to zero.

Handling Deposits and Refunds from Vendors

This section covers how to handle more complicated transactions between you and your vendors. These transactions include deposits paid to vendors in advance of receiving the bill, refunds received from vendors for overpayment of a bill, and refunds received from vendors when Accounts Payable is not involved.

Vendor Deposits — When You Use Accounts Payable

Sometimes vendors require you to give them a deposit before they will provide you with services or products. To do this, create a check for the vendor and code it to Accounts Payable. This creates a credit in QuickBooks for the vendor that you can apply to the bill when it arrives.

> DO NOT PERFORM THESE STEPS. THEY ARE FOR REFERENCE ONLY.

1. Click on the **Write Checks** icon on the *Home* page.
2. Enter the data as shown in Figure 4-53. Notice that this check is coded to Accounts Payable. You only code checks to A/P when you are sending deposits to a vendor prior to receiving the bill.
3. Click **Save & Close**.

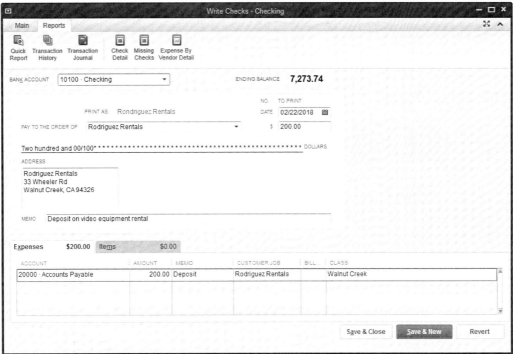

Figure 4-53 Coding check to Accounts Payable

Later, when the Bill is received from the vendor, enter it as you would any other Bill. Then apply the credit resulting from the check created above to the Bill by using the procedures outlined in the **Applying Vendor Credits** section of this chapter, beginning on page 133.

Vendor Refunds — When You Use Accounts Payable

When you receive a refund from a vendor, the kind of transaction you enter in QuickBooks will depend on how you originally paid the vendor.

If you prepaid the vendor using the method above and the amount of your prepayment was more than the bill, your Accounts Payable account will have a negative (debit) balance for that vendor. In this case, you will apply the refund check from the vendor to this credit balance in Accounts Payable.

On the other hand, if you simply wrote a check to the vendor and coded the check to an expense account, you will need to reduce the expense by the amount of the refund. The following tutorials address each of these situations.

To record a refund from a vendor that you prepaid using the deposit check in Figure 4-53, follow the steps below. In this example, you paid Rodriguez Rentals $200.00 in advance of receiving the bill. On a later date, Rodriguez Rentals sent a bill for $185.00. Since your deposit was more than the bill, the vendor also sent you a refund check for $15.00.

Start by entering the bill from the vendor just like any other bill. Then use the *Make Deposits* window to record your refund from the vendor.

> DO NOT PERFORM THESE STEPS. THEY ARE FOR REFERENCE ONLY.

1. Open the *Enter Bills* window and enter the bill from Rodriguez Rentals as shown in Figure 4-54. Click **Save & Close** to record the bill.

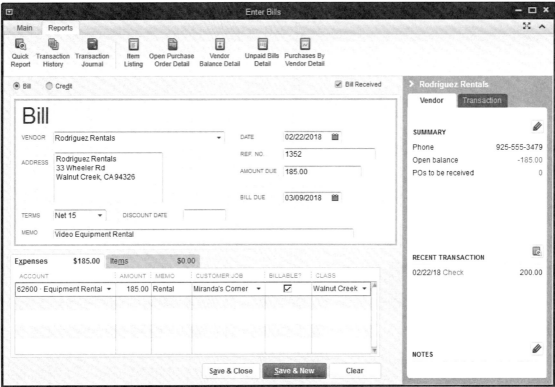

Figure 4-54 Enter Bill received from Rodriguez Rentals

2. Select the **Record Deposit** icon in the *Banking* section of the *Home* page.
3. Press **Tab** to leave *Checking* selected in the *Deposit To* field (see Figure 4-55).
4. Press **Tab** to leave the default date in the *Date* field.
5. Enter *Refund from Rodriguez* in the *Memo* field and press **Tab**.
6. Enter in the remaining data as shown in Figure 4-55. Enter the vendor's name in the Received From column so that QuickBooks will apply this refund to Rodriguez Rentals in A/P reports.

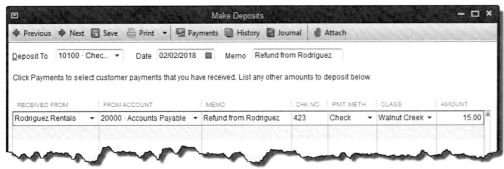

Figure 4-55 Make Deposits window to deposit refund check

Managing Expenses - Handling Deposits and Refunds from Vendors

7. Click **Save & Close** at the bottom of the window.

After you have recorded the deposit in Figure 4-55, apply the $200.00 prepayment check to both the bill and the refund check you just received (i.e. use the $200.00 prepayment check to *pay* the bill and the refund). Your Accounts Payable reports will not be correct until you make this application.

> DO NOT PERFORM THESE STEPS. THEY ARE FOR REFERENCE ONLY.

1. Select the **Pay Bills** icon from the *Home* page.
2. Click *Show all bills* in the *Show bills* field.
3. Leave **Check** in the *Payment Method* field and **Checking** in the *Account* field.
4. Enter *02/24/2018* in the *Payment Date* field.

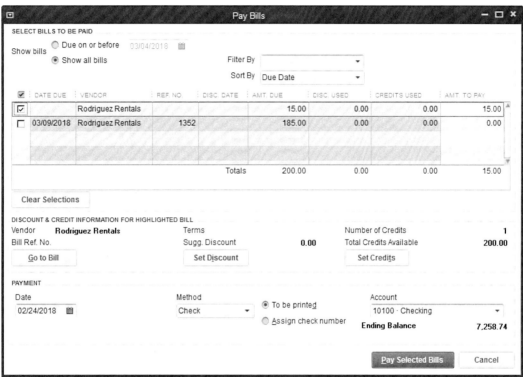

Figure 4-56 Pay Bill window; applying $200 deposit check to $15.00 refund

5. Place a checkmark on the first line in the *Pay Bills* window ($15.00 deposit) and click **Set Credits** as shown in Figure 4-56.

   Though this window seems to show two bills for Rodriguez Rentals, the first line is actually the refund check you recorded using the *Make Deposits* window as shown in Figure 4-55.

6. In the *Discounts and Credits* window, QuickBooks automatically applies $15.00 of the $200.00 credit to the refund check (see Figure 4-57).

7. Click **Done**.

Figure 4-57 Apply Credits window

8. The second line in the *Pay Bills* window is the actual Bill from Rodriguez Rentals. Select this Bill and click **Set Credits** (Figure 4-58).

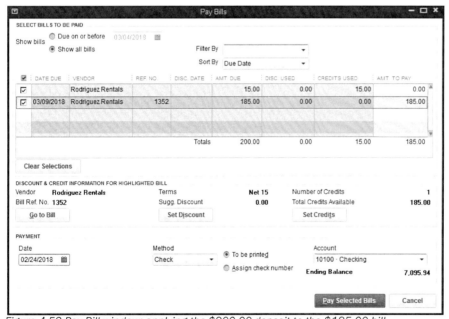

Figure 4-58 Pay Bill window; applying the $200.00 deposit to the $185.00 bill

9. In the *Discounts and Credits* window, QuickBooks automatically applies $185.00 of the $200.00 credit to Bill #1352 (see Figure 4-59).

10. Click **Done**.

Managing Expenses - Handling Deposits and Refunds from Vendors   **141**

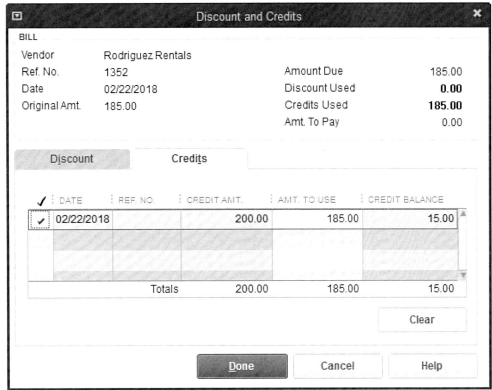

Figure 4-59 Discounts and Credits window

11. Since the amount of the prepayment ($200.00) is the same as the bill ($185.00) plus the refund check ($15.00), the total in the *Amt. To Pay* field is zero (see Figure 4-60).

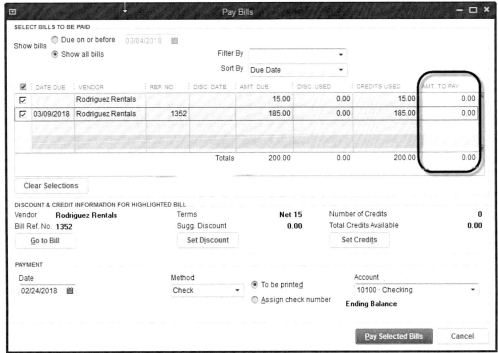

Figure 4-60 Pay Bills window with the deposit applied

12. Click **Pay Selected Bills**. QuickBooks will link these transactions together, clearing them from the Unpaid Bills and Accounts Payable Aging reports. A Bill Payment for zero will appear in the Check Register. This entry can be used to print a bill payment stub to send the vendor if needed.

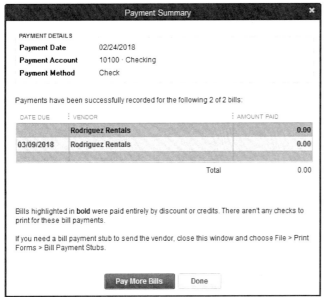

Figure 4-61 Payment Summary for $0 to link and clear transactions

13. Click **Done** on the Payment Summary dialog box.

Vendor Refunds — When You Directly Expensed Payment

If you did not use the Accounts Payable features, but instead wrote a check to the vendor and coded the check to an expense account, record the refund using a deposit transaction. Use the same expense account you used on the original payment to the vendor (see Figure 4-62).

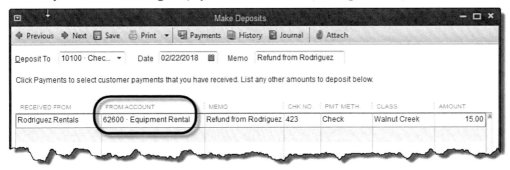

Figure 4-62 Make Deposit window coding the refund to an expense account

Tracking Petty Cash

It is sometimes necessary to use cash for minor expenditures, such as office supplies, postage, parking, or other small items. In order to track these expenditures, you can set up a separate bank account in QuickBooks called *Petty Cash*.

To track a deposit to your Petty Cash account (and the withdrawal of cash from your Checking account), simply write a check to a designated person, the *custodian*, who will cash the check at a local bank and place the money into Petty Cash. Code the check to the Petty Cash account.

When you use Petty Cash for a company expense, enter the expenditure in the *Payment* column of the Petty Cash account register. This reduces the balance in the Petty Cash account so that it always agrees with the actual amount of cash you have on hand. Code each cash expenditure to the appropriate *payee, account, class* and *job*. Click the **Splits** button to split the expenditure among multiple accounts or to assign customer names or classes to the transaction.

Tracking Company Credit Cards

To track charges and payments on your company credit card, set up a separate credit card account in QuickBooks for each card. Then enter each charge individually using the *Enter Credit Card Charges* window. To pay the credit card bill, use *Write Checks* and code the check to the credit card account.

> **Another Way:**
> You can also pay your credit card bill by using *Pay Bills* after recording a *Bill* for the balance due, coded to the credit card liability account.
>
> **Did You Know?**
> Many credit cards allow you to download your credit card charges into QuickBooks through the Internet, eliminating the need to enter each charge manually. For more information about the QuickBooks Credit Card download, select the *Banking* menu, select *Bank Feeds*, and then select *Set Up Bank Feeds for an Account*.

Entering Credit Card Charges

Each time you use a company credit card, use the *Enter Credit Card Charges* window to record the transaction.

> **The accounting behind the scenes:**
> When you record credit card charges, QuickBooks increases (credits) your Credit Card Payable liability account and increases (debits) the expense account shown at the bottom of the window.
>
> **Note:**
> You will need to create an account on your *Chart of Accounts* for each company credit card. Use the *Credit Card* type when creating the account.

COMPUTER PRACTICE

Step 1. Click the **Enter Credit Card Charges** icon on the *Home Page*. Alternatively, from the *Banking* menu, select **Enter Credit Card Charges**.

Step 2. Press **Tab** to accept **National Bank VISA Gold** in the *Credit Card* field.

Step 3. **Purchase/Charge** is already selected. Press **Tab** twice.

If you used your card when receiving a refund or credit from a vendor, you would select **Refund/Credit** instead of **Purchase/Charge** on this step. QuickBooks will then reduce the balance on your credit card when you record a Credit transaction.

Step 4. Enter *Bay Office Supply* in the *Purchased From* field and press **Tab**.

Step 5. Enter *02/24/2018* in the *Date* field. Press **Tab**.

Step 6. Enter *65432* in the *Ref No.* field and press **Tab**.

The *Ref No.* field is optional. Its purpose is to tag each charge with the number on the charge slip.

Step 7. Enter *86.48* in the *Amount* field and press **Tab**.

Step 8. Enter *Purchase Office Supplies* in *Memo* field and press **Tab**.

Step 9. Enter the *Account*, *Amount*, *Memo*, and *Class* fields as displayed in Figure 4-63.

Step 10. Verify that your screen matches Figure 4-63. Click **Save & New** to record the credit card charge.

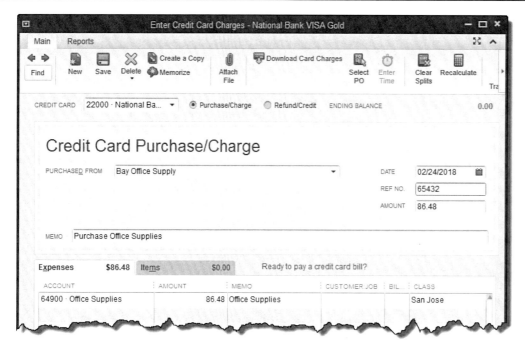

Figure 4-63 Enter Credit Card Charges window for Bay Office Supplies purchase

Step 11.   Enter another credit card charge that matches Figure 4-64. Click **Save & Close**.

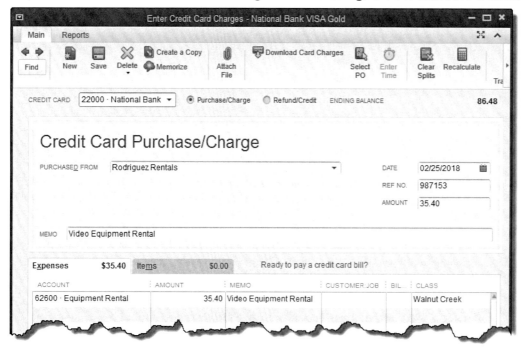

Figure 4-64 Enter Credit Card Charges window for equipment rental

Paying the Credit Card Bill

Follow the steps below to write a check to pay your credit card bill.

Managing Expenses - Tracking Company Credit Cards

> **The accounting behind the scenes:**
> When you record a credit card payment, QuickBooks reduces (credits) the Checking account and reduces (debits) the Credit Card liability account.
> **Note:** There is another method of paying the credit card bill that is part of the reconciliation process. In the reconciliation chapter, you'll learn more about reconciling the credit card account, and then creating a *Bill* for the balance due.

COMPUTER PRACTICE

Step 1. Click the **Write Checks** icon on the *Home* page.

Step 2. Enter the check as shown in Figure 4-65. Notice that you will enter the credit card account name in the *Account* column of the *Expenses* Tab.

Step 3. Click **Save & Close** to record the transaction.

Step 4. Click **Save Anyway** to bypass *Items not assigned classes* window.

You do not need to enter a class when posting to a credit card account or to any other Balance Sheet account.

Figure 4-65 Write Checks window to pay credit card bill

To see the detail of your credit card charges and payments, look in the *National Bank VISA Gold* account register (see Figure 4-66). This register can be accessed by pressing **Ctrl+A** to open the Chart of Accounts, and then double-clicking on the *National Bank VISA Gold* credit card account. You can also pay credit cards as part of the reconciliation process. For more information, see 176.

Figure 4-66 National Bank VISA Gold account register

Paying Sales Tax

Many QuickBooks users need to collect sales tax each time they sell products and certain types of services. This sales tax needs to be paid to the appropriate state or local agency. Academy Photography files its sales tax return to a single vendor called the State Board of Equalization. In this example, we will run reports for the first quarter of 2018. For more on collecting sales tax, see page 91.

Paying Sales Tax

After you prepare your sales tax return and make necessary adjustments for discounts, interest, penalties or rounding, create a sales tax payment for the amount you owe.

When you pay your sales tax, do not use the *Write Checks* window because the payment will not affect the *Sales Tax Items*. It also will not show properly on the *Sales Tax Liability* reports. To correctly pay your sales tax liability, use the *Pay Sales Tax* window.

COMPUTER PRACTICE

Step 1.   From the *Home* page, select the **Manage Sales Tax** icon.

Step 2.   Click the **Pay Sales Tax** button in the *Manage Sales Tax* dialog box. Alternatively, from the *Vendors* menu, select **Sales Tax** and then select **Pay Sales Tax**.

Step 3.   The *Pay Sales Tax* window displays. In the *Pay From Account* field, **Checking** already displays so press **Tab**. This field allows you to select the account from which you wish to pay your sales tax.

Step 4.   Enter *04/15/2018* in the *Check Date* field and press **Tab**. This field is the date of *when* you are paying the sales tax.

Step 5.   Enter *03/31/2018* in the *Show sales tax due through* field and press **Tab**. In this field, enter the last day of the sales tax reporting period. For example, if you are filing your sales tax return for the first quarter, enter the last day of March in this field.

QuickBooks shows the total tax you owe for each county as well as any adjustments. To pay all the tax and the adjustments for all rows, click the **Pay All Tax** button. You can create a Sales Tax Adjustment by clicking Adjust on this screen.

Step 6.   Leave **333** in the *Starting Check No.* field and press **Tab**. QuickBooks automatically enters the next check number sequentially.

Managing Expenses - Accounts Payable Reports

Step 7. Click in the **Pay** column (see Figure 4-67) on the line with a balance or alternatively click **Pay All Tax**.

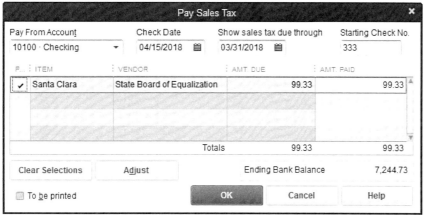

Figure 4-67 Pay Sales Tax window

Step 8. Click **OK** to record the Sales Tax Payment.

Step 9. Close the *Manage Sales Tax* window.

After you record the sales tax payment, QuickBooks will create a special type of check called a *Sales Tax Payment* (TAXPMT) in your checking account for the total tax due to each sales tax agency (Vendor).

> **Important:**
> QuickBooks allows you to adjust the amounts in the *Amt. Paid* column. However, if you do you will retain an incorrect (overstated) balance *in Sales Tax Payable* for the period. If you need to change the amount of sales tax due, use a *Sales Tax Adjustment*. To quickly access *the Sales Tax Adjustment* window, click **Adjust** on the *Pay Sales Tax* window.

Accounts Payable Reports

QuickBooks has several reports that you can use to analyze and track your purchases and vendors. Following are two sample reports for you to create. See the Reports chapter for more information on creating reports.

Vendor Balance Detail

The *Vendor Balance Detail* report shows the detail of each *Bill* and *Bill Payment* to each vendor. However, this report only includes transactions that "go through" Accounts Payable. That is, it only shows transactions such as *Bills* and *Bill Payments*. If you write checks to your vendors directly, without first entering a *Bill*, those transactions will not show in this report.

COMPUTER PRACTICE

Step 1. From the *Reports* menu, select **Vendors & Payables** and then select **Vendor Balance Detail** (see Figure 4-68).

Step 2. To print the report, click **Print** and click **Report** at the top of the report window. Close the report, and click **No** if the *Memorize Report* message appears.

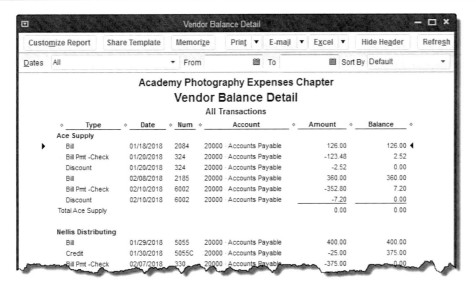

Figure 4-68 Vendor Balance Detail Report

Transaction List by Vendor

The *Transaction List by Vendor* report shows all transactions associated with your vendors, even if the transactions did not "go through" Accounts Payable (e.g., checks and credit card charges).

COMPUTER PRACTICE

Step 1.   From the *Reports* menu, select **Vendors & Payables** and then select **Transaction List by Vendor** (see Figure 4-69).

Step 2.   Set the date fields on the report to *01/01/2018* through *03/31/2018*.

Step 3.   Close all open windows and click **No** if the *Memorize Report* message appears.

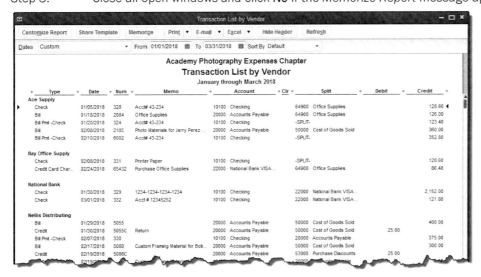

Figure 4-69 Transaction List by Vendor report

Sales Tax Liability

The *Sales Tax Liability* report shows the details of Total Sales broken down into Non-Taxable and Taxable groups along with the Tax Rate and Tax Collected. This report is useful for verifying the amount of sales tax collected for a specific period of time.

Managing Expenses - Tracking Loans using the Loan Manager

COMPUTER PRACTICE

Step 1. From the *Reports* menu, select **Vendors & Payables** and then select **Sales Tax Liability**. (See Figure 4-70)

Step 2. Set the date fields on the report to *01/01/2018* through *03/31/2018*.

Step 3. Close all open windows and click **No** if the *Memorize Report* message appears.

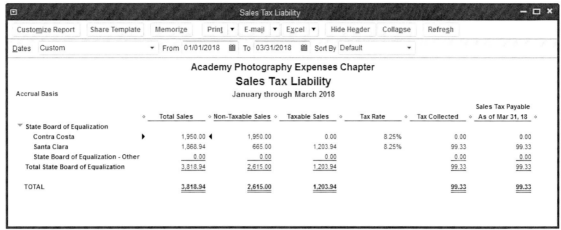

Figure 4-70 Sales Tax Liability report

Tracking Loans using the Loan Manager

If you have QuickBooks Pro or Premier, you can track detailed information about your loans. You can individually track and amortize each of your loans so that QuickBooks will automatically allocate the principal and interest on each payment.

Setting up a Loan in the Loan Manager

The details of each loan can be set up in the **QuickBooks Loan Manager** to automatically amortize and track each loan. If you plan to have QuickBooks track loan details using the Loan Manager, you'll need to gather the details on each loan so that you have all of the information shown in Table 4-2.

Truck Loan Detail	
Account Name	Truck Loan
Lender	National Bank
Origination Date	12/31/2017
Original Amount	$ 24,000.00
Term	60 Months
Due Date of Next Payment	01/31/2018
Payment Amount	$ 452.16
Next Payment Number	1
Payment Period	Monthly
Does loan have escrow payment?	No
Alert me 10 days before a payment is due	Leave unchecked
Interest Rate	5%
Compounding period	Monthly
Payment Account	Checking
Interest Expense Account	Interest Expense
Fees/Charges Expense Account	Bank Service Charges

Table 4-2 Truck Loan Detail

> **DO NOT PERFORM THESE STEPS. THEY ARE FOR REFERENCE ONLY.**

For this example, Academy Photography owns a Delivery Truck that they purchased on 12/31/2017. When they purchased the truck, they took out a loan with National Bank for $24,000.00 that carries an interest rate of 5% per year, for 5 years.

1. From the *Banking Menu*, select **Loan Manager**.
2. In the *Loan Manage* setup window, click **Add a Loan**.

> **Note:**
> The liability account and the balance for this loan were set up in the data file for this chapter. It is necessary to set up the account and the beginning balance first to ensure correct linking of the loan detail to the General Ledger. For more information click **What you need to do before you add a loan** on the *Loan Manager* setup window (see Figure 4-71).

Figure 4-71 Loan Manager setup window

3. Complete the loan information in the *Add Loan* window using the data from Table 4-2. Complete the *Enter account information for this* loan section. When completed your screen should look like Figure 4-72.

Managing Expenses - Tracking Loans using the Loan Manager **151**

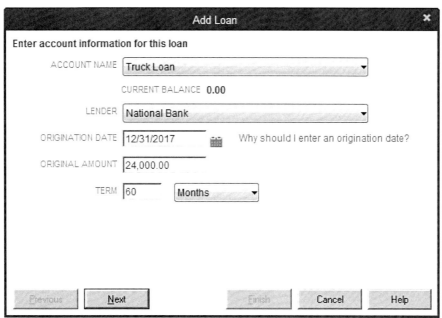

Figure 4-72 Truck loan information – your screen may vary

4. Click **Next**.

5. Complete the *Enter payment information for this* loan section using data from Table 4-2. When completed, your screen should look like Figure 4-73.

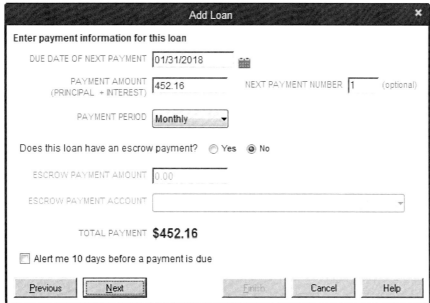

Figure 4-73 Payment information for Truck loan

> **Note:**
> QuickBooks allows you to track escrow amounts separately from principal and interest so you can automatically record these expenditures with each payment. For example, taxes added to your mortgage payment automatically could be posted each month, rather than by a separate manual entry.

6. Click **Next**.

7. Complete the *Enter interest information for this* loan section using data from Table 4-2. When completed, your screen should look like Figure 4-74.

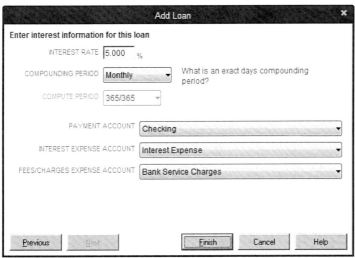

Figure 4-74 Interest information for Truck loan

8. Click **Finish** to save the Truck Loan.

Making Loan Payments using the Loan Manager

In our example, Academy Photography purchased a truck and took out a loan with National Bank for $24,000.00. The loan has been set up in Loan Manager; therefore, all payments on the loan should originate in Loan Manager.

> **Note:**
> The loan manager will only display the Payment Schedule after the origination date of the loan.

> **DO NOT PERFORM THESE STEPS. THEY ARE FOR REFERENCE ONLY.**

1. If Loan Manager is not already open, from the *Banking* menu select **Loan Manager**. QuickBooks displays the *Loan Manager* window as shown in Figure 4-75. Click the *Payment Schedule* tab to see a list of all the payments.

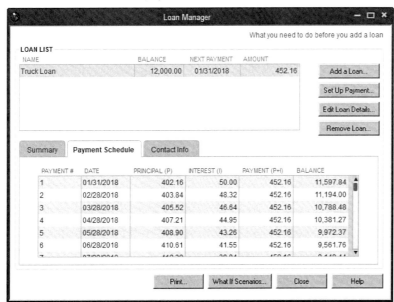

Figure 4-75 Loan Manager window – your screen may vary

Managing Expenses - Tracking Loans using the Loan Manager **153**

2. **Truck Loan** in the *Loan List* is already selected. Click **Set Up Payment** to make a payment for the Truck Loan. QuickBooks displays the window shown in Figure 4-76.

3. Confirm that **A regular payment** is selected in the *This payment is* drop-down list as shown in Figure 4-76.

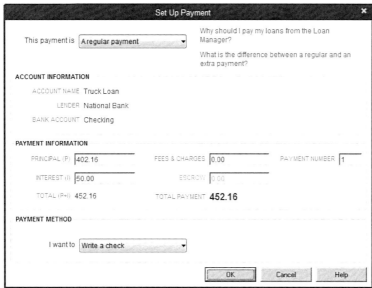

Figure 4-76 Set Up Payment window

> **Note:**
> Select **An extra payment** when you are making a payment in addition to your regular monthly amount.
>
> QuickBooks automatically calculates the amounts for the *Principal* and *Interest* fields based on the information you entered when you set up the loan. Confirm that these amounts agree to your loan statement and enter any fees or charges for the month in the *Fees & Charges* field.

4. In the *I want to* field, leave **Write a check** selected.

5. Click **OK** to create a check to make a payment for this loan. QuickBooks displays the *Write Checks* window and populates each field with the correct information as shown in Figure 4-77. If a manual check number displays in the **No.** field, check the *Print Later* box so that a voucher check can be used.

> **Note:**
> If you want to enter a Bill instead of a Check, select **Enter a bill** in the *I want to* drop-down list in the *Set Up Payment* window in the *Loan Manager*.

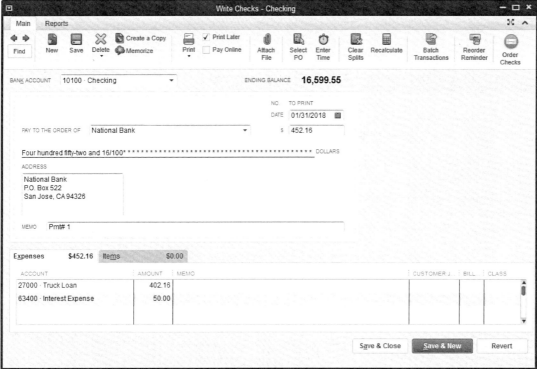

Figure 4-77 Write Checks window for Truck loan payment

6. Enter *01/31/2018* in the *Date* field. QuickBooks uses the current date when creating a **Check** or **Bill** through the *Loan Manager*. Edit the date field as necessary so the **Check** or **Bill** has the correct date.
7. Confirm that your screen matches Figure 4-77.
8. Click **Save & Close**.

Review Questions

Comprehension Questions

1. Describe how classes are used in QuickBooks.
2. Describe how to track expenses by job in QuickBooks.
3. Describe the steps in tracking Accounts Payable transactions in QuickBooks.
4. Under what circumstances is it important to use Bill Credits to record discounts?
5. To track credit card charges and payments in a separate liability account, describe the steps you must use to record charges and payments on the credit card.

Multiple Choice

Select the best answer(s) for each of the following:

1. You may record payments to your vendors by:
   a) Recording a manual entry directly into the check register.
   b) Using *Write Checks* to write and print a check without using Accounts Payable.
   c) Using *Enter Bills* to record Accounts Payable and then using *Pay Bills* to pay open Bills.
   d) all of the above.

2. To display the *Vendor Center:*
   a) Click *Vendors* on the QuickBooks *Home* Page.
   b) Click the *Vendor Center* icon on the Icon Bar.
   c) Select the *Vendor* menu and then select *Vendor Center*.
   d) a, b, or c.

3. You can add a vendor:
   a) Only at the beginning of the fiscal year.
   b) Only if you will purchase over $600 from that particular vendor and a Form 1099 will be issued.
   c) Only at the beginning of the month.
   d) At any time by selecting *New Vendor* in the *Vendor Center*.

4. Which statement is true?
   a) QuickBooks records each *Bill Payment* in a bank account register (or credit card account register) and the Accounts Payable register.
   b) *Bill Payments* increase the balance in both the Checking account and the Accounts Payable account.
   c) You should assign *Jobs* to all discounts taken.
   d) You cannot make partial payments on a *Bill*.

5. Which QuickBooks feature allows you to separate your income and expenses by line of business, department, location, profit center, or any other meaningful breakdown of your business?
   a) Job costing.
   b) Class tracking.
   c) Customer types.
   d) Vendor types.

6. If you void a Bill Payment check, all of the following occur, except:
   a) QuickBooks retains a trail of the check number, but the amount becomes zero.
   b) The Bill becomes unpaid.
   c) The Checking account balance increases.
   d) The Accounts Payable account decreases.

7. If you want to track the expenses for each customer or job:
   a) Enter each expense in the job-cost section.
   b) Use the pay liabilities function.
   c) Link each expense with the customer or job to which it applies.
   d) Create a separate expense account for each job.

8. To make a loan payment, you can:
   a) Select the loan liability account in the Chart of Accounts and choose Make Deposit from the Activities Menu.
   b) Choose Pay Loan from the Banking Menu.
   c) Use the **Loan Manager** to calculate the interest and principal amounts. Select the **Loan Manager**, then select the Loan to pay, and then select **Set Up Payment**.
   d) All of the Above.

9. When a vendor credits your account, you record it in:
   a) The *Write Checks* window.
   b) The *Enter Bills* window.
   c) The *Pay Bills* window.
   d) The *Accounts Payable* Register.

10. Which Account-type should you use to track Petty Cash:
    a) Credit Card.
    b) Equity.
    c) Bank.
    d) Checking.

11. The Vendor Balance Detail Report:
    a) Shows the detail of each Bill, Bill Credit, Discount, and Bill Payment to each vendor.
    b) Shows the detail of each payment created using the *Write Checks* window.
    c) Can be created by selecting *Vendor Balance Detail* report from the **Vendor Center**.
    d) None of the above.

12. What is the accounting behind the scenes for the *Pay Bills* window:
    a) Increase (debit) Accounts Payable, Decrease (credit) the Checking Account.
    b) Decrease (debit) Accounts Payable, Decrease (credit) the Checking Account.
    c) Decrease (debit) Accounts Payable, Increase (credit) the Checking Account.
    d) Decrease (debit) Accounts Payable, Decrease (debit) the Checking Account.

13. It's best not to use which field in the new vendor setup window:
    a) Opening Balance.
    b) Vendor Name.
    c) Address.
    d) Terms.

14. In the *Pay Bills* window, you can sort the Bills by:
    a) Due Date.
    b) Vendor.
    c) Discount Date.
    d) All of the above.

15. Which statement is true regarding bill payments:
    a) Bill Payments *increase* the balance in the Accounts Payable account.
    b) When you use a check to pay bills, QuickBooks records each Bill Payment in the Checking account register and in the Accounts Payable account register.
    c) If you select more than one Bill for the same vendor, QuickBooks creates a separate Bill Payment for each Bill.
    d) Bill Credits that are created from a vendor are automatically applied to Bills that are due for that same vendor.

Completion Statements

1. The _____ _____ shows a graphical representation of the steps involved in recording your expenses.

2. Terms of 2% 10 Net 30 on a bill means that if you pay the bill within _____ days, you are eligible for a(n) _____ discount.

3. To separately track income and expenses for multiple departments, locations, or profit centers, use _____ tracking.

4. To track job costs in QuickBooks, link each expense with the _____ or _____ to which it applies.

5. For a Bill to be considered paid by QuickBooks, you must pay the Bill using the _____ _____ window.

Expenses Problem 1

> Restore the Expenses-14Problem1.QBM file.

1. Activate *Class* tracking in the data file.

2. Add a new vendor to the Vendor list using the data in the table below. Fields that are not provided below can be left blank.

Field Name	Data
Vendor Name	Batish Video Services
Company Name	Batish Video Services
Mr./Ms./...	Ms.
First Name	Karen
Last Name	Batish
Main Phone	510-555-8682
Main Email	karen@batishonsite.us
Name and Address	Batish Video Services Karen Batish 90 Sunset Ave. Dublin, CA 94508
Account #	89766-56
Terms	Net 30
Print on Check as	Batish Video Services
Tax ID	888-77-9999
Check Box	Vendor eligible for 1099
Account Prefill	Professional Fees
Vendor Type	Consultant
County	Alameda

Table 4-3 Use this data to enter a new vendor

3. Print the **Vendor List**. (From the *Reports* menu, select **Vendors & Payables** and then select **Vendor Contact List**.)

4. Enter check number *331* directly in the **Checking** register on *01/08/2018* to *Green Office Supply* for $*800.00*. Use **Quick Add** to add the Vendor. Split the expense to $*400.00* for **Office Supplies** for the **San Jose** store and $*400.00* for **Office Supplies** for the **Walnut Creek** store.

5. Enter *Bill* number *84-6542* from *Sinclair Insurance* on *01/17/2018* for $*1,730.00* with Terms of **Net 30**. Code the *Bill* to **Insurance Expense**. Allocate 100% of the cost to the **San Jose** store.

6. Create and print an **Unpaid Bills Detail** report dated 01/20/2018.

7. Pay all of the **Bills** due on or before 02/20/2018. Pay the **Bills** from the Checking account on 02/20/2018. Starting check number is *332*.

Expenses Problem 2 (Advanced)

APPLYING YOUR KNOWLEDGE

> Restore the Expenses-14Problem2.QBM file.

1. Activate *Class* tracking in the data file.

2. Add a new vendor to the Vendor list using the data in the table below. Fields that are not provided below can be left blank.

Field Name	Data
Vendor Name	Prado Photography Services
Company Name	Prado Photography Services
Mr./Ms./...	Ms.
First Name	Joy
Last Name	Prado
Main Phone	510-555-1414
Main Email	joy@pradophoto.biz
Name and Address	Prado Photography Services Joy Prado 755 Market Ave. Castro Valley, CA 94500
Account #	89766-46
Terms	Net 30
Print on Check as	Prado Photography Services
Tax ID	111-22-3333
Check Box	Vendor eligible for 1099
Account Prefill	Professional Fees
Vendor Type	Consultant
County	Alameda

Table 4-4 Use this data to enter a new vendor

3. Print the **Vendor List**. (From the *Reports* menu, select **Vendors & Payables** and then select **Vendor Contact List**.)

4. Enter check number *331* directly in the **Checking** register on *01/12/2018* to *Carl's Hardware* for $*325.00*. Use **Quick Add** to add the Vendor. Split the expense to $*125.00* for **Office Supplies** for the **San Jose** store and $*200.00* for **Repairs and Maintenance** for the **Walnut Creek** store.

5. Using **Write Checks**, enter a check (*Print Later*) to *Orlando Properties* dated *01/12/2018* for $*1,500.00* for **Rent** at the **San Jose** store. Make the check printable but don't print the check.

6. Enter *Bill* number *1500* from *Nellis Distributing* on *01/18/2018* for $*896.00* with Terms of **Net 15**. The *Bill* is for the purchase of supplies for the Bob Mason job, so code the *Bill* to **Cost of Goods Sold**. Bob Mason is a customer in the San Jose store, so link the cost with the appropriate *Job* and *Class*.

7. Enter *Bill* number *3453* from *Sinclair Insurance* on *01/19/2018* for $*1,680.00* with Terms of **Net 30**. Code the *Bill* to **Insurance Expense**. Allocate 100% of the cost to the **San Jose** store.

Managing Expenses - Expenses Problem 2 (Advanced)

8. Create and print an **Unpaid Bills Detail** report dated *1/20/2018.*

9. Pay all of the *Bills* due on or before **02/28/2018**. **Pay Bills** from the *Checking* account on **01/19/2018**. Make the *Bill Payments* "printable" checks.

10. Print all of the checks that you recorded with a *Print Later* status. Print them on blank paper and start the check numbers at *6001.*

11. Enter a credit card charge on the **National Bank VISA** card from **Bay Office Supply** (Use *Quick Add* to add the vendor), reference number *1234*, dated *1/25/2018*. The purchase was for $*61.33* for **office supplies** for the **Walnut Creek** store.

12. Enter *Bill* number *4635* from *Ace Supply* on *01/25/2018* for $*992.84* with terms of **Net 30**. Code the *Bill* to **Cost of Goods Sold** since it was for supplies for the **Ron Berry** *Job*. Ron Berry is a *Customer* at the **San Jose** store. Keep the default terms for Ace Supply.

13. Enter a *Bill Credit* from *Ace Supply* on *01/30/2018* for $*150.00*. Use reference number *4635C* on the credit. Code the credit to **Cost of Goods Sold** and link the credit with the **Ron Berry** *Job* and the **San Jose** *Class*.

14. Apply the credit to *Bill* number 4635 and pay the remainder of the *Bill* on 01/30/2018 using a printable check.

15. Print the check using number **6005** on blank paper.

16. Print a **Vendor Balance Detail** report for **All** transactions.

QUICKBOOKS AND BEYOND – *TAKE THE NEXT STEP WITH THE SLEETER GROUP BLOG*

"Hail the Vendor Neutral, Frictionless, Zero Data Entry World!"

Greg Lam writes, "(Recently), I attended the Sleeter Group Accounting Solutions Conference for the first time. At the end of it all, what stuck with me were a few pieces of jargon: *Vendor Neutral*, *Frictionless*, and *Zero Data Entry*. What does the jargon actually mean?"

In this *QuickBooks and Beyond* section, Greg Lam shares his thoughts on recent trends in the accounting software world. Read the full post at www.sleeter.com/blog/?p=8984.

New Terminology

Cloud Computing – Storing, managing, or processing data through remote servers accessed through the Internet rather than on a personal computer.

QuickBooks Online – A cloud-based application created by Intuit, the makers of QuickBooks Desktop Edition.

Xero – A cloud-based accounting application for small and medium-sized businesses. Xero is a competitor to QuickBooks Online.

Harmony Update – Name given to a redesign of QuickBooks Online released in 2013 that included significant changes to the user interface.

Putting New Knowledge to Use

1. What are the advantages to your company or workplace of being "vendor neutral?"

2. Using the definition of *friction* used in this blog post, what is a source of friction in your company or workplace?

Chapter 5
Bank Reconciliation and Bank Transactions

Topics

In this chapter, you will learn about the following topics:

- Reconciling Bank Accounts (page 161)
- Bank Reconciliation Reports (page 167)
- Finding Errors During Bank Reconciliation (page 168)
- Handling Bounced Checks (page 173)
- Reconciling Credit Card Accounts and Paying the Bill (page 176)
- Bank Feeds (page 179)

> **Restore this File:**
> This chapter uses BankRec-14.QBW. To open this file, restore the BankRec-14.QBM file to your hard disk. See page 9 for instructions on restoring files.

At the end of each month, you must compare the transactions you have entered into QuickBooks with your bank statement to ensure that QuickBooks matches the bank's records. This process is called *reconciling*. It is a very important step in the overall accounting process and ensures the accuracy of your accounting records.

In addition to reconciling bank accounts, you can also reconcile other accounts, such as credit card accounts, using the same process. In fact, you can reconcile almost any Other Current Asset, Fixed Asset, Credit Card, Other Current Liability, Long Term Liability, or Equity account using the same process presented in this chapter. However, even though QuickBooks *allows* you to reconcile many accounts, the primary accounts you'll reconcile are bank and credit card accounts since these types of accounts always have monthly statements.

Reconciling Bank Accounts

Figure 5-1 shows Academy Photography's bank statement for the checking account as of January 31, 2018. Before reconciling the account in QuickBooks, make sure you've entered all of the transactions for that account. For example, if you have automatic payments from your checking account (EFTs) or automatic charges on your credit card, it is best to enter those transactions before you start the reconciliation.

Business Checking Account				
Statement Date:	January 31, 2018			Page 1 of 1

Summary:

Previous Balance as of 12/31/17:		$	14,384.50
Total Deposits and Credits:	+	$	3,386.02
Total Checks and Debits:	-	$	12,345.60
Statement Balance as of 1/31/18	=	$	5,424.92

Deposits and Other Credits:

DEPOSITS

Date	Description	Amount	
22-Jan	Customer Deposit	$	249.54
30-Jan	Customer Deposit	$	1,950.00
31-Jan	Customer Deposit	$	1,177.86
	3 Deposits:	$	3,377.40

INTEREST

Date	Description	Amount	
31-Jan	Interest Earned	$	8.62
	Interest:	$	8.62

Checks and Other Withdrawals:

CHECKS PAID:

Check No.	Date Paid	Amount	
325	2-Jan	$	465.00
326	7-Jan	$	276.52
327	10-Jan	$	128.60
6001**	10-Jan	$	3,200.00
6003**	25-Jan	$	142.00
6004	26-Jan	$	123.48
	6 Checks Paid:	$	4,335.60

OTHER WITHDRAWALS/PAYMENTS

Date	Description	Amount	
31-Jan	Transfer	$	8,000.00
	2 Other Withdrawals/Payments:	$	8,000.00

SERVICE CHARGES

Date	Description	Amount	
31-Jan	Service Charge	$	10.00
	1 Service Charge:	$	10.00

Figure 5-1 Sample bank statement

COMPUTER PRACTICE

Using the sample data file for this chapter, follow these steps to reconcile the QuickBooks Checking account with the bank statement shown in Figure 5-1.

Step 1. Before you begin the reconciliation process, first review the account register to verify that all of the transactions for the statement period have been entered (e.g., deposits, checks, other withdrawals, and payments.) The Academy Photography sample data file for this section already has the deposits, checks, other withdrawals, and payments entered into the register.

Step 2. If the *Home* page is not already open, select the **Company** menu and then select **Home Page**.

Step 3. Click the **Reconcile** Icon in the *Banking* section of the *Home* page.

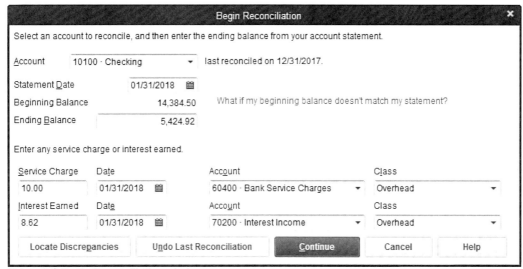

Figure 5-2 Begin Reconciliation window

Step 4. In the *Begin Reconciliation* window (see Figure 5-2), the *Account* field already shows *Checking*. The account drop-down list allows you to select other accounts to reconcile, however since *Checking* is the account you're reconciling, you don't need to change it now. Press **Tab**.

Step 5. Leave **01/31/2018** in the *Statement Date* field and press **Tab**.

The default statement date is one month after your last reconciliation date. Since this exercise file was last reconciled on 12/31/2017, QuickBooks entered *01/31/2018*.

> **Tip:**
> If your bank does not date statements at the end of the month, ask the bank to change your statement date to the end of the month. This makes it easier to match the bank statement with your month-end reports in QuickBooks.

Step 6. Look for the *Previous Balance as of 12/31/17* on the bank statement (see Figure 5-1). Compare this amount with the *Beginning Balance* amount in the *Begin Reconciliation* window (see Figure 5-2). Notice that they are the same.

> **Note:**
> QuickBooks calculates the *Beginning Balance* field in the *Begin Reconciliation* window by adding and subtracting all previously reconciled transactions. If the beginning balance does not match the bank statement, you probably made changes to previously cleared transactions. See *Finding Errors During Bank Reconciliation* on page 168 for more information.

Step 7. Enter **5,424.92** in the *Ending Balance* field. This amount is the *Statement Balance as of 1/31/18* shown on the bank statement in Figure 5-1. Press **Tab**.

> **Note:**
> If you already recorded bank charges in the check register, skip Step 8 through Step 11 to avoid duplicate entry of the charges.

Step 8. Enter **10.00** in the *Service Charge* field and press **Tab**.

If you have any bank service charges or interest earned in the bank account, enter those amounts in the appropriate fields in the *Begin Reconciliation* window. When you enter these amounts, QuickBooks adds the corresponding transactions to your bank account register.

Step 9. Leave **01/31/2018** in the *Date* field and press **Tab**.

Step 10. Select *Bank Service Charges* from the *Account* drop-down list and press **Tab**.

Each time you reconcile, this field will default to the account you used on the last bank reconciliation. Confirm that this is the correct expense account before proceeding to the next field.

Step 11. Select *Overhead* from the *Class* drop-down list and press **Tab**.

> **Note:**
> If you already recorded interest income in the check register, skip Step 12 through Step 15 to avoid duplicate entry of the interest income.

Step 12. Enter *8.62* in the *Interest Earned* field and press **Tab**.

Step 13. Leave **01/31/2018** in the *Date* field and press **Tab**.

Step 14. Select *Interest Income* from the *Account* drop-down list and press **Tab**.

Step 15. Select *Overhead* from the *Class* drop-down list and click **Continue**.

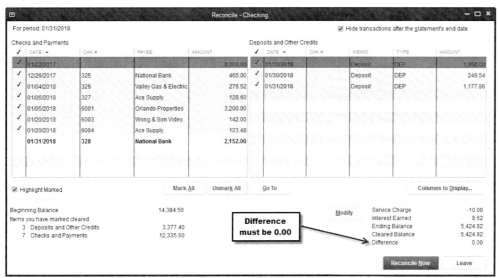

Figure 5-3 Reconcile – Checking window

Step 16. At the top of the *Reconcile – Checking* window (see Figure 5-3), check the box labeled "Hide transactions after the statement ending date".

☑ Hide transactions after the statement's end date

This removes transactions dated after the statement date from being displayed on the screen. Since they could not possibly have cleared, this simplifies your life so you only have to look at transactions that *could* have cleared the bank as of the statement date.

Step 17. In the *Deposits and Other Credits* section of the *Reconcile – Checking* window, match the deposits and other credits on the bank statement (see Figure 5-1 on page 162) with the associated QuickBooks transactions. Click anywhere on a line to mark it cleared. The checkmark (✓) indicates which transactions have cleared.

Step 18. In the *Checks and Payments* section of the *Reconcile – Checking* window, match the checks and other withdrawals on the bank statement with the associated QuickBooks transactions.

> **Tip:**
> Notice that QuickBooks calculates the sum of your marked items at the bottom of the window in the *Items you have marked cleared* section. This section also shows the number of deposits and checks you have marked cleared. Compare the figures to your bank statement. If you find a discrepancy with these totals, you most likely have an error. Search for an item you forgot to mark or one that you marked in error.

> **Tip:**
> You can sort the columns in the *Reconcile - Checking* window by clicking the column heading. If you would like to change the columns displayed in the *Reconcile – Checking* window, click the *Columns to Display* button. This will allow you to select which columns you would like to see when you are reconciling (see Figure 5-4).

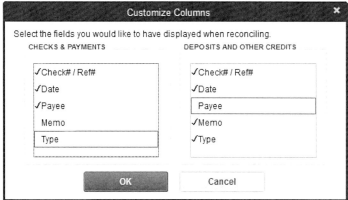

Figure 5-4 Customizing the Bank Reconciliation with Columns to Display

Step 19. After you've marked all the cleared checks and deposits, look at the *Difference* field. It should be **0.00**, indicating that your bank account is reconciled.

If the *Difference* field is not zero, check for errors. For help in troubleshooting your bank reconciliation, see *Finding Errors During Bank Reconciliation* on page 168.

> **Tip:**
> If you need to wait until another time to complete the bank reconciliation, you can click **Leave**. When you click **Leave**, QuickBooks will save all of your changes so you can complete the reconciliation later.

Step 20. If the *Difference* field is zero, you've successfully reconciled. Click ***Reconcile Now***. If you see a window offering online banking, click **OK** to close.

> **Note:**
> It is very important that you do not click **Reconcile Now** unless the *Difference* field shows **0.00**. Doing so will cause discrepancies in your accounting records. See page 171 for more information.

Step 21. The *Select Reconciliation Report* dialog box displays. The **Both** option is already selected, so click **Display** to view your reports on the screen (see Figure 5-5).

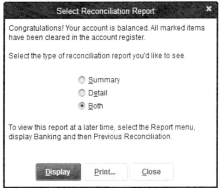

Figure 5-5 Select Reconciliation Report window

Step 22.   Click **OK** on the *Reconciliation Report* window.

Step 23.   QuickBooks creates both a *Reconciliation Summary* report (Figure 5-6) and a *Reconciliation Detail* report (Figure 5-7). The length of the detail report will depend upon how many transactions you cleared on this reconciliation and how many uncleared transactions remain in the account.

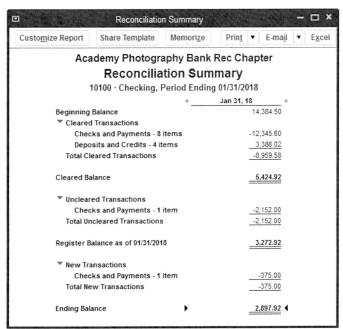

Figure 5-6 Reconciliation Summary report

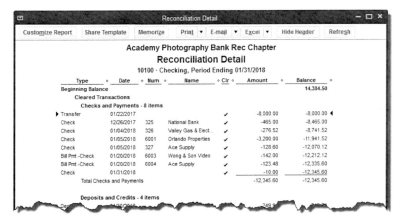

Figure 5-7 Reconciliation Detail report

Bank Reconciliation and Bank Transactions - Bank Reconciliation Reports **167**

Step 24. Close all open report windows.

Bank Reconciliation Reports

Each time you complete a bank reconciliation, QuickBooks walks you through creating a bank reconciliation report for that reconciliation. You can recreate your bank reconciliation reports at any time by following the steps below.

> **Note:**
> If you are using QuickBooks Pro you can create Bank Reconciliation reports for the most recently reconciled month only.

COMPUTER PRACTICE

Step 1. From the *Reports* menu select **Banking** and then select **Previous Reconciliation**. The *Select Previous Reconciliation Report* window displays (see Figure 5-8).

Step 2. Confirm that **Checking** is selected in the *Account* field.

If you have more than one bank account, you can select another bank account using the *Account* drop-down list.

Step 3. Confirm that **01/31/2018** is selected in the *Statement Ending Date* field.

QuickBooks automatically selects the report for your most recent bank reconciliation. You can select another report by highlighting the statement date in this section.

Step 4. Confirm that **Detail** is selected in the *Type of Report* section.

Step 5. Confirm that **Transactions cleared at the time of reconciliation** in the *In this report, include* section is selected. When you select this option, QuickBooks displays an Adobe Acrobat PDF file with the contents of the reconciliation report. The Acrobat (PDF) report does not include any changes you may have made to reconciled transactions. See Figure 5-8.

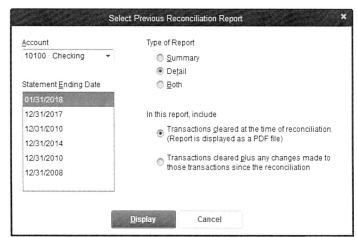

Figure 5-8 Printing a Previous Bank Reconciliation

Step 6. Click **Display** to view your bank reconciliation reports on screen.

> **Note:**
> If your screen does not show the Balance column in the window shown in Figure 5-9, you need to set your Printer Setup settings to fit the report to 1 page wide before you perform the bank reconciliation. This is because Acrobat creates the report when you finish the reconciliation and uses the settings in your Printer Setup to determine how to lay out the page.
>
> If you have already created the report, you can undo the reconciliation (see page 169) and then select *Printer Setup* from the *File* menu. When the *Printer setup* window displays, select *Report* from the *Form Name* drop down list. At the bottom of the window you can check the *Fit report to* option and enter *1* for the number of pages wide you want reports to display, as illustrated below.
>
>

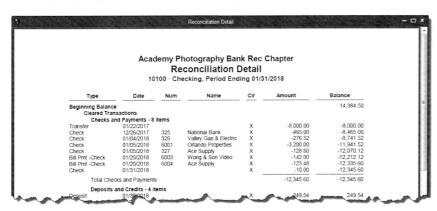

Figure 5-9 Adobe Acrobat (PDF) bank reconciliation report – your screen may vary

Step 7.   Close the Reconciliation Detail report.

> **Note:**
> If you prefer to create a normal QuickBooks reconciliation report (as opposed to an Acrobat PDF report), select the option, *Transactions cleared plus any changes made to those transactions since the reconciliation* in Step 5 above.

Finding Errors During Bank Reconciliation

If you have finished checking off all of the deposits and checks but the *Difference* field at the bottom of the window does not equal zero, there is an error (or discrepancy) that must be found and corrected. To find errors in your bank reconciliation, try the following steps:

Step 1: Review the Beginning Balance Field

Verify that the amount in the *Beginning Balance* field matches the beginning balance on your bank statement. If it does not, you are not ready to reconcile. There are two possibilities for why the beginning balance will no longer match to the bank statement:

1. One or more reconciled transactions were voided, deleted, or changed since the last reconciliation; and/or,
2. The checkmark on one or more reconciled transactions in the account register was removed since the last reconciliation.

To correct the problem you have two options:

Option 1: Use the Reconciliation Discrepancy Report to Troubleshoot

Review the report for any changes or deletions to cleared transactions. The *Type of Change* column shows the nature of the change to the transaction. Notice that a user deleted a cleared check.

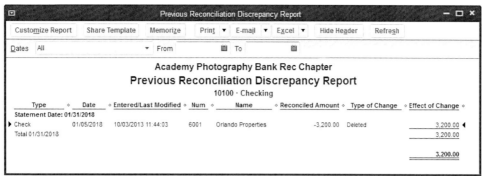

Figure 5-10 Reconciliation Discrepancy report

1. For each line of the report with "Deleted" in the Type of Change column, re-enter the deleted transaction. Then, use the Bank Reconciliation window to re-reconcile the transaction that had been deleted.
2. For each line of the report with "Amount" in the *Type of Change* column, double-click the transaction in the *Reconciliation Discrepancy* report to open it (i.e., QuickZoom). Then, change the amount back to the reconciled amount.

After returning all transactions to their original state (as they were at the time of the last reconciliation), you can then proceed to investigate whether the changes were necessary, and if so, enter adjustment transactions.

Option 2: Undo the Bank Reconciliation

The *Previous Reconciliation Discrepancy* report only shows changes to cleared transactions since your most recent bank reconciliation. If the beginning balance was incorrect when you performed previous bank reconciliations, the *Previous Reconciliation Discrepancy* report will not fully explain the problem.

If this is the case, the best way to find and correct the problem is to undo the previous reconciliation(s).

Figure 5-11 Begin Reconciliation window

> **Note:**
> When you undo a reconciliation, QuickBooks resets your beginning balance to the previous period. However, the bank service charges and interest income that you entered in the prior reconciliation will remain in the check register and will not be deleted.

> Therefore, do not enter bank service charges and interest income when repeating the bank reconciliation. Instead, clear those transactions along with the other checks and deposits when you re-reconcile the account.

Step 2: Locate and Edit Incorrectly Recorded Transactions

When you find a discrepancy between a transaction in QuickBooks and a transaction on the bank statement, you need to correct it. You will use different methods to correct the error, depending upon the date of the transaction.

Correcting or Voiding Transactions in the Current Accounting Period

If you find that you need to correct a transaction in QuickBooks and the transaction is dated in the **current accounting period** (i.e., a period for which financial statements and/or tax returns have not yet been issued), correct the error as described in the following paragraphs.

If You Made the Error

If you made an error in your records, you must make a correction in QuickBooks so that your records will agree with the bank. For example, if you wrote a check for $400.00, but you recorded it in QuickBooks as $40.00, you will need to change the check in QuickBooks. Double-click the transaction in the **Reconcile** window, or highlight the transaction and click **Go To.** Make the correction, and then click **Save & Close**. This will return you to the *Reconcile* window and you will see the updated amount.

If the Bank Made the Error

If the bank made an error, enter a transaction in the bank account register to adjust your balance for the error and continue reconciling the account. Then, contact the bank and ask them to post an adjustment to your account. When you receive the bank statement showing the correction, enter a subsequent entry in the bank account register to record the bank's adjustment. This register entry will show on your next bank reconciliation, and you can clear it like any other transaction.

For example, Figure 5-12 displays a check register with an adjusting entry of $90.00 on 1/31/2018 where the bank made a deposit error during the month. The $90.00 shortage is recorded on the *Payment* side of the check register so that the register will reconcile with the bank statement. Subsequently, another adjusting entry is made on the *Deposit* side of the check register to record the bank's correction of the previous month's deposit. The $90.00 deposit will show on February's bank statement and can be cleared during the reconciliation process. Notice that *both* adjusting entries in the register are recorded to the same account, *Reconciliation Discrepancies*.

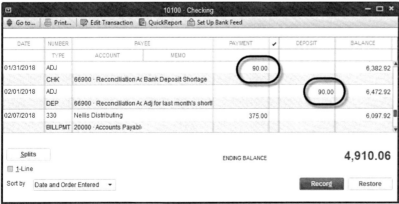

Figure 5-12 Adjusting entries for bank deposit error

Voiding Checks and Stop Payments

When you find a check dated in the **current accounting period** that you know will not clear the bank (e.g., if you stop payment on a check), you will need to void the check. Double-click the check from the *Reconcile* window. Select the **Edit** menu and then select **Void Check**. Click **Save & Close** to return to the *Reconcile* window.

Correcting or Voiding Transactions in Closed Accounting Periods

A *closed accounting period* is the period prior to and including the date on which a company officially "closes" its books (for example, 12/31/2017), creates its final financial reports, and presents its finalized reports to external stakeholders such as the IRS and investors. You do not want to change transactions dated in a closed accounting period because doing so will change financial reports during a period for which you have already issued financial statements or filed tax returns.

In QuickBooks, for the closing date protection to work, you must use the *closing date* to indicate the date on which you last closed the accounting period. For example, if you issued financial statements on 12/31/2017, you can set the closing date in QuickBooks to 12/31/2017. This will essentially "lock" your QuickBooks file so that only the administrator (or other authorized users) will be able to modify transactions before 12/31/2017.

To correct or void a check that is dated in a **closed accounting period**, follow the procedure described below.

> DO NOT PERFORM THESE STEPS NOW. THEY ARE FOR REFERENCE ONLY.

1. Display the check in the register as shown in Figure 5-13 and click on the transaction that needs to be voided to select it.

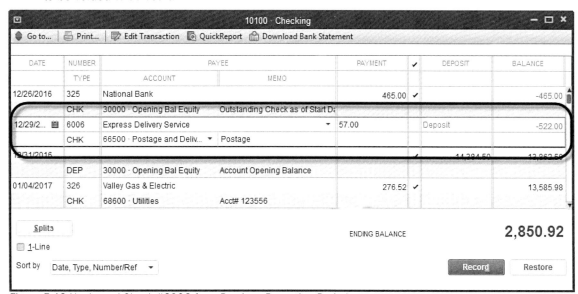

Figure 5-13 Uncleared Check #6006 from Previous Reporting Period

2. From the **Edit** menu, select **Void Check**. QuickBooks zeroes all dollar amounts and adds a "VOID" note in the Memo field as shown in Figure 5-14. Click **Record**.

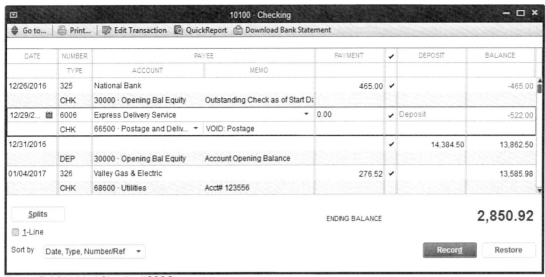

Figure 5-14 Voided Check - #6006

3. QuickBooks prompts you that the transaction you are voiding is cleared and that it is dated in a closed accounting period (Figure 5-15). Click **Yes**.

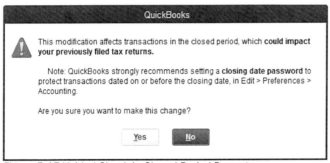

Figure 5-15 Voided Check in Closed Period Prompt

4. QuickBooks then displays the window shown in Figure 5-16. Click **Yes (Recommended).** This is the default response.

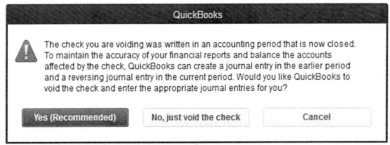

Figure 5-16 Voided Check Adjustment Prompt

5. QuickBooks performs three actions when you click **Yes (Recommended)** on the window shown in Figure 5-16 above.

   a) QuickBooks adds wording to the Memo field of the check showing that the program reversed the impact of the void on the General Ledger.

Figure 5-17 Voided Check - Additional Memo Text

b) QuickBooks posts a General Journal Entry (GJE) dated the same date that reverses the impact on the General Ledger caused by the voided check.

Figure 5-18 Journal Entry - Reverses GL Changes from Voiding the Check

c) QuickBooks then enters a Reversing General Journal Entry (RGJE) in the current period. The default date for the reversing entry is "today."

01/08/2017	2016-4R	Express Delivery Service			✓	57.00	10,314.38
	GENJRN	66500 · Postage and Delivery	Reverse of GJE 2016-4 – For CHK 6006 voide				

Figure 5-19 Journal Entry that "moves" the GL Change to the Current Reporting Period

> **Note**
> QuickBooks clears all entries. However, the entries will appear in the Bank Reconciliation window until the client reconciles them using the Bank Reconciliation feature.
>
> **Important:**
> The *Void Checks* tool only works with *Check(CHK)* transactions that are coded to one or more *Expense* and/or *Other Expense* accounts. The following transactions are not protected with the *Void Checks* tool:
> 1. Checks coded to accounts other than *Expense/Other Expense*
> 2. Checks that include Items
> 3. Checks that are not "Check" transaction types (e.g., Bill Payment, Payroll Liability Payment, Sales Tax Payment, Paycheck)

6. Next, enter the correct amount in a new transaction. Use the date of the current bank statement for the new transaction.

When QuickBooks Automatically Adjusts your Balance

If the difference is not zero when you click **Reconcile Now** in the *Reconcile* window, QuickBooks creates a transaction in the bank account for the difference. The transaction is coded to the *Reconciliation Discrepancies* expense account. You should not leave this transaction in the register, but research why the discrepancy exists and properly account for it. A balance in this account usually indicates an over- or under-statement in net income.

Handling Bounced Checks

Banks and accountants often refer to bounced checks as NSF (non-sufficient funds) transactions. This means there are insufficient funds in the account to cover the check.

When Your Customer's Check Bounces

If your bank returns a check from one of your customers, enter an NSF transaction in the banking account register.

For example, Bob Mason bounced the check #2526 for $1,177.86 and the bank charged the Company $10.00. Complete the steps below to complete the NSF transaction.

COMPUTER PRACTICE

Step 1. Open the *Receive Payments* window and click **Previous.** The Customer Payment window for *Bob Mason* opens (see Figure 5-20).

Step 2. Click the Record Bounced Check button in the top of the window.

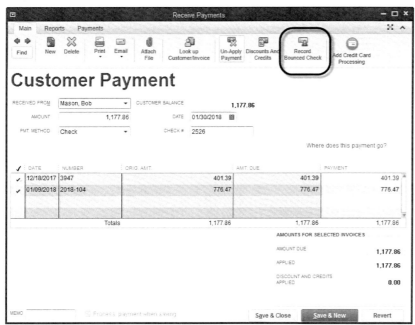

Figure 5-20 Record Bounced Check button in Customer Payment window

Step 3. The *Manage Bounced Check* window opens. Enter the information in Figure 5-21. When finished click **Next**.

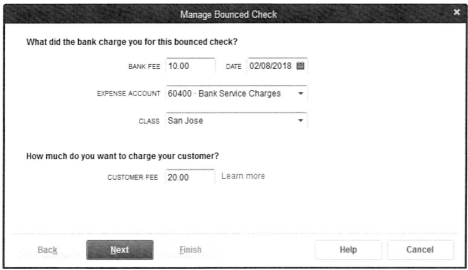

Figure 5-21 Manage Bounced Check window

Step 4. The *Bounced Check Summary* window opens (see Figure 5-22). Review and click **Finish**.

The *Bounced Check Summary* window explains the three changes that will take place once you record this bounced check. First, all the invoices connected with this check will be marked *Unpaid*, so the aging for these invoices will be correct. Second, fees for the check amount and for the service fee will be deducted from the bank account. Third, an invoice for the fee you are charging your customer will be created.

Bank Reconciliation and Bank Transactions - Handling Bounced Checks   **175**

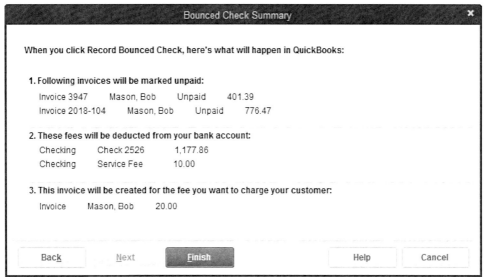

Figure 5-22 Bounced Check Summary window

Step 5.   The Customer Payment window is now marked with a Bounced Check alert (see Figure 5-23).

Figure 5-23 Customer Payment window after recording Bounced Check

Receiving and Depositing the Replacement Check

COMPUTER PRACTICE

To record the transactions for receiving and depositing a replacement check, follow these steps:

Step 1.   Select the **Customers** menu, and then select **Receive Payments**.

Step 2.   In this example, Bob Mason sent a replacement check #2538 on 2/10/18 for $1,197.86 that includes the amount of the check plus the NSF service charge of $20.00. Fill in the customer payment information as shown in Figure 5-24.

Make sure you apply the payment against the original *Invoices* and the service charge *Invoice* you just created earlier.

Step 3.   Click Save & Close.

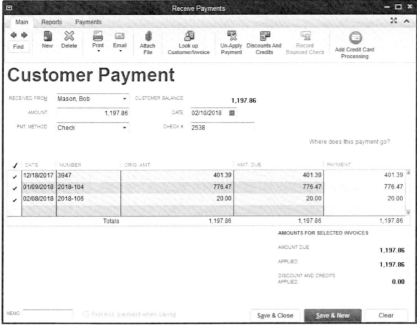

Figure 5-24 The Receive Payments window showing the replacement check

When Your Check Bounces

If you write a check that overdraws your account and your bank returns the check, follow these steps:

1. Decide with your vendor how you will handle the NSF Check (e.g., send a new check, redeposit the same check, or pay by credit card).
2. When the bank sends you the notice that your check was returned, there will be a charge from your bank. Enter a transaction in the bank account register. Code the transaction to Bank Service Charges and use the actual date that the bank charged your account.
3. If your balance is sufficient for the check to clear, tell the vendor to redeposit the check.
4. If your balance is not sufficient, consider other ways of paying the vendor, such as paying with a credit card. Alternatively, negotiate delayed payment terms with your vendor.
5. If your vendor charges an extra fee for bouncing a check, enter a *Bill* (or use *Write Checks*) and code the charge to the Bank Service Charge account.
6. If you bounce a payroll check, use the same process as described. It is good practice, and may be required by law, to reimburse your employee for any bank fees incurred as a result of your mistake.

Reconciling Credit Card Accounts and Paying the Bill

If you use a credit card liability account to track all of your credit card charges and payments, you should reconcile the account every month just as you do with your bank account. The credit card reconciliation process is very similar to the bank account reconciliation, except that when you finish the reconciliation, QuickBooks asks you if you want to pay the credit card immediately or if you want to enter a bill for the balance of the credit card.

Bank Reconciliation and Bank Transactions - Reconciling Credit Card Accounts and Paying the Bill

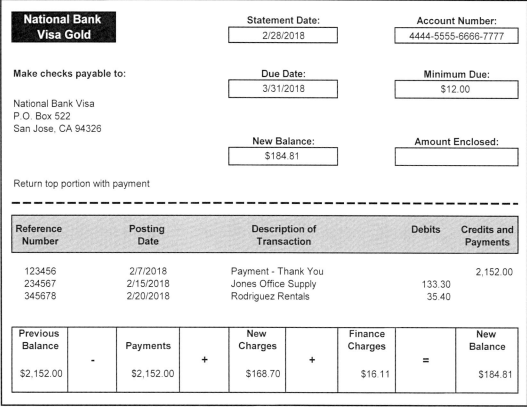

Figure 5-25 National Bank Visa credit card statement

Use the National Bank Visa Gold credit card statement shown in Figure 5-25 to reconcile your account.

COMPUTER PRACTICE

Step 1. Select the **Banking** menu and then select **Reconcile**.

Step 2. On the Begin Reconciliation window, enter the information from the Credit Card statement as shown in Figure 5-26. Click **Continue**.

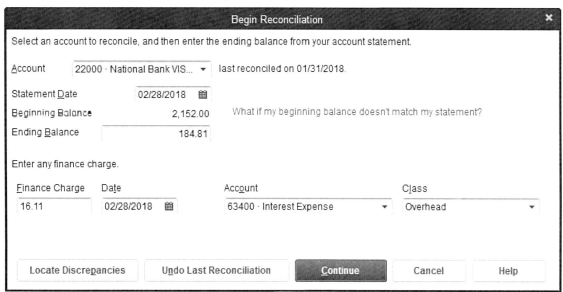

Figure 5-26 Enter your credit card statement information on the Begin Reconciliation window

Step 3. Click each cleared transaction in the *Reconcile Credit Card* window as you match it with the credit card statement.

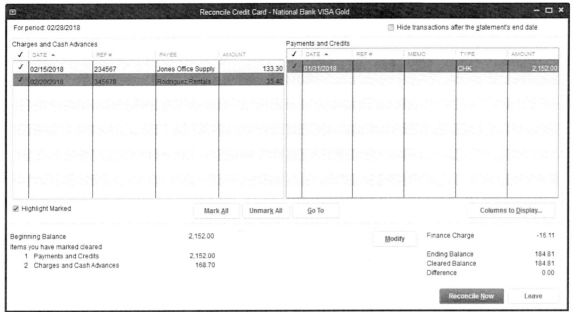

Figure 5-27 The Difference field should show a difference of 0.00 after reconciling

Step 4.   Verify that the *Difference* field shows **0.00** (see Figure 5-27). If it doesn't, look for discrepancies between your records and the credit card statement.

Step 5.   Verify that your screen looks like Figure 5-27 and click **Reconcile Now**.

Step 6.   On the *Make Payment* dialog box, click to select **Enter a bill for payment later** and click **OK** (see Figure 5-28).

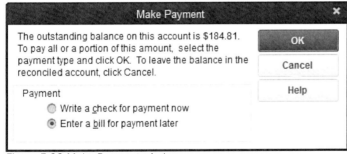

Figure 5-28 Make Payment window

Step 7.   On the *Select Reconciliation Report* window, click **Close**. Normally you would select **Both** and then click **Print**. However, for this exercise, skip this step. See page 167 for more information about Bank Reconciliation reports.

Step 8.   Enter the additional information to complete the **Bill** for the VISA payment as shown in Figure 5-29.

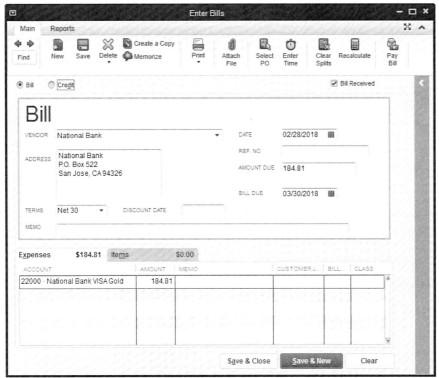
Figure 5-29 Use this data to pay the VISA Bill

> **The accounting behind the scenes:**
> QuickBooks selects the **National Bank VISA Gold** account on the Expenses tab. This reduces the Credit Card liability account (debit) and increases Accounts Payable (credit).
> **Note:**
> Although the bill in Figure 5-29 includes the Overhead class, the transaction will not affect the **Profit & Loss by Class** report because the bill does not post to any income or expense accounts.

Step 9.   Click **Save & Close** to record the Bill.

This bill for $184.81 will display in the *Pay Bills* window the next time you select **Pay Bills** from the *Vendor* menu.

> **Important tip for partial payments of credit card bills:**
> If you don't want to pay the whole amount due on a credit card, don't just change the amount in the *Pay Bills* window. Instead, edit the original *Bill* to match the amount you actually intend to pay. By changing the *Bill*, you reduce the amount that is transferred out of the Credit Card account (and into A/P) to the exact amount that is paid. This way, the amount you don't pay remains in the balance of the Credit Card liability account and will match the account balance on your next credit card statement.

Bank Feeds

The QuickBooks Bank Feeds feature allows you to process online transactions, such as payments and transfers, and download bank transactions into your QuickBooks file. Downloaded transactions save you time by decreasing manual entry and increasing accuracy. It is important to review each downloaded transaction to avoid bringing errors into your company file.

Online banking is secure. QuickBooks uses a secure Internet connection and a high level of encryption when transferring information from your financial institution. Bank fees may apply.

Bank Feed Setup

To begin to use Bank Feeds, you will need to set up the appropriate accounts to communicate with the bank. Steps vary by institution. To complete this process, refer to the QuickBooks help files or the video tutorial.

Processing Online Transactions

You may have the option to enter online transactions, such as online payments, bill payments, or transfers (depending on your financial institution). Figure 5-30 displays an example of an online payment. You can create an online payment by opening the **Write Checks** window and checking **Pay Online**. Notice that there are several differences between a standard check form and an online payment form. For example, the check number field displays the word *SEND*.

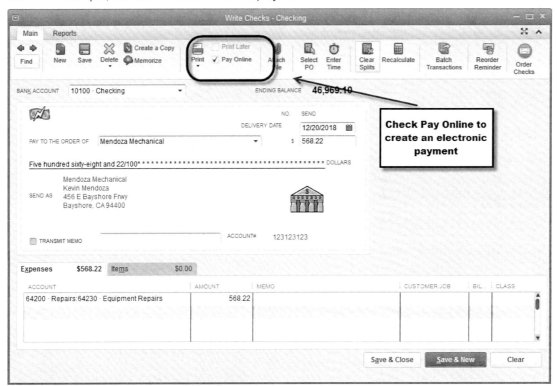

Figure 5-30 Check to be sent as an Online Payment

After saving an online payment, the transaction is queued up in the *Bank Feed Center*. By clicking the *Send Items* button in the *Bank Feed Center*, you can send the online payments and other online transactions to, as well as download transactions from, your financial institution.

Your financial institution may require additional steps. Follow any guidelines given after clicking the *Send Items* button. Do not click the *Send Items* button now.

Figure 5-31 Bank Feeds Center – your screen may vary

Opening the Sample File

With Bank Feeds, transactions are processed and downloaded directly from your financial institution through your internet connection. For this section, we will open a sample QuickBooks file for *Sample Rock Castle Construction*. This file contains downloaded transactions pre-loaded in the file.

We will not be able to use this file to set up an online banking connection or to send or receive transactions, since this would require a live account at a financial institution and cannot be simulated in an educational environment. We will use this sample file to process downloaded transactions that have already been loaded into the sample file.

> **Restore this File**
> This section uses **BankFeeds-14.QBW**. To open this file, restore the BankFeeds-14.QBM file to your hard disk. See page 9 for instructions on restoring files. Click *OK* in the QuickBooks Information window notifying you that the file will use 12/15/2018 as the date. For more on sample files see page 6.

Downloaded Transactions

When you click the *Download Transactions* button in the *Bank Feeds Center*, you download all the new transactions from your financial institution. After downloading, the transactions are ready for review. (Do not click the *Download Transactions* button now.)

As the transactions are downloaded, QuickBooks searches for similar transactions that have previously been entered. If an existing transaction is similar to the downloaded transaction, such as by having the same date and amount, QuickBooks *matches* the downloaded transaction with this entry. Any downloaded transaction that is unpaired with an existing entry is *unmatched*.

> **Note:**
> Some transactions will be downloaded with payee names that do not match the names in the *Vendor Center*. Downloaded transactions often include names appended with a numerical code. It is important to avoid creating duplicate vendors. QuickBooks allows you to create *renaming rules* so that these downloaded transactions are linked to the appropriate existing vendor. You can access the renaming rules by clicking the Rules button in the upper left of the *Bank Feeds Center*; however, the renaming rules window is not accessible in the sample file.

COMPUTER PRACTICE

Step 1. Select **Bank Feeds Center** from the *Bank Feeds* option under the *Banking* menu.

Step 2. The *Bank Feeds* window opens (see Figure 5-32).

A list of your Bank and Credit Card accounts that have been set up to receive downloaded transactions appears on the left. Information about the selected account, including a button for downloading transactions appears on the right.

Step 3. Click on **ANYTIME Financial account** ending in *1235* (the second bank account from the top). This account has 7 transactions downloaded and waiting to be added to QuickBooks.

Figure 5-32 Bank Feeds window

Step 4. Click the **Transaction List** button on the right side of the window.

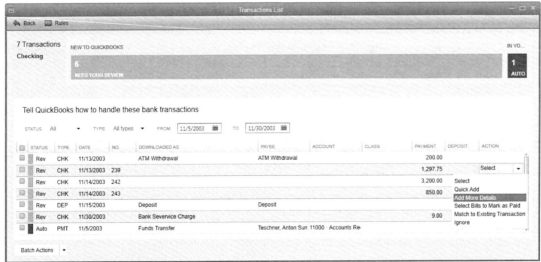

Figure 5-33 Transaction List

Step 5. The Transaction List window opens (see Figure 5-33). Click on the second line to select *Check 239* dated 11/13/2003.

Of the 7 Transactions that have been downloaded from the bank, 1 transaction has already been entered and 6 transaction need review. The matched transaction is at the bottom of the list and has a status of *Auto*. After reviewing each transaction, you can either select individual transactions for approval or for adding further detail, or approve all transactions in one batch action.

> **Note:**
> Observant readers may notice that the downloaded transactions are dated 2003, while most of the transactions in the sample file are dated 2018. Please disregard this discrepancy in the sample file.

Step 1. An action menu appears on the right end of the row for Check 239. Select **Add More Detail** in this action menu.

The bank has not downloaded details about check 239, so this information needs to be added manually to properly link this transaction with the right *Customer* and *Account*. If you need to enter information (such as *Items*) that are not available in the *Transaction Detail – Add More Details* window, you can always enter the transaction normally and match the entered transaction with the downloaded transaction.

Step 2. The *Transaction Detail – Add More Details* window opens. Enter the information in Figure 5-34. Make sure that account *60130 Repairs and Maintenance* is entered in the *Account* field. This account should automatically populate when *Dianne's Auto Shop* is selected.

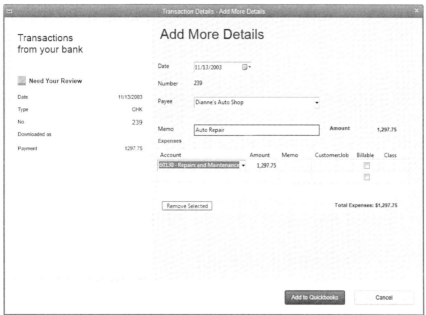

Figure 5-34 The Add Transactions To QuickBooks window

Step 3. Click the **Add to QuickBooks** button to accept the downloaded transaction into your QuickBooks file.

Step 4. Close the *Transaction List*.

Step 5. Close the *Bank Feeds* window

Review Questions

Comprehension Questions

1. Explain how QuickBooks calculates the *Beginning Balance* field in the *Begin Reconciliation* window. Why might the beginning balance calculated by QuickBooks differ from the beginning balance on your bank statement?

2. Explain why it's important not to change transactions in closed accounting periods.

3. How is the credit card reconciliation process different from the bank account reconciliation?

Multiple Choice

Select the best answer(s) for each of the following:

1. When the *Beginning Balance* field on the *Begin Reconciliation* window doesn't match the beginning balance on the bank statement, you should:
    a) Call the bank.
    b) Change the amount in QuickBooks to match the bank's amount.
    c) Click **Locate Discrepancies** in the *Begin Reconciliation* window. Click **Discrepancy Report** and/or **Previous Reports** to research what has been changed since the last reconciliation. Then fix the problem before reconciling.
    d) Select the **Banking** menu and then select *Enter Statement Charges*.

2. Which statement is false?
    a) You can enter bank service charges using *Enter Statement Charges*.
    b) You can enter bank service charges on the *Begin Reconciliation* window.
    c) You can enter bank service charges using the *Splits* button on a register transaction.
    d) You can enter bank service charges using *Write Checks* before you start your reconciliation.

3. When you find an erroneous amount on a transaction while reconciling, correct the amount by:
    a) Selecting the **Banking** menu and then selecting **Correct Error**.
    b) Double-clicking on the entry and changing the amount on the transaction.
    c) Selecting the entry in the **Reconcile** window, then clicking **Go To** and changing the amount on the transaction.
    d) Performing either b or c.

4. To properly record a voided check from a closed accounting period:
    a) Delete the check in the register.
    b) Make a deposit in the current period and code it to the same account as the original check you want to void. Then delete both transactions in the **Reconciliation** window.
    c) Find the check in the register, select the **Edit** Menu, and then select **Void Check**.
    d) Change the amount of the check to zero.

5. Which of the following columns cannot be displayed in the *Checks and Payments* section of the *Reconcile* window?
    a) Check #.
    b) Class.
    c) Date.
    d) Payee.

6. You know you have reconciled your bank account correctly when:
    a) You make a *Balance Adjustment* entry.
    b) The *Difference* field shows **0.00.**
    c) There are no more register entries to select in the *Reconcile* window.
    d) All of the above.

7. The Reconciliation Summary report shows:
    a) The Beginning Balance shown on the Bank Statement.
    b) Detail of all the entries for the month in the register.
    c) The Ending Balance shown in the register in QuickBooks.
    d) Both a and c.

8. What accounts should be reconciled?
    a) Any account that receives regular statements.
    b) Any bank, income or expense account.
    c) Only bank accounts can be reconciled.
    d) Reconciling is optional for all account types.

9. When you "undo" a bank reconciliation, which statement is true?
    a) Undoing a bank reconciliation does not affect the Beginning Balance.
    b) Balance Adjustments are deleted from the check register.
    c) Interest Income amounts that are entered during the prior bank reconciliation are deleted.
    d) Undoing a bank reconciliation does not delete the Bank Service Charges recorded on the "undone" bank reconciliation.

10. When a customer bounces a check, you should:
    a) Delete the *Deposit* that contained the bounced check.
    b) Mark the customer's invoice as *Unpaid*.
    c) Create an *Invoice* to the customer for NSF charges.
    d) Click the **Record Bounced Check** button in the *Receive Payments* window.

11. When you finish reconciling a credit card account, you:
    a) Can only create a check for the total amount due.
    b) Can create a check for an amount equal to or less than the total amount due.
    c) Cannot choose to bypass making a payment.
    d) Cannot choose to enter a bill for later payment.

12. What is the accounting behind the scenes for a Bill coded to a Credit Card liability account?
    a) Decrease (debit) Accounts Payable, Increase (credit) Credit Card liability.
    b) Decrease (debit) Accounts Payable, Decrease (credit) Credit Card liability.
    c) Increase (credit) Accounts Payable, Decrease (debit) Credit Card liability.
    d) Increase (credit) Accounts Payable, Increase (credit) Credit Card liability.

13. In what account is a transaction created if you complete a reconciliation and your difference is not 0.00?
    a) Opening Balance Equity.
    b) Uncategorized Income.
    c) Reconciliation Discrepancies.
    d) Other Expense.

14. When you void a check written in a closed accounting period, QuickBooks automatically creates:
    a) An adjustment in the *Reconciliation Discrepancies* account.
    b) A new check to be dated to the current date.
    c) Two journal entries in the closed accounting period.
    d) A journal entry in the closed accounting period and a journal entry during the open accounting period.

15. After notifying a customer that his check bounced, he asks you to deposit it again. What should you record in QuickBooks?
    a) Enter the same transactions as you would for any bounced check, and receive the check as a new payment or create a new deposit using the current date.
    b) Delete the original deposit.
    c) Change the date on the original deposit to the current date.
    d) You do not need to record the deposit in QuickBooks because the check was previously deposited.

Completion Statements

1. QuickBooks calculates the *Beginning Balance* field in the *Begin Reconciliation* window by adding and subtracting all previously _____ transactions.

2. Voiding, deleting or changing the amount of a transaction you previously cleared in a bank reconciliation causes the _____ _____ field on the *Begin Reconciliation* window to disagree with your bank statement.

3. The **Previous Reconciliation Discrepancy** report shows changes to cleared transactions since your most recent bank _____.

4. You don't want to change transactions dated in a(n) _____ accounting period because doing so would change net income in a period for which you have already issued _____ statements and/or filed the tax returns.

5. Banks and accountants often refer to bounced checks as _____ transactions.

Bank Reconciliation Problem 1

APPLYING YOUR KNOWLEDGE

Restore the BankRec-14Problem1.QBM file.

1. Using the sample bank statement shown below, reconcile the checking account for 01/31/2018.

Business Checking Account

Statement Date: January 31, 2018 — Page 1 of 1

Summary:

Previous Balance as of 12/31/17:	$	17,385.30
Total Deposits and Credits	+ $	4,561.08
Total Checks and Debits	- $	7,876.12
Statement Balance as of 1/31/18:	**= $**	**14,070.26**

Deposits and Other Credits:

DEPOSITS

Date	Description	Amount
12-Jan	Customer Deposit	$ 1,709.53
30-Jan	Customer Deposit	$ 2,848.27
	2 Deposits: $	**4,557.80**

INTEREST

Date	Description	Amount
31-Jan	Interest Earned	$ 3.28
	Interest: $	**3.28**

Checks and Other Withdrawals:

CHECKS PAID:

Check No.	Date Paid	Amount
325	2-Jan	$ 324.00
326	7-Jan	$ 276.52
327	17-Jan	$ 128.60
6001**	25-Jan	$ 3,000.00
6003**	25-Jan	$ 142.00
	5 Checks Paid: $	**3,871.12**

OTHER WITHDRAWALS/PAYMENTS

Date	Description	Amount
31-Jan	Transfer	$ 4,000.00
	1 Other Withdrawals/Payments: $	**4,000.00**

SERVICE CHARGES

Date	Description	Amount
31-Jan	Service Charge	$ 5.00
	1 Service Charge: $	**5.00**

Figure 5-35 Bank statement for January 31, 2018

2. Print a **Reconciliation Detail** report dated 1/31/2018.

Bank Reconciliation Problem 2 (Advanced)

APPLYING YOUR KNOWLEDGE

Restore the BankRec-14Problem2.QBM file.

Bank Reconciliation and Bank Transactions - Bank Reconciliation Problem 2 (Advanced)

187

1. Record a bounced check from Maria Cruz on **02/12/2018** (check #9563, received on 1/27/18 for Invoice #2018-105 and the Walnut Creek class). The amount of the check was **$880.00**. The bank charged you an NSF Fee of **$10.00**. Your company's NSF Charge is $20.00.

2. Enter the transactions necessary to record the receipt and redeposit of Maria Cruz's replacement check for $880.00 (Check #*9588*) that did **not** include the bounce charge. Date the payment *02/14/2018* and apply it to invoice #**2018-105**. Date the deposit on *02/14/2018*.

3. Using the sample bank statement shown below, reconcile the checking account for 02/28/2018.

Business Checking Account

Statement Date: **February 28, 2018**   Page 1 of 1

Summary:

Previous Balance as of 1/31/17:		$	14,070.26
Total Deposits and Credits: 6	+	$	5,800.46
Total Checks and Debits: 7	-	$	4,532.83
Statement Balance as of 2/28/18:	=	$	15,337.89

Deposits and Other Credits:

DEPOSITS

Date	Description	Amount
3-Feb	Customer Deposit	$ 119.08
4-Feb	Customer Deposit	$ 2,460.13
10-Feb	Customer Deposit	$ 809.03
11-Feb	Customer Deposit	$ 753.41
13-Feb	Customer Deposit	$ 775.98
14-Feb	Customer Deposit	$ 880.00
	6 Deposits:	$ 5,797.63

INTEREST

Date	Description	Amount
28-Feb	Interest Earned	$ 2.83
	Interest:	$ 2.83

Checks and Other Withdrawals:

CHECKS PAID:

Check No.	Date Paid	Amount
329	14-Feb	$ 2,152.00
330	15-Feb	$ 342.35
331	24-Feb	$ 375.00
332 **	28-Feb	$ 645.00
6004	2-Feb	$ 123.48
	5 Checks Paid:	$ 3,637.83

OTHER WITHDRAWALS/PAYMENTS

Date	Description	Amount
12-Feb	Returned Item	$ 880.00
12-Feb	NSF Charge	$ 10.00
	2 Other Withdrawals/Payments:	$ 890.00

SERVICE CHARGES

Date	Description	Amount
28-Feb	Service Charge	$ 5.00
	1 Service Charge:	$ 5.00

Figure 5-36 Bank statement for February 28, 2018

4. Print a *Reconciliation Detail* report dated 02/28/2018.

5. Print a customer *Statement* for Maria Cruz's Branch Opening job for the period 01/1/2018 through 02/28/2018.

QUICKBOOKS AND BEYOND – *TAKE THE NEXT STEP WITH THE SLEETER GROUP BLOG*

"Cloud Accounting Comparison – Introduction"

Greg Lam writes in this blog post, "I started reviewing cloud accounting software in 2012 as an effort to figure out how to work with my clients more efficiently. I had tried networking computers with VPNs, logging in to clients' computers remotely, and even tried using QuickBooks in Dropbox, but all those solutions didn't work for one reason or another. Enter cloud accounting software."

In this *QuickBooks and Beyond* section, Greg Lam introduces several different cloud accounting applications. This is the first of several posts that review each of these applications. Read the full post at www.sleeter.com/blog/?p=7201.

New Terminology

VPN – Virtual Private Network, or a private network that uses a public network infrastructure, such as the Internet.

Dropbox – A company that provides free online storage.

Putting New Knowledge to Use

1. What criteria would you use to evaluate your company's needs from its accounting software?

Chapter 6
Reports

Topics

In this chapter, you will learn about the following topics:
- Types of Reports (page 189)
- Cash Versus Accrual Reports (page 190)
- Accounting Reports (page 192)
- Business Management Reports (page 202)
- QuickBooks Graphs (page 207)
- Building Custom Reports (page 209)
- Memorizing Reports (page 215)
- Processing Multiple Reports (page 217)
- Finding Transactions (page 218)
- Exporting Reports to Spreadsheets (page 225)

> **Restore this File:**
> This chapter uses Reports-14.QBW. To open this file, restore the Reports-14.QBM file to your hard disk. See page 9 for instructions on restoring files.

QuickBooks reports allow you to get the information you need to make critical business decisions. In this chapter, you'll learn how to create a variety of reports to help you manage your business. Every report in QuickBooks gives you immediate, up-to-date information about your company's performance.

There are literally hundreds of reports available in QuickBooks. In addition to the built-in reports, you can *modify* reports to include or exclude whatever data you want. To control the look of your reports, you can customize the formatting of headers, footers, fonts, or columns. When you get a report looking just the way you want, you can *memorize* it so that you can quickly create it again later. Or you can export it into a spreadsheet program for more customization.

This chapter also looks at the different search features to allow you to find transactions.

Types of Reports

There are two major types of reports in QuickBooks – accounting reports and business management reports. In addition, most reports have both "detail" and "summary" styles. Detail reports show individual transactions and summary reports show totals for a group of transactions.

Accounting reports contain information about transactions and accounts. For example, the *Profit & Loss* report is a summary report of all transactions coded to income and expense accounts for a specified period of time. Your accountant or tax preparer will need several accounting reports from QuickBooks in order to provide accounting and tax services for your company.

Business management reports are used to monitor different activities of a business to help plan workflow and review transactions that have already occurred. These reports provide critical information that you need to operate your business. For example, the *Customer Contact List* report shows addresses, phone numbers, and other information about Customers.

Report Type	Example Reports
Accounting	Profit & Loss, Balance Sheet, Trial Balance, Cash Flow Forecast, General Ledger, Trial Balance
Business Management	Open Invoices, Unpaid Bills Detail, Check Detail, Sales by Item Detail, Item Profitability, Customer Contact List, Item Price List, Time by Name, Stock Status by Item

Table 6-1 Types of QuickBooks reports

Cash Versus Accrual Reports

QuickBooks can automatically convert reports from the accrual basis to the cash basis, depending on how you set your Preferences or how you customize reports.

If you use cash basis accounting, you regard income or expenses as occurring at the time you actually receive a payment from a customer or pay a bill from a vendor. The cash basis records (or recognizes) income or expense only when cash is received or paid, no matter when the original transaction occurred. If you use accrual basis accounting, you regard income or expenses as occurring at the time you ship a product, render a service, or receive a bill from your vendors. Under this method, the date that you enter a transaction and the date that you actually pay or receive cash may be two separate dates, but income (or expense) is recognized on the day of the original transaction.

You can set the default for all QuickBooks summary reports to the cash or accrual basis by selecting *Cash* or *Accrual* in the *Summary Reports Basis* section of the *Reports & Graphs Preferences* window. Follow these steps:

COMPUTER PRACTICE

Step 1. Select the **Edit** menu and then select **Preferences**.

Step 2. Click on the **Reports and Graphs** preference.

Step 3. Click the Company Preferences tab.

> **Note:**
> If you are in multi-user mode you will need to first switch to single-user mode to change company preferences.

Step 4. To set the basis to match your company's finances, click **Cash** or **Accrual** in the *Summary Reports Basis* section (see Figure 6-1). For this chapter, leave the basis set to **Accrual**.

> **Note:**
> You can also change the default font size and font color on your reports using the *Reports & Graphs Company Preferences*. Click the **Format** button in the *Preferences* window.

Step 5. Click **OK** to save your changes (if any) and close the *Preferences* window.

> **Did You Know?**
> In QuickBooks, you can leave the *Reporting Preferences* set to the accrual basis for internal management reporting purposes and then create cash-basis reports for tax purposes.

Irrespective of the default setting in your *Preferences*, you can always switch between cash and accrual reports by modifying reports. To convert the report basis from accrual to cash on any report, follow these steps:

Reports - Cash Versus Accrual Reports

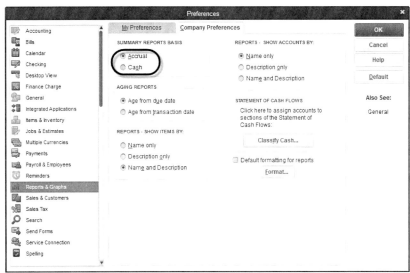

Figure 6-1 Preferences for Reports and Graphs

COMPUTER PRACTICE

Step 1. Click the *Reports* icon on the *Icon Bar*. There are three different views for previewing the reports, *Carousel*, *List,* and *Grid*.

Step 2. Click on **Carousel View** in the upper right corner of the *Report Center*.

Step 3. Select **Company & Financial** from the list on the left of the window, if it is not already selected. *Profit & Loss Standard* is the first report (see Figure 6-2).

You can choose other reports by moving the slider at the bottom of the window. You can also choose a date range from the *Dates* fields at the bottom of the window.

Step 4. Double click the **Profit & Loss Standard** report image in the *Report Center*.

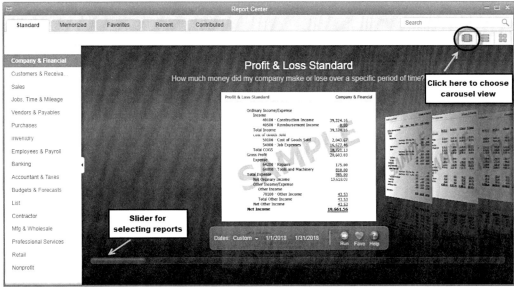

Figure 6-2 Carousel View in the Report Center

Step 5. Click the **Customize Report** button at the top left of the *Profit & Loss* window.

Step 6. Set the *Dates* fields From *01/01/2018* and To *01/31/2018*. Press **Tab**.

Step 7. Click **Cash** in the *Report Basis* section (see Figure 6-3).

Step 8. Click **OK** to save your changes and display a Cash Basis *Profit & Loss* report for January 2018.

Step 9. Close the *Profit & Loss* report window.

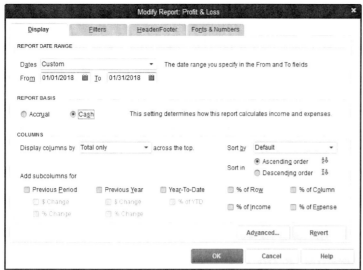

Figure 6-3 Select the Cash report basis in the Modify Report window

Accounting Reports

There are several built-in reports that summarize a group of transactions. These reports help you analyze the performance of your business.

Profit & Loss

The *Profit & Loss* report (also referred to as the *Income Statement*) shows all your income and expenses for a given period. As discussed earlier, the goal of accounting is to provide the financial information you need to measure the success (or failure) of your organization, as well as to file proper tax returns. The *Profit & Loss* report is one of the most valuable sources of this financial information.

COMPUTER PRACTICE

Step 1. From the *Report Center*, click **Grid View** to choose a report from a different view (see Figure 6-4).

Step 2. Select **Company & Financial** from the list on the left of the window if it is not already selected, and then double click the **Profit & Loss Standard** report in the upper left of the Grid View.

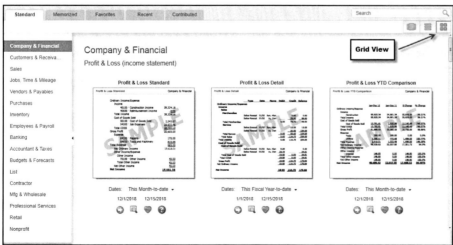

Figure 6-4 Grid View of the Report Center

Step 3.   Set the *Dates* fields *From 01/01/2018* and *To 01/31/2018*. Press **Tab**.

Step 4.   The *Profit & Loss* report (see Figure 6-5) summarizes the totals of all your *Income* accounts, followed by *Cost of Goods Sold* accounts, then *Expenses*, then *Other Income*, and finally *Other Expenses*. The total at the bottom of the report is your *Net Income* (or loss) for the period you specified in the *Dates* fields. The *Profit & Loss* report is a company's operating results, normally for a period of 12 months or less.

Note that the window shown in Figure 6-5 is not the complete report. You will have to scroll down to see the remainder of the report. Do not close this report.

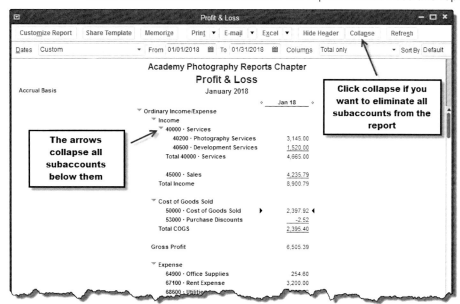

Figure 6-5 Upper portion of the Profit & Loss report (scroll down to see the remainder)

Analyzing the Profit & Loss Report

The first section of the *Profit & Loss* report shows the total of each of your income accounts for the period specified on the report. If you have subaccounts, QuickBooks indents those accounts on the report and subtotals them. Notice on Figure 6-5 that the *Services* income category has two subaccounts: *Photography Services* and *Development Services*. To hide subaccounts on this report (or any summary report), click the *Collapse* button at the top of the report.

The next section of the report shows your *Cost of Goods Sold* accounts. You use these accounts to record the costs of the products and services you sell in your business (e.g., inventory, cost of labor, etc.). If you use *Inventory Items*, QuickBooks calculates *Cost of Goods Sold* as each *Inventory Item* is sold, using the *average cost method*.

The next section of the report shows your expenses of the business. Use these accounts to record costs associated with operating your business (e.g., rent, salaries, supplies, etc.). Expenses are generally recorded in QuickBooks as you write checks or enter bills, but can also be recorded directly into a register or as a journal entry.

The next section of the report shows your *Other Income/Expenses* accounts. Use these accounts to record income and expenses that are generated outside the normal operation of your business. For example, if you provide accounting services but sold an old business computer, the income generated from the sale would be classified as *Other Income* because it was generated outside the normal operation of your business.

At the bottom of the report, QuickBooks calculates your *Net Income* – the amount of your revenue less your Cost of Goods Sold and your operating expenses. You may want to view your expenses (such as rent, office supplies, employee salaries, etc.) as a percentage of total income to help you locate excessive expenses in your business.

COMPUTER PRACTICE

Step 1.	Click the **Customize Report** button at the top left of the *Profit & Loss* report.

Step 2.	Click the **% of Income** box (see Figure 6-6).

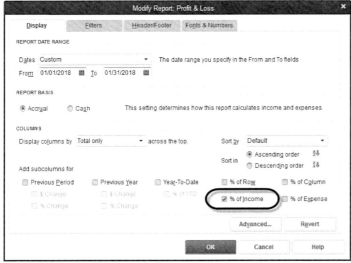

Figure 6-6 The Modify Report window

Step 3.	Click OK.

The *Profit & Loss* report now has a *% of Income* column (see Figure 6-7), allowing you to quickly identify numbers that deviate from the norm. Familiarize yourself with the percentages of expenses in your business and review this report periodically to make sure you stay in control of your expenses.

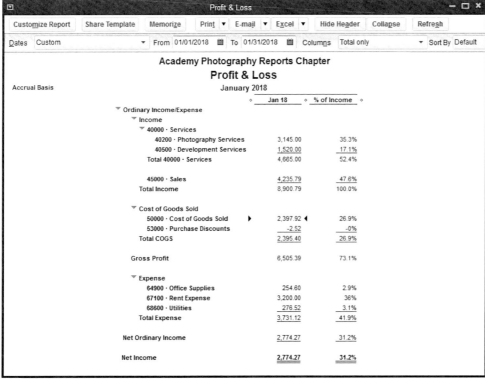

Figure 6-7 Modified Profit & Loss report

Step 4. To find the details behind any of these numbers, you can use *QuickZoom* (explained on page 224). Double-click the *Cost of Goods Sold* line item amount of **2,397.92** in the report (see Figure 6-7).

The report shown in Figure 6-8 shows each transaction coded to the *Cost of Goods Sold* account. Double-click on any of these numbers to see the actual transaction.

Figure 6-8 Transaction Detail by Account report for the Cost of Goods Sold account

Step 5. Close both open reports.

Profit & Loss by Class Report

To divide your *Profit & Loss* report into departments (or Classes), use the *Profit & Loss by Class* report.

COMPUTER PRACTICE

Step 1. From the *Report Center*, click the *List* view (see Figure 6-9)

Step 2. Select **Company & Financial** from the menu on the left if it is not already selected, then double click the **Profit & Loss By Class** report in the *Profit & Loss (income statement)* section.

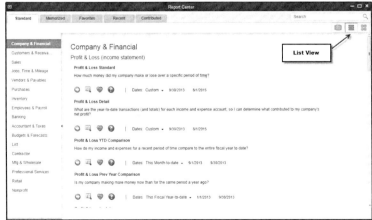

Figure 6-9 List View in the Report Center

Step 3. Enter *01/01/2018* in the *From* field, enter *01/31/2018* in the *To* field at the top of the report, and press **Tab**.

Step 4. Your report should look like the one shown in Figure 6-10. Notice that totals for each Class are displayed in a separate column.

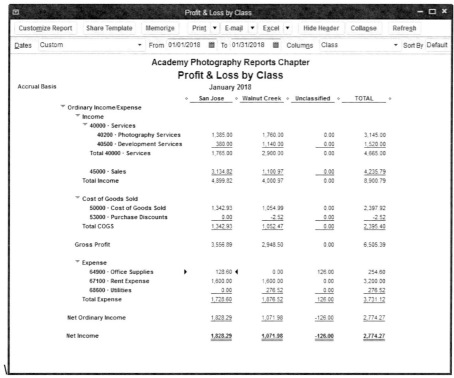

Figure 6-10 Profit and Loss by Class report

This report includes an *Unclassified* column, as shown in Figure 6-10, which means that some of the transactions were not assigned a Class. To classify the unclassified transactions, follow these steps:

Step 5. Double-click to QuickZoom on the 126.00 amount in the *Unclassified* column under Office Supplies. This will bring up the *Transaction Detail by Account* report.

Step 6. Double-click to QuickZoom on the 126.00 amount again. This opens the *Bill* from Ace Supply.

Step 7. Assign the Class **San Jose** to the *Bill* as shown in Figure 6-11.

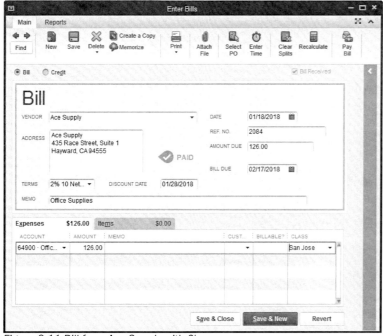

Figure 6-11 Bill from Ace Supply with Class

Step 8. Save and Close the *Bill*.

Step 9. The *Report needs to be refreshed* window appears. Click **Yes** to refresh the open reports.

Step 10. Close the *Transaction Detail by Account* report. Notice the *Profit & Loss by Class* report no longer has an *Unclassified* column (see Figure 6-12).

Step 11. Close the Profit & Loss by Class report.

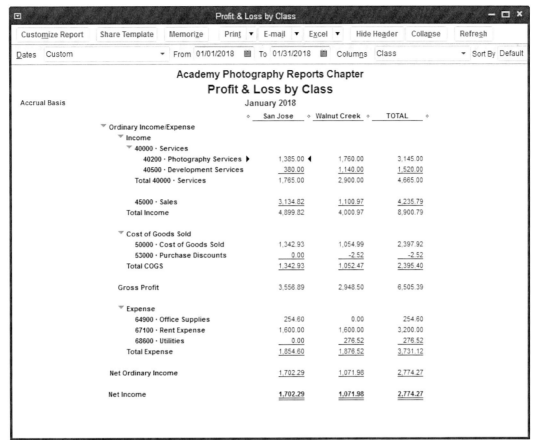

Figure 6-12 Profit & Loss by Class without Unclassified Column

> **Note:**
> When using Classes, be sure to always enter the Class as you are recording each transaction. This prevents any transaction from being recorded as "Unclassified." For transactions that do not fall within the normal operating activities of one of the classes in your company file, use a general Class such as *Overhead*.

To ensure that transactions are always assigned to Classes, set *Preferences* so that QuickBooks will prompt you to assign a Class before completing the transaction. To learn more about these *Preferences*, see page 285.

Profit & Loss by Job Report

To divide your *Profit & Loss* report into *Customers* or *Jobs*, use the *Profit & Loss by Job* report. This report, sometimes called the Job Cost report, allows you to see your profitability for each *Customer* or *Job*. This information helps you to spot pricing problems, as well as costs that are out of the ordinary. For example, if this report showed that you lost money on all the Jobs where you did an outdoor session, you would probably want to adjust your prices for outdoor photo shoots. Similarly, if the cost on one Job is significantly higher or lower than other Jobs of similar size, you might look closer at that Job to see if adjustments are needed to control costs.

COMPUTER PRACTICE

To create a *Profit & Loss by Job* report, follow these steps:

Step 1.   From the *Report Center*, select **Company & Financial** and then double click the **Profit & Loss By Job** link in the *Profit & Loss (income statement)* section.

Step 2.   Enter *01/01/2018* in the *From* field, enter *01/31/2018* in the *To* field, and press **Tab** (see Figure 6-13).

Step 3.   After you view the *Profit & Loss by Job* report, close all open report windows.

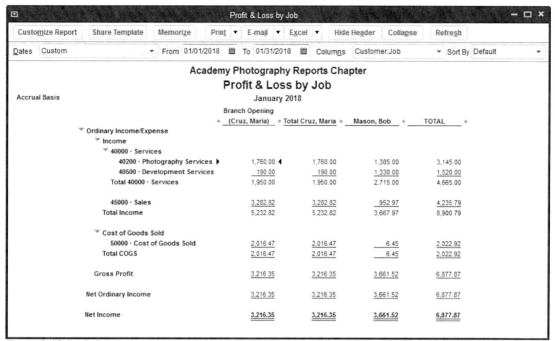

Figure 6-13 Profit & Loss by Job report

> **Note:**
> New with QuickBooks 2014, you can filter *Job Status* in reports, for example to examine the profitability of closed jobs. For more on filtering reports, see page 209.

Balance Sheet

Another important report for analyzing your business is the *Balance Sheet*. The Balance Sheet shows your financial position, as defined by the balances in each of your assets, liabilities, and equity accounts on a given date.

COMPUTER PRACTICE

Step 1.   From the *Report Center*, select **Company & Financial** and then double click the **Balance Sheet Standard** report in the *Balance Sheet & Net Worth* section. You may need to scroll down.

Step 2.   Enter *01/31/2018* in the *As of* field and press **Tab**. In Figure 6-14, you can see a portion of the *Balance Sheet* for Academy Photography on 01/31/2018.

> **Tip:**
> Familiarize yourself with how your Balance Sheet changes throughout the year. Banks examine this report very closely before approving loans. Often, the bank will calculate the ratio of your current assets divided by your current liabilities. This ratio, known as the current ratio, measures your ability to satisfy your debts.

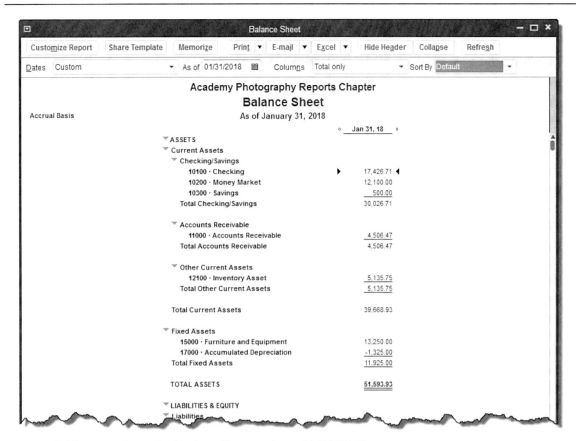

Figure 6-14 Balance Sheet for Academy Photography on 01/31/2018

Statement of Cash Flows

The *Statement of Cash Flows* provides information about the cash receipts and cash payments of your business during a given period. In addition, it provides information about investing and financing activities, such as purchasing equipment or borrowing. The *Statement of Cash Flows* shows the detail of how you spent the cash shown on the company's *Balance Sheet*.

COMPUTER PRACTICE

Step 1. From the *Report Center*, select **Company & Financial** and then double click the **Statement of Cash Flows** report in the *Cash Flow* section.

Step 2. Enter *01/01/2018* in the *From* field, enter *01/31/2018* in the *To* field, and press **Tab**.

On the report shown in Figure 6-15, you can see that although there was a net income of $2,774.27, there was a net decrease in cash of $532.89 during the first month of the year. Bankers look closely at this report to determine if your business is able to generate a positive cash flow, or if your business requires additional capital to satisfy its cash needs.

Step 3. After you view the *Statement of Cash Flows* report, close all open report windows.

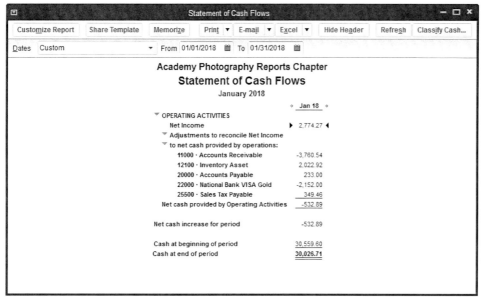

Figure 6-15 Statement of Cash Flows report

General Ledger

The *General Ledger* shows you all of the activity in all of your accounts for a specific period.

COMPUTER PRACTICE

Step 1. From the *Report Center*, select **Accountant & Taxes** from the list of report categories on the left of the window and then double click the **General Ledger** report in the *Account Activity* section. If the *Collapsing and Expanding Transactions* window appears, read it and click **OK**.

Step 2. Enter *01/01/2018* in the *From* field, enter *01/31/2018* in the *To* field, and press **Tab** (see Figure 6-16).

Step 3. Close the *General Ledger* report.

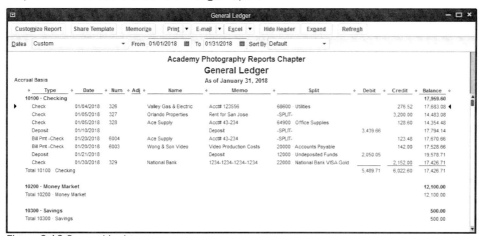

Figure 6-16 General Ledger

> **Note:**
> The *General Ledger* is a very long report. Every account, even accounts that have a zero balance or that have never been used, are included by default. You can condense the report to only show accounts with a balance by selecting the *In Use* option in the *Advanced Options* window (see Figure 6-17). You can open the *Advanced Options* window from the *Advanced* button in the *Modify Reports* window.

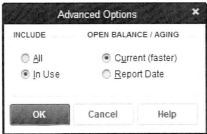

Figure 6-17 Advanced Options window

Trial Balance

The *Trial Balance* report shows the balance of each of the accounts as of a certain date. The report shows these balances in a Debit and Credit format. Your accountant will usually prepare this report at the end of each fiscal year.

COMPUTER PRACTICE

Step 1. From the *Report Center*, select **Accountant & Taxes** and then double click the **Trial Balance** report in the *Account Activity* section.

Step 2. Enter *01/01/2018* in the *From* field, enter *01/31/2018* in the *To,* field and press **Tab** (see Figure 6-18).

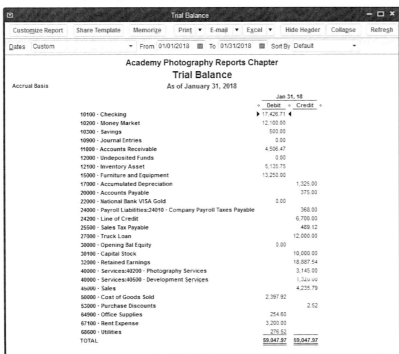

Figure 6-18 Trial Balance - Balance of each account as of a specific date

Step 3. Close all open reports.

Voided/Deleted Transactions Summary Reports

The *Voided/Deleted Transactions Summary* report shows transactions that have been voided or deleted in the data file. This report assists accountants in detecting errors or fraud and are available under the *Accountant & Taxes* submenu of the *Reports* menu. This feature is very useful when you have a number of users in a file and transactions seem to "disappear" or change without explanation. The standard version of this report presents the transactions in a summary format (see Figure 6-19).

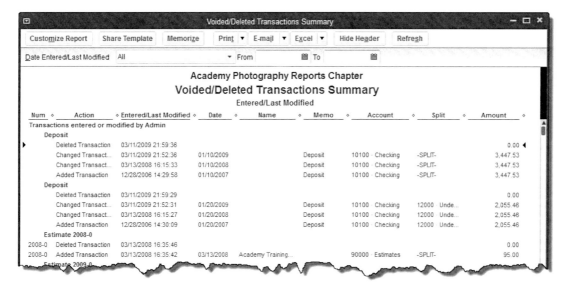

Figure 6-19 Voided/Deleted Transactions Report

The *Voided/Deleted Transactions Detail* report shows all of the line items associated with each affected transaction. This feature makes the original transaction information available so that it can be recreated if necessary (see Figure 6-20).

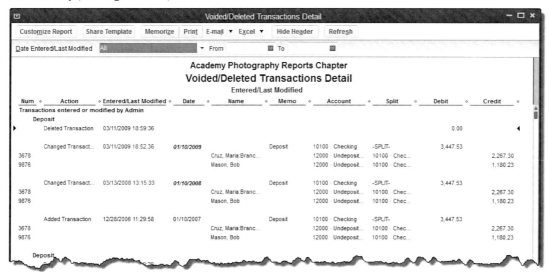

Figure 6-20 Voided/Deleted Transactions Detail Report

Business Management Reports

In the following Computer Practice exercises, you will use QuickBooks to create several different reports that help you manage your business.

Customer Phone List

The *Customer Phone List* shown in Figure 6-21 is a listing of each of your customers and their phone numbers. To create this report, follow these steps:

COMPUTER PRACTICE

Step 1. From the *Report Center*, select **List** and then double click the **Customer Phone List** report in the *Customer* section to display the report (see Figure 6-21).

Figure 6-21 Customer Phone List report

Vendor Contact List

The *Vendor Contact List* shown in Figure 6-22 is a listing of your vendors along with each vendor's contact information. To create this report, follow these steps:

COMPUTER PRACTICE

Step 1.   From the *Report Center*, select **List** and then double click the **Vendor Contact List** report in the *Vendor* section to display the report (see Figure 6-22).

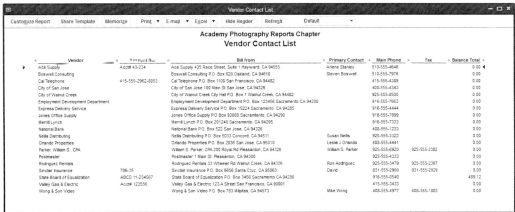

Figure 6-22 Vendor Contact List report

Item Price List

The *Item Price List* shown in Figure 6-23 is a listing of your *Items*. To create this report, follow these steps:

COMPUTER PRACTICE

Step 1. From the *Report Center*, select **List** and then double click the **Item Price List** report in the *Listing* section to display the report (see Figure 6-23).

Step 2. After viewing the **Item Price List** report, close all open report windows. Click **No** if QuickBooks prompts you to memorize the reports.

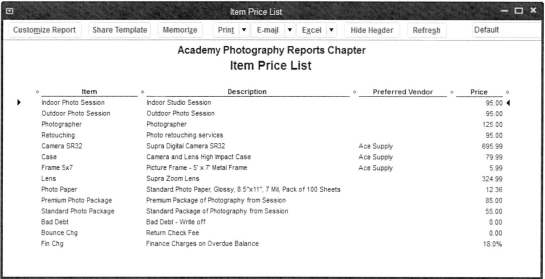

Figure 6-23 Item Price List report

Check Detail Report

The *Check Detail* report is quite valuable if you use accounts payable or payroll. It is frequently necessary to see what expense account(s) are associated with a bill payment. However, the *Register* report only shows that bill payments are associated with accounts payable. That's because a bill payment only involves the checking account and accounts payable. Similarly, paychecks only show in the register report as "Split" transactions because several accounts are associated with each paycheck. The *Check Detail* report shows the detailed expense account information about these types of transactions.

COMPUTER PRACTICE

Step 1. From the *Report Center*, select **Banking** and then double click the **Check Detail** report in the *Banking* section.

Step 2. Enter *01/01/2018* in the *From* field and enter *01/31/2018* in the *To* field. Then, press **Tab**.

Step 3. Scroll down until you see Bill Pmt -Check 6004 (near the bottom of the report).

In Figure 6-24, notice bill payment number 6004. The report shows that QuickBooks split the total amount due of $126.00 between the accounts payable account ($2.52) and the checking account ($123.48).

The amount for $-2.52 is the discount that you took when you paid the *Bill*. Although this report does not show it, you coded this amount to the Purchase Discounts account.

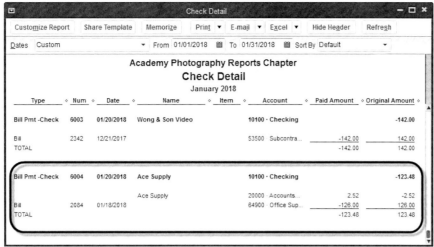

Figure 6-24 Check Detail report

Step 4. Close all open report windows. Click **No** if QuickBooks prompts you to memorize the reports.

> **Tip:**
> In order to make your *Check Detail* reports easier to read and understand, consider recording your purchase discounts differently. Instead of taking the discount on the *Pay Bills* window (as you did in the example on page 125), consider recording your purchase discounts using *Bill Credits*.

Accounts Receivable and Accounts Payable Reports

There are several reports that you can use to keep track of the money that your Customers owe you (*accounts receivable*) and the money that you owe to your vendors (*accounts payable*).

Collections Report

The *Collections Report* is a report that shows each Customer's outstanding *Invoices* along with the Customer's telephone number.

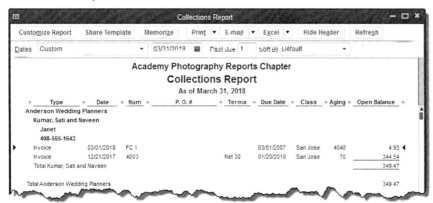

Figure 6-25 Accounts Receivable Collections Report

COMPUTER PRACTICE

Step 1. From the *Report Center*, select **Customers & Receivables** and then double click the **Collections Report** in the *A/R Aging* section.

Step 2. Enter *03/31/2018* in the *Dates* field and press **Tab** (see Figure 6-25).

Customer Balance Detail Report

Use the *Customer Balance Detail* report to see the details of each Customer's transactions and payments. This report shows all transactions that use the accounts receivable account, including *Invoices, Payments, Discounts,* and *Finance Charges.*

COMPUTER PRACTICE

Step 1. From the *Report Center*, select **Customers & Receivables** and then double click the **Customer Balance Detail** report in the *Customer Balance* section (see Figure 6-26). The *Dates* field on this report defaults to *All*.

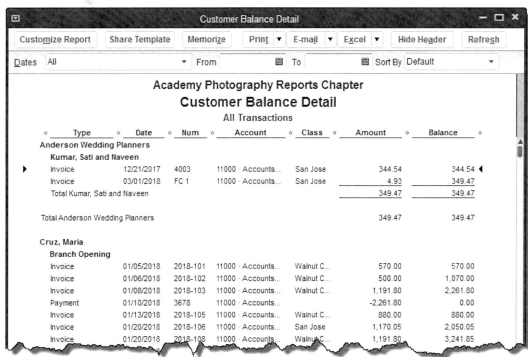

Figure 6-26 Customer Balance Detail report

Vendor Balance Detail Report

The *Vendor Balance Detail* report is similar to the *Customer Balance Detail* report, but it shows transactions that use *Accounts Payable*, including *Bills, Bill Credits, Bill Payments,* and *Discounts*.

COMPUTER PRACTICE

Step 1. From the *Report Center*, select **Vendors & Payables** and then double click the **Vendor Balance Detail** report in the *Vendor Balances* section (see Figure 6-27). The *Dates* field on this report defaults to *All*.

Step 2. Close all open report windows.

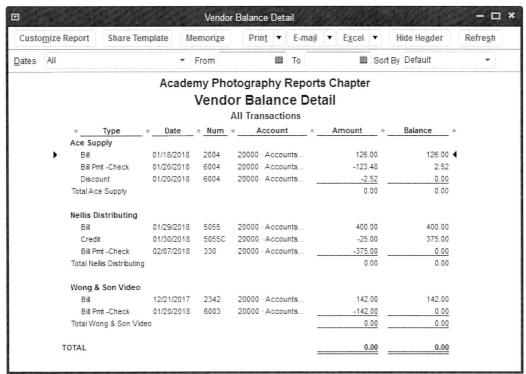

Figure 6-27 Vendor Balance Detail report

QuickBooks Graphs

One of the best ways to quickly get information from QuickBooks is to create a graph.

The *Income and Expense Graph* shows your income and expenses by month, and displays a pie chart showing a summary of your expenses.

COMPUTER PRACTICE

Step 1. From the *Report Center*, select **Company & Financial** and then double click **Income and Expense Graph** in the *Income & Expenses* section.

Step 2. Click **Dates** at the top left of the graph.

QuickBooks will display the *Change Graph Dates* window (see Figure 6-28).

Figure 6-28 Enter the dates for your graph in the window.

Step 3. Enter *01/01/2018* in the *From* field and enter *01/31/2018* in the *To* field. Then, click **OK**.

Step 4. QuickBooks displays the graph shown in Figure 6-29.

Step 5. After viewing the graph, close the graph window.

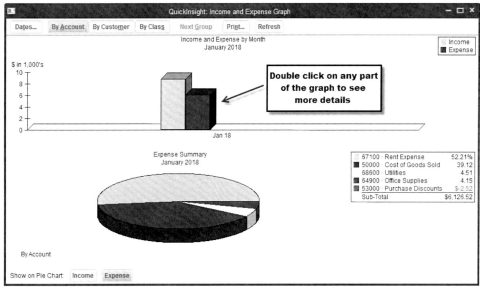

Figure 6-29 Income and Expense by Month graph

QuickBooks graphs highlight interesting facts about your company that are not easy to see from normal reports. For example, you can create a graph that shows your largest Customers or your biggest selling Items, and then you can visually inspect the relative sizes of each section of the graph.

COMPUTER PRACTICE

Step 1. From the *Report Center*, select **Sales** and then double click **Sales Graph** in the *Sales by Customer* section (see Figure 6-30).

Step 2. Click **Dates** at the top left of the graph. QuickBooks will display the *Change Graph Dates* window. Press **Tab**.

Step 3. Enter *01/01/2018* in the *From* field, enter *02/28/2018* in the *To* field, and click **OK**.

Step 4. Click the **By Customer** button on the top of the *QuickInsight: Sales Graph* window. This redraws the graph to show sales by Customer.

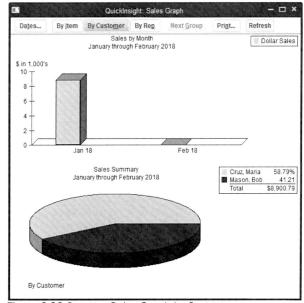

Figure 6-30 Create a Sales Graph by Customer

Step 5. After viewing the graph, close the window.

Building Custom Reports

To make reports that show only the information you want, you can modify (i.e., customize) an existing report. All reports include at least some modification and filtering options, so familiarize yourself with the tabs in the *Modify Report* window as they are described below.

The *Modify Report* window displays when you click the *Customize Report* button on any report. Four tabs make up the *Modify Report* window. Use the *Display* tab to change the date range, select a report basis, add or delete columns, change how columns are displayed, or add subcolumns on a report. The *Display* tab will show different sections depending upon the report being modified. For example, the *Display* tab for a *Profit and Loss* report does not allow you to select or deselect columns for the report (see Figure 6-31), while the *Display* tab for an *Item Price List* only allows you to select or deselect columns for the report (see Figure 6-32). The *Display* tab shows those sections particular to the report being modified.

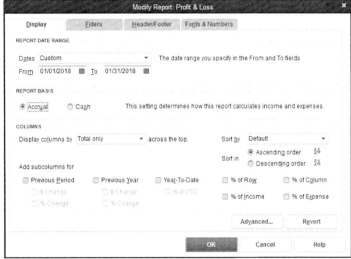

Figure 6-31 Display tab on the Modify Report: Profit & Loss window

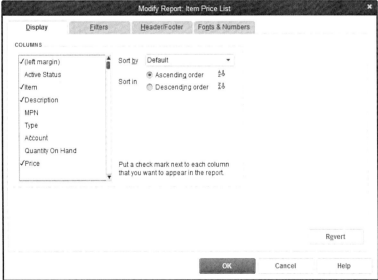

Figure 6-32 Display tab on the Modify Report: Item Price List window

Use the *Filters* tab to narrow the contents of the report so that you can analyze specific areas of your business. On the *Filters* tab, you can filter or choose specific accounts, dates, names, or Items to include in the report (see Figure 6-33).

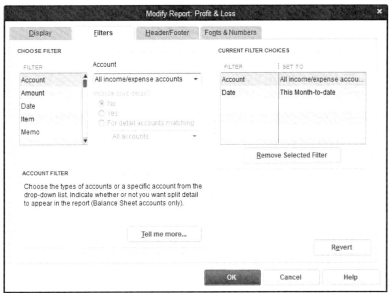

Figure 6-33 Filters tab on The Modify Report: Profit & Loss window

Use the *Header/Footer* tab to select which headers and footers will display on the report. In addition, the *Header/Footer* tab allows you to modify the *Company Name*, *Report Title*, *Subtitle*, *Date Prepared*, *Page Number*, and *Extra Footer Line* (see Figure 6-34).

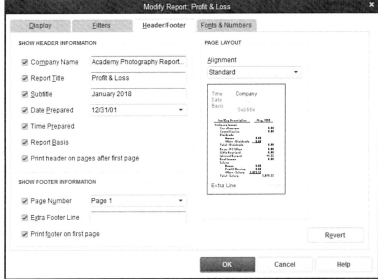

Figure 6-34 Header/Footer tab on The Modify Report: Profit & Loss window

Use the *Fonts & Numbers* tab to change the font and how numbers are displayed on the report. In addition, the *Fonts & Numbers* tab allows you to reduce numbers to multiples of 1000, hide amounts of 0.00, and show dollar amounts without cents (see Figure 6-35).

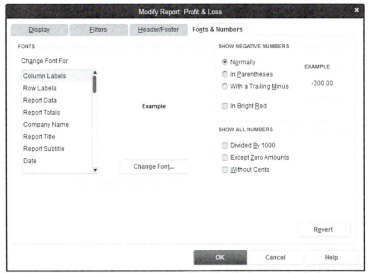
Figure 6-35 Fonts & Numbers tab on The Modify Report: Profit & Loss window

To practice modifying reports, suppose you want to get a report of all transactions that include all *Service Items* (*Photography Service* and *Development Services*) that you sold to Customers who live in *Walnut Creek* during January and February of 2018. In addition, you want QuickBooks to sort and total the report by Customer. The report should only display the type of transaction, the date, transaction number, customer name, city, Item, account, credit and debit. Finally, the report should be titled *Sales of Services to Walnut Creek Customers*.

> **Note:**
> Although Academy Photography uses Classes to track which store their Customers buy from, we want a report about where customers *live*. Specifically, we want the *City* from the Customer's address. This information comes from the field called "Name City" that is used as part of the Customer's billing address.

COMPUTER PRACTICE

Begin by creating a *Custom Transaction Detail* report and then modify the report so that it provides the information you need.

Step 1. From the *Reports* menu, select **Transaction Detail** from the *Custom Report* submenu. The **Modify Report: Custom Transaction Detail Report** window displays.

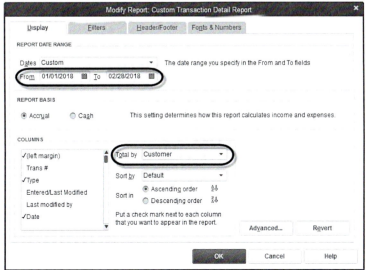
Figure 6-36 Modify Report: Custom Transaction Detail Report window

Step 2.   Enter *01/01/2018* in the *From* field and enter *02/28/2018* in the *To* field.

Step 3.   Select **Customer** from the *Total by* drop-down list and click **OK**.

This report will now show all transactions during January and February, totaled by Customer (see Figure 6-37).

Figure 6-37 Transaction Detail by Account report totaled by Customer

For our purposes there are four problems with this report:

- The report shows more columns than we want to display.
- The report shows all transactions, not just the Service Items sold to Customers.
- The report is not filtered to only show Customers who live in Walnut Creek.
- The report has the wrong title.

We will modify the report to correct the four problems listed above.

Step 4.   Click Customize Report.

Step 5.   In the **Columns** section of the *Display* tab, notice that several fields have check marks (see Figure 6-38). The check marks indicate which columns show on the report. Select **Name City** and **Item** to turn those columns on. Then deselect **Memo, Class, Clr, Split,** and **Balance**. You will need to scroll up and down in the list to find each field.

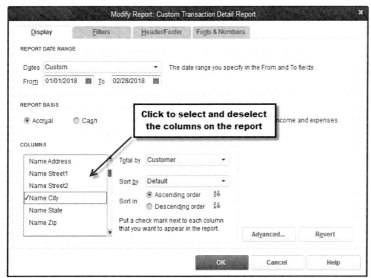

Figure 6-38 Modify columns by checking and unchecking lines in the Columns list

Reports - Building Custom Reports

> **Note:**
> There are several other settings on the **Display** tab that you can choose if you want to modify the report further. For example, you could change the basis of the report from Accrual to Cash, or you could set the sorting preferences. Click the **Advanced** button for even more settings. Explore these settings to learn how they affect your reports. For descriptions of each selection, use the QuickBooks **Help** menu.

Step 6. Click the **Filters** tab.

Step 7. To filter the report so that it includes only Service Items, select the **Item** filter in the *Choose Filter* section and select **All services** from the *Item* drop-down list (see Figure 6-39) to show only the transactions that involve **service** items.

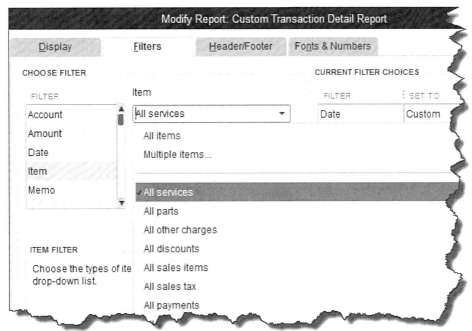

Figure 6-39 Item drop-down list in the Filters window

Step 8. To filter the report so that it includes only those Customers who live in Walnut Creek, scroll down the *Choose Filter* section and select the **Name City** filter. This displays a **Name City** field to the right of the *Choose Filter* section. Enter *Walnut Creek* in the **Name City** field (see Figure 6-40). Press the **Tab** key.

> **Did You Know?**
> Many fields on the Filter tab act like wildcards. If you enter a portion of the text in a field for a particular filter, QuickBooks will display all records containing that text. For example, if you only type in *nut* or *eek* in the *City* field, all customer records in the city of Walnut Creek will still display, but other cities that contain *nut* or *eek* in their names will also appear. Therefore, be careful when using a wildcard in a field because it can produce an unintended result.

Figure 6-40 Entering a filter for a report

Step 9. Click the **Header/Footer** tab on the *Modify Report* window.

Step 10. To modify the title of the report so that it accurately describes the content of the report, enter *Sales of Services to Walnut Creek Customers* in the *Report Title* field as shown in Figure 6-41.

Step 11. Click **OK** on the *Modify Report* window.

> DO NOT CLOSE THE REPORT. YOU WILL USE IT IN THE NEXT PRACTICE.

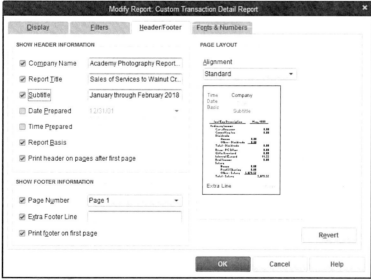

Figure 6-41 Change the report title on the Header/Footer tab

In Figure 6-42 you can see your modified report. Notice that its heading reflects its new content. You can modify the width of columns by dragging the diamond on the top right of the column to reduce or expand the width. Also, if you want to move a column left or right, move your cursor over the column header until you see the hand icon. Then, hold your left mouse button down as you drag the column to the left or right.

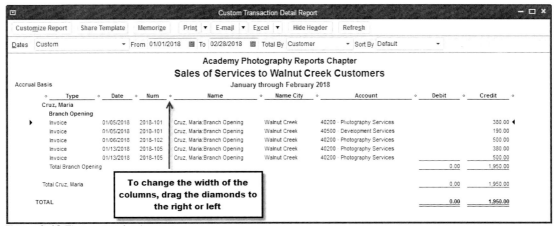

Figure 6-42 The customized report

Memorizing Reports

After you have modified a report, you can *memorize* the format and filtering so that you don't have to perform all of the modification steps the next time you want to view the report.

> **Note:**
> Memorizing a report does not memorize the data on the report, only the format, dates, and filtering.

If you enter specific dates, QuickBooks will use those dates the next time you bring up the report. However, if you select a *relative* date range in the *Dates* field (e.g., Last Fiscal Quarter, Last Year, or This Year to Date) before memorizing a report, QuickBooks will use the relative dates the next time you create the report.

For example, if you memorize a report with the *Dates* field set to *This Fiscal Quarter*, that report will always use dates for the current fiscal quarter as of the date you run the memorized report (see Figure 6-43).

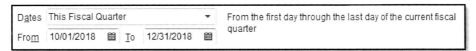

Figure 6-43 The Dates field showing a relative date range

COMPUTER PRACTICE

Step 1. With the *Sales of Services to Walnut Creek Customers* report displayed, click **Memorize** at the top of the report.

Step 2. In the *Memorize Report* window, the name for the report is automatically filled in. QuickBooks uses the report title as the default name for the memorized report (see Figure 6-44). The name can be modified if desired.

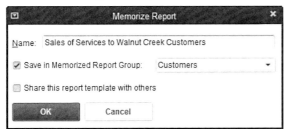

Figure 6-44 Memorize Report window

Step 3. Click the Checkbox next to **Save in Memorized Report Group:** and select **Customers** from the drop-down list as shown in Figure 6-44.

You can group your reports into similar types when you memorize them. This allows you to run several reports in a group by selecting them in the *Process Multiple Reports* window.

Step 4. Leave *Share this report template with others* unchecked.

If checked, this feature would allow you to share your report template with the greater QuickBooks user community. For more on *Contributed Reports*, see page 216.

Step 5. Click **OK** and close the report.

Viewing Memorized Reports

The next time you want to see this report follow these steps:

COMPUTER PRACTICE

Step 1. From the *Report Center*, click on the **Memorized** tab at the top of the window.

Notice that QuickBooks displays the reports in groups according to how you memorized them.

Step 2. Select the report you just memorized by selecting **Customers** on the menu on the left of the window and double click **Sales of Services to Walnut Creek Customers** (see Figure 6-45).

Figure 6-45 Memorized Report in the Report Center

Step 3. Close all open report windows.

Contributed Reports

When you memorize a report, you are given the option of sharing the report template with others. You can access contributed reports from the Reports Center. Be aware that you may not be able to use certain reports if they utilize features that you do not use, such as multi-currency.

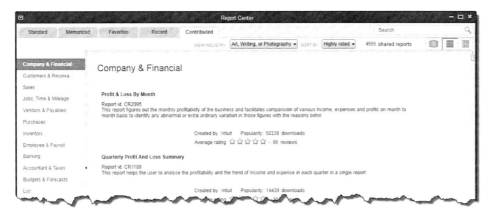

Figure 6-46 Contributed Reports in the Reports Center

Processing Multiple Reports

QuickBooks allows you to combine several reports into a group, so that you can later display and/or print the reports in the group as a batch.

You may want to use this feature to print a series of monthly reports for your files (e.g., monthly *Profit and Loss* and *Balance Sheet* reports).

COMPUTER PRACTICE

Step 1. From the *Reports* menu select **Process Multiple Reports** (see Figure 6-47).

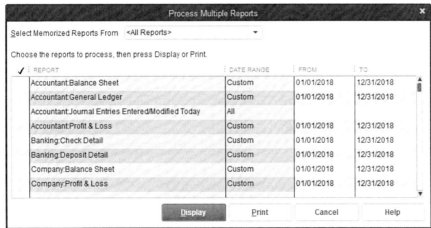

Figure 6-47 Process Multiple Reports window

> **Note:**
> Click in the column to the left of the report you want to include when you print or display your reports. Select the *From* and *To* date ranges of the report you wish to print in the columns on the right. Your date ranges will not match the ones displayed in Figure 6-47 and Figure 6-48. If you print the same group of reports on a regular basis, create a new Report Group in the *Memorize Reports List* window to combine the reports under a single group. Then you can select the group name in the *Select Memorized Reports From* field.

Step 2. Select **Customers** from the *Select Memorized Reports From* drop-down list (see Figure 6-48).

Figure 6-48 Customers Report Group

Step 3. If you do not want to display or print all the reports in the group, uncheck (√) the left column to deselect the reports you want to omit. Click **Display** to show the reports on the window (see Figure 6-49) or click **Print** to print all the reports.

> If your *Home* page is maximized, make sure to **Restore Down** the window so that your reports will display in the cascade style shown in Figure 6-49.

Step 4. Close all open report windows. Click **No** if QuickBooks prompts you to memorize the reports.

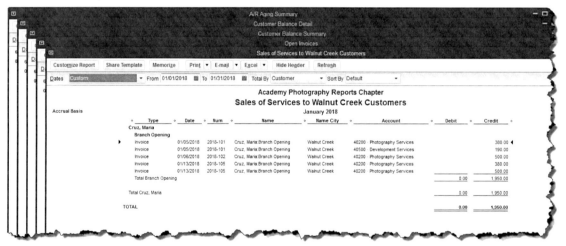

Figure 6-49 All of the reports in the Customer report group

Printing Reports

Every report in QuickBooks is printable. When you print reports, QuickBooks allows you to specify the orientation (landscape or portrait) and page-count characteristics for the reports.

COMPUTER PRACTICE

Step 1. Create a **Profit & Loss by Job** report dated *01/01/2018* to *01/31/2018* (see page 197).

Step 2. To print the report, click **Print** at the top of the window and select **Report**.

> **Another Way:**
> To print a report, press Ctrl+P or select the **File** menu and then select **Print Report**.

Reports - Memorizing Reports

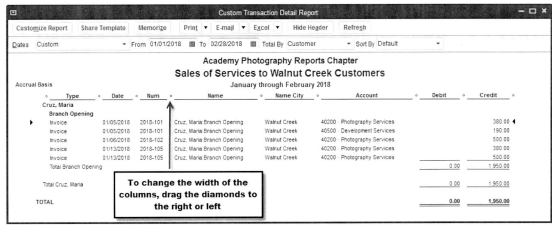

Figure 6-42 The customized report

Memorizing Reports

After you have modified a report, you can *memorize* the format and filtering so that you don't have to perform all of the modification steps the next time you want to view the report.

> **Note:**
> Memorizing a report does not memorize the data on the report, only the format, dates, and filtering.

If you enter specific dates, QuickBooks will use those dates the next time you bring up the report. However, if you select a *relative* date range in the *Dates* field (e.g., Last Fiscal Quarter, Last Year, or This Year to Date) before memorizing a report, QuickBooks will use the relative dates the next time you create the report.

For example, if you memorize a report with the *Dates* field set to *This Fiscal Quarter*, that report will always use dates for the current fiscal quarter as of the date you run the memorized report (see Figure 6-43).

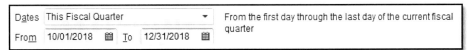

Figure 6-43 The Dates field showing a relative date range

COMPUTER PRACTICE

Step 1.   With the *Sales of Services to Walnut Creek Customers* report displayed, click **Memorize** at the top of the report.

Step 2.   In the *Memorize Report* window, the name for the report is automatically filled in. QuickBooks uses the report title as the default name for the memorized report (see Figure 6-44). The name can be modified if desired.

Figure 6-44 Memorize Report window

Step 3. Click the Checkbox next to **Save in Memorized Report Group:** and select **Customers** from the drop-down list as shown in Figure 6-44.

You can group your reports into similar types when you memorize them. This allows you to run several reports in a group by selecting them in the *Process Multiple Reports* window.

Step 4. Leave *Share this report template with others* unchecked.

If checked, this feature would allow you to share your report template with the greater QuickBooks user community. For more on *Contributed Reports*, see page 216.

Step 5. Click **OK** and close the report.

Viewing Memorized Reports

The next time you want to see this report follow these steps:

COMPUTER PRACTICE

Step 1. From the *Report Center*, click on the **Memorized** tab at the top of the window.

Notice that QuickBooks displays the reports in groups according to how you memorized them.

Step 2. Select the report you just memorized by selecting **Customers** on the menu on the left of the window and double click **Sales of Services to Walnut Creek Customers** (see Figure 6-45).

Figure 6-45 Memorized Report in the Report Center

Step 3. Close all open report windows.

Contributed Reports

When you memorize a report, you are given the option of sharing the report template with others. You can access contributed reports from the Reports Center. Be aware that you may not be able to use certain reports if they utilize features that you do not use, such as multi-currency.

Figure 6-46 Contributed Reports in the Reports Center

Processing Multiple Reports

QuickBooks allows you to combine several reports into a group, so that you can later display and/or print the reports in the group as a batch.

You may want to use this feature to print a series of monthly reports for your files (e.g., monthly *Profit and Loss* and *Balance Sheet* reports).

COMPUTER PRACTICE

Step 1.   From the *Reports* menu select **Process Multiple Reports** (see Figure 6-47).

Figure 6-47 Process Multiple Reports window

> **Note:**
> Click in the column to the left of the report you want to include when you print or display your reports. Select the *From* and *To* date ranges of the report you wish to print in the columns on the right. Your date ranges will not match the ones displayed in Figure 6-47 and Figure 6-48. If you print the same group of reports on a regular basis, create a new Report Group in the *Memorize Reports List* window to combine the reports under a single group. Then you can select the group name in the *Select Memorized Reports From* field.

Step 2.   Select **Customers** from the *Select Memorized Reports From* drop-down list (see Figure 6-48).

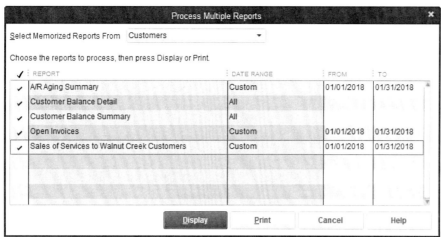

Figure 6-48 Customers Report Group

Step 3.   If you do not want to display or print all the reports in the group, uncheck (√) the left column to deselect the reports you want to omit. Click **Display** to show the reports on the window (see Figure 6-49) or click **Print** to print all the reports.

> If your *Home* page is maximized, make sure to **Restore Down** the window so that your reports will display in the cascade style shown in Figure 6-49.

Step 4.   Close all open report windows. Click **No** if QuickBooks prompts you to memorize the reports.

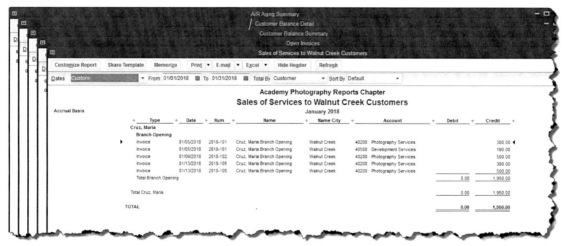

Figure 6-49 All of the reports in the Customer report group

Printing Reports

Every report in QuickBooks is printable. When you print reports, QuickBooks allows you to specify the orientation (landscape or portrait) and page-count characteristics for the reports.

COMPUTER PRACTICE
Step 1.   Create a **Profit & Loss by Job** report dated *01/01/2018* to *01/31/2018* (see page 197).
Step 2.   To print the report, click **Print** at the top of the window and select **Report**.

> **Another Way:**
> To print a report, press Ctrl+P or select the **File** menu and then select **Print Report**.

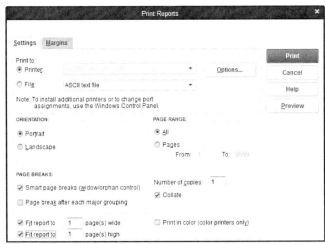

Figure 6-50 Print Report window – your screen may vary

Step 3. The **Print Reports** window displays. Your settings will be different than the settings shown in Figure 6-50.

Step 4. QuickBooks normally selects your default printer, but you can select another printer from the *Printer* drop-down list.

Step 1. Select **Landscape** in the *Orientation* section.

The Portrait setting makes the print appear from left to right across the 8½-inch dimension of the page ("straight up"), while the Landscape setting makes the print appear across the 11-inch dimension of the page ("sideways").

Step 2. Confirm that the **Smart page breaks (widow/orphan control)** setting is selected (see Figure 6-51). This setting keeps related data from splitting across two pages.

Figure 6-51 Page Breaks setting

Using **Smart page breaks**, you can control (to some extent) where page breaks occur on reports so that your pages don't break in inappropriate places. Using **Page break after each major grouping**, you can have QuickBooks break the pages after each major grouping of accounts. For example, in the Profit & Loss report, all Income and Cost of Goods Sold accounts will be on the first page (or pages), and all the Expense accounts will begin on a new page. In other reports, like the Customer Balance Detail and Vendor Balance Detail reports, this setting will cause each Customer and Vendor to begin on a new page, respectively.

Step 3. Select **Fit report to 1 page(s) wide** and **Fit report to 1 page(s) high** (see Figure 6-52). When you select these options, QuickBooks reduces the font size of the report so that it fits into the desired number of page.

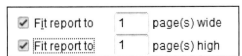

Figure 6-52 Fit report to 1 page wide and 1 page high

Before you print any report, it's a good idea to preview the report to make sure it will print the way you want.

Step 4. Click the **Preview** button on the *Print Reports* window.

Step 5. If everything looks right, click **Print** to print the report.
Step 6. Close all open report windows.

> **Note:**
> QuickBooks saves the setting on the *Print Reports* window when a report is memorized.

Finding Transactions

There are several ways to find transactions in QuickBooks depending on what you are trying to find. Sometimes you only know the date of a transaction and other times you know only the Customer, Item, or amount. Some of the ways you can search for a transaction include finding it in the register, using the **Search** command, using **QuickReports**, or using **QuickZoom**.

Using the Find Button

Unless you just completed a transaction, finding it by clicking the Previous button on the transaction form can be impractical. Clicking the Find button on the form, such as on the Invoice form on Figure 6-53, allows you to search for a transaction by *Name, Date, Transaction Number,* or *Amount*.

Figure 6-53 Find button

Using the Search Command

If you are looking for a transaction and you do not know which register to look in, or if you want to find more than just a single transaction, you can use the **Search** command.

COMPUTER PRACTICE

You want to find a recent payment by Maria Cruz.

Step 1. Enter **Cruz** in the *Search* field on the top of the *Icon Bar* and select **Search company file** from the drop-down menu (see Figure 6-54). Click the **Search** icon (see Figure 6-55)

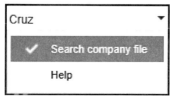

Figure 6-54 The Search field

Figure 6-55 Search icon

Step 2.   The *Search* window opens. QuickBooks returns a keyword search including any transaction or *Name* record that contains the word, or string, "Cruz" (see Figure 6-56). If the *Search* returns no transactions, click the **Update search information** link on the left side of the Search window.

You will notice that the search results include both the customer Maria Cruz, as well as Sinclair Insurance which is located in Santa Cruz, CA. Notice that different forms and name entries are included, such as *Customers*, *Vendors*, and *Invoices*.

> **Note:**
> QuickBooks 2014 includes a new auto suggestion feature in the *Search* window. As you enter characters in the *Search* field in the *Search* window, suggested words will appear in a drop down box below the field. Auto suggestion is not available in the *Search* field in the *Icon Bar*.

Step 3.   Close the *Search* window.

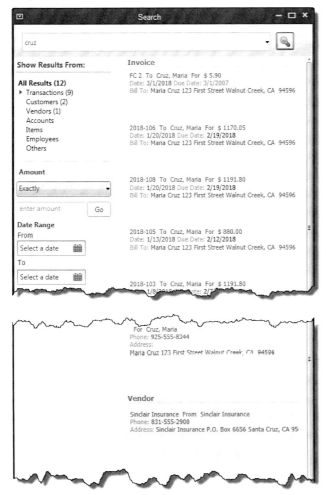

Figure 6-56 The Search Window

QuickReports

A *QuickReport* can quickly give you detailed transactions about an *Account*, *Item*, *Customer*, *Vendor*, or other payee. You can generate QuickReports from the *Chart of Accounts*, *Centers*, *Lists*, *Account Registers*, or forms. Table 6-2 shows different types of *QuickReports*.

When you are in...	The QuickReport shows you...
Chart of Accounts	All transactions involving that account
Centers and *Lists* (with an *Item* or *Name* selected)	All transactions for that *Item* or *Name*
Registers (with a transaction selected)	All transactions in that register for the same *Name*
Forms (*Invoice, Bill,* or *Check*)	All transactions for that particular customer, vendor, or payee within the same *Name* as the current transaction

Table 6-2 Types of QuickReports

COMPUTER PRACTICE

Step 1. Click the **Chart of Accounts** icon in the *Company* section of the **Home** page.

Step 2. Select the **Inventory Asset** account.

Step 3. Click the *Reports* button and select **Quick Report: Inventory Asset**. Alternatively, press **Ctrl+Q** (see Figure 6-57).

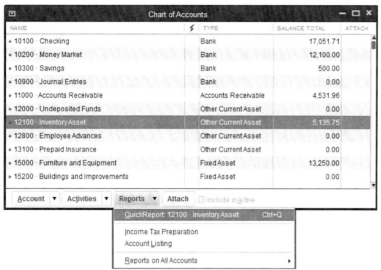

Figure 6-57 QuickReport of the Inventory Asset account

Step 4. QuickBooks displays all transactions involving the **Inventory Asset** account (see Figure 6-58).

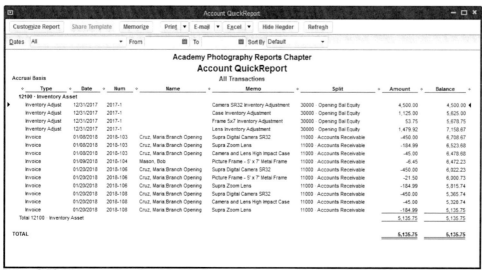

Figure 6-58 All transactions involving the Inventory Asset account

Reports - Finding Transactions

Step 5. Close the Account QuickReport and Chart of Accounts window.

Step 6. From the *Lists* menu select **Item List**.

Step 7. Select **Camera SR32** from the *Item list*.

Step 8. Click the *Reports* button and select **Quick Report: Camera SR32**. Alternatively, press **Ctrl+Q**.

Step 9. Change the *Dates* range to **All** by typing *A* in the Dates field. QuickBooks displays all transactions involving the **Camera SR32** Item (see Figure 6-59).

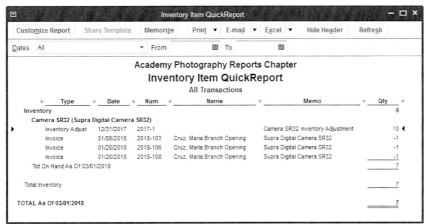

Figure 6-59 All transactions involving the Camera SR32 Item

Step 10. Close the Item QuickReport and Item List window.

Step 11. Click the **Check Register** icon in the *Banking* section of the *Home* page.

Step 12. Confirm that *Checking* displays in the *Select Account* field of the *Use Register* dialog box. Click **OK**.

Step 13. Scroll up and select **BILLPMT #6004**.

Step 14. Click the **QuickReport** icon at the top of the register (see Figure 6-60) or press **Ctrl+Q**.

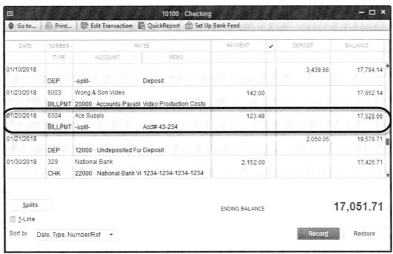

Figure 6-60 Select the Check and click QuickReport icon

Step 15. QuickBooks displays a report of all transactions in the Checking register using the same name as the selected transaction (see Figure 6-61).

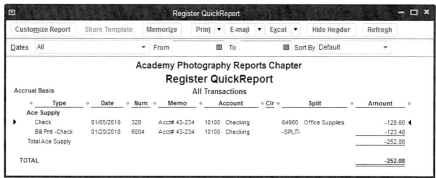

Figure 6-61 QuickReport for Vendor

Step 16. Close the Register QuickReport and Checking register.

> **Did You Know?**
> You can also generate QuickReports from the Customer Center, Vendor Center, or Employee Center by selecting the Customer, Vendor, or Employee and clicking on the **QuickReport** link in the upper right-hand corner of the window.

Using QuickZoom

QuickBooks provides a convenient feature called *QuickZoom*, which allows you to see the details behind numbers on reports. For example, the Profit & Loss report in Figure 6-62 shows $3,145.00 of *Photography Services* income. Double-click on the amount to see the details behind the number.

Figure 6-62 QuickZoom allows you to see the details behind a number

As your cursor moves over numbers on the report, it will turn into a magnifying glass with a "z" in the middle. The magnifying icon indicates that you can double-click to see the details behind the number on the report. After you double-click the number, *QuickZoom* displays a *Transaction Detail By Account* report (see Figure 6-63) that shows the details of each transaction in the account that you zoomed in on.

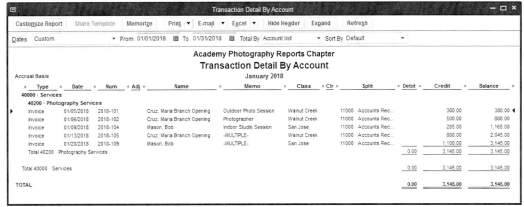

Figure 6-63 Transaction Detail by Account report

Exporting Reports to Spreadsheets

When you need to modify reports in ways that QuickBooks does not allow (e.g., changing the name of a column heading), you will need to export the report to a spreadsheet program.

> **Note:**
> *QuickBooks Statement Writer* is a utility for creating reports in Excel using live QuickBooks data. It is included in QuickBooks Accountant and QuickBooks Enterprise Solutions.

Exporting a Report to Microsoft Excel

COMPUTER PRACTICE

Step 1.   From the *Report Center*, select **Sales** and then double click the **Sales by Customer Detail** report in the *Sales by Customer* section to display the report.

Step 2.   Enter *01/01/2018* in the *From* field and enter *01/31/2018* in the *To* field. Press **Tab** twice (see Figure 6-64).

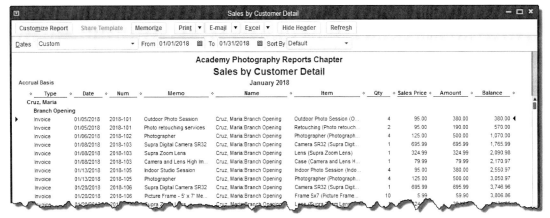

Figure 6-64 Click Excel button to export the report to a Microsoft Excel spreadsheet

Step 3.   Click **Excel** at the top of the report and choose **Create New Worksheet** from the dropdown menu.

Step 4.   In the *Send Report to Excel* window, make sure *Create new worksheet* and *in new workbook* are selected. This will export your report to a new Excel worksheet (see Figure 6-65).

> **Note:**
> The *Advanced* button of the *Send Report to Excel* window has many useful features for working with your QuickBooks data in Excel, including Auto Outline, which allows you to collapse and expand detail.

Figure 6-65 Send Report to Excel window

Step 5. Click **Export** in the *Send Report to Excel* window. QuickBooks will export your report directly to an Excel spreadsheet (see Figure 6-66).

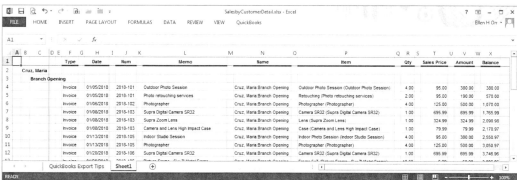

Figure 6-66 The report is now in an Excel spreadsheet.

> **Note:**
> After opening a QuickBooks exported report, Excel will display a QuickBooks Tips tab on the Excel ribbon. Once you save the file, you will be able to use the *Update Report* feature to refresh the report with updated information from QuickBooks. Although you can bring in new information to your Excel report from QuickBooks, it is not possible to import changes from this Excel report back into QuickBooks.

Review Questions

Comprehension Questions

1. Explain how the *QuickZoom* feature helps you see more detail about a report.
2. Name an example of how the *Check Detail* report is valuable.
3. How can you hide the subaccounts on the *Profit & Loss* report?
4. Explain how using *Filters* helps you get the reports you want.
5. Explain how memorized reports help you save time.

Multiple Choice

Choose the best answer(s) for each of the following:

1. What are the two major types of reports in QuickBooks?
    - a) Register and List.
    - b) Monthly and Annual.
    - c) Accounting and Business Management.
    - d) Balance Sheet and Profit & Loss.

2. Use the **Customize Report** button on any report to:
    - a) Add or delete columns or change the accounting basis of the report.
    - b) Change the width of columns on the report.
    - c) Print the report on blank paper.
    - d) Memorize the report for future use.

3. You cannot create a **QuickReport** for:
    - a) Customers.
    - b) Vendors.
    - c) Items.
    - d) Incorrectly posted entries.

4. To create a report that lists each of your vendors along with their address and telephone information:
    - a) Display the Vendor Contact List.
    - b) Open the *Search* window and do a search for Vendors and the corresponding Address and Phone Numbers.
    - c) Customize the Vendor database.
    - d) You must create a *Modified Report* to see this information.

5. In order to analyze the profitability of your company, you should:
    - a) Only analyze if the company is profitable.
    - b) Create a *Profit & Loss* report.
    - c) Review all detailed transaction reports.
    - d) Review the financial exceptions report.

6. Which statement is false? You may analyze your income and expenses for a given period:
   a) By class.
   b) By job.
   c) By vendor.
   d) For the whole business.

7. Which report shows monies owed to your company by customer?
   a) The **Balance Sheet** report.
   b) The **Accounts Receivable Aging** report.
   c) The **Accounts Payable Aging** report.
   d) The **Daily Charges** report.

8. In order to modify the header and footer of your report:
   a) Click the **Customize Report** button and then click the **Filters** tab.
   b) Click the **Titles** button and then click the **Customization** tab.
   c) Click the **Header/Footer** button.
   d) Click the **Customize Report** button and then click the **Header/Footer** tab.

9. Report Groups allow you to:
   a) Rearrange the report center.
   b) Organize the memorized report list into groups of related reports.
   c) Create groups of filters for your reports.
   d) Group reports by date.

10. The **Profit & Loss** report shows which of the following:
    a) Assets, Liabilities, and Equity accounts.
    b) Checks written for the period.
    c) Income, Cost of Goods Sold, Expenses, Other Income, and Other Expenses.
    d) A/R increases for the period.

11. If the **Profit & Loss by Class** report has an *Unclassified* column:
    a) There is an error in the filters on the report.
    b) You must refresh the report.
    c) You should eliminate the column using the **Modify Report** window.
    d) Some of the transactions for the period were not assigned to a class.

12. The report that shows total sales in each sales tax district (item) and shows the taxable sales separately from the nontaxable sales is called:
    a) The **Sales Tax Liability** report.
    b) **Tax by County** report.
    c) **Balance Sheet** report.
    d) **Sales by Tax Location** report.

13. Which is a feature of the **Filters** tab on the *Modify Report* window?
    a) Filters allow you select the columns on a report so that you can analyze specific areas of your business.
    b) Filters allow you to change how reports total and subtotal.
    c) Filters allow you to choose specific accounts, dates, names, or items to include on a report.
    d) Filters allow you to modify the date range on most reports.

14. To modify which columns are displayed on a report, click **Customize Report** and then check the names of columns to be displayed on the:
    a) Header/Footer tab.
    b) Display tab.
    c) Filters tab.
    d) Fonts & Numbers tab.

15. The **Fit report to 1 page(s) wide** feature does the following:
    a) Fits the report into a single page for each column.
    b) Eliminates columns from the report until it fits on a single page.
    c) Reduces the font size of the report so the width of all columns does not exceed 8½" (in portrait mode) or 11" (in landscape mode).
    d) Increases the margins on reports to make sure everything fits on one page.

Completion Statements

1. The _____ _____ _____ is a listing of your vendors along with each vendor's address and telephone information.

2. To modify the contents of a report, you can _____ it to include certain accounts, names, columns, or transaction types.

3. QuickBooks provides a convenient feature called _____, which allows you to see the detail behind numbers on reports.

4. If you're looking for a transaction and you don't know which register to look in, or if you want to find more than just a single transaction, you can use the _____ command.

5. The _____ _____ is a report that shows your financial position, as defined by the balances in each of your asset, liabilities, and equity accounts on a given date.

Reports Problem 1

APPLYING YOUR KNOWLEDGE

> Restore the Reports-14Problem1.QBM file.

1. Print the Profit & Loss Standard Report for January 2018.
2. Print the Balance Sheet Standard Report for January 2018.
3. Print the Statement of Cash Flows Report for January 2018.
4. Print the Customer QuickReport for Bob Mason for January 2018.
5. Print the Vendor Contact List Report.
6. Open the Sales by Customer Detail Report for January 2018.
7. Filter the report to only display Sales which total an amount greater than or equal (>=) to $500.
8. Print the customized Sales by Customer Detail Report for January 2018.

Reports Problem 2 (Advanced)

APPLYING YOUR KNOWLEDGE

> Restore the Reports-14Problem2.QBM file.

1. Print the reports listed below for Academy Photography.

a) Customer Phone List.
b) Check Detail Report for January and February of 2018 with split detail, sorted by Num.
c) Customer QuickReport for Maria Cruz for January and February 2018.
d) Profit & Loss Standard Report for January and February 2018.
e) Profit & Loss by Job Report for January and February 2018.
f) Trial Balance Report for January 2018.
g) Balance Sheet Standard Report for January 31, 2018.

2. Create a custom report showing the customers who had paid an amount over $300 in January 2018. Modify the report so that it totals by Customer and includes the title and columns displayed in Figure 6-67.

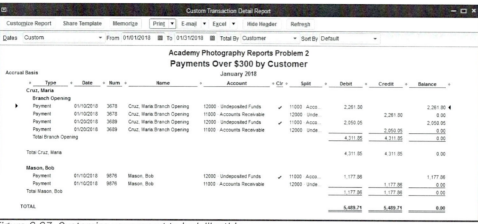

Figure 6-67 Customize your report to look like this.

> **Important:**
> When you complete #2, do not close the report. You will use the modified report in the next step.

3. Print the report you created in Step 2 and then memorize it in the Customers report group. Name the memorized report "Payments Over $300 by Customer."

4. Create and print a graph of your Income and Expenses (by Class, Show Expense on Pie Chart) for January and February 2018.

QUICKBOOKS AND BEYOND – *TAKE THE NEXT STEP WITH THE SLEETER GROUP BLOG*

How to Record Sales on Consignment in QuickBooks "

Many retail businesses are engaged in the practice of selling on consignment. This means that the owner of the products places them in the hands of a store owner, and that store owner only pays for the goods the store sells. This keeps the risk entirely on the owner of the goods and not the person selling them.

In this four-part video series, Seth David discusses how to set up and use a QuickBooks file if you use consignment goods. The second and fourth videos show examples of how to use reports to display needed information. Although in this chapter you learned about many reports, this video blog explains how versatile reports can be. Some concepts, such as inventory, are discussed later in this book. Read and view the first post and video at www.sleeter.com/blog/?p=5791.

New Terminology

Consignor – The company or person who owns the consignment inventory and has given the stock to another merchant.

Consignee – The merchant who does not own but is selling the consignment inventory.

Putting New Knowledge to Use

1. Does your workplace or business work with consignment goods?
2. How could you customize reports used in your workplace or business to display needed information?

Chapter 7
Company File Setup

Topics

In this chapter, you will learn about the following topics:
- Choosing a Start Date – Step 1 (page 233)
- Creating the Company File – Step 2 (page 234)
- Setting Up the Chart of Accounts and Other Lists – Step 3 (page 243)
- Setting Up Opening Balances – Step 4 (page 254)
- Entering Open Items – Step 5 (page 260)
- Entering Year-to-Date Income and Expenses – Step 6 (page 264)
- Adjusting Opening Balance for Sales Tax Payable – Step 7 (page 265)
- Adjusting Inventory and Setting up Fixed Assets – Step 8 (page 266)
- Setup Payroll and YTD Payroll Information – Step 9 (page 267)
- Verifying your Trial Balance – Step 10 (page 267)
- Closing Opening Bal Equity – Step 11 (page 268)
- Setting the Closing Date - Backing up the File – Step 12 (page 270)
- Users and Passwords (page 270)

In this chapter, you will learn how to create a new QuickBooks data file, set up the Chart of Accounts, and enter opening balances. You will also learn how to set up user access rights and passwords for each person who will use QuickBooks.

Creating a new company file can be done at the inception of a new company or when an existing company decides to start using QuickBooks. It is also appropriate for a company that is already using QuickBooks to create a new company file when the existing one has many errors and fixing it is not possible.

In this section, you will learn about the 12-Step setup process for completing your QuickBooks file setup (see Table 7-1).

Choosing a Start Date – Step 1

Before you create your company file, choose a start date for your company file. Your start date is the day before you start using QuickBooks to track your daily transactions. You will need complete information for your opening balances as of this start date. Assuming you file taxes on a calendar-year basis, the best start date for most companies is December 31. If you file taxes on a fiscal year, choose the last day of your fiscal year as your start date.

Do not use January 1 (or the first day of your fiscal year) for your start date, because doing so would cause the opening balances to affect your first year's *Profit & Loss Report*. This could affect your taxes and distort the picture of the company's financial history.

The 12-Step Setup Checklist

1. Choose the Start Date (see page 233).
2. Create the QuickBooks company file (see page 234).
3. Create the Chart of Accounts and company Lists (see page 243).
4. Enter opening balances for most Balance Sheet accounts (see page 254).
5. Enter outstanding transactions as of the start date (see page 260).
6. If needed, enter your year-to-date income and expenses (see page 264).
7. Adjust Sales Tax Payable (see page 265).
8. Adjust Inventory to match physical counts and set up Fixed Assets (see page 266).
9. Set up Payroll Lists and year-to-date (YTD) payroll information (see page 267).
10. Verify that the Trial Balance report matches your previous trial balance (see page 267).
11. Close the Opening Bal Equity account into Retained Earnings (see page 268).
12. Set the Closing Date and backup your company file (see page 270).

Table 7-1 The 12-Step Setup Checklist

Keep in mind that you will need to enter all of the transactions (checks, invoices, deposits, etc.) between your start date and the day you perform the QuickBooks setup. Because of this, your start date has a big impact on how much work you will do during setup. If you do not want to go back to the end of last year, choose a more recent date, such as the end of last quarter or the end of last month.

> **Note:**
> In order for your records to be complete and accurate, you should enter every transaction (check, invoice, deposits etc.) that your company performed between the start date and the day you perform the QuickBooks setup. For example, if you are setting up the QuickBooks company file on January 5 with a start date of December 31, you will need to enter all transactions that the company performed on January 1 through January 5 for your records to be complete and accurate.

If you are starting a new business, your start date is the day you formed the company.

Creating the Company File – Step 2

There are two ways to create a file, through the *Express Start* and the *Detailed Start*. In the following section, we will show you how to create a file using both methods. *Express Start* creates a file with minimal entries and a default set of *Preferences*. Only users who are familiar with QuickBooks *Preferences* and the impact of creating a QuickBooks file without a start date should use *Express Start*. *Detailed Start* allows you to set up a number of *Preferences,* as well as set the start date for a company.

Express Start

When you first create a new file, you are given the option of choosing *Express Start* or *Detailed Start*, as well as several other options such as converting a file from another format, for example Quicken or Peachtree (see Figure 7-1).

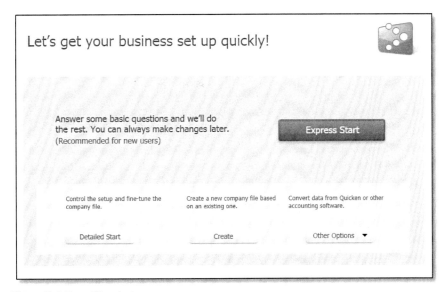

Figure 7-1 New File window

If you choose *Express Start*, you only need to enter your Company information before creating a file. Once the file is created you can enter *Customers*, *Vendors*, *Employees*, *Items*, and *Bank Accounts*, then start using the file. QuickBooks chooses default *Accounts* and *Preferences* for you based on the *Industry* you select (see Figure 7-2).

Figure 7-2 Express Start Tell us about your business screen

After completing the file setup, whether using Express Start or Advanced Setup, you can access and edit the Company Information, such as business name, address, or phone number by selecting the Company menu and selecting My Company (see Figure 7-3).

Figure 7-3 My Company window

Detailed Start

The *Detailed Start*, also called the *EasyStep Interview,* allows you to enter your Company information as in the Express Start, however, it also asks you to customize some of the most common preferences and set a start date.

COMPUTER PRACTICE

Step 1.   Select the **File** menu and then select **New Company**.

Step 2.   A new file window appears. Click **Detailed Start** to launch the *EasyStep Interview* (see Figure 7-4).

Step 3.   The *EasyStep Interview* window appears. Enter the information in the Company information screen as shown in Figure 7-4. Click **Next** when done.

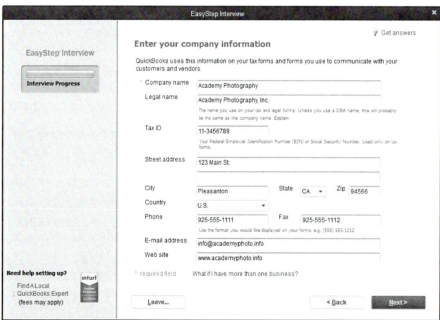
Figure 7-4 Company Information in EasyStep Interview

Company File Setup - Creating the Company File – Step 2

> **Note:**
> As you answer questions in the *EasyStep Interview*, QuickBooks creates your company file, *Lists*, and *Preferences*. To proceed to the next step in the process click **Next**. To go back to a previous window in the interview, click **Back**. To exit the Interview and retain all changes, click **Leave**. When you open the company file again after clicking *Leave*, you will be taken back to the Easy Step Interview.
>
> To make changes to the company information after you have completed the *EasyStep Interview*, select *My Company* from the *Company* menu.

Step 4. Select **Art, Writing, or Photography** from the list of industry types. QuickBooks uses the industry information to suggest the appropriate income and expense accounts later in the *EasyStep Interview*. Click **Next** when finished.

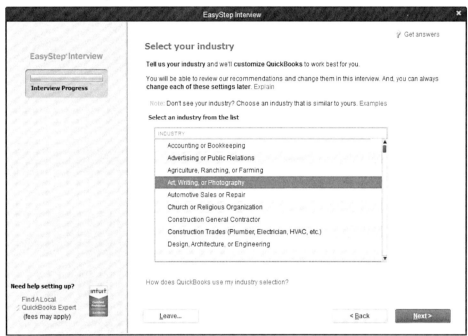

Figure 7-5 Select your industry in EasyStep Interview

> **Tip:**
> If you are unsure how to answer the questions in the Easy Step Interview, consider contacting a QuickBooks expert. *QuickBooks ProAdvisors* are bookkeepers, accountants, software consultants, and CPAs who offer QuickBooks-related consulting services. In addition, *QuickBooks Certified ProAdvisors* are those *ProAdvisors* who have completed a comprehensive training and testing program. For more information on QuickBooks *ProAdvisors* and *Certified ProAdvisors*, refer to QuickBooks in-product Help.

Step 5. The *How is your company organized?* window appears. Select the **S Corporation** radio button and click **Next**.

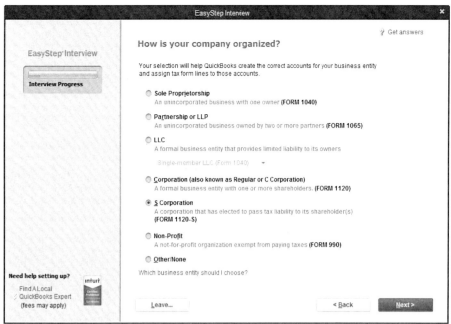

Figure 7-6 How your company is organized window in the EasyStep Interview

Step 6. The next window prompts the user to select the first month of the company's fiscal or income tax year. Leave **January** selected and click the **Next** button.

This field indicates the beginning of the year for year-to-date reports, such as the *Profit & Loss* report.

Figure 7-7 Select the first month of your fiscal year window in the EasyStep Interview

> **Note for new businesses:**
> The first month of your fiscal or income tax year is **NOT** necessarily the month you started your business. Setting the first month in your fiscal year correctly is important as it specifies the default date range for accounting reports such as the Profit & Loss and Balance Sheet. The first month in your tax year specifies the default date range for **Income Tax Summary** and **Detail** reports. If you make an error in this selection, you can correct it later by selecting *My Company* from the *Company* menu.

Step 7. The Administrator password setup screen will appear (see Figure 7-8). Although it's optional, creating an Administrator password is highly recommended. The Administrator is the only person who has access to all functions within a company file. Establishing an Administrator password restricts other users so that they cannot execute tasks that are normally reserved for the Administrator.

However, since you are just creating a sample data file for this lesson, do not create an Administrator password at this time. Click **Next** to move to the next step.

Company File Setup - Creating the Company File – Step 2   **239**

Figure 7-8 The Administrator Password Screen in the EasyStep Interview

> **Tip:**
> If you need help during the interview, click the **Get answers** link at the top of the interview window.

Step 8. The next window in the *EasyStep Interview* window contains a message about creating your company file. Click **Next** to create the file.

Step 9. The *Filename for New Company* window (see Figure 7-9) is where you specify the filename and location for your company file. QuickBooks automatically enters your company name and adds .QBW to the end of your filename.

In the *Save in* field, select your student data folder. Use the default file name, Academy Photography.QBW.

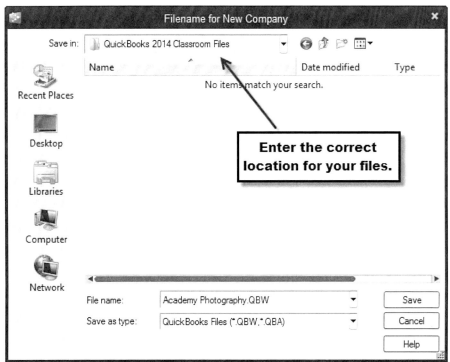

Figure 7-9 Filename for New Company window

Step 10. Click **Save** to create your company file.

Step 11. QuickBooks displays the *Customizing QuickBooks for your business* step. Click **Next** to begin the customizing process.

Step 12. The next several screens of the *EasyStep Interview* will guide you through customizing your company file and setting up *Preferences*. Use the data in Table 7-2 to answer initial questions about your business.

Company Setup and Preferences	
Question From EasyStep Interview	Response
What do you sell?	Both services and products
Do you charge sales tax?	Yes
Do you want to create estimates in QuickBooks?	Yes
Do you want to track sales orders before you invoice your customers?	Yes (Note: This option is not available in QuickBooks Pro.)
Do you want to use billing statements in QuickBooks?	Yes
Do you want to use progress invoicing?	Yes
Do you want to keep track of bills you owe?	Yes
Do you want to track inventory in QuickBooks?	Yes
Do you want to track time in QuickBooks?	Yes
Do you have employees?	Yes (check the boxes for both W-2 employees and 1099 contractors)

Table 7-2 Data for the Company Setup

Step 13. In the next section of the interview, QuickBooks creates your Chart of Accounts. Click **Next** on the *Using accounts in QuickBooks* screen.

Step 14. In the *Select a date to start tracking your finances* screen, select **Use today's date or the first day of the quarter or month.** Then enter *12/31/17* in the date field. Click **Next**.

If you are setting up your file to begin at the start of the fiscal year, it is best to choose the last day of the previous fiscal year as the start date. (see page 233).

Figure 7-10 Select a date to start tracking your finances window in EasyStep Interview

Step 15. The following screen contains a list of suggested income and expense accounts based on the industry selected earlier in the *EasyStep Interview*. These accounts can be edited after completing the *EasyStep Interview*.

Leave the default accounts checked and click **Next**.

Company File Setup - Creating the Company File – Step 2   **241**

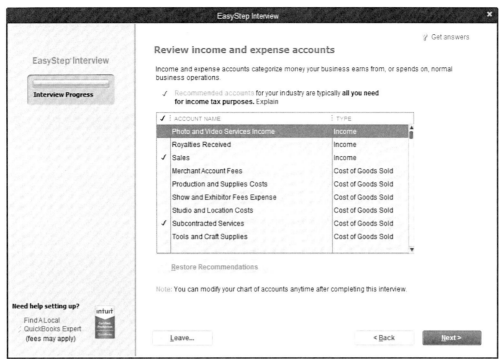

Figure 7-11 Review income and expense accounts window in the EasyStep Interview

Step 16.   Click **Go to Setup** to complete the interview.

Figure 7-12 Final screen in EasyStep interview

Step 17.   The *QuickBooks Setup Add Info* window is displayed. This window offers a quick way to enter *Customers*, *Vendors*, *Employees*, *Items,* and *Bank Accounts*. We will use this window to create a bank account. Click the **Add** button in the *Add your bank accounts* section in the lower part of the window.

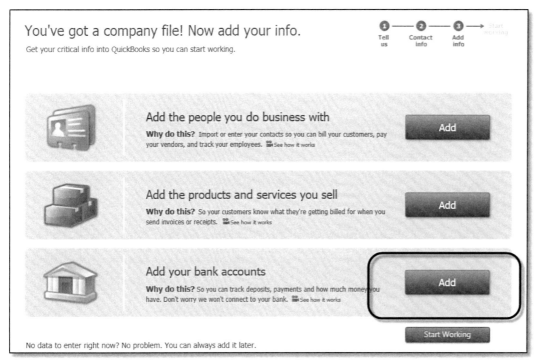

Figure 7-13 QuickBooks Setup Add Info

Step 18.   Enter the information in Figure 7-14 to setup the *Checking* account. For now, enter an *Opening Balance* of **0.00**. We will discuss setting up *Opening Balances* on page 268.

Figure 7-14 Add your bank accounts window

> Note:
> The *Account number* field in the *Add you bank accounts* window is for the account number assigned from your bank. This is a different number than the five digit QuickBooks Account Number discussed on page 243.

Step 19.   Click Continue.

Step 20.   Click **No Thanks** to the offer to order Intuit checks. If necessary, decline any additional offers.

Step 21.   Click Continue.

Step 22.   Click the **Start Working** link at the bottom of the window (see Figure 7-15).

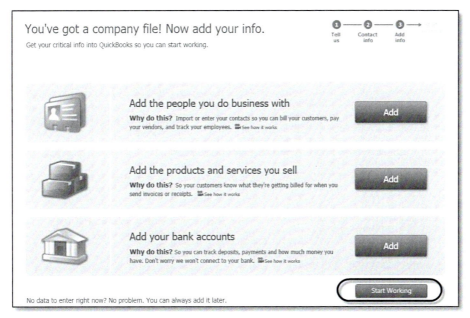

Figure 7-15 Start Working Link in QuickBooks Setup Add Info

Step 23. QuickBooks has now created your company file with a default *Chart of Accounts* and a bank account, and has configured your *Company Preferences*.

Step 24. If necessary, close the *Accountant Center* window.

Step 25. Close the *Quick Start Center* window.

Step 26. Close the company file by selecting **Close Company** from the *File* menu.

Setting Up the Chart of Accounts and Other Lists – Step 3

> Restore the **Setup-14.QBM** file to your hard disk. See page 9 for instructions on restoring files.

Setting Up the Chart of Accounts

The *Chart of Accounts* is one of the most important lists in QuickBooks. It is a list of all the accounts in the General Ledger. If you are not sure how to design your *Chart of Accounts*, ask your accountant or QuickBooks ProAdvisor for help.

Account Types

There are five basic account types in accounting: assets, liabilities, equity, income, and expenses.

QuickBooks breaks these basic account types into subtypes. For example, QuickBooks uses five types of asset accounts: *Bank*, *Accounts Receivable*, *Other Current Asset*, *Fixed Asset*, and *Other Asset*. QuickBooks offers four types of liability accounts: *Accounts Payable*, *Credit Card*, *Other Current Liability*, and *Long Term Liability*. Income accounts can be divided into *Income* or *Other Income* types. Expenses can be classified as *Expense*, *Other Expense*, or *Cost of Goods Sold*. *Equity* doesn't have subtypes.

Activating Account Numbers

QuickBooks does not require account numbers. If you prefer, you can use just the account *name* to differentiate between accounts. However, if you prefer to have account numbers, you can activate them in the *Accounting Company Preferences*.

For this section, you will turn on the account numbers, but at the end of *Setting up the Chart of Accounts* section, you will turn them off again.

COMPUTER PRACTICE

Step 1. Select the **Edit** menu and then select **Preferences**.

Step 2. On the *Preferences* window, click on the **Accounting** option and select the **Company Preferences** tab.

Step 3. Check the **Use account numbers** box and click **OK**.

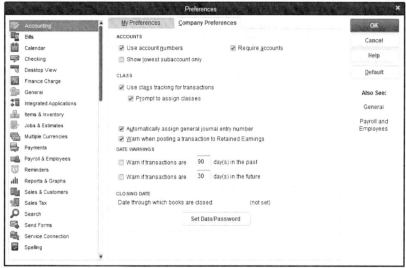

Figure 7-16 The Accounting—Company Preferences window

> **Did You Know?**
> All of the *Preferences* in Figure 7-16 are used to configure the way QuickBooks operates. For more information on these and other *Preferences*, see page 285.

Adding Accounts

COMPUTER PRACTICE

Step 1. Select the **Chart of Accounts** icon on the *Company* section of the *Home page*.

The *Chart of Accounts* list from your sample file is displayed, showing account numbers as well as account names (see Figure 7-17).

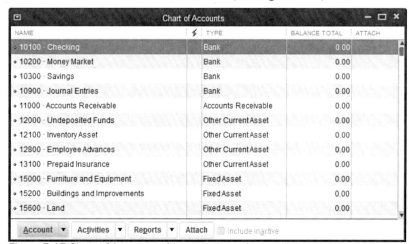

Figure 7-17 Chart of Accounts with account numbers

> **Another way:**
> To open the *Chart of Accounts*, you may also select **Chart of Accounts** from the *List* menu, or press **Ctrl+A**.

Step 2. Select the **Account** drop-list button at the bottom of the *Chart of Accounts* window and select **New**. Another way to add a new account is to press **Ctrl+N**.

Step 3. Select **Expense** from the choice of account types in the *Add New Account: Choose Account Type* window (see Figure 7-18). Click Continue.

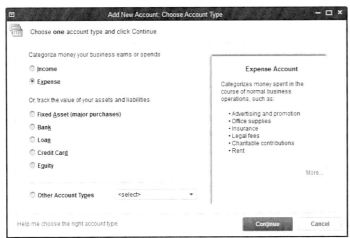

Figure 7-18 Add New Account: Choose Account Type Window

Step 4. Enter *62600* in the *Number* field and then press **Tab**.

Step 5. Enter *Entertainment* in the *Name* field and then press **Tab** twice.

Step 6. Enter *Entertainment Expenses* in the *Description* field and then press **Tab** twice. The *Description* field is optional.

Step 7. Select **Deductions: Other miscellaneous taxes** from the *Tax-Line Mapping* drop-down list.

If you or your accountant uses TurboTax, ProSeries, Lacerte, or other QuickBooks-compatible tax software to prepare your tax return, specify the line on your tax return that this account will feed. This allows the tax software to fill out your tax return automatically, based on the data in QuickBooks. If you do not use one of the supported tax programs to prepare your taxes, or if you do not wish to otherwise take advantage of any of the income tax reports in QuickBooks, you can leave this field blank.

Step 8 Your screen should look like Figure 7-19. Click **Save & Close** at the bottom of the window to save the account.

Figure 7-19 Add New Account window

Adding Subaccounts

If you want more detail in your *Chart of Accounts*, you can add *Subaccounts*. Account types for the main account and its subaccounts *must* be same. You can add up to five levels of subaccounts.

> **Did You Know?**
> Clicking the **Collapse** button on *Reports* that include Subaccounts (e.g., *Balance Sheet* and *Profit & Loss Reports*) removes the Subaccount detail from the report. The balance of each primary account on the collapsed report is the total of its subaccount balances.

COMPUTER PRACTICE

Step 1. Display the **Chart of Accounts** using any method shown previously, if it is not already displayed.

Step 2. Select the **Account** drop-list button at the bottom of the *Chart of Accounts* window and select **New**.

Step 3. Select the **Expense** option from *the Add New Account: Choose Account Type* window. Click **Continue**.

Step 4. Fill out the **New Account** window as shown in Figure 7-20. Notice that the *Subaccount of* field is checked and the main account is selected in its field.

Step 5. Click **Save & Close** to save the record.

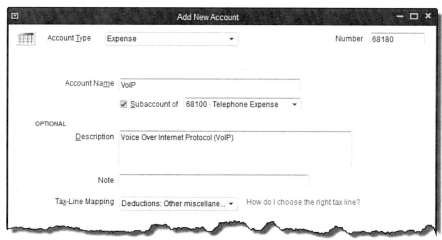

Figure 7-20 Add a Subaccount for more detail in the Chart of Accounts.

Step 6. Now the *Chart of Accounts* shows your new subaccount slightly indented under its master account (see Figure 7-21).

> **Tip**
> Once subaccounts are set up under a main account, you should only use subaccounts and not the main account in transactions. Using the main account defeats the purpose of getting more detail.
>
> **Note:**
> In reports, whenever you see an account name with the string "-Other", it means that you used a main account instead of a subaccount. To avoid this problem, you might choose to show only subaccounts and not the main accounts in the drop-down list by selecting the **Show lowest subaccount only** checkbox in *Accounting Company Preference* (see Figure 7-22).

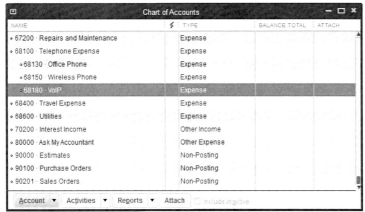

Figure 7-21 Subaccounts appearance in the Chart of Accounts

Figure 7-22 Account Numbers Preferences

Removing Accounts from the Chart of Accounts

When you no longer need an account, it is best to remove the account from the *Chart of Accounts* List. Removing unnecessary accounts helps avoid data entry errors by ensuring that no transactions are accidentally posted to these accounts. There are three ways to remove an account from the *Chart of Accounts* List: deleting the account, deactivating the account, or merging the account with another account.

Deleting Accounts – Option 1

To delete an account, follow these steps:

> DO NOT PERFORM THESE STEPS NOW. THEY ARE FOR REFERENCE ONLY.

1. Select the account in the **Chart of Accounts** List.
2. Select the **Account** menu at the bottom of the *Chart of Accounts* window and select **Delete** or press **Ctrl+D**.

QuickBooks list entries cannot be deleted if they are in use. This is true for Accounts, Items, Customers, Vendors, Employees, Payroll Items or any other list entry. An account can be in use in many different ways, such as in an Item, in a transaction, or in a Preference. In cases where you are not able to delete an account or other list item, use either Option 2 or Option 3 below.

Deactivating Accounts – Option 2

If you cannot delete an account but you still want to remove it from your list, you can deactivate it. Deactivating an account causes it to be hidden in the *Chart of Accounts* List. Deactivating an old account reduces the clutter in your Lists while preserving your ability to see the account in historical transactions and reports.

> **Note:**
> Even if an Account (or Item or Name) is inactive, all transactions using that account (or Item or Name) will show on reports.

To make an account inactive, follow these steps:

> **DO NOT PERFORM THESE STEPS NOW. THEY ARE FOR REFERENCE ONLY.**

1. Select the account in the **Chart of Accounts** list.
2. Select the **Account** button and then select **Make Account Inactive** from the menu (see Figure 7-23).

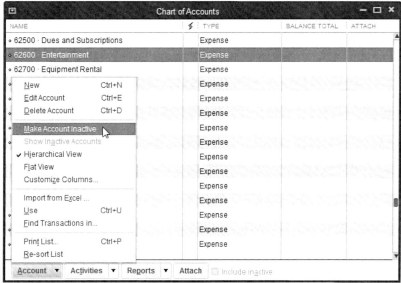

Figure 7-23 Making an account inactive in the Chart of Accounts

To view all accounts in the *Chart of Accounts*, including the inactive accounts, click **Include inactive** at the bottom of the *Chart of Accounts* window (see Figure 7-24). The icon in the far left column indicates that an account is inactive. To reactivate the account, click on the large X icon next to the inactive account.

> **Note:**
> You can make entries in most lists inactive through this same process, including *Customers*, *Vendors* and *Items*.

Figure 7-24 When Include inactive is checked, all accounts appear in the list.

> **Did You Know?**
> You can also deactivate *Customers*, *Vendors*, *Employees*, or *Items* using this same method. Click in the Inaction column (indicated by a large X) to make lines on any list active or inactive.

Merging Accounts – Option 3

When you merge two accounts, QuickBooks edits each transaction from the merging account so that it posts to the merged (combined) account. For example, if you merge the *Entertainment* account into the *Meals and Entertainment* account, QuickBooks will edit each transaction that had been posted to *Entertainment*, making it post to *Meals and Entertainment* instead. Then QuickBooks will remove the *Entertainment* account from the *Chart of Accounts* List.

You can only merge accounts of the same type. In this example, both accounts are Expense accounts.

> **Important:**
> Merging cannot be undone. Once you merge accounts together, there is no way to find out which account the old transactions used (except by reviewing a backup file). In this example, all transactions that were originally coded to *Entertainment* will post to *Meals and Entertainment*.

COMPUTER PRACTICE

Step 1. Display the **Chart of Accounts** List.

Step 2. Select the account whose name you <u>do not</u> want to keep. Here you will merge the *Entertainment* account into *Meals and Entertainment*, so select **62600 Entertainment**.

Step 3. Right-click on **62600 Entertainment** and then select **Edit Account**. Alternatively, press Ctrl+E.

Step 4. Enter *Meals and Entertainment* in the *Name* field (see Figure 7-25) and then click **Save & Close**. You must enter the account name <u>exactly</u> as it appears in the *Chart of Accounts*. One way of ensuring this is to copy and paste the account name from the merged account to the merging account.

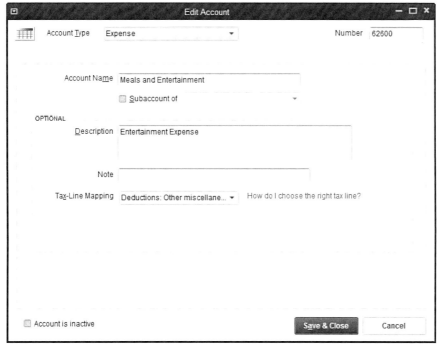

Figure 7-25 Change the name of the account to exactly match the name of another account.

Step 5. Now that this account has the same name as the other account, QuickBooks asks if you want to merge the two accounts (see Figure 7-26). Click **Yes**.

Figure 7-26 Click Yes to merge the accounts.

> **Did You Know?**
> If account numbers are in use, another way to merge accounts is to change the account number of one account to match the account number of another. This has the same effect as replacing the account name of the merging account with the account name of the merged account.
>
> **Note:**
> The merge feature is not limited to just the *Chart of Accounts* List; it can be used on most Lists within QuickBooks, including *Customers* and *Vendors*.

Reordering the Account List

There are several ways to reorder the *Chart of Accounts* list. By default, the Chart of Accounts list sorts first by account type and then alphabetically by account name within the account type if account numbers are not in use or numerically by account number within the account type if account numbers are in use. For example, all of the bank accounts come first, followed by Accounts Receivable, Other Current Assets, and so on. The account types are arranged in the order in which they appear on financial statements.

> **DO NOT PERFORM THESE STEPS NOW. THEY ARE FOR REFERENCE ONLY.**

1. Display the **Chart of Accounts** (see Figure 7-27).
2. Click the **Name** column heading to sort the list.

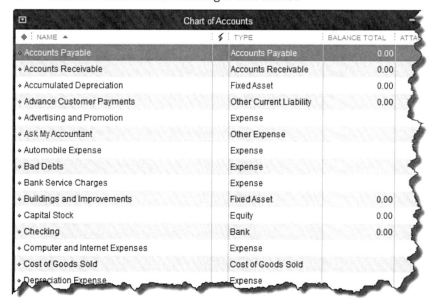

Figure 7-27 Chart of Accounts sorted by name

> **Note:**
> When account numbers are inactive and you click the *Name* header, QuickBooks sorts the account list alphabetically by account name.
>
> However, when account numbers are active and you click the *Name* header, QuickBooks sorts the list by account number. Click the other headers to sort by ⚡ (*Online status*), *Type,* or *Balance*.
>
> **Tip:**
> When you assign account numbers, set numbering breaks that correspond to the account types. For example, number all of your asset accounts 10000-19999 and all of your liability accounts 20000-29999, and so forth. When you click the Name header to sort the *Chart of Accounts*, QuickBooks does not also sort the list by account type. Therefore, if you assign an account number of 70000 to a Bank account, QuickBooks will place that account near the bottom of the *Chart of Accounts*, regardless of its type. If you do not use account numbers, it is best not to use the Name header to sort the *Chart of Accounts*. Instead, select the **Account** menu and choose **Re-sort List**. This will sort the list by Account name (or number) while respecting the account types.

You can also use the mouse to drag the accounts up or down within the same account type. Within each account type, the order of the accounts in the Chart of Accounts determines the order of the accounts in financial statements and other reports.

> **Tip:**
> Once you have manually reordered the *Chart of Accounts*, all new accounts will automatically be added to the top of the list within its type, rather than in alphabetical order.

To reorder the *Chart of Accounts* List using the mouse, follow these steps:

> **DO NOT PERFORM THESE STEPS NOW. THEY ARE FOR REFERENCE ONLY.**

1. If you have sorted the list by *Name, Online Status, Type,* or *Balance* by clicking on the column headers, click on the diamond to the left of the **Name** column header. This will remove the sorting (see Figure 7-28).

Figure 7-28 Chart of Accounts, sorted by account name

2. Hold down the mouse button on the small diamond to the left of each Account name. Drag the account up or down (see Figure 7-29).

> **Note:**
> You can reorder other lists and centers as well by dragging the diamond next to the name.

Figure 7-29 Reorder the list by moving an account with the mouse.

> **Tip:**
> To preserve proper financial statement presentation, you can only rearrange accounts within their account type. In addition, QuickBooks treats accounts with subaccounts as a group, so if you want to move your account above or beneath an account with subaccounts, you'll need to drag it above or below the group.
>
> **Tip:**
> If you use account numbers, it may be best to edit the numbers to move accounts up or down in the list. For example, if you want account #10400 to be above account #10300, you can edit its account number so that it is #10200. Then, you may need to select the **Account** menu and then select **Re-sort List**.

Turning Off Account Numbers

For the rest of this chapter, we'll turn off the display of account numbers in the Chart of Accounts.

COMPUTER PRACTICE

Step 1. Select the **Edit** menu and then select **Preferences**.

Step 2. In the *Preferences* window, click on the **Accounting** option and then select the **Company Preferences** tab.

Step 3. Deselect the *Use account numbers* box and then click **OK**.

Step 4. Close any open windows.

Setting Up Other Lists

At this point in the 12-Step process, you would enter additional information in lists, such as *Customers* and *Vendors*. You can use the *QuickBooks Setup Add Info* (see page 234) to import *Customers*, *Vendors*, and *Employees* from contact lists in other formats, such as your Outlook contact list. For this exercise, the Setup-14.QBM file you restored earlier already has this data entered. Refer to page 35 and 108 for more information on adding *Customers* and *Vendors*.

Add/Edit Multiple List Entries

You can add multiple list entries, such as *Customers, Vendors* or *Inventory Items* using a feature called *Add/Edit Multiple List Entries*. This is particularly useful when you already have a list of these entities, such as in a database or in an Excel spreadsheet. Using the *Add/Edit Multiple List Entries*, columns of data can be copied from your original file and pasted into the QuickBooks file. This can also be used to enter data into many list entries at one time.

> **DO NOT PERFORM THESE STEPS. THEY ARE FOR REFERENCE ONLY.**

Company File Setup - Setting Up the Chart of Accounts and Other Lists – Step 3

1. Select **Add/Edit Multiple Entries** from the *List* menu. The *Add/Edit Multiple List Entries* window opens.
2. Select **Customers** from the *List* field. You also have the option to choose *Vendors, Service Items, Inventory Parts, Non-Inventory Parts* or *Inventory Assemblies* (see Figure 7-30).

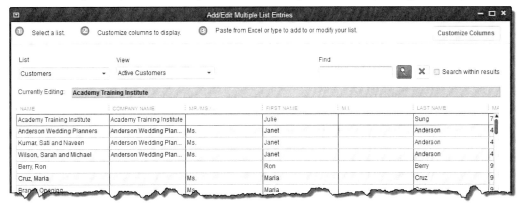

Figure 7-30 – Add/Edit Multiple Customer Items

3. Click on the **Customize Columns** button on the right. The *Customize Columns* window opens.
4. Select the fields you want to import and click the **Add** button. This copies the columns from *Available Columns* list on the left of the window to the *Chosen Columns* on the right of the window. Select *Credit Limit* and click **Add**. Then, click the **Move Up** button so that *Credit Limit* is below *Last Name* in the *Chosen Column* field. Click **OK**.

Figure 7-31 - Select Fields to Add

5. Enter **5,000** in the *Academy Training Institute* row under the *Credit Limit* column. Then right click the **5,000** entry and choose **Copy Down**. All Customers now have a $5,000 *Credit Limit*.

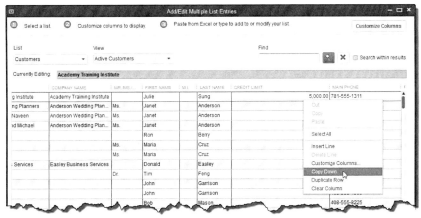

Figure 7-32 – Entering multiple fields in Add/Edit Multiple List Entries

> **Note:**
> You can also use the *Add/Edit Multiple List Entries* to enter multiple new list items by pasting in columns from a spreadsheet that contains the new data.

6. When all the information is complete, click on **Save Changes**.

Setting Up Opening Balances – Step 4

Gathering Your Information

After you've set up your *Chart of Accounts*, you're ready to enter your opening balances. To set up your opening balances, you will need to gather several documents prepared as of your start date. The following is a list of items needed to complete your setup:

Trial Balance: Ask your accountant to provide you with a trial balance for your start date. If your start date is the end of your fiscal year, ask your accountant for an "after-closing" trial balance. The term "after-closing" means "after all of the income and expenses have been closed into Retained Earnings."

If a trial balance is not available, use an after-closing Balance Sheet and a year-to-date Income Statement as of your start date. Table 7-3 shows a sample after-closing trial balance for Academy Photography on the start date of 12/31/2017.

Academy Photography

Trial Balance
December 31, 2017

	Debit	Credit
Checking	$17,959.60	
Money Market	12,100.00	
Savings	500.00	
Accounts Receivable	1,253.41	
Inventory	7,158.67	
Furniture and Equipment	13,250.00	
Fixed Assets:Accumulated Depreciation		$1,325.00
Accounts Payable		142.00
National Bank VISA Gold		2,152.00
Payroll Liabilities:Company PR Taxes		368.00
Sales Tax Payable		141.79
Line of Credit		6,700.00
Truck Loan		12,000.00
Common Stock		10,000.00
Retained Earnings		19,392.89
TOTAL	$52,221.68	$52,221.68

Table 7-3 Trial Balance on Academy Photography's start date

Bank Statement (for all bank accounts): You will need the most recent bank statement prior to your start date. For example, if your start date is 12/31/2017 you will need the 12/31/2017 bank statements for all of your accounts.

Business Checking Account

Statement Date:	December 31, 2017	Page 1 of 1

Summary:

Previous Balance as of 11/30/17:		$	12,155.10
Total Deposits and Credits: 2	+	$	10,157.28
Total Checks and Debits: 9	-	$	7,027.40
Total Interest Earned	+	$	8.62
Total Service Charge:1	-	$	10.00
Statement Balance as of 12/31/17:	=	**$**	**15,283.60**

Deposits and Other Credits:

DEPOSITS

Date	Description		Amount
8-Dec	Customer Deposit	$	6,150.00
20-Dec	Customer Deposit	$	4,007.28
	2 Deposits:	$	10,157.28

INTEREST

Date	Description		Amount
31-Dec	Interest Earned	$	8.62
	Interest:	$	8.62

Checks and Other Withdrawals:

CHECKS PAID:

Check No.	Date Paid		Amount
316	2-Dec	$	324.00
317	3-Dec	$	128.60
318	5-Dec	$	83.00
319	8-Dec	$	285.00
320	10-Dec	$	1,528.00
321	12-Dec	$	3,000.00
322	13-Dec	$	276.52
323	15-Dec	$	142.00
324	28-Dec	$	1,260.28
	6 Checks Paid:	$	7,027.40

SERVICE CHARGES

Date	Description		Amount
31-Dec	Service Charge	$	10.00
	1 Service Charge:	$	10.00

Figure 7-33 Bank Statement for Academy Photography on 12/31/2017

> **Tip:**
> If your bank statements are not dated on the end of each month, ask your bank to change your statement date to the end of the month. You may also be able to run a statement on your bank's Web site that ends on the date you choose.

Unpaid Bills: List each vendor bill by date of the bill, amount due, and what items or expenses you purchased on the bill (see Table 7-4).

Bill Number	Bill Date	Vendor	Amt. Due	Account/Item	Job	Class	Terms
2342	12/21/17	Wong & Son Video	$142.00	Subcontractors Expense	Mason, Bob (Not Billable)	San Jose	Net 30

Table 7-4 Unpaid bills on Academy Photography's start date

Outstanding Checks and Deposits: You'll need a list of all of your checks and deposits that have not cleared the bank as of the bank statement dated on or prior to your start date.

OUTSTANDING DEPOSTIS AT 12/31/17		
Date	Description	Amount
12/30/17	Customer Deposit	$3,000.00
OUTSTANDING CHECKS AT 12/31/17		
Check No.	Date Paid	Payee	Amount
325	12/26/17	National Bank	$324.00

Table 7-5 Outstanding deposits and checks on Academy Photography's start date

Open Invoices: List each customer invoice including the date of the invoice, amount due, and the items sold on the invoice (see Table 7-6).

Inv #	Invoice Date	Customer:Job	Class	Terms	Item	Qty	Amt Due
3947	12/18/17	Mason, Bob	San Jose	Net 30	Camera Santa Clara Tax Total	1	$695.99 8.25% $753.41
4003	12/21/17	Cruz, Maria: Branch Opening	San Jose	2% 10 Net 30	Photographer $125/hr Total	4	$500.00 $500.00

Table 7-6 Open Invoices on Academy Photography's start date

Employee list and W-4 information for each employee: Gather complete name, address, social security number, and withholding information for each employee.

> **Note:**
> The next three payroll-related lists are necessary only if your start date is in the middle of a calendar year and you want to track payroll details with QuickBooks. If your start date is 12/31, skip these lists and enter the opening balances for payroll liabilities in the liability accounts as shown later in this section.
>
> If your start date is 12/31, you need to enter the detail from these lists only if you want to use QuickBooks to create payroll reports, Form 940, Form 941, or W-2s for the previous year.

Payroll Liabilities by Item: List the amount due for each of your payroll liabilities as of your start date. For example, list the amounts due for federal withholding tax, social security (employer), social security (employee), and any other payroll liabilities.

Year-to-Date Payroll Detail by Employee: If your start date is not 12/31 and you want QuickBooks to track your payroll, you will need gross earnings, withholdings, employer taxes, and any other deductions for each employee so far this year. For the most detail, this list should include each employee's earnings *for each month* this year.

Year-to-Date Payroll Tax Deposits: If your start date is not 12/31, list each payroll tax deposit during the year by *Payroll Item*.

Physical Inventory by Inventory Part: List the quantity and cost for each product in inventory (see Table 7-7).

> **Tip:**
> If you don't have actual counts and costs for your inventory, you'll need to estimate. However, the accuracy of your reports will be compromised if you don't have accurate setup numbers. If possible, we strongly recommend conducting a physical inventory as of your QuickBooks start date.

Company File Setup - Setting Up Opening Balances – Step 4   **257**

Physical Inventory at 12/31/17		
Item	Qty. on Hand	Value
Camera	10	$4,500.00
Case	25	1,125.00
Frame	25	53.75
Lenses	8	1,479.92

Table 7-7 Physical inventory on Academy Photography's start date

Opening Balances for Accounts

To enter opening balances, you can either edit the account in the *New Account* or *Edit Account* window, or create a *General Journal Entry*. Entering the *Opening Balance* in the *New Account* or *Edit Account* window is a good method for setting up a single account. General Journal Entries allow you to set up the Opening Balances for several accounts at once.

When entering opening balances for bank accounts and credit cards, it is very important to use the ending balance from the bank statement dated on (or just prior to) your start date.

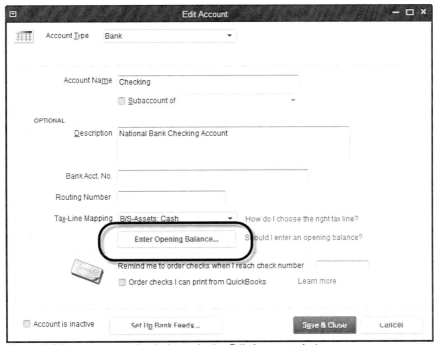

Figure 7-34 Enter an opening balance in the Edit Account window.

Directly Editing the Account

To enter the opening balances, repeat the following steps for each of your Balance Sheet accounts:

COMPUTER PRACTICE

Step 1. Display the Chart of Accounts.

Step 2. Select the **Checking** bank account by clicking on the account name one time.

Step 3. Select the **Account** button at the bottom of the window and then select **Edit Account**.

Step 4. Click on the **Enter Opening Balance** Button (see Figure 7-34).

Step 5. In the *Enter Opening Balance: Bank Account* window (see Figure 7-35), enter *15,283.60* in the *Statement Ending Balance* field. This amount is the ending balance on the bank statement.

Step 6.   Enter **12/31/17** in the *Statement Ending Date* field.

Figure 7-35 Enter Opening Balance for a Bank Account window

Step 7.   Click **OK** to finalize the *Enter Opening Balance: Bank Account* window. Then, click **Save & Close** on the *Edit Account Window*. Repeat Steps 2 through 7 for the *Money Market* account. Enter an opening balance of *$12,100.00* as of *12/31/2017* (see Figure 7-36).

Figure 7-36 Edit the Money Market account to enter an opening balance

You can also enter bank account balances as part of a *General Journal Entry*. We will use this method to enter the opening balance for the *Savings* bank account balance. However with this method, the starting balance on your first *Bank Reconciliation* will be zero. If you want your starting balance to equal your *Opening Balance*, enter the bank account's *Opening Balance* in the *Edit Account* window.

> **Accounting Behind the Scenes:**
> When you enter an opening balance in an account, a transaction posts to the account and to *Opening Balance Equity*. Also, the opening balance in a bank type account becomes the *Beginning Balance* for the first bank reconciliation.
>
> **Note:**
> QuickBooks does not allow you to directly enter the opening balance for *Accounts Receivable, Undeposited Funds, Accounts Payable, Sales Tax Payable,* or *Opening Balance Equity*. To enter opening balances for these accounts, see later in this chapter.

Recording Opening Balances Using a General Journal Entry

General Journal Entries allow you to record debits and credits to specific accounts. Other forms in QuickBooks, such as *Invoices* or *Bills*, take care of the credits and debits for you behind the scenes (See page 2). *General Journal Entries* record transactions that cannot otherwise be recorded using QuickBooks forms.

Because total debits always equal total credits, the total of the debit column and the total of the credit column must be equal or you will not be able to save the *General Journal Entry*. QuickBooks automatically calculates the amount required to make these entries balance as you create each new line in the *General Journal Entry*. Even though QuickBooks automatically enters this amount, it is only correct when you reach the last entry line. To change the amount, simply enter the correct number over the automatic number. For the final line of this *General Journal Entry*, code the amount QuickBooks calculates to the *Opening Bal Equity* account. This amount may be a debit or a credit, depending on the other figures in the entry.

Although the *Trial Balance* doesn't show any balance in Opening Bal Equity, you use this account during setup to keep everything in balance. At the end of the setup process, you'll transfer the balance from this account into Retained Earnings, as shown later in the setup steps.

You can use a *General Journal Entry* to record some, but not all, of your opening balances. Do not include the following accounts in the *General Journal Entry*: Accounts Receivable, Accounts Payable, Inventory, Sales Tax Payable, and Retained Earnings. You will enter the opening balance for these accounts later in the 12-Step setup. For example, you'll exclude Accounts Receivable and Accounts Payable because you will create *Invoices* and *Bills* to enter these accounts, respectively. See *Entering Open Bills (Accounts Payable)* on page 261.

COMPUTER PRACTICE

Use the information from the Trial Balance on page 254 to complete the following steps:

Step 1. Select the **Company** menu and then select **Make General Journal Entries**. If necessary, click **OK** in the *Assign Numbers to Journal Entries* dialog box. If you are not using QuickBooks Accountant, your *Make General Journal Entries* window will appear differently.

Step 2. Fill in the **Make General Journal Entries** window as shown in Figure 7-37. Make sure to uncheck *Adjusting Entry*.

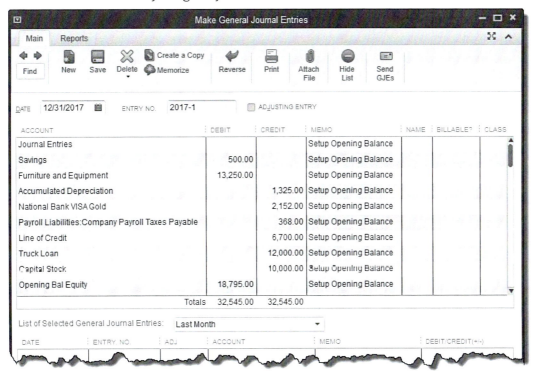

Figure 7-37 Enter opening balances using a General Journal Entry – Your window may appear differently

> **Note:**
> It is a best practice to use an account called Journal Entries on the top line of each General Journal Entry, as shown in Figure 7-37. Use the *Bank* account type when setting up this account in your *Chart of Accounts*. The *Journal Entries* account will never have a balance, so it will never show on financial statements, but it will have a register where you'll be able to look at all of your *General Journal Entries*.

Step 3. Click **Save & Close** to save the entry.

Step 4. QuickBooks will warn you that you can set up Fixed Asset Items from the *Fixed Asset Item List*. Click **OK**. If you see the *Items not assigned classes* dialog box, click the **Save Anyway** button.

> **Important Note:**
> In this example, you're setting up the opening balances for Payroll Liabilities directly in the accounts instead of first setting up the Payroll function. This way, you can finalize your opening balances before worrying about the Payroll setup, and you can separate the tasks of Company setup and Payroll setup.
>
> Remember though, because we've set up the liabilities outside of the Payroll system, your first Payroll Liability payment (for last year's liability), must be entered using the *Write Checks* window instead of the *Pay Liabilities* window. Alternatively, you could set up the Payroll Liability Balances using the *Adjust Liabilities* window with the *Do not Affect Accounts* setting. Then, you would use the *Pay Liabilities* window to pay your opening Payroll Liability balances.

Understanding Opening Bal Equity

As you enter the opening balances for your assets and liabilities, QuickBooks automatically adds offsetting amounts in the *Opening Bal Equity* account. This account, which is created automatically by QuickBooks, is very useful if used properly. As you'll see later in this section, each of the opening balance transactions you enter into QuickBooks will affect this account. Then, after you have entered all of the opening balances, you'll "close" *Opening Bal Equity* into *Retained Earnings* (or *Owner's Equity*). After the set up process is complete, the Opening Balance Equity account must always maintain a zero balance.

> **Tip:**
> By using the *Opening Bal Equity* account during setup, you will quickly be able to access the detail of your setup transactions by looking at the *Opening Bal Equity* register.

Entering Open Items – Step 5

Entering Outstanding Checks and Deposits

To help with the first bank reconciliations, you want all of the outstanding checks and deposits to show in QuickBooks so that you can match them with your first bank statement after the start date. If you don't enter the individual transactions, you won't see them in the QuickBooks reconciliation window. In addition, if a transaction never clears the bank, you won't know which transaction it was without going back to your old records.

COMPUTER PRACTICE

For each of your bank accounts and credit cards, enter all outstanding checks (or charges) and deposits (or payments) as additional transactions in the account register. Enter each outstanding check and deposit with the date the check was written or the deposit made, and post each transaction to *Opening Bal Equity*.

Step 1. With the **Chart of Accounts** open, double-click on the **Checking** account to display its register.

Step 2. Enter new transactions directly in the register for each outstanding check and deposit (see Figure 7-38). See the list of outstanding checks and deposits in Table 7-5 on page 256.

	By default, the outstanding checks and deposits will sort into date order in the register, before the Opening Balance transaction. The balance including the outstanding checks and deposits must match your accountant's trial balance.
Step 3.	Notice that the ending balance in the account now matches the balance on the 12/31/2017 Trial Balance.
Step 4.	Close all open windows.

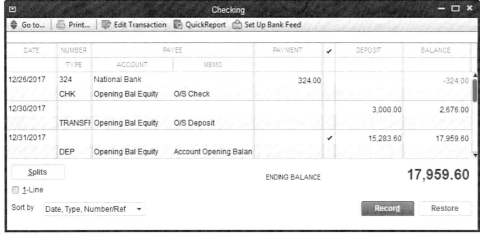

Figure 7-38 Checking account register with outstanding checks and deposits

Entering Open Bills (Accounts Payable)

COMPUTER PRACTICE

Enter your **Unpaid Bills** and **Vendor Credits** as of the start date. Use the original date of the bill (or credit) along with all of the details (terms, vendor, etc.) of the bill. By entering the individual bills, you can preserve detailed job costing and class tracking data if needed.

Step 1.	Click **Enter Bills** on the *Home page*, or select **Enter Bills** from the *Vendors* menu.
Step 2.	Enter the **Bill** as shown in Figure 7-39.
Step 3.	Click **Save & Close** to save the transaction.

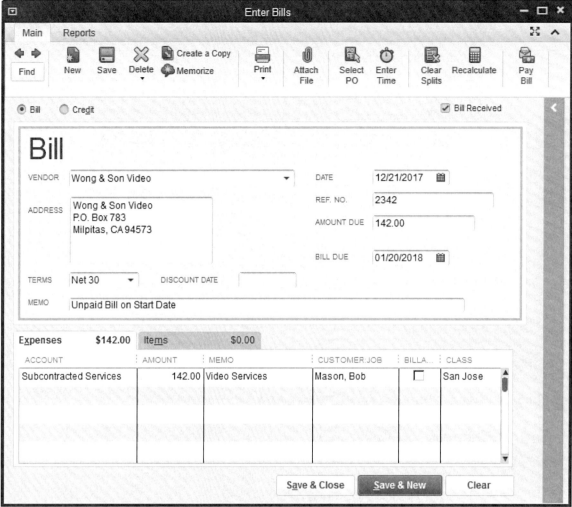

Figure 7-39 Enter the open Bill with the actual Bill date and the Bill due date.

Entering Open Invoices (Accounts Receivable)

Enter each *Invoice* or *Credit Memo* as of the Start Date. Enter each *Invoice* with its original date along with all of the details (terms, customer, etc.) of the original *Invoice*.

COMPUTER PRACTICE

Step 1. From the *Home page* click **Create Invoices** or select **Create Invoices** from the *Customers* menu. If you see the *Professional Services Form* dialog box, click **OK**.

Step 2. Enter the **Invoice** as shown in Figure 7-40. When you see the warning about insufficient quantities, click **OK**. If you receive a warning in the *Not Enough Quantity* and/or *the Tracking Customer Orders* windows, click **OK**. Make sure the **Academy Photo Service Invoice** is selected in the *Template* field.

Step 3. Click **Save & New** to save the transaction and display a new *Invoice*.

Company File Setup - Entering Open Items – Step 5

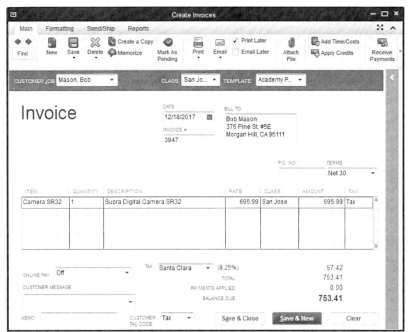

Figure 7-40 Enter the open Invoice with the original Invoice date.

Step 4.   Enter another Invoice as shown in Figure 7-41. The *Customer:Job* is *Cruz, Maria: Branch Opening*. Click **Save & Close** to save the *Invoice*.

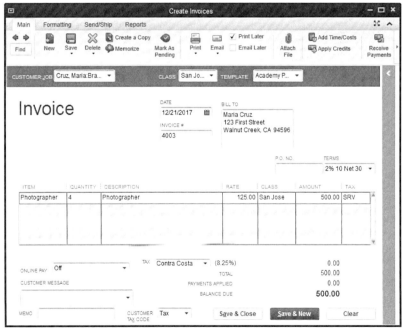

Figure 7-41 Enter this open Invoice.

> **Note:**
> When you set up your company file, it is important that you enter all *Invoices*, *Credit Memos*, *Bills*, and *Bill Credits* separately. QuickBooks needs the details of the transactions, such as the date, terms, and Customer or Vendor information, to prepare accurate aging reports (e.g., *Unpaid Bills Detail* and *A/R Aging Summary*).
>
> In addition, when you receive money against one of your prior year *Invoices* or pay a prior year *Bill*, you will need individual *Invoices* and *Bills* against which to match the receipts and payments.

Entering Open Purchase Orders

If you have open *Purchase Orders*, enter them individually, just as you did with *Bills*, *Bill Credits*, *Invoices*, and *Credit Memos*. Enter each *Purchase Order* with its original date and all of its details. If you have partially received items on the *Purchase Order*, enter only the quantities yet to be received from the Vendor.

Entering Open Estimates and Sales Orders

If you have open *Estimates* and/or *Sales Orders* (not available in QuickBooks Pro), enter them individually, just as you did with *Bills*, *Bill Credits*, *Invoices*, and *Credit Memos*. Enter each *Estimate* and/or *Sales Order* with its original date and all of its details. If you have already progress-billed a portion of the *Estimate* or delivered part of the *Sales Order*, enter only the remaining amount to be invoiced.

Entering Year-to-Date Income and Expenses – Step 6

Earlier you learned that Income and Expense accounts are totaled at the end of the fiscal year as the Net Profit (or Loss) and are combined with Retained Earnings (see page 2). In this chapter's exercise the start date is the end of the fiscal year. Later in the 12-Step process you will see the Income and Expense accounts zeroed out and their balances combined with Retained Earnings on the first day of the year (1/1/18). However, when your company file has a start date that is *not* the end of the fiscal year, the year-to-date amounts for the Income and Expense accounts will need to be entered as a *General Journal Entry* (see Figure 7-42).

All the income amounts should be entered into the Credit column. All the expense amounts should be entered into the Debit column. Use your Opening Balance Equity account to record your net income (or loss) to date.

> THE *GENERAL JOURNAL ENTRY* SHOWN IN FIGURE 7-42 IS FOR REFERENCE ONLY. IT SHOWS A MID-YEAR SETUP ENTRY. DO NOT ENTER IT NOW.

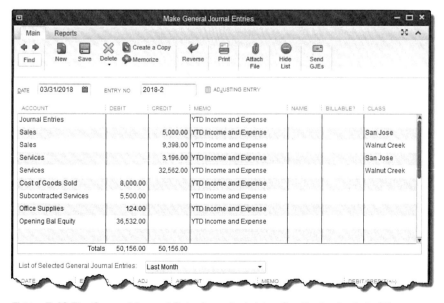

Figure 7-42 The General Journal Entry for a start date after the beginning of the year

Adjusting Opening Balance for Sales Tax Payable – Step 7

To enter the opening balance for *Sales Tax Payable*, begin by opening the *Sales Tax Payable* register to view the activity in the account. Notice that there are entries for each of the open *Invoices* you just entered. This is your *uncollected* tax. Since the total Sales Tax Liability is a combination of the *collected* tax and the *uncollected* tax, you will need to subtract the current balance in the account (the *uncollected* tax) from the amount shown on the trial balance from your accountant (or your 12/31/2017 sales tax return) to arrive at the unpaid *collected* tax.

$$TotalTaxDue = CollectedTax + UncollectedTax$$
$$CollectedTax = AmountsAlreadyCollectedButNotPaid$$
$$UncollectedTax = TaxOnOpenInvoices$$
$$...therefore$$
$$AdjustmentAmount = CollectedTax = TotalTaxDue - UncollectedTax$$

Equation 7-1 Calculating the amount of your sales tax adjustment

For example, you know from the trial balance that Academy Photography's Total Tax Due is $141.79. The Uncollected Tax has already been entered with *Invoice* #3947. The sales tax on this *Invoice* was $57.42. By subtracting the Uncollected Sales Tax ($57.42) from the Total Tax Due ($141.79), you can calculate the Collected Tax, $84.37.

You must create a *Sales Tax Adjustment* for the collected tax amount.

COMPUTER PRACTICE

Step 1.   Select the **Vendors** menu, then select **Sales Tax**, and then select **Adjust Sales Tax Due**.

Step 2.   Complete the *Sales Tax Adjustment* window as shown in Figure 7-43 and then click **OK**. If you see the *Items not assigned classes* dialog box, click the **Save Anyway** button.

If you pay sales tax to more than one sales tax agency, you will need to enter a separate adjustment for each agency.

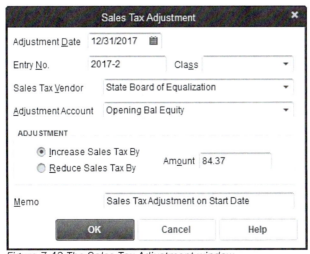

Figure 7-43 The Sales Tax Adjustment window

> **Did You Know?**
> The *Sales Tax Adjustment* window creates a *General Journal Entry* transaction in QuickBooks. Therefore, the Entry No. field will display the next *General Journal Entry* number in sequence. If you prefer, you could instead enter this adjustment using a *General Journal Entry*.

Adjusting Inventory and Setting up Fixed Assets – Step 8

If you have inventory, you will need to create an inventory adjustment to enter the actual quantity and value on hand as of your start date. This is done *after* you enter your outstanding *Bills* and *Invoices*, so that the actual inventory counts and costs will be accurate even if some of the *Bills* and/or *Invoices* include *Inventory Items*.

As with the adjustment to Sales Tax Payable, begin by opening the *Inventory* register to view the activity and the current balance. Also, open the *Item List* to view the current stock status of each Inventory Item. Then adjust the quantity on hand and value of each item so that Inventory will agree with the physical inventory counts and the company's trial balance as of your start date.

Adjusting Inventory for Actual Counts

COMPUTER PRACTICE

Step 1. Select the Vendors menu, then select Inventory Activities, and then select Adjust Quantity/Value on Hand.

Step 2. Choose **Quantity and Total Value** from the *Adjustment Type* field (see Figure 7-44).

Step 3. Enter *12/31/2017* in the *Adjustment Date* field. Press **Tab**.

Step 4. Select **Opening Bal Equity** in the *Adjustment Account* field.

Step 5. Click **OK** on the *Income or Expense expected* warning window.

Step 6. Enter *2017-3* in the *Ref. No.* field. Press **Tab**.

Step 7. Leave both the *Customer:Job* and *Class* fields blank.

Step 8. Enter the information in Figure 7-44.

If your *Qty on Hand* column does not match, check the *Adjustment Date* to make sure it says *12/31/2017* as this column is calculated as of the adjustment date. If your date is correct and you still don't match, then make sure you entered Invoice 3947 correctly earlier in this chapter.

Step 9. Click **Save & Close** to record the transaction. If you see the *Items not assigned classes* dialog box, click the **Save Anyway** button.

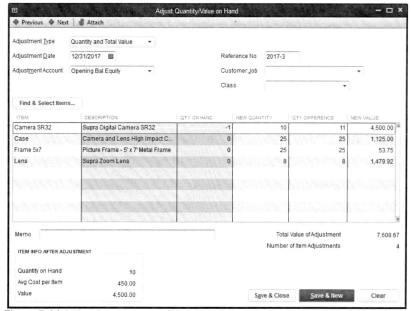

Figure 7-44 Adjust inventory as of the start date

Setting up Fixed Assets

You can track detailed information about your company's Fixed Assets. You can set up detailed information about each asset using the *Fixed Asset Item* List. Then, if you use QuickBooks Accountant, your accountant can use the *Fixed Asset Manager* to individually calculate and track depreciation on each asset.

Setting up Loans

You can track detailed information about your loans. You can individually track and amortize each of your loans so that QuickBooks will automatically allocate the principal and interest on each payment.

Setup Payroll and YTD Payroll Information – Step 9

Setting up Payroll in QuickBooks is a lengthy and involved process. Refer to our companion textbook *QuickBooks Complete* for more information about setting up the Payroll feature.

Verifying your Trial Balance – Step 10

Before you complete the set up process by transferring the balance of *Opening Bal Equity* into *Retained Earnings*, make sure the account balances in QuickBooks match your accountant's trial balance.

COMPUTER PRACTICE

Step 1.   Select the **Reports** menu, then select **Accountant & Taxes**, and then select **Trial Balance**.

Step 2.   Set the *From* and *To* date field to your start date as shown in Figure 7-45.

Step 3.   After reviewing the *Trial Balance*, write down the balance of the *Opening Bal Equity* account, and close the window. Click **No** if you are given the option to memorize the report.

Notice that the *Trial Balance* in Figure 7-45 looks slightly different from your accountant's report (in Table 7-3). For example, there are balances in several income and expense accounts as well as in *Opening Bal Equity*. Do not worry about this difference at this point as you are not finished with the setup yet. The income and expense accounts have balances because you just entered *Invoices* and *Bills* for the open invoices and unpaid bills. Those *Invoices* and *Bills* were dated during the prior year, so those transactions add to income and expenses for that year. QuickBooks will automatically close the balances in the income and expense accounts to Retained Earnings at the start of the next year on 01/01/2018.

Your *Trial Balance* could also differ from your accountant's report if the reporting basis on the two reports is not the same. For example, if you create an accrual basis *Trial Balance* and your accountant's *Trial Balance* is cash basis, the balances in the income and expense accounts may be different. Regardless of which method of accounting you use, the income and expense accounts will automatically be closed to Retained Earnings. Therefore, at this point in your setup, you should create an accrual basis *Trial Balance*, regardless of which basis you will ultimately use on reports. Just verify that all of the *Balance Sheet* account balances are accurate with the exception of Retained Earnings.

> **Note:**
> To learn more about the cash or accrual basis of accounting see the section beginning on page 190.

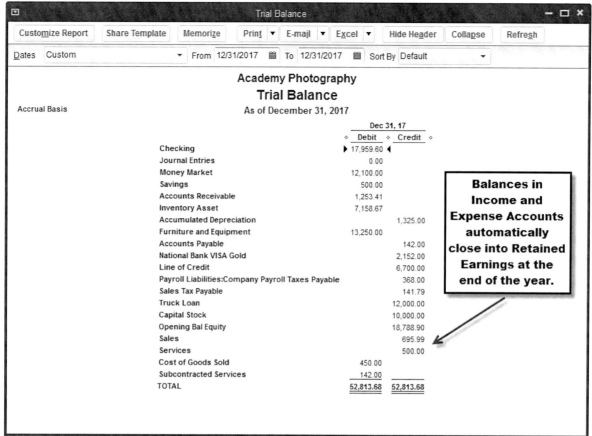

Figure 7-45 Trial Balance for Academy Photography as of the start date

Closing Opening Bal Equity – Step 11

Once you have compared your *Trial Balance* report to your accountant's report, use a *General Journal Entry* to transfer (close) the balance in *Opening Bal Equity* into *Retained Earnings*.

> **Note:**
> If your company is a sole proprietorship, use this same process, but instead of *Retained Earnings*, the account should be called *Owner's Equity*. If your company is a partnership, split the balance of *Opening Bal Equity* between each of the partners' profit accounts.

COMPUTER PRACTICE

Step 1. Select the **Company** menu and then select **Make General Journal Entry**. If necessary, click **OK** in the *Assign Numbers to Journal Entries* dialog box. The screenshot below is from QuickBooks Accountant. If you are using a different edition of QuickBooks, your window may appear differently.

Step 2. Set the **Date** field to your start date.

Step 3. Enter the **General Journal Entry** as shown in Figure 7-46 and then click **Save & Close**.

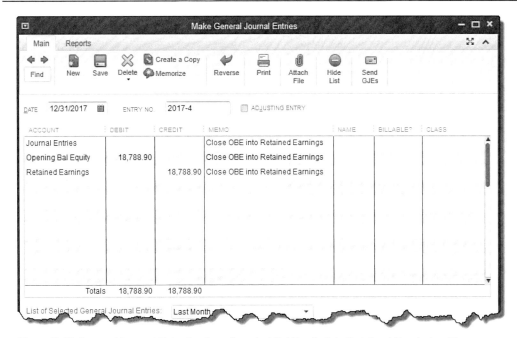

Figure 7-46 General Journal Entry to close Opening Bal Equity into Retained Earnings – Your screen may vary

Step 4. If the *Retained Earnings* window appears, click **OK**. If you see the *Items not assigned classes* dialog box, click the **Save Anyway** button.

When you are finished entering all of the opening balances and you have closed the *Opening Bal Equity* account into *Retained Earnings*, verify your *Balance Sheet*. Create a *Balance Sheet* for *the day after* your start date and verify that the numbers match your accountant's trial balance.

COMPUTER PRACTICE

Step 1. Select the **Reports** menu, then select **Company & Financial**, and then select **Balance Sheet Standard**.

Step 2. Set the *As of* field to *01/01/2018*, the day after your start date (see Figure 7-47).

Step 3. Print the report and then close the window.

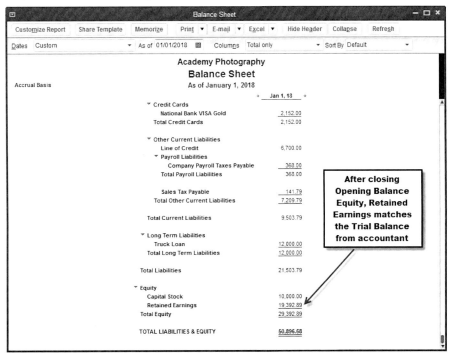

Figure 7-47 Academy Photography Balance Sheet

Setting the Closing Date - Backing up the File – Step 12

Now that you have entered all of your opening balances in the file, create a backup of the file. It is a good idea to keep this backup in a secure location so that you always have a clean record of your setup transactions. This is in addition to your regular backup process.

Setting the Closing Date to Protect your Setup Balances

For details on setting the *Closing Date* and the *Closing Date password*, see our companion textbook *QuickBooks Complete*.

Congratulations! You have finished the setup of your company file and are ready to begin entering transactions. First you need to set up users of the file so you can control which areas of QuickBooks can be accessed by individuals.

Users and Passwords

QuickBooks provides a feature for defining "users" of the file. This feature allows the "administrator" (the owner of the file) to set privileges for each user of the file. This provides security and user tracking when several people have access to the same data file.

Setting Up Users in the Company File

Each user should have a separate user name and password. Once users have been setup, QuickBooks will require a user name and password when a company file is opened. The privileges granted to that user by the administrator determine what functions of QuickBooks they can access. For example, a user might have access to Accounts Receivable, Accounts Payable, and Banking functions, but not Payroll or "sensitive activities" like online banking. For a complete description of each privilege, click the **Help** button on the *User Setup* windows.

COMPUTER PRACTICE

Step 1. First you will setup the Administrator's password. Select the **Company** menu, select **Set Up Users and Passwords**, and then select **Change Your Password**. The *Change QuickBooks Password* window will appear (Figure 7-48).

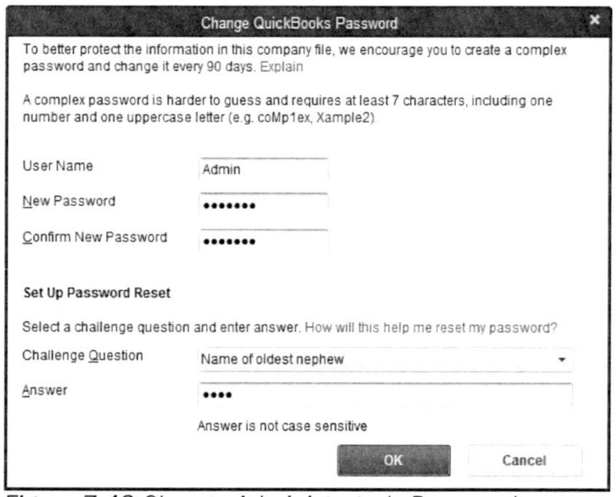

Figure 7-48 Change Administrator's Password

Step 2. Leave **Admin** in the *User Name* field and then press **Tab** (see Figure 7-48).

You could, of course, change the administrator's *User Name*, but even if you do, you'll

Company File Setup - Users and Passwords   **271**

always be able to log in (or open the file) as the administrator if you enter *Admin* in the user name field and if you enter the administrator's correct password.

Step 3.   Enter *Abc1234* in the *Administrator's Password* and *Confirm Password* fields. Once you enter this password, you will need to remember this password to open this exercise file in the future.

Several privileges are reserved exclusively for the administrator of the file. For example, the administrator is the only one who can view or change the company information (name, address, etc.). Also, the administrator is the only one who can make any changes to the *Company Preferences* tabs in the *Preferences* section. For more information about the file administrator, see QuickBooks online Help.

> **Note:**
> To protect and secure your QuickBooks data file, always use a complex password. Complex passwords use at least seven characters, including capital and lowercase letters, numbers, and special characters. At least one of the characters should be a number and another should be an uppercase letter.

Step 4.   In the *Challenge Question* field, select **Name of oldest nephew**.

Step 5.   Enter **Bill** in the *Answer* field. Click **OK**. After reading the password reminder window, click **OK** again.

Step 6.   Now you will set up the user's privileges for an individual. Select **Set Up Users** from the *Set Up Users and Passwords* submenu of the *Company* menu. The *QuickBooks Login* window displays (see Figure 7-49).

Step 7.   Type *Abc1234* in the *Password* field and click **OK**.

Figure 7-49 QuickBooks Login window

Step 8.   The window in Figure 7-50 shows the *User list* for this company file. To create an additional user, click **Add User**.

Figure 7-50 The User List for a company file

Step 9. When you click **Add User**, QuickBooks walks you through a series of windows (a Wizard) where you set privileges for each user (see Figure 7-51). Make your selections as appropriate.

Step 10. On the *User Name and Password* window, enter *Kathy* in the *User Name* field, and enter *Abc4321* in the *Password* and *Confirm Password* fields. Click **Next**.

Figure 7-51 The User Name and Password window

Step 11. On the *Access for user: Kathy* window, select **Selected areas of QuickBooks** (see Figure 7-52). Click **Next**.

As the Administrator, you can give users access to all areas of QuickBooks or you can restrict access to selected areas of the program.

Company File Setup - Users and Passwords   **273**

Figure 7-52 You can restrict a user's access

> **Did you know?**
> By selecting *Access to All areas of QuickBooks*, you give a user permission to change transactions in closed periods. Even if you want a user to have access to all areas, it's better to choose *Selected areas of QuickBooks* for all users. Then select *Full Access* in all areas but say *No* on the allow users to change or delete transactions that were recorded before the closing date. This protects your prior period accounting data without limiting the users' access to any other transactions or reporting.

Step 12.   On the *Sales and Accounts Receivable* window, select **Full Access** and click **Next** (see Figure 7-53).

Figure 7-53 The Sales and Accounts Receivable window

Step 13.   Click **Next** on each of the following windows to view the default settings.

When setting up your own file, set access rights for each new user as appropriate. If you are not sure what to select, click **Help**. Online Help will fully explain each privilege.

Each user should be restricted from *Changing or Deleting Transactions recorded before the closing date* (see Figure 7-54). This setting creates additional protection for your accounting data once you have closed the books for a period.

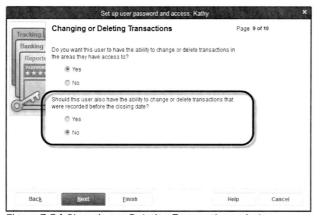
Figure 7-54 Changing or Deleting Transactions window

Step 14. On the final window, review the privileges that you have set for this user (see Figure 7-55). If you want to make any changes, click **Back** until you see the window you want to change. To save your new user settings, click **Finish**. If you receive an Intuit Sync Manager warning, click **OK**.

Figure 7-55 The Summary window

Step 15. Click **Close** on the *User List* window.

Multi-User and Single-User Modes

QuickBooks is often run in a networked environment, where multiple users access the file at the same time. In such an environment, you will need to have QuickBooks open in *multi-user* mode to allow these users to access the file. However, there are a few changes that cannot be made to a file while QuickBooks is in *multi-user* mode and require you to switch to *single-user* mode. When QuickBooks is in *single-user* mode, only one person can access the file at a time. Any user, not just those with *Administrator* privileges can use QuickBooks in *single-user* mode. Some of the changes that require *single-user* mode include making backups, exporting data, or deleting a list item.

> Note:
> Each user must have the same version of QuickBooks on their computer system to access the same company file. All versions of QuickBooks, including Pro, Premier, Accountant and Enterprise, support multiple users.

To switch to *single-user* mode, first contact the others in your company who are using your file and ask them to exit out of the QuickBooks file. Once they have exited the file, go to the *File* menu and select *Switch To Single-User Mode*. When you are done in *single-user* mode, you can switch back to *multi-user* from the same location on the *File* menu.

Figure 7-56 Switch to Multi-user Mode on File menu

Review Questions

Comprehension Questions

1. Explain how the Opening Balance Equity account is used when you set up a new bank account in the Chart of Accounts.

2. Explain how you would set up your Chart of Accounts to separately track state, county, and city taxes and provide a summary total of all taxes paid at the same time.

3. If you have been separately tracking your entertainment and meal expenses, what action would you take if you wanted to track them as one account?

4. Explain the importance of entering your outstanding checks as of the Start Date into the *Checking* account.

5. What information should you gather before setting up a QuickBooks file?

Multiple Choice

Select the best answer(s) for each of the following:

1. Your company has decided to begin using QuickBooks at the beginning of the 2018 calendar year, which is also the fiscal year. The best start date for your company file setup is:
    a) January 1, 2018.
    b) The date when you first decide to use QuickBooks.
    c) December 31, 2017.
    d) There is no best start date, you can use whatever date is convenient.

2. This chapter suggests that the best way to set up A/R and A/P balances in QuickBooks is to:
    a) Enter the total amount of A/R and A/P on a *General Journal Entry* dated on your start date.
    b) Enter the balance of each account by editing the accounts in the *Chart of Accounts*.
    c) Use a special account called A/R Setup (or A/P Setup) to record the opening balances.
    d) Enter a separate *Invoice* for each open invoice and enter a separate *Bill* for each unpaid bill.

3. Setting up a company file does not include:
   a) Obtaining a business license.
   b) Selecting the appropriate chart of accounts for your type of business.
   c) Adding accounts to the chart of accounts.
   d) Entering *Invoices*.

4. A good example of a liability account is:
   a) Inventory.
   b) Accounts Receivable.
   c) Advertising.
   d) Accounts Payable.

5. To ensure the accuracy of the information entered during setup, it is important to:
   a) Know your Retained Earnings.
   b) Verify that your *Trial Balance* matches the one provided by your accountant.
   c) Start at the beginning of the fiscal period.
   d) Know everything there is to know about accounting.

6. Close Opening Bal Equity into Retained Earnings by:
   a) Starting to enter new daily transactions.
   b) Creating a General Journal Entry.
   c) Setting the Closing Date. QuickBooks will then make the entry for you.
   d) Selecting **Close Opening Balance** on the **Activities** menu.

7. If you no longer need an account in the Chart of Accounts, you can delete it. However, if it has transactions posted to it, you cannot delete it. Instead:
   a) You should ignore it.
   b) You should rename it.
   c) You can merge it with another account, or you can deactivate it.
   d) You can move it to the bottom of the chart of accounts, which will cause it to no longer appear on reports.

8. Which of the following is NOT a way to deactivate an account?
   a) Right-click on the account and select **Make Inactive**.
   b) Select **Make Account Inactive** from the **Account** menu at the bottom of the Chart of Accounts.
   c) Edit the account and click **Account is Inactive**.
   d) Select the account and check the **Include Inactive** checkbox at the bottom of the Chart of Accounts.

9. When account numbers are inactive and you click the *Name* header:
   a) QuickBooks sorts the account list alphabetically by account name.
   b) You can rename the selected account.
   c) You will see all account names.
   d) You can rename the Chart of Accounts list.

10. As the administrator, you can set up new users of the file and restrict access to several areas in the program. Which is something you CANNOT restrict?
    a) Access to all bank accounts.
    b) Access to A/P transactions.
    c) Access to Payroll.
    d) Access to one bank account, but no access to another bank account.

Company File Setup - Review Questions **277**

11. When verifying your setup, create a Balance Sheet and verify that Retained Earnings matches the Trial Balance from the accountant. If your start date is 12/31, what date should you use on this Balance Sheet?

    a) Always use the Start Date.
    b) December 31.
    c) January 1.
    d) December 30.

12. To set up the opening balance in your *Sales Tax Payable* account, wait until after you've entered your open invoices. Then adjust the *Sales Tax Payable* account for the additional sales tax due. Why is this adjustment necessary?

    a) Because Opening Bal Equity is not involved.
    b) Because the total amount in Sales Tax Payable is the sum of the *uncollected* sales tax (from the open invoices) plus the *collected* sales tax. Since you already entered the open invoices, the Sales Tax Payable account only has the *uncollected* sales tax and you have to add in the *collected* sales tax by adjusting the account balance.
    c) Because there is no other way to set up the opening balance in Sales Tax Payable.
    d) All of the above.

13. Where does QuickBooks place new accounts in the Chart of Accounts after it has been manually reordered?

    a) Alphabetically within its account type.
    b) Alphabetically in the list, regardless of account type.
    c) At the top of the list, within its account type.
    d) At the bottom of the Chart of Accounts.

14. If you have an open Invoice for an inventory item on your start date, to properly set up your Inventory balances (Quantity and Value):

    a) Use a Journal Entry to debit Inventory for the total value of the inventory and then select **Setup Inventory Quantities** from the **Inventory** menu.
    b) Use an Inventory Adjustment transaction *after* you enter in your opening Invoices and Bills.
    c) Use an Inventory Adjustment transaction *before* you enter in your opening Invoices and Bills.
    d) Use the *Opening Balance* field in the *Edit Account* window.

15. Which of the following do you set up using the *EasyStep Interview*?

    a) Default Accounts.
    b) Outstanding Checks and Deposits.
    c) Inventory.
    d) Sales Tax.

Completion Statements

1. There are five basic account types in accounting: _____, _____, _____, _____, and _____.

2. It is impossible to _____ a QuickBooks account if you have used it in transactions.

3. At the end of your setup, close the _____ _____ _____ account into Retained Earnings.

4. You can use a(n) _____ _____ _____ to record multiple accounts' opening balances at one time.

5. The account balances on your _____ _____ from your previous books and your QuickBooks file should match at the end of your file setup.

Setup Problem 1

1. Create a *new* QuickBooks company file for Academy Photography. Use Express Start and the information from the following tables and figures to completely set up the file using 12/31/2017 as your start date. Call your file **Setup-14Problem1.QBW**.

Company Info	
Company name	Academy Photography
Industry	Art, Writing or Photography
Company Type	S Corporation
Tax ID	11-1111111
Do you have Employees?	Yes
Legal name	Academy Photography, Inc.
Address	123 Main Street Pleasanton, CA 94588
Country	U.S.
Phone	925-555-1111
E-mail Address	info@academyphoto.biz
Web site	http://www.academyphoto.biz
Company Filename	Setup-14Problem1.QBW Change the save location to your student data files folder.

Table 7-8 Express Start Setup Information

2. Add a bank account called Checking. Opening Balance is $0.00. Account Number is 12123456. Opening Balance date is 12/31/2017.

3. When finished, create an *Account Listing* report. (The *Account Listing* Report is in the *Reports* menu, under the *List* submenu).

Setup Problem 2 (Advanced)

p.236

APPLYING YOUR KNOWLEDGE

Create a *new* QuickBooks company file for Academy Photography. Use the information from the following tables and figures to completely set up the file using 12/31/2017 as your start date. Use the 12-Step setup process discussed in this chapter. Call your file **Setup-14Problem2.QBW**.

Company Info	
Company name	Academy Photography
Legal name	Academy Photography, Inc.
Tax ID	11-1111111
Address	123 Main Street Pleasanton, CA 94588
Country	U.S.
Phone	925-555-1111
Fax	925-555-1112
E-mail Address	info@academyphoto.biz
Web site	http://www.academyphoto.biz
Industry	Art, Writing or Photography
Income tax form	S Corporation
First month of fiscal year	January
Administrator password	*Leave blank*
Company Filename	Setup-14Problem2.QBW Change the save location to your student data files folder.

Table 7-9 Company Information

Detailed Start Settings	
Products and services	Academy Photography sells both products and services, although they do not sell products online.
Sales	Academy Photography charges sales tax and creates estimates. They want to track sales orders (not available in Pro), and use billing statements and progress invoicing.
Purchases & vendors	Academy Photography will need to track bills, inventory and time.
Employees	Academy Photography has both W-2 employees and 1099 contractors. They will want to track time.
Start Date	Use 12/31/2017

Table 7-10 EasyStep Interview settings

Accounts – In the Easy Step Interview, accept the default chart of account suggested for you industry. After completing the Interview, add the accounts listed in Table 7-11. Since QuickBooks automatically created a Sales Income Account, you will only need to change the account number for this account. It is not necessary to enter descriptions, bank account numbers, or assign tax line items to any of these accounts for this problem. You will also create subaccounts where names are separated from the main account by a colon (:). For example, Company Payroll Taxes Payable is a subaccount of Payroll Liabilities. For a full recommended *Chart of Accounts*, see Setup Problem 3.

Additional Accounts for the Chart of Accounts		
Acct #	Account Name	Account Type
10100	Checking	Bank
10200	Money Market	Bank
10900	Journal Entries	Bank
22000	National Bank VISA Gold	Credit Card
24010	Payroll Liabilities:Company Payroll Taxes Payable	Other Current Liability
24020	Payroll Liabilities:Employee Payroll Taxes Payable	Other Current Liability
24030	Payroll Liabilities:Other Payroll Liabilities	Other Current Liability
27000	Truck Loan	Long Term Liability
40000	Services	Income
45000	Sales (*note: change number of existing account*)	Income

Table 7-11 Additional Accounts for the Chart of Accounts

Items – Table 7-12 is the *Item List* that will be used to track products and services sold by Academy Photography. Leave any other fields blank or accept the defaults if not shown in the table.

You can add the Service, Inventory Part and Non-Inventory Part during the Easy Step Interview or wait and add all items using the Item List after the interview. Sales Tax Items must be added using the Item List.

Type	Item	Description	Tax Code	Account	Cost	Price
Service	Indoor Photo Session	Indoor Studio Session	Non	Services		$95.00
Service	Retouching	Photo retouching services	Non	Services		$95.00
Inventory Part	Camera SR32	Supra Digital Camera SR32	Tax	Sales	$450.00	$695.99
Inventory Part	Case	Camera and Lens High Impact Case	Tax	Sales	$45.00	$79.99
Non-Inventory Part	Standard Photo Package	Standard Package of Photography from Session	Tax	Sales		$55.00
Sales Tax Item	Contra Costa	Contra Costa Sales Tax Vendor: State Board of Equalization (Quick Add)		Sales Tax Payable		8.25%
Sales Tax Item	Out of State (Automatically Created)	Out of State Sales Tax - exempt from sales tax		Sales Tax Payable		0%
Sales Tax Item	Santa Clara	Santa Clara Sales Tax Vendor: State Board of Equalization (Quick Add)		Sales Tax Payable		8.25%

Table 7-12 Item List

Classes – Academy Photography uses *Classes* to separately track revenues and expenses from each of their locations. You will need to turn on class tracking in the *Accounting Company Preferences*.

Class Names	San Jose	Walnut Creek	Overhead

Table 7-13 Class Tracking

Terms – Verify the following terms in the **Terms List**.

Terms	Net 30	Net 15	2% 10, Net 30	Due on Receipt

Table 7-14 Terms List

Bank Statements – Figure 7-57 shows the Checking account bank statement for Academy Photography on their Start Date of 12/31/2017. There is no bank statement available for the money market and savings accounts, but you've been told that there are no outstanding deposits or checks in those accounts. Enter the **Bank Ending Balance** as the opening balance for Checking account.

Company File Setup - Setup Problem 2 (Advanced)

Business Checking Account

Statement Date: December 31, 2017   Page 1 of 1

Summary:

Previous Balance as of 11/30/17	$	32,624.52
Total Deposits and Credits: 2	+ $	10,157.28
Total Checks and Debits: 9	- $	7,027.40
Total Interest Earned: 1	+ $	8.62
Total Service Charge: 1	- $	10.00
Statement Balance as of 12/31/17:	= $	**35,753.02**

Deposits and Other Credits:

DEPOSITS

Date	Description	Amount
8-Dec	Customer Deposit	$ 6,150.00
20-Dec	Customer Deposit	$ 4,007.28
	2 Deposits:	$ 10,157.28

INTEREST

Date	Description	Amount
31-Dec	Interest Earned	$ 8.62
	Interest:	$ 8.62

Checks and Other Withdrawals:

CHECKS PAID:

Check No.	Date Paid	Amount
3466	2-Dec	$ 324.00
3467	3-Dec	$ 128.60
3468	5-Dec	$ 83.00
3469	8-Dec	$ 285.00
3470	10-Dec	$ 1,528.00
3471	12-Dec	$ 3,000.00
3472	13-Dec	$ 276.52
3473	15-Dec	$ 142.00
3474	28-Dec	$ 1,260.28
	9 Checks Paid:	$ 7,027.40

SERVICE CHARGES

Date	Description	Amount
31-Dec	Service Charge	$ 10.00
	1 Service Charge:	$ 10.00

Figure 7-57 Bank statement for checking account on 12/31/2017

Outstanding Checks and Deposits – Table 7-15 and Table 7-16 shows a list of outstanding checks and deposits in the Checking account on 12/31/2017. Enter the outstanding check and deposit in the checking account register using the original date and Opening Balance Equity as the offsetting account "Quick Add" each of the vendor names when prompted.

Outstanding Deposits at 12/31/17	
Date	Amount
12/30/2017	$1,500.00

Table 7-15 Outstanding deposits

Outstanding Checks at 12/31/17			
Date	Check #	Payee	Amount
12/26/2017	3475	Wong & Son Video	4,229.69

Table 7-16 Outstanding checks

Open Invoices - Table 7-17 shows a list of all open invoices for Academy Photography on 12/31/2017. Enter open **Invoices** using the original information and Intuit Product Invoice template. "QuickAdd" each of the customer names when prompted. Save the class, terms and tax information to be used again.

Inv #	Invoice Date	Customer:Job	Class	Terms	Item/Qty/Amt Due
2017-905	12/18/2017	Doughboy Donuts	San Jose	Net 30	Indoor Photo Session 2 Hours, $190.00 Retouching 1 Hour, $95.00 Out of State Sales Tax Total: $285.00
2017-942	12/21/2017	Scotts Shoes	San Jose	Net 30	Camera $695.99 Santa Clara Sales Tax Total $753.41

Table 7-17 Open Invoices

Unpaid Bills - Academy Photography had one unpaid bill at 12/31/2017. Enter the **Bill** with original information. "Quick Add" each of the vendor names when prompted. Save the terms information to be used again.

Bill #	Bill Date	Terms	Vendor	Amt Due	Account/Item	Job	Class
52773	12/21/17	Net 15	Boswell Consulting	$352.50	Subcontracted Services	Scotts Shoes	San Jose

Table 7-18 Unpaid bills

Physical Inventory– Below are the physical inventory counts and values at 12/31/2017. Enter the Ref. No. as 2017-1 and Opening Balance Equity as Adjusting account. If necessary, select **Save Anyway** option if a dialog box appears asking for class information.

Physical Inventory at 12/31/2017		
Item	Quantity on Hand	Value
Camera	20	$9,000.00
Case	20	900.00

Table 7-19 Physical Inventory by Inventory Part

Trial Balance – Table 7-20 shows the ending trial balance for Academy Photography on 12/31/2017. Enter opening balances as *General Journal Entries* for any remaining Asset, Liabilities (excluding Sales Tax Payable), and Equity accounts (excluding Retained Earnings) to match the trial balance amounts.

Adjust Sales Tax Payable to match trial balance amount, using *Vendor:* State Board of Equalization.

Close the Opening Balance Equity account to Retained Earnings. Verify the Opening Balance Equity account has a zero balance.

You will notice that the Trial Balance does not exactly match the one in Table 7-20. The income and expenses from the open *Invoices* and unpaid *Bills* shows in the income and expense accounts. This is CORRECT! When QuickBooks "closes" the year, those numbers will be posted into Retained Earnings. To see it work, change the date on the *Trial Balance* to 01/01/2018.

Company File Setup - Setup Problem 2 (Advanced)

Academy Photography		
Trial Balance		
December 31, 2017		
	Debit	Credit
Checking	$33,023.33	
Money Market	$68,100.00	
Accounts Receivable	$1,038.41	
Inventory	$9,900.00	
Furniture and Equipment	$85,365.00	
Accumulated Depreciation		$43,550.00
Accounts Payable		$352.50
National Bank VISA Gold		$2,152.00
Payroll Liabilities: Company Payroll Taxes Payable		$83.00
Payroll Liabilities: Employee Payroll Taxes Payable		$285.00
Sales Tax Payable		$327.03
Truck Loan		$28,625.00
Capital Stock		$10,000.00
Retained Earnings		$112,052.21
TOTAL	$197,426.74	$197,426.74

Table 7-20 Trial balance on 12/31/2017

After completing the setup, print the following reports:

1. Account Listing
2. Item Listing
3. Open Invoices Report at 12/31/2017
4. Unpaid Bills Detail Report at 12/31/2017
5. Inventory Valuation Summary Report at 12/31/2017
6. Trial Balance as of 12/31/2017
7. Trial Balance as of 01/01/18
8. Balance Sheet Standard on 01/01/2018

Notice that Retained Earnings on the 01/01/2018 Balance Sheet has been adjusted for the income and expenses from last year. This shows how QuickBooks automatically calculates Retained Earnings. If you change the date on the Balance Sheet to 12/31/2017, you'll see Net Income on the Balance Sheet and the Retained Earnings number will change back to the "before closing" amounts. Try it.

QUICKBOOKS AND BEYOND – TAKE THE NEXT STEP WITH THE SLEETER GROUP BLOG

"QuickBooks for Law Firms: Setup"

QuickBooks Desktop is in use in thousands of small law firms throughout the United States. The program is capable of handling many of the needs of these firms, as long as it is set up properly and transactions are entered correctly and consistently.

In this *QuickBooks and Beyond* section, Caren Schwartz discusses setup issues for a particular business type – law offices. This is the first in a series of posts about using QuickBooks in an attorney's office. Some of the topics covered in this post, such as double-sided items, are covered later in the book; others are beyond the scope of this book. Even if some of the concepts are new, reviewing the post will help you understand how to customize a QuickBooks setup for a particular industry. Read the full post at www.sleeter.com/blog/?p=6103.

New Terminology

Trust – Property (including funds) that is held for an individual, in this case, by a law firm.

General Retainer – A fee a client pays a law firm before services are delivered, for a specific period of time and not for a specific project.

Putting New Knowledge to Use

1. Even though your workplace or business may not be a law firm, understanding how QuickBooks can be set up for different types of businesses can be a useful exercise. What are the specific accounting needs of your business?

Chapter 8
Customizing QuickBooks

Topics

In this chapter, you will learn about the following topics:

- QuickBooks Preferences (page 285)
- Customizing QuickBooks Menus and Windows (page 288)
- QuickBooks Items and Other Lists (page 291)
- Custom Fields (page 304)
- Modifying Sales Form Templates (page 305)

> **Restore this File:**
> This chapter uses the Customizing-14.QBW. To open this file, restore the Customizing-14.QBM file to your hard disk. See page 9 for instructions on restoring files.

QuickBooks has many customizable options that allow you to configure the program to meet your own needs and preferences. This chapter introduces you to many of the ways you can make these configurations in QuickBooks using *Preferences*, customizing the *Home* page, menus, and toolbars, and creating templates for forms. This chapter also introduces some new lists, including the *Item List,* the *Terms List,* and the *Template List.*

QuickBooks Preferences

There are two types of *Preferences* in QuickBooks:

1. **User Preferences.** In QuickBooks, User Preferences are specific to the user who is currently logged on to the file. A user can make changes to his or her User Preferences as desired.

2. **Company Preferences.** Use Company Preferences to make global changes to the features and functionality of an individual company's data file. Only the *Administrator* of the data file can make changes to Company Preferences.

In this section, you will learn about a few of these *Preferences* and how they affect QuickBooks. Clicking the *Help* button in the *Preferences* window will launch QuickBooks Help with specific topics relevant to the *Preference* in the open window.

> **Note:**
> Many of the *Preferences* are discussed in detail in other chapters.

Setting User Preferences

COMPUTER PRACTICE

To access QuickBooks Preferences, follow these steps:

Step 1. Select the **Edit** menu, and then select **Preferences**.

User Preferences – Desktop View

Use the *Desktop View* User Preferences ("*My Preferences*" tab) to customize the view of the current user.

Step 2. Click the **Desktop View** icon. See Figure 8-1.

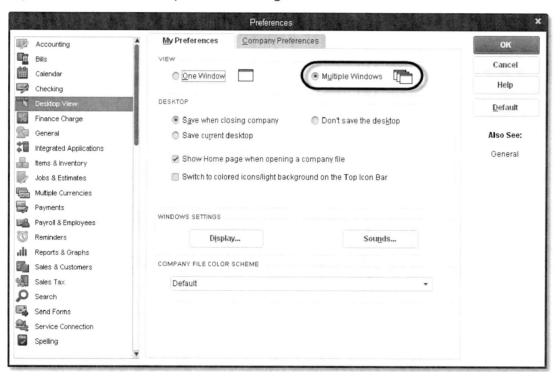

Figure 8-1 User Preferences - Desktop View

The user preferences for *Desktop View* allow you to customize the default windows that show when you open QuickBooks. We recommend selecting *Multiple Windows* as shown on Figure 8-1. Unless you change the Preference to *Multiple Windows*, you will not be able to display more than one QuickBooks window at a time, and you will not be able to change the size of QuickBooks windows.

There is also the *Show Home page when opening a company file* option. Activating this Preference causes the *Home* page window to be displayed whenever the company file is opened.

> **Tip:**
> If you use QuickBooks in a multi-user environment, it may be best to select the *Don't save the desktop* radio button on the window shown in Figure 8-1. If you save the desktop, each time you open QuickBooks it will re-open all of the windows and reports you were viewing when you last used the program. If you save the desktop, this may negatively impact performance for other users when they open the data file.

Company Preferences – Desktop View

Administrators may use the *Company Preferences* tab in the *Desktop View* Preferences to control which icons display on the *Home* page. These settings will affect every user who uses this company file.

Step 1. With the *Desktop View Preference* still selected, click the **Company Preferences** tab (see Figure 8-2).

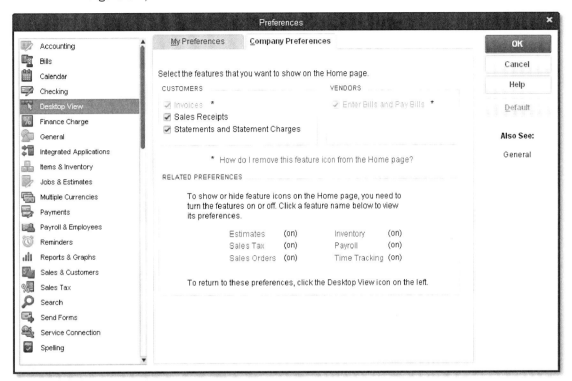

Figure 8-2 The Desktop View—Company Preferences window

Step 2. Click the **Statements and Statement Charges** checkbox to deselect.

In this window, you can remove some icons from displaying on the *Home* page. Turning off the icon on the *Home* page does not disable the feature, since you can access the command using the appropriate menu. Some features, such as *Estimates*, *Sales Tax,* and *Sales Orders* listed in the lower portion of the *Desktop View Company Preference* window can only be removed from the *Home* page by disabling the feature using the appropriate *Preferences*. You can access the appropriate *Preference* through the links in the *Desktop View Company Preferences* window.

> **Note:**
> You cannot remove the icons for *Invoices*, *Enter Bills*, or *Pay Bills* from the *Home* page if certain other features are enabled. For example, the *Invoices* icon must be turned on if your company uses *Estimates* or *Sales Orders*. For a complete list of *Preferences*, see QuickBooks Help.

Step 3. Click **OK** to close the *Preferences* window. Click **OK** in the dialog box that appears about closing open windows.

Step 4. Click the **Home** button on the *Icon Bar*. Notice that the *Statements* branch of the *Customers* section of the *Home* page no longer displays (see Figure 8-3).

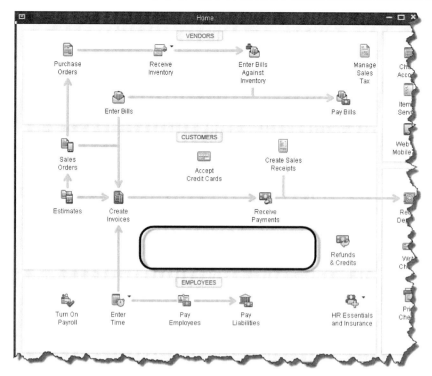

Figure 8-3 Home Page without Statements branch displaying

Customizing QuickBooks Menus and Windows

QuickBooks gives you the ability to set up some special customized features. You can create a *Favorites Menu* for your regular activities. You can also customize the *Icon Bar*, which gives you easy access to various commands.

Favorites Menu

The *Favorites* menu is a customizable menu where you can place your common QuickBooks commands.

COMPUTER PRACTICE

Step 1. Locate the *Favorites* menu between the *Lists* and *Company* menus on the menu bar. (Those using QuickBooks Accountant will see it between the *Lists* and *Accountant* menus).

> Note:
> If you do not see the *Favorites* menu, you can turn it on by selecting *Favorites Menu* from the *View* menu.

Step 2. Select the **Customize Favorites** option from the *Favorites* menu (see Figure 8-4).

Figure 8-4 Customize Favorites option in the Favorites menu

Customizing QuickBooks - Customizing QuickBooks Menus and Windows   **289**

Step 3.   The *Customize Your Menus* window includes all available menu items. You can select a menu item to be easily accessed through the *Favorites* Menu. Click **Chart of Accounts** and then click **Add** (see Figure 8-5).

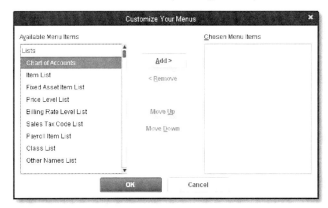

Figure 8-5 Chart of Accounts added to Favorites menu in the Customize Your Menus window

Step 4.   Click **OK** to close the *Customize Your Menus* window.

Step 5.   Select the **Favorites** menu and chose **Chart of Accounts** (see Figure 8-6).

Figure 8-6 Chart of Accounts in the Favorites menu

Step 6.   Close the Chart of Accounts.

QuickBooks Icon Bar

The *Icon Bar* appears at the left of the screen by default (see Figure 8-7). The buttons on the *Icon Bar* are shortcuts to QuickBooks windows. The *Icon Bar* allows you to create an icon shortcut to almost any window in QuickBooks.

You can customize the *Icon Bar* through several options under the *View Menu*. You can set the *Icon Bar* to display at the top of your screen, below the *Menu* by choosing *Top Icon Bar* from the *View Menu*. You can also *Hide the Icon Bar* from the *View* menu.

Figure 8-7 Default Location for the Icon Bar

Customizing the Icon Bar

You can customize the *Icon Bar* to include icons to commonly used transactions and reports.

Using the Customize Icon Bar Window

Use the *Customize Icon Bar* window to add icons to the *Icon Bar* or to edit or delete existing icons. You can also use this window to add separators between icons and to reposition icons.

COMPUTER PRACTICE

Step 1.   Select **Customize Icon Bar** from the *View* menu. QuickBooks displays the *Customize Icon Bar* window shown in Figure 8-8.

Figure 8-8 Customize Icon Bar window

Step 2.   To add an Icon to the *Icon Bar* click **Add**. QuickBooks opens the window.

Step 3.   Select **Calculator** from the list of icons as shown in Figure 8-9. Notice that QuickBooks automatically selects the preferred icon for calculator and recommends the label name and description.

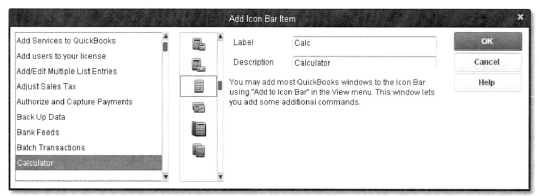

Figure 8-9 Add Icon Bar Item window with Calculator selected

Step 4.   Click **OK** to create the Calculator icon.

Step 5.   The order of the icons on this list dictates the order of the icons on the *Icon Bar*. To move the *Calc* icon, click the diamond next to **Calc** and then drag and drop *Calc* to move it right below the **Add Payroll** icon as shown in Figure 8-10.

Customizing QuickBooks - Customizing QuickBooks Menus and Windows

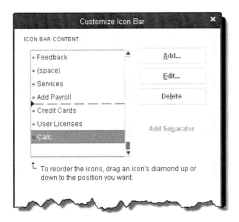

Figure 8-10 Use your mouse to move icons up or down in the list.

Step 6.   Click **OK** to save your changes. Figure 8-11 displays the customized *Icon Bar*.

Figure 8-11 Customized Icon Bar

Customizing the Icon Bar – Using Add "window-name" to Icon Bar

You can add Icons to the Icon Bar using the **Add "window-name" to Icon Bar** option from the *View* menu. For example, Academy Photography wants an icon for the **Customer Phone List** report, customized to include the customers' phones and total balances. Follow these steps to add this report to your Icon bar:

> DO NOT PERFORM THESE STEPS. THEY ARE FOR REFERENCE ONLY.

1.   From the *Reports* menu select **List**, and then select **Customer Phone List**. See Figure 8-12.

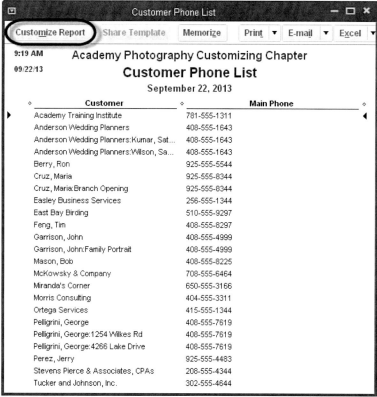

Figure 8-12 Customer Phone List Report

2. Click **Customize Report** and select the **Balance Total** field in the *Columns* list (see Figure 8-13). Click **OK** to save your changes.

Figure 8-13 Select Balance Total on the Columns List

3. With the modified report displayed, select the *View* menu and then select **Add "Customer Phone List" to Icon Bar**. QuickBooks displays the *Add Window to Icon Bar* window shown in Figure 8-14.

Figure 8-14 Add Window to Icon Bar window

4. Enter *Customer Report* in the Label field as shown in Figure 8-15. Click **OK** to save your changes. QuickBooks enters the title of your report in the Label and Description fields. It is usually best to condense the Label so the icon does not use as much space on the Icon Bar.

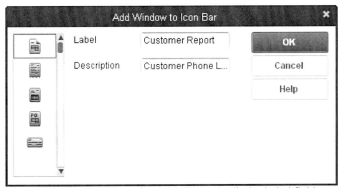

Figure 8-15 Select an icon from the list and edit the Label field.

5. You may need to expand the Icon Bar to see the **Customer Report** icon. Figure 8-16 displays a portion of the Icon Bar.

Figure 8-16 Expanded Icon Bar with Customer Report added

6. Close the Customer Phone List.

Open Window List

The QuickBooks **Open Window List** displays a selection box containing the titles of all open windows in the Icon Bar. To display the window, select **Open Window List** from the *View* menu or select the Open Windows icon in the Icon Bar (see Figure 8-17).

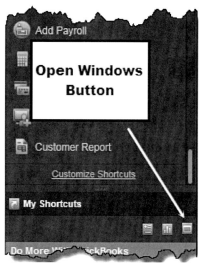

Figure 8-17 Open Window List button on the Icon Bar

The *Open Window List* includes window titles that are currently open, allowing you to quickly toggle between reports, forms, lists, or registers. This window is very helpful if you set your **Desktop** User Preferences to view *One Window* at a time. You cannot customize the *Open Windows List*. To return the *Icon Bar* to the list of Shortcuts, click the *My Shortcuts* bar below the *Open Windows list* on the *Icon Bar*.

Figure 8-18 Open Window List

QuickBooks Items and Other Lists

QuickBooks provides several *Lists* that allow you to add more information to each transaction and help you track more details. In this section, you will learn how to create items in the *Item List*, *Terms List* and *Price Level List*.

QuickBooks Items

In this section, you will learn more about QuickBooks *Items* and how they affect the "accounting behind the scenes" as you create transactions. Every time you use an item, the value of the item or items flow into the linked account. In this way, items affect the financial statements for a company. You will establish this link to the accounts with each Item created below.

The *Item List* is used to identify the products and services your business purchases and/or sells. *Items* in the *Item List* are also used as part of the sales tax tracking process as a means of generating subtotals and as a method of calculating discounts.

The *Item List* shows all *Items* you have already created (see Figure 8-19).

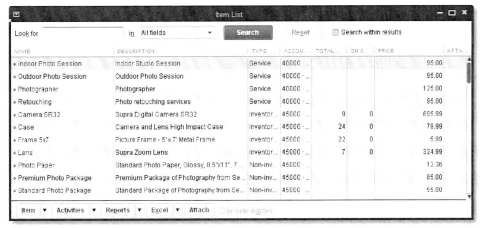

Figure 8-19 The Item list

Item Types

There are several different types of *Items* in QuickBooks (see Figure 8-20). When you create an *Item*, you indicate the *Item Type* along with the name of the *Item* and the *Account* with which the *Item* is associated.

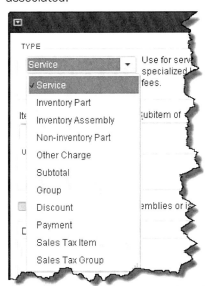

Figure 8-20 The Type menu in the New Item window

- *Service Items* track services you buy and/or sell.
- *Inventory Part Items* track your purchases and sales of inventory.
- *Inventory Assembly Items* track *Items* that contain assemblies of other *Items*. *Inventory Assembly Items* are not available in QuickBooks Pro.
- *Non-inventory Part Items* track products you buy and/or sell but don't keep in inventory.
- *Other Charge Items* track miscellaneous charges such as shipping and finance charges.
- *Subtotal Items* calculate and display subtotals on sales forms.
- *Group Items* allow you to use one *Item* to "bundle" several *Items* together. *Group Items* are similar to *Inventory Assembly Items*, but Group items do not track quantity on hand (or sold) of the Group. Rather, each *Item* within the Group is tracked separately.
- *Discount Items* calculate and display discounts on sales forms.
- *Payment Items* show payments collected on *Invoices* and refunds given on *Credit Memos*.

- *Sales Tax Items* track sales taxes in each location where you sell taxable goods and services.
- *Sales Tax Group Items* are used when you pay sales tax to more than one tax agency.

Service Items

Academy Photography sells photo sessions by the hour. To track the sales of a *Service Item*, create an *Item* called **Photo Session**, and associate the *Item* with the Services income account.

COMPUTER PRACTICE

Step 1. Select the **Lists** menu and then select **Item List**.

Step 2. Select the **Item** button and then select **New**.

Step 3. Select **Service** from the *Type* drop-down list as shown in Figure 8-20 if it is not already selected, and fill in the detail of the *Item* as shown in Figure 8-21.

Step 4. Click **OK** to save the Item.

Figure 8-21 Selecting items

If the price for this service fluctuates, you can override this amount when you use it on a sales form. Therefore, when you set up the *Item*, enter the rate you normally charge.

Subcontracted Services

To track your subcontracted services, you can set up a special "two-sided" *Service Item* to track both the income and the expense of the subcontractor. By using a single *Item* to track both the income and expense for the subcontracted service, you can automatically track the profitability of your subcontractors. You might want to have a separate *Item* for each subcontractor.

COMPUTER PRACTICE

Step 1. With the *Item List* displayed, press **Ctrl+N**. This is another way to set up a new *Item*.

Step 2. Select **Service** from the *Type* drop-down list if it is not already selected and press **Tab**.

Step 3. Enter **Video Photographer** in the *Item Name/Number* field and check the Subitem of box.

Step 4. Click the *Subitem of* checkbox and select **Photographer** from the *Subitem of* drop-down list.

Step 5. Check the box next to *This service is used in assemblies or is performed by a subcontractor or partner*.
Selecting this box allows you to use the same *Item* on purchase transactions and sales transactions, but have the *Item* affect different accounts depending on the transaction.

Step 6.   Enter the *Description on Purchase Transactions*, *Cost* (purchase price), *Expense Account*, and *Preferred Vendor* for this *Item* as shown in Figure 8-22.

Step 7.   Enter the *Description on Sales Transactions*, *Sales Price*, *Tax Code* and *Income Account* for this Item as shown in Figure 8-22.

Step 8.   Click **Next** to save the *Item* and open another *New Item* window.

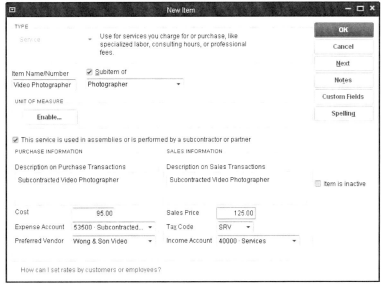

Figure 8-22 Subcontracted Service Item

Non-Inventory Parts

To track products that you buy and/or sell but don't monitor as inventory, set up *Non-Inventory Part Items*. Academy Photography doesn't track custom photo packages in inventory, so they use one generic *Item* called Custom Photo Package.

COMPUTER PRACTICE

Step 1.   Select **Non-inventory Part** from the *Type* drop-down list.

Step 2.   Enter **Custom Photo Package** in the Item Name/Number field.

Step 3.   Fill in the detail of the *Item* as shown in Figure 8-23.

Step 4.   Click **Next** to save the item.

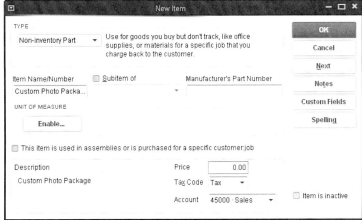

Figure 8-23 Non-inventory Part Item

Non-Inventory Parts - Passed Through

You can also specifically track the income and expenses for each *Non-Inventory Part*. In this case, you should create a "two-sided" *Non-inventory Part Item* to track the purchase costs in a Cost of Goods Sold (or Expense) account, and the sales amounts in an income account. This is particularly useful when you pass the costs on to your customers for special-ordered parts. For example, Academy Photography tracks video camera orders with one *Non-Inventory Part Item*.

COMPUTER PRACTICE

Step 1.   If necessary, select **Non-inventory Part** from the *Type* drop-down list. Fill in the detail of the *Item* as shown in Figure 8-24.

Step 2.   Click **Next** to save the item.

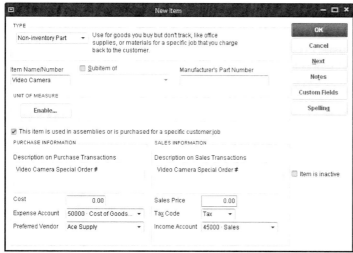

Figure 8-24 Non-inventory Part Item - passed through

Other Charge Items

To track charges like freight, finance charges, or expense reimbursements on your *Invoices*, use *Other Charge Items*.

COMPUTER PRACTICE

Step 1.   Select **Other Charge** from the *Type* drop-down list and fill in the detail of the *Item* as shown in Figure 8-25.

Step 2.   Click **Next** to save the Item.

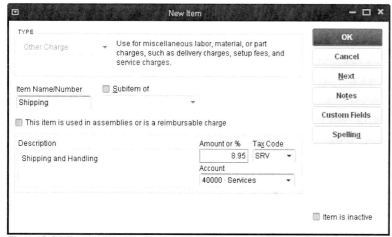

Figure 8-25 Track shipping charges with an Other Charge Item

Sales Tax Items

The *Sales Tax Items* are used to track sales tax.

COMPUTER PRACTICE

Step 1. Select **Sales Tax Item** from the *Type* drop-down list and fill in the detail of the *Item* as shown in Figure 8-26.

In this example, the *Tax Agency* is the *State Board of Equalization*. Make sure you enter the name of your tax collector in the Tax Agency field. QuickBooks needs this name for sales tax reports and sales tax payments.

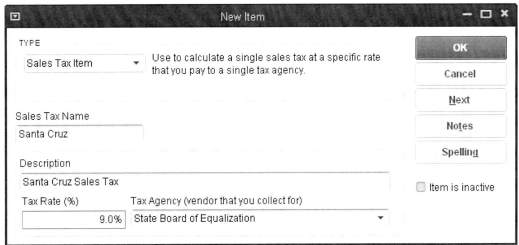

Figure 8-26 Track sales tax with the Sales Tax Item.

Step 2. Click **OK** to save this *Item* and close the *New Items* window.

You should create a separate *Sales Tax* Item for each tax imposed by each taxing jurisdiction. For example, if you have both state and county sales taxes, then create *Sales Tax Items* for the state taxes and each of the county taxes.

If multiple *Sales Tax Items* are to be billed on a particular sales transaction, then create a *Sales Tax Group Item* to join the individual *Sales Tax Items* together for billing purposes. This allows QuickBooks to correctly track sales taxes by taxing jurisdiction. In most states, you don't need to use *Sales Tax Groups*. Use *Sales Tax Group Items* only if you pay sales tax to more than one agency.

> Note:
> If you need to import a large number of *Items* (or other list entries) you can paste in a spreadsheet using the *Add/Edit Multiple List Entries* option, located in the *Lists* menu.

Printing the Item List

COMPUTER PRACTICE

To print the Item List, follow these steps:

Step 1. Select the *Reports* menu, select **List**, and then select **Item Listing** (see Figure 8-27).

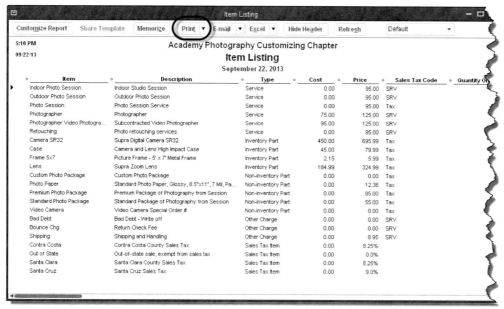

Figure 8-27 The Item Listing report

Step 2.   Click **Print** at the top of the report (or select **Print Report** from the *File* menu).

Step 3.   Close the Item Listing Report.

Step 4.   Close the **Item List** window.

The Terms List

The *Terms List* is the place where you define the payment terms for *Invoices* and *Bills*. QuickBooks uses terms to calculate when an *Invoice* or *Bill* is due. If the terms specified on the transaction include a discount for early payment, QuickBooks also calculates the date on which the discount expires.

QuickBooks allows you to define two types of terms:

- *Standard Terms* calculate based on how many days from the *Invoice* or *Bill* date the payment is due or a discount is earned.

- *Date-Driven Terms* calculate based on the day of the month that an *Invoice* or *Bill* is due or a discount is earned.

You can override the default terms on each sale as necessary. When you create reports for *Accounts Receivable* or *Accounts Payable*, QuickBooks takes into account the terms on each *Invoice* or *Bill*.

COMPUTER PRACTICE

Step 1.   Select the *Lists* menu, select **Customers & Vendor Profile Lists**, and then select **Terms List** (see Figure 8-28).

Figure 8-28 The Terms List window

Step 2. The practice file already includes several terms (see Figure 8-28). To set up additional terms, select the **Terms** menu from the *Terms List* window, and then select **New**, or press **Ctrl+N**.

Step 3. To set up a standard term, complete the *New Terms* window as shown in Figure 8-29, and click **Next**.

The window in Figure 8-29 shows how the 2% 7 Net 30 terms are defined. It is a *Standard Terms Item* indicating that full payment is due in 30 days. If the customers pay within 7 days of the *Invoice* date, however, they are eligible for a 2% discount.

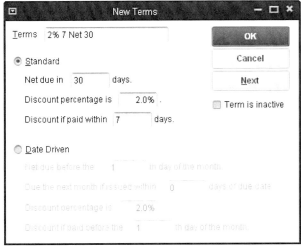

Figure 8-29 The New Terms window with standard terms

Step 4. To set up a date-driven term, select the **Date Driven** radio button.

Step 5. Fill in the fields as shown in Figure 8-30. Then click **OK**.

The terms in Figure 8-30 are an example of *Date Driven Terms*, where payment is due on the 10th of the month (e.g. February 10th). If the *Invoice* is dated less than 10 days before the due date, the *Invoice* (or *Bill*) is due on the 10th of the following month.

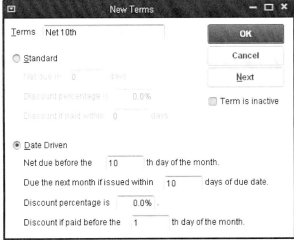

Figure 8-30 The New Terms window with date-driven terms

Step 6. Close the **Terms List** window.

Price Levels

> **Note:**
> *Per Item Price Levels* are available only in QuickBooks Premier and above.

Price Levels allow you to define custom pricing for different customers. Use *Price Levels* on *Invoices* or *Sales Receipts* to adjust the sales amount of particular items. There are several ways to use *Price Levels* on sales forms:

- You can adjust each item individually by selecting the applicable *Price Level* in the *Rate* column drop-down list (see Figure 8-31).

Figure 8-31 Selecting a Price Level on an Invoice

- You can assign a *Price Level* to a Customer's record so that when you use the customer's name in a sales form, QuickBooks will change the default sales price for each *Sales Item* on the form (see Figure 8-32).

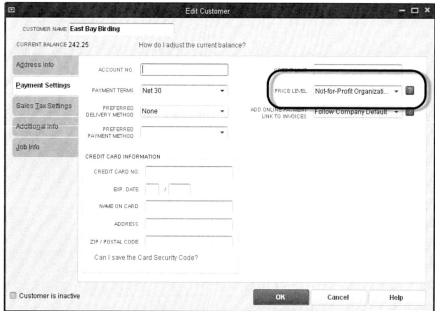

Figure 8-32 Setting a Price Level on a Customer's Record

Price Level Types

There are two types of *Price Levels*, *Fixed Percentage* and *Per Item*. You can create both types of *Price Levels* by opening the *Price Levels List* and selecting **New** from the *Price Levels Menu*.

Fixed Percentage Price Levels allow you to increase or decrease prices of *Items* for a *Customer* or *Job* by a fixed percentage(see Figure 8-33). This price level is recommended for customers who always receive a discount, since the discount will be generated automatically.

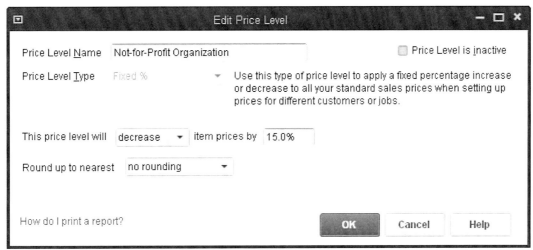

Figure 8-33 Defining a new price level

Per Item Price Levels let you set specific prices for *Items* (see Figure 8-34).

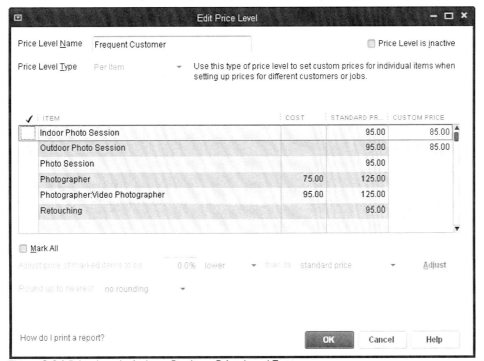

Figure 8-34 Price Level window - Per Item Price Level Type

> **Note:**
> New with *QuickBooks 2014 Enterprise,* you can now specify quantity discounts and complex pricing rules with an added-cost subscription feature called *Advanced Pricing.*

Custom Fields

When you set up a new *Customer* record, you can define *Custom Fields* for tracking additional information specific to your *Customers*, *Vendors*, and *Employees*.

Academy Photography tracks each *Customer* and *Vendor* by county in order to create reports of total purchases and sales in a city or county. This information allows them to determine the best area to expand business operations.

You can access the *Define Fields* button on the *Additional Info* tab of a *Customer* or *Vendor* record (see Figure 8-35).

Figure 8-35 Click Define Fields in the Additional Info Tab.

In the window shown in Figure 8-36, you can define up to fifteen *Custom Fields* in the QuickBooks data file, and any one name type, i.e., *Customer*, *Vendor*, or *Employee*, can have up to seven *Custom Fields*.

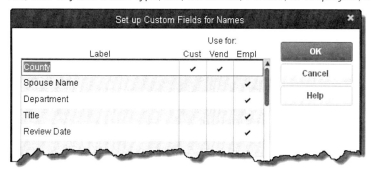

Figure 8-36 The Define Fields window

Adding Custom Field Data to Customer Records

After you have defined a *Custom Field* and checked the box in the *Customer:Job* column, the field appears on the *Customer* record (see Figure 8-37). Fill in the data just as you did for the other fields.

Customizing QuickBooks - Modifying Sales Form Templates

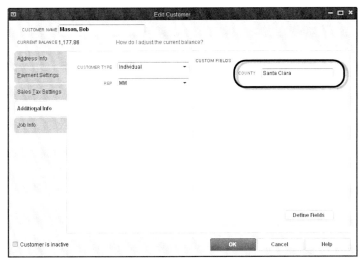

Figure 8-37 Fill in the Custom Fields for each customer.

Modifying Sales Form Templates

QuickBooks provides templates so that you can customize your sales forms. You can select from the standard forms that QuickBooks provides, or you can customize the way your forms appear on both the screen and the printed page. The first step in modifying your forms is to create a template for the form you want. The templates for all forms are in the *Templates List*.

COMPUTER PRACTICE

Step 1. Select the *Lists* menu, and then select **Templates** (see Figure 8-38). This list shows the standard templates that come with QuickBooks, as well as any form templates the user may have created.

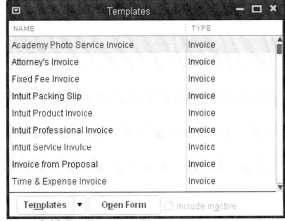

Figure 8-38 The Templates list

Step 2. Select **Intuit Service Invoice**. Then select the **Templates** menu button and select **Duplicate**. The *Intuit Service Invoice* is the template you are using as the basis for your custom template.

Step 3. Select **Invoice** on the *Select Template Type* window and click **OK** (see Figure 8-39).

Figure 8-39 Select Template Type window

Step 4. In the Templates List, *Copy of: Intuit Service Invoice* should already be selected. Select the **Templates** menu and select **Edit Template**.

Step 5. Click the **Manage Template** button in the *Basic Customization* window (see Figure 8-40).

Step 6. In the **Manage Templates** window, enter *My Invoice Template* in the *Template Name* field (see Figure 8-41).

You must enter a unique template name. You must give your template a descriptive name so that you will easily recognize it when selecting it from a form list.

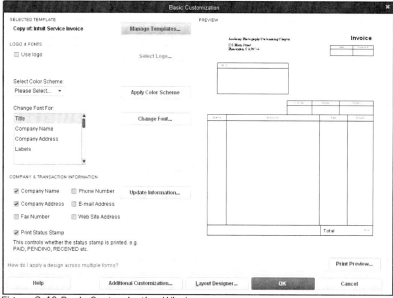

Figure 8-40 Basic Customization Window

> Note:
> You can download templates from the Intuit website – browse through the selection of pre-designed templates by clicking the *Download Templates* button on the *Manage Templates* window.

Customizing QuickBooks - Modifying Sales Form Templates   307

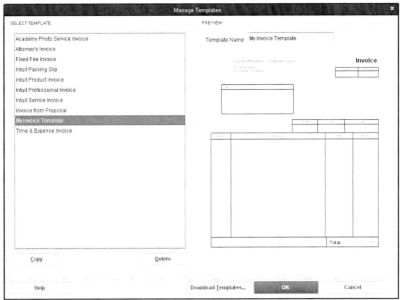

Figure 8-41 Manage Templates window

Step 7. Click **OK** to accept the name change and close the *Manage Templates* window.

Step 8. Click the **Additional Customization** button. The *Basic Customization* window changes to the *Additional Customization* window.

Step 9. Review the fields in the *Header* tab. Do not edit any of the fields on this window (see Figure 8-42).

> You would click the boxes in the *Screen* and *Print* columns to indicate which fields will show on the screen and which fields will be printed. You could also modify the titles for each field by changing the text in the *Title* fields.

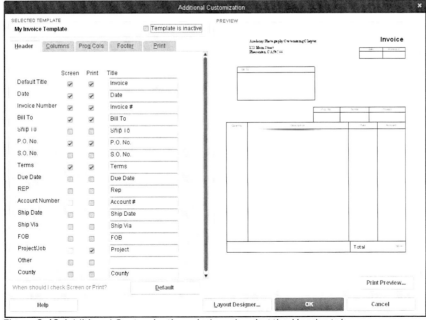

Figure 8-42 Additional Customization window showing the Header tab

Step 10. Click the **Columns** tab to modify how the columns display on the *Invoice*. Change the order of the columns by entering the numbers in the *Order* column as shown in Figure 8-43. If you see the *Layout Designer* warning box, click **OK**.

308 Customizing QuickBooks - Modifying Sales Form Templates

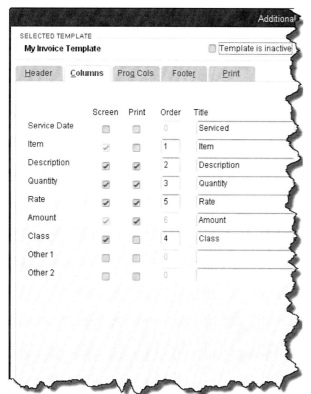

Figure 8-43 Additional Customization window showing the Columns tab

Step 11. Click the **OK** button to return to the *Basic Customization* window.

Step 12. Next, add a logo to the template by checking the **Use logo** checkbox (see Figure 8-44).

Adding a business logo to an *Invoice* helps customers familiarize themselves with your company. It can also help them identify your *Invoice*.

Figure 8-44 The Use logo option in the Basic Customization window

Step 13. In the *Select Image* dialog box, navigate to your student files. Select **logo.gif** and click **Open**.

> **Note:**
> If you encounter a warning telling you that the filename is too long, you may be experiencing a bug that occurs when the QBW file is located on a removable drive, such as a flash drive. For more information visit
> http://support.quickbooks.intuit.com/support/articles/SLN42488.

Customizing QuickBooks - Modifying Sales Form Templates

Step 14. A dialog box warns that the logo graphic file will be copied to a subfolder of the location of your working file. Click **OK** to accept. You should see the logo in the upper left side of the preview pane of the *Managing Templates* window.

Step 15. Click the **Select Color Scheme** drop down menu. You can choose six preset colors. Choose **Maroon** and then click the **Apply Color Scheme** button. The text and border lines on the *Invoice* change to the selected color.

Step 16. Next, change the color of the *Invoice* title to black. Verify that **Title** is selected in the *Change Font For:* box and click the **Change Font** button.

Step 17. The *Example* window opens (Figure 8-45). You can use this window to change font, size, style, and color of the title of the invoice. In the **Color** field, choose **Black**. When finished, click **OK**.

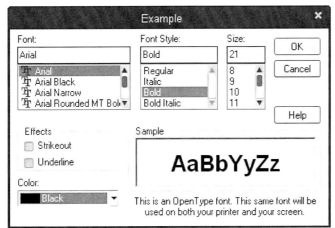

Figure 8-45 Example dialog box for changing font of labels on a template

Step 18. Click **OK** to close the *Basic Customization* window.

Step 19. Close the **Templates** window.

Step 20. From the *Home Page*, click the **Create Invoices** icon.

Step 21. To use the new template, choose **My Invoice Template** from the *Template* drop down list.

Step 22. To view how the *Invoice* will print, click the down arrow next to **Print** button at the top of the *Create Invoices* window and select **Preview**.

Step 23. Click **Close** to close the *Print Preview* window.

Step 24. Close the **Create Invoices** window.

> **Note:**
> You can make further changes to the position of elements in the form by opening the *Layout Designer*. Click the **Layout Designer** button on the bottom of the *Basic Customization* window. From the *Layout Designer*, you can change the position of design elements, such as the textboxes and the logo.

Review Questions

Comprehension Questions

1. Describe the difference between *User Preferences* (i.e., My Preferences) and *Company Preferences*.
2. What commands should you put in the *Favorites* menu?
3. Describe the purpose of the *Open Window List*.
4. How would setting a customer's default price level affect their future invoices?
5. Describe the process of adding a Custom Field to a customer record.

Multiple Choice

Select the best answer(s) for each of the following:

1. You can create *Custom Fields* for:
    - a) Customers.
    - b) Templates.
    - c) Vendors.
    - d) Both a and c.

2. The two types of *Preferences* are:
    - a) User and Company Preferences.
    - b) User and Accountant Preferences.
    - c) Favorite and General Preferences.
    - d) Income and Expense Preferences.

3. If you don't see the *Favorites* menu in your menu bar, you can turn it on in the:
    - a) *Customize Templates* window.
    - b) *Customize Icon Bar* window.
    - c) *View* menu.
    - d) *Windows* menu.

4. Which of the following is not an available Template type in QuickBooks?
    - a) Credit Memo.
    - b) Statement.
    - c) Check.
    - d) Sales Receipt.

5. If you pay sales tax to more than one agency, you should use which of the following *Item* types?
    - a) Sales Tax Group.
    - b) Group.
    - c) Inventory Assembly.
    - d) Subtotal.

Customizing QuickBooks - Review Questions

6. Which of the following can be displayed vertically on the far left side of the screen or horizontally along the top of the screen?
   a) The Home Page
   b) The Icon Bar
   c) The Open Window List
   d) None of the above

7. You cannot customize which of the following?
   a) The layout of Statements
   b) The Icon Bar
   c) The layout of the Estimate forms
   d) The Open Window list

8. To add an Icon to the Icon Bar, you can use:
   a) The *Add "window-name" to Icon Bar* option.
   b) The *Customize Icon Bar* Window.
   c) The User Preferences for Desktop View.
   d) Either a or b.

9. How do you display the *Open Window List*?
   a) Add the *Open Window List* to the *Favorites* menu.
   b) Select the *List* menu and choose *Open Window List*.
   c) Select the *Open Windows* icon in the *Icon Bar*.
   d) Click the shortcut to the *Open Window List* on the *My Shortcuts* section of the *Icon Bar*.

10. Use which of the following to manually design the layout of an Invoice?
    a) The *Company* tab of the *Customize Invoice* window
    b) The *Format* tab of the *Customize Invoice* window
    c) QuickBooks *Company Preferences*
    d) *The Layout Designer*

11. The two types of Price Levels are:
    a) Fixed percentage and per item.
    b) Fixed percentage and per customer.
    c) Per item and per customer.
    d) Per customer and per vendor.

12. You would like to offer a discount when some customers pay their invoice early. What List would you open to start creating this discount?
    a) Terms
    b) Item
    c) Price Levels
    d) None of the above. You can't create this type of discount in QuickBooks..

13. The simplest way to offer a regular discount to a customer is to:
    a) Set the price level on the customer's invoices.
    b) Add a Discount Item to each of the customer's invoices.
    c) Enter the discount in the *Customer Discount* field in the *Edit Customer* window.
    d) Set the default price level for that customer

14. To include shipping charges on an Invoice, it is best to use which type of item?
    a) Inventory Part
    b) Other Charge
    c) Service
    d) Non-inventory Part

15. You can rearrange the order of columns in a template using the:
    a) *Managing Templates* window.
    b) *Template List*.
    c) *Basic Customization* window
    d) *Additional Customization* window.

Completion Statements

1. Use a(n) _____ Item (item type) to track subcontracted labor.

2. Use the _____ _____ *User Preferences* to set default windows that show when you open QuickBooks and to change the color and graphics of QuickBooks toolbars and windows.

3. The _____ _____ displays common commands along with an icon representing that command along the side edge or the top of the QuickBooks window.

4. _____-_____ terms calculate based on the day of the month that an Invoice or Bill is due or a discount is earned.

5. Use a(n) _____ Item on Invoices or Sales Receipts to calculate the subtotal of the Items above that line.

Customizing Problem 1

APPLYING YOUR KNOWLEDGE

Restore the Customizing-14Problem1.QBM file.

1. Create the following new *Item*.

Field Name	Data
Item Type	Service
Item Name/Number	Consultation
Description	Consultation on photography services
Price	95
Tax Code	SRV
Account	Services

Table 8-1 New Item data

2. Create a new payment term called *Net 45*. Customers who have these terms should pay within 45 days and are not offered a discount for early payment.

3. Enter the following *Invoice*:

Field Name	Data
Customer	Feng, Tim
Class	San Jose
Date	02/24/2018
Invoice #	2018-106
Terms	Net 45
Tax	Santa Clara
Quantity	2
Item Code	Consultation

Table 8-2 Use this data for the Invoice

4. Print the Invoice.
5. Print the *Item List*.

Customizing Problem 2 (Advanced)

APPLYING YOUR KNOWLEDGE

> Restore the Customizing-14Problem2.QBM file.

1. Set up the following *Terms*:
   a) 1% 5 Net 30
   b) 1% 7th Net 20th (Due next month if issued within 10 days of the due date)
   c) Net 20
   d) 3% 10th Net 30th (Due next month if issued within 10 days of the due date)

2. Create a **Terms Listing** report (Select the **Reports** menu, **Lists**, and then **Terms Listing**). Add the **Discount on Day of Month** and **Min Days to Pay** columns. Expand the columns so you can see the entire column headers. Print the report.

3. Add a *Custom Field* to your *Customers* called **Referred by**. Add these referrers to the following customer records:

Customer:Job Name	Referred by
Anderson Wedding Planners: Kumar, Sati and Naveen	Cruz, Maria
Anderson Wedding Planners: Wilson, Sarah and Michael	Cruz, Maria
Anderson Wedding Planners	Cruz, Maria
Pelligrini, George	Mason, Bob
Pelligrini, George:1254 Wilkes Rd	Mason, Bob
Pelligrini, George: 4266 Lake Drive	Mason, Bob

Table 8-3 Referred by data for custom fields

4. Create a **Customer Contact List**, modified to display the *Customer Name* and **Referred by** only. Print the report.

5. Create a **Sales Tax Item** for Santa Cruz, payable to the State Board of Equalization. The sales tax rate is 9.75%.

6. Create a duplicate **Invoice** of the *Intuit Service Invoice Template*. Then, make the following changes:

a) Change the name of the template to *Academy Photo Invoice*.
b) Add the **Referred by** custom field to the screen and printed *Invoice* using the *Additional Customization Header* tab.
c) When prompted, click **Default Layout** and confirm your choice.

7. Create a new *Non-inventory Part* called *Custom Package*. Set up the new *Item* using the following information:

Field Name	Data
Item Name/Number	Custom Package
Description	Customized Photography Package from Session
Price	0 (leave 0 because it's a custom package)
Tax Code	Tax
Account	Sales

Table 8-4 Item setup data

8. Create an **Invoice** for Pelligrini, George, for the 1254 Wilkes Rd job, using the *Academy Photo Invoice* template. Enter the following information on the header and footer of the *Invoice*:

Field Name	Data
Class	San Jose
Date	02/28/2018
Invoice #	2018-106
Terms	1% 5 Net 30
Tax	Santa Cruz

Table 8-5 Use this data for the Invoice header.

9. Enter the following information into the body of the *Invoice*:

Item	Qty	Description	Rate	Tax
Outdoor Photo Session	4	Outdoor Photo Session	95.00	SRV
Custom Package	2	Customized Photography Package from Session	750.00	Tax

Table 8-6 Item descriptions

10. Accept the default for all other fields on the *Invoice*. Click **OK** if you get a pop-up window regarding custom price levels. Save and print the **Invoice**.

11. Save the new **Terms** and **Tax Items** when prompted.

QUICKBOOKS AND BEYOND – *TAKE THE NEXT STEP WITH THE SLEETER GROUP BLOG*

"Custom Fields in QuickBooks"

Every business has some sort of unique information that is important to its operation. While QuickBooks provides the places to store the basic information that every business needs, you will often find that you need to store additional data, such as a customer's vehicle registration number or the weight of an inventory item – information that QuickBooks doesn't already accommodate. To address this, QuickBooks provides us with custom fields, a way that you can define your own places to store information in the QuickBooks database.

In this *QuickBooks and Beyond* section, Charlie Russell discusses the many ways to use custom fields to customize your QuickBooks data. Read the full post at www.sleeter.com/blog/?p=9087.

New Terminology

QQube – Software that extracts QuickBooks data to generate effective reports, created by Clearify.

Putting New Knowledge to Use

1. What custom fields might you create for your company's or workplace's QuickBooks data?
2. How might you display your company's or workplace's custom fields in QuickBooks forms and reports?

Chapter 9
Walker Graphic Design Business Scenario

Description of Company

Sarah Walker has decided to follow her dream and start her own business. She developed a well thought out business plan for a graphic design business with an online store. She took her accumulated savings and started Walker Graphic Design.

Sarah lives in a metropolitan city with a growing economy and many potential clients. She decided to offer web and print graphics services, including ad layout, logo creation, and website design. She will also offer consulting services to help clients focus their design towards target markets.

In addition to working with clients, she will have an online store selling gift items printed with her designs. To do this, she utilizes an online service that handles the production, inventory, shipping, and sales tax.

To help her new start-up, she selected QuickBooks software to help manage the business. To start with she will have no employees and has organized her company as a sole proprietorship. She has leased 600 square feet of office space.

Goals

Using QuickBooks and the sample file (Walker-14.QBW), you will perform the following:
- Record initial start-up costs.
- Record a month of business transactions, including purchases, sales, deposits, Accounts Receivable and Accounts Payable.
- Reconcile bank accounts.
- Answer several questions about the finances for Walker Graphic Design (WGD).

Revenue and expense transactions will be recorded into one of the three classes that WGD uses to track performance. At the end of the month, you will reconcile the bank statement and then produce financial statements and sales analysis reports, including a report of business performance by class.

Company Set Up

> **Restore this File**
>
> This chapter uses Walker-14.QBW. To open this file, restore the Walker-14.QBM file to your hard disk.

The company file for this exercise is mostly set up for you. Begin by familiarizing yourself with the setup of the file so you can correctly record the transactions and complete the exercises as instructed below.

Instructions

1. Restore the Walker-14.QBM file to Walker-14.QBW file.
2. Enter the transactions for May 2018 beginning on page 318.
3. Reconcile the bank account for May from the statement shown on page 323.
4. Prepare the following reports and graphs:
   - a) Reconciliation Summary Report for 05/31/18
   - b) Balance Sheet Standard as of 05/31/2018
   - c) Profit and Loss Standard for May 2018
   - d) Profit and Loss by Class for May 2018
   - e) Statement of Cash Flows for May 2018
   - f) Sales by Item Summary for May 2018
   - g) Graph – Sales by Month by Customer for May 2018
5. Complete the analysis questions on page 324.

Business Transactions

May 2018

May	Business Transaction	Transaction Details
1	Deposited owner investment from Sarah Walker to provide cash for operations.	Transaction type: **Deposit** Deposit to: **National Bank Checking** Date: **5/1/2018** Memo: *Deposit Owner's Investment* Received From: **Walker, Sarah** From Account: **Investments** (Equity Account) Check #: **401** Class: **Admin/Other** Amount: **$30,000.00**
1	Paid rent plus refundable deposit to Commerce Realty.	Transaction type: **Check** Date: **5/1/2018** Pay to the Order of: **Commerce Realty** Check#: **1001** Memo: *May Rent plus $800 Deposit* Account: **Rent - $800.00** Account: **Refundable Deposits - $800.00** Total Check: **$1,600.00** Class: **Admin/Other**
2	Received bill from Apex Online for setup of store.	Transaction type: **Bill** Vendor: **Apex Online - V** Date: **5/2/2018** Bill Due: **6/1/2018** Account: **Computer and Internet Expenses** Amount: **$426.00** Terms: **Net 30** Ref No: **65189** Memo: *Store Setup Fees* Class: **Online Sales**

Walker Graphic Design Business Scenario

May	Business Transaction	Transaction Details	
2	Received bill from Office Supply Depot.	Transaction type: **Bill** Vendor: **Office Supply Depot** Date: **5/2/2018** Bill Due: **6/1/2018** Account: **Furniture and Equipment** Amount: **$1,150.00** Terms: **Net 30** Ref No: **68-20** Memo: *Office Equipment* Class: **Admin/Other**	✓
3	Received bill from Legacy Office Supply.	Transaction type: **Bill** Vendor: **Legacy Office Supply** Date: **5/3/2018** Bill Due: **6/2/2018** Account: **Office Supplies** Amount: **$452.00** Terms: **Net 30** Ref No: **6433** Memo: *Office Supplies* Class: **Admin/Other**	✓
3	Issued check to Office Furniture Rentals, Inc. for rental of office furniture for May.	Transaction type: **Check** Date: **5/3/2018** Pay to the Order of: **Office Furniture Rentals** Check#: **1002** Memo: *Furniture Rental* Account: **Equipment Rental** Amount: **$711.00** Class: **Admin/Other**	✓
4	Issued check to All American Insurance for liability insurance premium for May.	Transaction type: **Check** Date: **5/4/2018** Pay to the Order of: **All American Insurance** Check#: **1003** Memo: *May General Liability Insurance* Account: **Insurance Expense** Class: **Admin/Other** Total: **$425.00**	✓
8	Prepared invoice for consulting with Maple Lane Salon.	Transaction type: **Invoice** Customer: **Maple Lane Salon** Class: **Design/Consulting** Template: **Intuit Service Invoice** Date: **5/8/2018** Invoice #: **2018-101** Terms: **2% 10 Net 30** Items: **Consultation (5 @ $60.00/Hour)** Total: **$300.00** Memo: *Marketing Consultation*	✓

May	Business Transaction	Transaction Details
14	Prepared invoice for consulting and design work for East Bay Boutique	Transaction type: **Invoice** Customer: **East Bay Boutique** Class: **Design/Consulting** Template: **Intuit Service Invoice** Date: **5/14/2018** Invoice #: **2018-102** Terms: **Net 30** Items: **Consultation (2 @ $60.00/Hour)** Items: **Design (5 @ $50.00/Hour)** Total: **$370.00** Memo: *2 Consulting, 5 Design*
15	Received payment from Maple Lane Salon. Maple Lane Salon paid within 10 days and took the discount for early payment.	Transaction type: **Payment** Customer: **Maple Lane Salon** Date: **5/15/2018** Amount: **$294.00** Check No: **9864** Payment Method: **Check** Memo: *Payment Received – Inv. #2018-101* Discount Account: **Sales Discounts** Discount Class: **Design/Consulting** Apply to: **Invoice #2018-101**

16	Recorded receipt for first two weeks of sales from online store.	Transaction type: **Sales Receipt**
		Customer: **Apex Online – C**
		Class: **Online Sales**
		Sales No.: **2018-101**
		Date: **5/16/2018**
		Check No: **26967**
		Items:
		    T-Shirts – Qty 9
		    Caps – Qty 14
		    Mugs – Qty 8
		    Clocks – Qty 1
		Sales Tax: **Out of State**
		Total: **$260.00**
		Memo: *Biweekly Store Revenue*

17	Received bill from Image Contacts, Inc. for printing of flyers.	Transaction type: **Bill** Vendor: **Image Contacts, Inc.** Date: **5/17/2018** Bill Due: **6/16/2018** Amount: **$1,450.00** Terms: **Net 30** Ref No: **2856** Memo: *Flyer Printing* Account: **Printing and Reproduction** Class: **Design/Consulting**
22	Received bill from Zenith Productions.	Transaction type: **Bill** Vendor: **Zenith Productions** Date: **5/22/2018** Bill Due: **6/21/2018** Amount: **$2,100.00** Terms: **Net 30** Ref No: **8248** Memo: *Fees for Product Designs* Account: **Professional Fees** Class: **Design/Consulting**

May	Business Transaction	Transaction Details
24	Prepared Invoice for Computer Manufacturers USA for design services.	Transaction type: **Invoice** Customer: **Computer Manufacturers USA** Class: **Design/Consulting** Template: **Intuit Service Invoice** Date: **5/24/2018** Invoice #: **2018-103** Terms: **Net 30** Items: **Design (164 @ $50/Hour)** Total: **$8,200.00** Memo: *Magazine Campaign*
26	Received check from Computer Manufacturers USA.	Transaction type: **Payment** Customer: **Computer Manufacturers USA** Date: **5/26/2018** Amount: **$8,200.00** Check No: **1079** Payment Method: **Check** Memo: *Payment Received – Inv. #2018-103* Apply to: **Invoice #2018-103**
28	Received check from East Bay Boutique.	Transaction type: **Payment** Customer: **East Bay Boutique** Date: **5/28/2018** Amount: **$370.00** Check No: **3065** Payment Method: **Check** Memo: *Payment Received – Inv. #2018-102* Apply to: **Invoice #2018-102**
29	Prepared Invoice for Western Energy Corporation.	Transaction type: **Invoice** Customer: **Western Energy Corporation** Class: **Design/Consulting** Template: **Intuit Service Invoice** Date: **5/29/2018** Invoice #: **2018-104** Terms: **Net 30** Items: **Design (52 @ $50.00/Hour)** Total: **$2,600.00** Memo: *Brochure and Ad*
29	Received bill from Cal Light & Power for utilities.	Transaction type: **Bill** Vendor: **Cal Light & Power** Date: **5/29/2018** Bill Due: **6/28/2018** Amount: **$322.00** Terms: **Net 30** Ref No: **7599** Memo: *Utility Bill* Account: **Utilities** Class: **Admin/Other**
29	Received bill from Western Bell for telephone.	Transaction type: **Bill** Vendor: **Western Bell** Date: **5/29/2018** Bill Due: **6/28/2018** Amount: **$58.00** Terms: **Net 30** Ref No: **2332** Memo: *Telephone Bill* Account: **Telephone Expense** Class: **Admin/Other**

May	Business Transaction	Transaction Details

30	Recorded receipt for two weeks of sales from online store.	Transaction type: **Sales Receipt**
		Customer: **Apex Online - C**
		Class: **Online Sales**
		Sale No.: **2018-102**
		Date: **5/30/2018**
		Check No: **27345**
		Items:
		    T-Shirts – Qty 22
		    Caps – Qty 27
		    Mugs – Qty 22
		    Clocks – Qty 6
		    Tote Bags – Qty 6
		Sales Tax: **Out of State**
		Total: **$700.00**
		Memo: *Biweekly Store Revenue*

31	Received check from Western Energy Corporation.	Transaction type: **Payment** Customer: **Western Energy Corporation** Date: **5/31/2018** Amount: **$2,600.00** Check No: **2021** Payment Method: **Check** Memo: *Payment Received – Inv. #2018-104* Apply to: **Invoice #2018-104**
31	Deposited all funds held in Undeposited Funds account to National State Bank.	Transaction type: **Deposit** Deposit to: **National Bank Checking** Memo: **Deposit** Date: **5/31/2018** Total Deposit Amount: **$12,424.00**
31	Paid all bills in a batch sorted by Vendor.	Select **Pay Bills**, and then pay the following bills: Apex Online Cal Light & Power Image Contacts, Inc., Legacy Office Supply Office Supply Depot Western Bell 1013 Zenith Productions, Inc. Total payments: **$5,958.00** Bill Payment Date: **5/31/2018**
31	Printed all checks (Chk#1004-1010).	#1004 – Apex Online #1005 – Cal Light & Power #1006 – Image Contacts, Inc. #1007 – Legacy Office Supply #1008 – Office Supply Depot #1009 – Western Bell #1010 – Zenith Production
31	Issued check to Open Door Computing for computer repairs.	Transaction type: **Check** Date: **5/31/2018** Pay to the Order of: **Open Door Computing** Check#: **1011** Memo: *Computer Repairs* Account: **Repairs and Maintenance** Class: **Admin/Other** Total: **$186.00**

Business Checking Account

Statement Date: May 31, 2018   Page 1 of 1

Summary: **Walker Graphic Design**

Previous Balance as of 4/30/18	$	-
Total Deposits and Credits	+ $	42,424.00
Total Checks and Debits	- $	8,704.00
Statement Balance as of 5/31/18:	= $	**33,720.00**

Deposits and Other Credits:

DEPOSITS

Date	Description	Amount
1-May	Customer Deposit	$ 30,000.00
31-May	Customer Deposit	$ 12,424.00
	2 Deposits:	**$ 42,424.00**

INTEREST

Date	Description	Amount
	Interest:	**$ -**

Checks and Other Withdrawals:

CHECKS PAID:

Check No.	Date Paid	Amount
1001	1-May	$ 1,600.00
1002	3-May	$ 711.00
1003	4-May	$ 425.00
1004	31-May	$ 426.00
1005	31-May	$ 322.00
1006	31-May	$ 1,450.00
1007	31-May	$ 452.00
1008	31-May	$ 1,150.00
1009	31-May	$ 58.00
1010	31-May	$ 2,100.00
	10 Checks Paid:	**$ 8,694.00**

OTHER WITHDRAWALS/PAYMENTS

Date	Description	Amount
	0 Other Withdrawals/Payments:	**$ -**

SERVICE CHARGES

Date	Description	Amount
31-May	Service Charge	$ 10.00
	1 Service Charge:	**$ 10.00**

Figure 9-1 Bank Statement

Analysis Questions

Use the completed reports from step 4 of the instructions and your QB company file to answer the following questions. Write your answer in the space to the left of each question.

1. _____ What is the net income or net loss for May?

2. _____ What is the total Expenses for May?

3. _____ What is the amount of Total Product Sales for May?

4. _____ What is the amount of rent paid for May?

5. _____ What is the net cash increase for May?

6. _____ What percentage of total sales were T-Shirts in May?

7. _____ What percentage of total sales was to Computer Manufacturers USA?

8. _____ How much does Walker Graphic Design have in total assets on May 31?

9. _____ What was the net income for the Online Sales Class?

10. _____ What was the amount of Total Uncleared Transactions from the May bank reconciliation?

Appendix

Keyboard Shortcuts

Date Shortcuts

When cursor is in a date field, this key	Causes the date to become...
y	First day of displayed calendar year
r	Last day of displayed calendar year
m	First day of displayed month
h	Last day of displayed month
t	Today
w	First day of displayed week
k	Last day of displayed week
+	Next day
-	Previous day

Cut, Copy & Paste

When text is selected in any field	Causes...
Ctrl + x	Cut the text to the Clipboard
Ctrl + c	Copy the text to the Clipboard
Ctrl + v	Paste the text to the Clipboard
Ctrl + z	Undo last change
Ctrl + d	Delete selected transaction or list Item

Making Changes

When editing a transaction, this key	Causes ...
Tab	Move the cursor to the next field.
Shift + Tab	Move the cursor to the previous editable field
Return (or Enter)	Record the transaction (when black border is highlighting OK, Next, or Previous button)
Esc	Cancel editing and close the current window
Ctrl + h	Get the history (A/R or A/P) for the currently selected transaction
Ctrl + g	Go to the other account register affected by this transaction
Ctrl + y	Display transaction journal
Ctrl + n	New transaction (Bill, Check, Deposit, List Item, Invoice)
Ctrl + r	Go to the register associated with the current transaction.
Page Up	Scroll register view or reports 1 page up
Page Down	Scroll register view or reports 1 page down
Home, Home, Home	Go to the top of a register (first transaction)
End, End, End	Go to the bottom of a register (last transaction)
Ctrl + 1	Display information about QuickBooks and your company file details
Ctrl + e	Edit transaction or list item
Space	To check or uncheck checkbox when selected

Answer Key for End of Chapter Questions

This section shows the answers to the questions at the end of each chapter.

Introducing QuickBooks

Comprehension Questions:

1. QuickBooks has three primary files: Data files, Backup files, and Portable Company files. Data files are used when QuickBooks is open and transactions are being recorded. Portable are compressed and are useful for moving data from one computer to another. Backup files are used to safeguard the company data.

2. Portable files are used for transporting QuickBooks data from one computer to another. They are compact and can be used to send QuickBooks data as email attachments. Portable files should not be used as backups.

3. The Home page is an easily accessible window that displays the most common QuickBooks tasks. It is divided into regions with flowcharts that make the sequence of workflow easier to understand. The flow charts are comprised of icons for different tasks. The Home page is automatically displayed when a file is opened and can be accessed by clicking the *Home* button on the *Icon Bar*.

4. Transactions are created by filling out familiar-looking forms such as invoices, bills, and checks. As you fill out forms, you choose from lists such as the customer center, the item list, and the account list. When you finish filling out a form, QuickBooks automatically records the accounting entries behind the scenes. For example, using the Write Checks window provides options not available in the checking account register like an items tab and access to customer/class columns without having to click **Split**. The check printing process (to be printed or individual check printing) is also much easier when working with the form. By using sales forms (e.g. Invoices, Sales Receipts and Credit Memos) QuickBooks populates sales reports and provides additional fields like sales rep that are not available in the Accounts Receivable register or Customer Register.

5. Accounting's primary concern is the accurate recording and categorizing of transactions so that you can produce reports that accurately portray the financial health of your organization. Put another way, accounting's focus is on whether your organization is succeeding and how well it is succeeding. The purpose of accounting is to serve management, investors, creditors, and government agencies. Accounting reports allow any of these groups to assess the financial position of the organization relative to its debts (liabilities), its capabilities to satisfy those debts and continue operations (assets), and the difference between them (net worth or equity).

Multiple Choice:

1. c
2. c
3. b
4. d
5. d

Completion Statements:

1. forms, accounting
2. back up
3. Home page
4. Items
5. Chart of Accounts

The Sales Process

Comprehension Questions:

1. When customers pay at the time of the sale either by check or by credit card, create a Sales Receipt transaction.

2. Setting the *Payments* Company Preference option to **Use Undeposited Funds as a default deposit to account** causes the funds from your sale to increase the balance in the *Undeposited Funds* account. Later, when you **Make Deposits**, you'll group all of the funds from several sales into one deposit in the bank. This will decrease your *Undeposited Funds* account. In most cases, the *Undeposited Funds* account should be zero after you record all of your deposits and credit card batches for the day. It is best to use *Undeposited Funds* when recording receipts because you can then group the receipts together when you record the deposit, by payment method. If you post each Sales Receipt and Payment directly to a bank account, QuickBooks will record a separate increase in cash for each customer receipt/payment. As a result, bank reconciliation will be more difficult since QuickBooks deposits won't match with the bank statement.

3. When you enter a payment amount, QuickBooks looks at all of the open Invoices for that customer. If it finds an amount due on an open Invoice that is the exact amount of the payment, it matches the payment with that Invoice. If there is no such match, it applies the payment to the *oldest* Invoice first and continues applying to the next oldest until the payment is completely applied. If this auto application of payments results in a partially paid Invoice, QuickBooks holds the balance on that Invoice open for the unpaid amount.

4. When this preference is on, you can select an invoice in the table of the *Receive Payments* form before entering an Amount Received, QuickBooks prefills the amount of that selected invoice into the *Amount Received* field. QuickBooks continues to automatically calculate the Amount Received based on the invoices you select or deselect for that payment. When this preference is off, QuickBooks does not automatically calculate payments. You need to click **Auto Apply** to see the results of your payment on the amounts for selected invoices. **Where to find this preference:** From the *Edit* menu, choose Preferences, and then select the *Payments* icon. Click the Company Preferences tab.

Multiple Choice:

1. d
2. a
3. b
4. d
5. d
6. c

7. d
8. a
9. a
10. d
11. c
12. c
13. b
14. b
15. c

Completion Statements:

1. Quick Add
2. bank, Undeposited Funds
3. calculating
4. Accounts Receivable
5. QuickMath

Additional Customer Transactions

Comprehension Questions:

1. Refunds are given to customers who return merchandise or who have unused services after these items have been paid for. Refunds should be given in the same type as the payment. If a customer paid with a check, he or she should be issued a refund check. If a customer paid by credit card, the refund should be issued to the same credit card type.

2. Customers who return merchandise or cancel an order after it has been invoiced but before it has been paid should be issued a credit using a Credit Memo. This credit can be immediately applied to the unpaid invoice.

    Customers who have paid for the merchandise or services but who have existing open invoices may request to have the credit used again the unpaid invoice, rather than receive a refund.

Multiple Choice:

1. a
2. d
3. b
4. d
5. d
6. d
7. b
8. a

9. c

10. a

11. c

12. d

13. a

14. c

15. c

Completion Statements:

1. cash, check, credit card
2. Credit Memos
3. write-off
4. Finance Charges
5. Statement

Managing Expenses

Comprehension Questions:

1. In QuickBooks, classes give you a way to *classify* your transactions. You can use QuickBooks classes to separate your income and expenses by line of business, department, location, profit centers, or any other meaningful breakdown of your business.

   For example, a dentist might classify all income and expenses as relating to either the dentistry or hygiene department. A law firm formed as a partnership might classify all income and expenses according to which partner generated the business. If you use classes, you'll be able to create separate reports for each class of the business. Therefore, the dentist could create separate Profit & Loss reports for the dentistry and hygiene departments, and the law firm could create separate reports for each partner.

2. If you want to track the expenses for each customer or job (i.e., track job costs), you'll need to link each expense with the customer or job to which it applies. When you record an expense transaction, use the **Customer:Job** column to link each expense account or Item with the customer or job to which it applies.

3. The steps in tracking A/P in QuickBooks are:

   a) When you receive a bill from a vendor, enter it into QuickBooks using the *Enter Bills* window. Recording a bill allows QuickBooks to track the amount you owe to the vendor along with the detail of what you purchased.

   b) Pay the bill using the *Pay Bills* window.

   c) If you want to make a partial payment on a bill, enter only the amount you want to pay in the *Amt. To Pay* column. If you pay less than the full amount due, QuickBooks will track the remaining amount due for that bill in Accounts Payable. The next time you go to the *Pay Bills* window, the partially paid bills will show with the remaining amount due.

   d) When a vendor credits your account, record that transaction in the *Enter Bills* window as a Credit and apply it to one of your unpaid bills.

e) When you select a Bill in the *Pay Bills* window from a vendor for whom one or more unapplied credits exist, QuickBooks displays the total amount of all credits for the vendor in the *Total Credits Available* field. Click **Set Credits** to apply the credit.

f) To record a discount on a bill, select the bill and look for the discount terms in the *Discount & Credit Information for Highlighted Bill* section. If a discount is available on the bill, use the **Set Discount** button to record the discount.

4. In many cases, it's better to use a bill credit instead of recording a discount. For example, when you want to associate the discount with a job, or if you want to track discount items, use Bill Credits instead of using discounts in the *Pay Bills* process.

5. To track your charges and payments on your company credit card, set up a separate credit card account in QuickBooks for each card. Use the *Credit Card* type when creating each account. Then enter each charge individually using the *Enter Credit Card Charges* window. To pay the credit card bill, use *Write Checks* and code the check to the credit card account.

Multiple Choice:

1. d
2. d
3. d
4. a
5. b
6. d
7. c
8. c
9. b
10. c
11. a
12. b
13. a
14. d
15. b

Completion Statements:

1. Home Page
2. 10, 2%
3. Class
4. customer, job
5. Pay Bills

Bank Reconciliation

Comprehension Questions:

1. QuickBooks calculates the *Beginning Balance* field by adding and subtracting all previously cleared transactions. The resulting calculation is shown on the *Begin Reconciliation* window. The amount in the *Beginning Balance* field will differ from your bank statement if the user(s) delete or change one or more reconciled transactions. The balance will also differ if the user(s) remove the checkmark from one or more reconciled transactions (using the bank account register). Users can also adjust the *Beginning Balance* field by clicking **Undo Last Reconciliation** in the *Locate Discrepancies* window.

2. You don't want to change transactions dated in a closed accounting period because doing so would change financial information in a period for which you have already issued financial statements and/or filed tax returns.

3. The credit card reconciliation process is very similar to the bank account reconciliation, except that when you finish reconciling a credit card account, QuickBooks asks you if you want to pay the credit card immediately or if you want to enter a bill for the balance of the credit card. Additionally, you enter Finance Charges, rather than Bank Charges and Interest Income, in the *Begin Reconciliation* window.

Multiple Choice:

1. c
2. a
3. d
4. c
5. b
6. b
7. d
8. a
9. d
10. d
11. b
12. c
13. c
14. d
15. a

Completion Statements:

1. reconciled
2. Beginning Balance
3. reconciliation
4. closed, audited

5. NSF (non-sufficient funds)

Reports and Graphs

Comprehension Questions:

1. QuickBooks provides a convenient feature called **QuickZoom**, which allows you to see the detail behind numbers on reports. As your cursor moves over numbers on a report, it will turn into a magnifying glass with a "z" in the middle. The magnifying icon indicates that you can double-click to see the details behind the number on the report. After you double-click the number, QuickZoom displays a **Transaction Detail by Account** report that shows the details of each transaction in the account that you zoomed in on.

2. The Check Detail report is very useful if you use Accounts Payable or Payroll. It is frequently necessary to see what expense account(s) are associated with a Bill Payment. However, most transaction reports don't give the detailed information on what expenses are associated with the Bill Payment. They only show that Bill Payments are associated with Accounts Payable. That's because a Bill Payment only involves the Checking account and Accounts Payable. Similarly, Paychecks only show in the register report as "Split" transactions because several accounts are associated with each paycheck. The Check Detail report shows the detailed expense account information about these types of transactions.

3. To hide subaccounts on the Profit & Loss report (or any summary report), click **Collapse** at the top of the report.

4. Use the **Filters** tab on the *Modify Report* window to narrow the contents of reports so that you can analyze specific areas of your business. On the **Filters** tab, you can filter for (select) specific accounts, dates, names, or items to include in the report.

5. After customizing a report, you can *memorize* it so you won't have to go through all of the modification steps the next time you want to view the report.

Multiple Choice:

1. c
2. a
3. d
4. a
5. b
6. c
7. b
8. d
9. b
10. c
11. d
12. a
13. c
14. b
15. c

Completion Statements:

1. Vendor Contact List
2. filter
3. QuickZoom
4. Search
5. Balance Sheet

Company File Setup and Maintenance

Comprehension Questions:

1. As you enter opening balances in your QuickBooks accounts, an offsetting transaction is entered into an automatically created account calling *Opening Balance Equity*.

   This transaction is recorded differently depending on which method you use for the opening balance. If you enter the opening balance by writing a value in the *Opening Balance* field in the *New Account* window, the amount is automatically added to *Opening Bal Equity* as well as the new account. If you enter the opening balance in the new account's register, the transaction should be coded to *Opening Bal Equity*.

   Opening Bal Equity is closed into *Retained Earnings* or *Owner's Equity* at the end of setting up the company file.

2. To separately track state, county, and city taxes in the Chart of Accounts and provide a summary total of all taxes paid, set up a main account called Taxes Paid. Then, set up subaccounts of that account called State Taxes Paid, County Taxes Paid, and City Taxes Paid.

3. Rename the Entertainment account to "Meals." Doing so will prompt QuickBooks to merge the Entertainment and Meals accounts. When you merge accounts these two accounts in this way, QuickBooks changes each transaction that posts to Entertainment, making it post to Meals instead. Then QuickBooks will remove the Entertainment account from the Chart of Accounts list.

4. It is important to enter all outstanding checks and deposits as of your start date so that your first bank reconciliation goes smoothly. In order for the reconciliation to go smoothly, you want all of the checks and deposits to show in QuickBooks so that you can match them with your first bank statement after the start date. If you don't enter the individual transactions, you won't see them in the QuickBooks reconciliation window. Also, if a transaction never clears the bank, you won't know which transaction it was without going to your old records.

5. You should have each of the following before setting up a QuickBooks file:

   a) Trial Balance

   b) Bank Statement for all bank accounts

   c) Outstanding Checks and Deposits

   d) Open Invoices

   e) Unpaid Bills

   f) Employee List and W-4 information for each employee

   g) Payroll Liabilities by Item

   h) Year-to-Date Payroll Detail for Employee

i) Year-to-Date Payroll Tax Deposits

j) Physical Inventory by Inventory Part

Multiple Choice:

1. c
2. d
3. a
4. d
5. b
6. b
7. c
8. d
9. a
10. d
11. c
12. b
13. c
14. b
15. a

Completion Statements:

1. Assets, Liabilities, Equity, Income, Expense
2. delete
3. Opening Balance Equity
4. General Journal Entry
5. Trial Balance

Customizing QuickBooks

Comprehension Questions:

1. *Company Preferences* are used to make global changes to the features and functionality of the data file. Only the Administrator of the data file can make changes to *Company Preferences*. *User Preferences* will not affect other users of the data file. Each user can make changes to his or her own *User Preferences*.

2. Any command that you use frequently can be put in the Favorites menu. You can also put items that are usually only accessible through submenus so that the options are more easily accessible.

3. The *Open Window List* shows a brief description of each open window. You can click on the description to move between windows. The *Open Window List* is most helpful when you select

the *One Window Desktop View* User Preference. With this preference selected, the *Open Window List* is the most convenient way to move between open windows.

4. Price levels allow you to customize different pricing for your customers. For example, some high volume customers may have negotiated discount pricing for all of their purchases. By setting the customer's default pricing level, every invoice and sales receipt will automatically use this discount pricing.

    To add *Price Level* defaults to customer records, create the *Price Level* in the *Price Level List*. Then, in the *Edit Customer* window, choose the *Additional Info* tab and set the *Price Level* field to the appropriate price level for the customer.

5. To add a **Custom Field** to a customer's record, open the customer's record, click the **Additional Information** tab and then click **Define Fields.** QuickBooks displays the *Define Fields* window where you can create a Custom Field. After you create the Custom Field, click the corresponding checkbox in the *Customers:Jobs* column.

Multiple Choice:

1. d
2. a
3. c
4. c
5. a
6. b
7. d
8. d
9. d
10. d
11. a
12. a
13. d
14. b
15. d

Completion Statements:

1. Service
2. Desktop View
3. Icon Bar
4. Date-driven
5. Subtotal

Walker Business Scenarios

Answers to the questions at the end of the Walker problem are available in the Instructor's Manual for this book.

Index

1099s 111
Academy Photography 5
Accountant's Review 6
Accounting Behind the Scenes 4
Accounts
   Account Numbers 243, 251, 252
   Account Types 243
   Adding Accounts 244
   Adding Subaccounts 246
   Chart of Accounts 22, 243
   Deactivating Accounts 247
   Deleting Accounts 247
   Include Inactive 248
   Make Inactive 248
   Merging Accounts 249
   Modifying the Chart of Accounts 244
   Reconciling 161
   Reordering the Account List 250
   Show lowest subaccount only 246
   Tax Line 245
Accounts Payable 120
   Discounts using Bill Credits 126
   Entering Bills 120
   Paying Bills 123
   Repaying a Bill After Voiding a Bill Payment
   132
Accrual Basis of Accounting
   .... 4, 190, 267
Add/Edit Multiple List Entries 299
Administrator 271
   Administrator Password 238, 270
Administrators
   Preferences 285
Adobe Acrobat 167
Alerts 17
Alt 45
Assets 243
ATM Withdrawal 116
Attaching Documents 122
Bad Debts 84
Bank Deposits 56
   Depositing Credit Cards 66
   Holding Cash Back from Deposits
   63
   Printing Deposit Slips 64
Bank Feeds 179
Bank Statements
   .... 254, Also See Reconciling
Batch Invoices
   Invoices 87
Bid (Customer Bid) 34
Bill Due field on Bills 121
Billing Statements
   .... See Customer Statements

Bills
   Bill Credits 133
   Bill Payment 126
   Bill Payment Stub 131
Bounced Checks 173
Calculating Items 50
Cash Basis of Accounting 5, 190, 267
Certification ix
Chart of Accounts 22, 243
Check Numbers 128
   Check Number Field 43
Classes 5, 43, 112
   Unclassified Column on Reports 60
Closed Accounting Period 171
Closing Date 171, 234
Closing the QuickBooks Program 9
Commissions 39
Company File 234
Company Information 237
Company Snapshot 19
Contributed Reports 216
Credit Cards 143
   Credit Card Discount Fees 67
   Entering Charges You Make 143
   Merchant Accounts 38
   Paying Bills by Credit Card 124
   Paying the Credit Card Bill 144, 179
   Reconciling Credit Card Accounts 176
Credit Memos 77
Current Accounting Period 170
Current Ratio 198
Custom Fields 40, 112, 304
Customer Statements 89
Customer:Job List 35
Customers
   Adding Jobs in the Customer list 40
   Credit Limit 37
   Custom Fields 304
   Customer Type 39
   Discounts 37
   Preferred Payment Method 38
   Price Levels 302
   Rep Field 39
   Setting up Customers 35
   Terms 37
Data Files
   Backing Up Your Data File 13
   Closing Company Files 9
   Opening Company Files 6
   Portable Company Files 9
Debit Card 116
Define Fields 40, 112
Departments 5, 43
Deposit Slips - Printing 64

Deposits, Making Bank 61
Detailed Start 236
Discount Date field on Bills 121
Discount Terms 300
Discounts 133
    Discounts on Bill Payments 125
    Discounts on Invoices 51
    Discounts Taken when Paying Bills 123
    Recording Discounts on Customer Payments
    58
Document Management Center 122
Double-Entry Accounting 3
Downloaded Transactions 181
EasyStep Interview 236
Editing Forms 51
Electronic Funds Transfer 116
Employees 304
Enterprise Solutions .... vii, 1
Equity 3, 243
Estimates 34
Excel .... vii, 225
Expenses 243, 264
Exporting Data 225
Express Start 6, 234
Files Types 5
Finding Transactions 220
Fiscal Year 238
Fit to 1 page wide 219
Fixed Asset Manager 267
Forms 31
    Entering Data on Forms 21
    Templates 305
Funds 5
General Journal Entries 258
    Tracking Journal Entries with a Special
        Account 260
General Ledger 34
Go to Bill 125
Graphs
    Sales by Customer 208
Help - Getting Help 25
History Pane 42, 48
Home Page 18
Icon Bar 19
Income 243, 264
Industry Type 237
Inserting or Deleting Lines on Forms 51
Installing QuickBooks Updates 2
Inventory 233, 234, 256, 266, 282
    Average Cost 193
Invoices 31, 48
    Applying Payments to Invoices 54
Items 24, 294
    Calculating Items 50, 51
    Discount Items 51, 295
    Group Items 295
    Inventory Assembly Items 295
    Inventory Parts 295
    Item List 294

Item Types 295
Non-inventory Parts 295, 297, 298
Other Charge Items 295
Payment Items 295
Price Levels 302
Printing the Item List 299
Sales Tax Group Items 296
Sales Tax Items 296, 299
Service Items 295, 296
Subcontracted Services 296
Subtotal Items 295
Two-Sided Non-inventory Part 298
Two-Sided Service Items 296
Job Costing 5, 114
Keyboard Shortcuts (Dates) 43
Liabilities 243
Lists
    Center-based 18
    Menu-based 22
    Printing the Item List 299
    Using Lists in QuickBooks 22
Loan Manager 149, 152
Maintenance Releases 2
Merging Accounts or other list items 249
Missing Checks 131
Multiple Window View Preference 286
Multi-user 274
    Preferences 190
New Business - Start Date for 234
Non-Posting Entries 34
Non-profit Organizations 112
Online Banking
    Bank Feeds 179
Open Window List 293
Opening Balance Equity
    .... 234, 258, 259, 260, 267, 269
Opening Balances
    Accounts Opening Balances 257
    Accounts Payable 282
    Accounts Recievable 281
    Directly Entering 257
    Entering with Journal Entry 258
Opening QuickBooks Data Files 7
Outstanding Checks and Deposits 260
Owner's Equity 260
Passwords 270
Payroll 234
PDF reports
    Bank Reconciliations 167
Petty Cash 64, 115, 142
PO Number Field - On Invoices 49
Portable Company Files 9
Preferences 285
    Account Numbers 243
    Accounting Preferences 244
    Activating Class Tracking 113
    Automatically apply payments 57
    Automatically calculate payments 57
    Company Preferences 285

Desktop Preferences 286
Don't save the desktop 286
Sales Tax 91
Use Account Numbers 244
User Preferences 285
Preferred Payment Method 38
Premier 1
Price Levels 302
Printing
Fit report to 1 page wide 219
Problems 131
ProAdvisors 26, 237
Profit Centers 5, 43
Quick Add 116
QuickBooks Editions 1
QuickBooks Accountant .... viii, 267
QuickBooks Mobile 20
QuickBooks Statement Writer 225
QuickFill 48, 117
QuickMath 67
QuickZoom 195, 196, 224
Receiving Payments
Automatically Apply Payments 57
Automatically Calculate Payments 57
Customer Discounts 58
How Payments Apply 57
Partial Payments 55
Payment By Credit Card 55
Payments by Check 53
Reconciling
Adjusting the Beginning Balance 173
Bank Accounts 161
Correcting Errors 170
Difference not Zero 168
Finding Reconciliation Errors 168
PDF reports 167
Previous Reconciliation Reports 167
Redepositing Bounced Checks 175
Stop Payments 171
Refunds 79
Customer Refunds 78
Refunding Credit Cards 81
Vendor Refunds 136
Registers 23
Reorder Lists
Chart of Accounts 250
New entry after sorting 251
Report Center 19, 191
Reports
A/R Aging Reports 205
A/R Collections Report 205
Accounting 189, 192
Accrual Basis 190
Balance Sheet 198, 234, 269
Business Management 189
Cash Basis 190
Check Detail Report 204
Collapsed Reports 246
Collapsing Subaccounts 193

Column Widths 53
Contributed 216
Customer Balance Detail 206
Customer Open Balance Report 97
Customizing Reports 209
Details Behind Reports (QuickZoom) 224
Exporting Reports to Spreadsheets 225
Filtering 209
General Ledger 200
Graphs 207
Memorizing Reports 215
Missing Checks Report 131
Open Invoices 52
Printing Reports 218
Processing Multiple Reports 217
Profit & Loss 192, 233, 238
Profit & Loss by Class 5, 113, 195
Profit & Loss by Job 197
QuickReports 221
Sales by Customer Summary Report 98
Statement of Cash Flows 199
Summary 189
Transaction 189
Transaction Detail by Account 211
Trial Balance 201, 254, 267
Vendor Balance Detail 206
Voided/Deleted Transactions History Report
....202
Voided/Deleted Transactions Report 201
Retained Earnings 234, 269
Returns 79
Returns and Credits 77
Sale Number 43, 49
Sales 31
Sales Orders 34
Sales Receipts 31, 41
Sales Tax 234, 299
Collecting Sales Tax 91
Customer Tax Code 95
Default Sales Tax Code 93
Managing Sales Tax 91, 146
Most comon sales tax 92
Paying Sales Tax 146
Preferences 91
Sales Tax Codes 39, 94
Sales Tax Group Items 296
Sales Tax Items 93, 296
Sales Tax on Forms 97
Search 220
Setup
12-Step Setup Process 233
Accounts Payable Opening Balance
....255, 261
Accounts Receivable Opening Balance
....256, 262
Backing up the File 270
Bank Statement for Setup Balance 254
Closing Opening Bal Equity to Retained
Earnings 233, 268

Detailed Start 236
EasyStep Interview 236
Entering Purchase Orders 264
Express Start 6, 234
Fixed Assets 267
Inventory Opening Balance 233, 259, 266
Opening Balances 234, 254
Outstanding Checks and Deposits 255
Payroll 256
Payroll Liabilities Opening Balances 256
Payroll Taxes 256
Retained Earnings Opening Balance 259
Sales Tax Opening Balance 259, 265
Setting the Closing Date 270
Start Date 234
Trial Balance on Start Date 254
Users and Passwords 270
Single-user 274
Preferences 190
Snapshot 19
Spacebar 46
Start Date 233, 234, 254
Statements
.... *See* Customer Statements
Stop Payments on Checks 171
Subaccounts 246
Subcontracted Services 296

Technical Support 25
Templates 305
Terms 49, 111, 300
TurboTax 245
Uncategorized Income 36
Unclassified 60
Undeposited Funds 46, 61
Undo Bank Reconciliation 169
User Profiles 270
Users and Passwords 270
Vendors
    1099s 111
    Credits 133
    Custom Fields 304
    Discounts 111
    Entering Bills From Vendors 120
    Paying Vendors 115
    Refunds from Vendors 136
    Setting up Vendors 108
    Terms 111
    Tracking and Classifying 111
    Vendor Balance Detail Report 147
    Vendor Type 112
Voiding Bill Payments 132
Voiding Checks 131
When Customers are Vendors 37
Writing Checks 119

Index

SOLUTIONS
THE SLEETER GROUP ACCOUNTING SOLUTIONS CONFERENCE

The Premier Event of the Year for Today's Leading Accounting Technologies

The Solutions Annual Conference is the one annual event where you will discover best practices in QuickBooks and *all* of today's leading accounting technologies, network with "rock stars" and colleagues in your field and obtain new strategies, tactics, and skills critical to moving your business forward.

Tracks and In-depth topics Include:
- QuickBooks Solutions
- Core Technologies & Productivity Solutions
- Cloud Applications
- Mobile Solutions
- Connecting the Pieces Using the Cloud
- Chunkification & Vertical Market Solutions
- Growing & Marketing Your Practice
- Ignite Sessions
- Product Specific Solutions

"An awesome event! Amazing learning and networking opportunities. Never a dull moment!"
—Robyn Burns

Receive the latest updates and special offers right in your email. Sign up today.
www.sleeterconference.com

Locations
Locations include Las Vegas, Orlando, Phoenix, Los Angeles and more!

Dates
3-4 days in early November each year

Special Events
Receptions, Raffles, Awards, Solutions Expo Exhibit Hall Walking Tours, Contests, Ignite Sessions, and faciliated discussions.

Conference and Tradeshow
Over 70 education sessions, more than 30 CPE credits and over 70 vendors in the Solutions Expo Hall.

"The Sleeter Conference is a great opportunity to sharpen your QuickBooks and Technical knowledge and to meet some of the most knowledgeable and generous people in the world."
—J. Kane, North Hollywood, CA

THE MOST COMPREHENSIVE GUIDE TO QUICKBOOKS
Consultant's Reference Guide

The *QuickBooks Consultant's Reference Guide* will help you through the most difficult issues you'll confront as a consultant. Packed with techniques to diagnose and fix your clients' QuickBooks files, this is a must-have tool in your toolbox.

The *QuickBooks Consultant's Reference Guide* includes easy-to-read graphics, screen shots, and detailed explanations. QuickBooks sample data files that accompany step-by-step descriptions are available for download at no additional cost. Editions updated yearly.

Order today
www.sleeter.com

Topics include:
- Extensive Inventory Chapter
- Troubleshooting QuickBooks Data Files
- Tricky Transactions
- Data File Management
- Networking QuickBooks
- And Much, Much More

"Anyone who works with QuickBooks should have this book."
— Michelle L. Long, CPA, MBA
Principal, Long for Success, LLC

REACH POTENTIAL CLIENTS AND
GROW YOUR BUSINESS

The QuickBooks® Step-by-Step Seminar System is a complete, turn-key system that empowers accountants and consultants to teach QuickBooks® in classrooms and industry settings. Get started now.

Our QuickBooks® Seminar System is fully designed for teaching QuickBooks® seminars. From planning, to marketing, to delivering a quality course, this system has everything you need to succeed with your seminars—and our Seminar System is the most affordable seminar package on the market. The system includes all the materials for teaching two unique QuickBooks® seminars:

Order today
www.sleeter.com

- Print copy of *QuickBooks® Seminar I*
- Print copy of *QuickBooks® Seminar II*
- Seminar Planning Guide (PDF)
- Companion PowerPoint presentations for each chapter
- Agenda with topic-by-topic instruction
- Sample QuickBooks® data files
- Seminar Planning/Marketing Templates

"There really isn't a better set of materials for workshops or seminars on QuickBooks®."
— Pat Hartley, Menifee, CA

KNOW A PROSPECTIVE EMPLOYEE'S SKILLS
BEFORE YOU HIRE THEM

QuickBooks Assessment Exams

An unqualified bookkeeper or consultant can wreak havoc on a QuickBooks file in no time. You need a reliable way to gauge the skill level of potential hires before they touch your QuickBooks files. QuickBooks Assessments from The Sleeter Group take the guesswork out of determining if a prospective new hire truly has the skills that you or your client's business needs.

Available Assessments:

QuickBooks Bookkeeper emphasizes correct data entry and basic accounting concepts.

QuickBooks Controller focuses on accounting knowledge as well as basic QuickBooks literacy.

QuickBooks Consultant assumes a very high level of both QuickBooks and accounting knowledge.

"The Sleeter Conference is a great opportunity to sharpen your QuickBooks and Technical knowledge and to meet some of the most knowledgeable and generous people in the world."
—J. Kane, North Hollywood, CA

Members Get 50 Exams Free

Members of The Sleeter Group Consultant Network receive 50 assessment exams each year as a benefit of membership.

Join Today!

ORDER TODAY
www.sleeter.com

JOIN THE GROUP THAT CAN HELP YOU
PLAN A SUCCESSFUL CAREER
AND STAY AHEAD OF THE TECHNOLOGY CURVE.

Build For Your Future

The Sleeter Group Consultants Network is the nation's premier membership organization supporting accountants, bookkeepers and CPAs— an active community of experts and new professionals.

When you join the Sleeter Group Consultant's Network you are joining a team of professional accounting experts and moving from an army of one to a worldwide army of many. In addition, members receive thousands of dollars in Product, Education & Event Savings...at a steal of a price for individuals and firms. The Sleeter Group mission is to bring you vendor-neutral solutions, advice, and education that will help you make the best decisions to build your career.
Join today.

A Network of 800+ Members
Our Members' #1 Recommended Benefit

Annual Solutions Conference Discount
A members-only deep discount to the leading accounting technology conference

LinkedIn Forum of Members
Network and talk to others at all stages in the accounting field.

Free QuickBooks® Assessment Exams
Prequalify yourself before applying for jobs with our qualified tools, includes Bookkeeper, Controller and Consultant exams

Discounts on CPE-Earning Webinars, Products & more
Continue your education and grow your business at a discounted price.

Discounts on Best-in-Class Solution Partners
Great products and great savings by Sleeter-vetted solutions partners for you and your clients

- Monthly Members-Only Webinar with Doug Sleeter
- Free Subscription to CPA Practice Advisor Magazine
- Exclusive, Members Only OfficeDepot Discount
- Discount on Sleeter Group products
- Plus new benefits continually added

JOIN TODAY www.sleeter.com